Matteo Ricci

Matteo Ricci

A Jesuit in the Ming Court

Michela Fontana

ROWMAN & LITTLEFIELD PUBLISHERS, INC.

Lanham • Boulder • New York • Toronto • Plymouth, UK

Published by Rowman & Littlefield Publishers, Inc.
A wholly owned subsidiary of The Rowman & Littlefield Publishing Group, Inc.
4501 Forbes Boulevard, Suite 200, Lanham, Maryland 20706
http://www.rowmanlittlefield.com

Estover Road, Plymouth PL6 7PY, United Kingdom

English translation by Paul Metcalfe for Scriptum, Rome

British Library Cataloguing in Publication Information Available

Library of Congress Cataloging-in-Publication Data
Fontana, Michela, 1950-
  [Matteo Ricci. English]
  Matteo Ricci : A Jesuit in the Ming Court / Michela Fontana.
      pages cm
  Translation of: Matteo Ricci / Michela Fontana. — Milano : Mondadori, c2005. — 347 pages ; 23 cm
  Includes bibliographical references and index.
  ISBN 978-1-4422-0586-4 (cloth : alk. paper) — ISBN 978-1-4422-0588-8 (electronic)
  1. Ricci, Matteo, 1552–1610. 2. Jesuits—China—Biography. 3. China—History—Ming dynasty, 1368-1644. I. Title.
  BV3427.R46F6613 2011
  266'.2092—dc22
  [B]

                                        2010050586

∞™ The paper used in this publication meets the minimum requirements of American National Standard for Information Sciences—Permanence of Paper for Printed Library Materials, ANSI/NISO Z39.48-1992.

Printed in the United States of America

For my husband
In memory of my father
and for my mother

Contents

~

Prologue: The Mandarin's Clothes

Zhaoqing, China, September 10, 1583

Japan looks onto an immense empire that enjoys great peace and is considered superior to all the Christian states as regards the workings of justice by the Portuguese merchants. . . . The Chinese I have seen . . . are bright and eager to learn. . . . Nothing leads me to imagine the presence of any Christians there.

—Francis Xavier

The Audience

The prefect[1] Wang Pan wore a loose robe of red silk and a mandarin square elaborately embroidered with two wild geese. The sleeves of the garment were so long and wide as to conceal his hands. Ornaments of silver, wood, and ivory hung from the richly decorated belt. His boots and hat were both black, the latter a rigid skullcap with a rounded brim on either side pointing down toward the shoulders.

Everything in the dress and bearing of the middle-aged official responsible for governing a region in the south of China the size of a small Italian state denoted prestige. The choice of ornaments was not left to chance, personal taste, or any wish to flaunt opulence, but was dictated by a precise protocol codified at the imperial court in Beijing. The details of the apparel, first of all the type of embroidered bird used as a badge of office, indicated that the "mandarin"—a term derived by the Portuguese from their verb *mandar*, meaning to command, and used by them to designate important Chinese dignitaries—held the fourth-highest rank of the nine in the imperial bureaucracy. Even though he was not at the very top of the administrative ladder, his power was sufficient to intimidate anyone admitted to his presence.

He sat on a chair with high armrests and an imposingly tall back at a table of dark wood bearing a number of books bound in damask fabric. Calligraphic brushes of different sizes in wood and bamboo were arrayed on a small and elegant vertical rack of wood and polychromatic china with a painted dragon motif, beside which was the customary slab of black stone for ink and a special bird-shaped water jug of white jade. Vases of blue and white porcelain and jade sculptures embellished with minute inlay were displayed behind him on top of a bookcase with asymmetrical shelves.

Kneeling before the prefect together with a number of Chinese citizens were two young missionaries with European features. Their heads were shaven, and they wore modest robes of grey cotton similar to those of Buddhist monks.

The priests had as yet a very limited knowledge of the difficult language and the history, culture, and customs of that remote empire in the farthest East, so different from the world they knew. The China with which they were now coming into apprehensive contact was a mysterious and hostile land that refused entry to foreigners, who were regarded as illiterate barbarians and dangerous enemies.

Helped by an interpreter and obeying the rules of a complex and alien procedure, the two Italian Jesuits, Matteo Ricci and Michele Ruggieri, asked the mandarin for permission to reside in his country. They wanted to purchase a site where they could build a house and a church and worship their god, the Lord of Heaven and Earth, in peace and in accordance with the laws of the land.

It was a fateful moment, and the date, September 10, 1583, was to remain imprinted in the Jesuits' memory forever. After at least thirty years of fruitless attempts by Western priests to establish a foothold on imperial territory, the first Jesuit mission in the China of the Ming dynasty was becoming a reality, and one that would mark the beginning of one of the most significant periods in the history of cultural exchange between East and West. For Matteo Ricci, then thirty years of age, it was the start of a human, intellectual, and spiritual adventure that was to continue for the rest of his life.

Thirty years earlier . . .

Note

1. The term used by Ricci in his writings is *governatore*, which corresponds in the Ming bureaucratic nomenclature to *zhifu*, meaning an official in charge of a prefecture (*fu*). This is translated here as "prefect" in line with current terminology.

◡

CHAPTER ONE

The Jesuit and Mathematics

From Macerata to Rome, 1552–1576

Whatever the present or other Roman pontiffs order that concerns the saving of souls and the spread of the faith, and to whatever provinces he shall wish to send us, this let us strive to accomplish as far as in us lies, without any turning back or excuse.

—Ignatius Loyola, Constitution of the Society of Jesus (1540)

Geometry is one and eternal shining in the mind of God. That share in it accorded to humans is one of the reasons that humanity is the image of God.

—Johannes Kepler, *Harmonices Mundi* (1618)[1]

The Choice

Matteo Ricci was born in Macerata, a town of the Papal States with a population of just under thirteen thousand, perched on a hill between the parallel valleys of the Potenza and Chienti rivers, on October 6, 1552.[2] In addition to various other municipal councils, his father, Giovanni Battista Ricci, an apothecary by profession, is thought to have served on the *Consiglio di Credenza*, membership of which was an exclusive prerogative of the city's dignitaries, in 1596.[3] The Ricci family had belonged to the lesser nobility of Macerata for centuries, their coat of arms being a blue hedgehog (*riccio* in Italian) on a vermilion field, and were to be granted the marquisate of Castel

1

Vecchio at the end of the seventeenth century. His mother, Giovanna Angiolelli, was also born into a noble family.

Matteo, the firstborn of a numerous family, had four sisters and eight brothers, including Antonio Maria, who was to become the canon of Macerata, and Orazio, who was to hold important positions in the government of the city.[4] Entrusted to the care of his grandmother, Laria, he studied under the guidance of Father Niccolò Bencivegni from Siena until the age of seven, when the priest left his post as tutor to enter the Society of Jesus, one of the most important orders founded in connection with the Counter-Reformation.

Matteo continued his studies at the new Jesuit college opened in the city in 1561, where he distinguished himself as one of the best pupils and manifested a religious vocation at a very early age, according to Sabatino de Ursis, his first biographer.[5] His father is reported to have had other plans for him, however, and he was sent to Rome immediately on completion of his basic education in order to study jurisprudence at the university, probably with a view to a career in the papal administration.

He arrived in Rome in 1568. The capital then had a population of nearly one hundred thousand and was one of the world's greatest cities of art. Work was still underway on Saint Peter's, the symbol of the Church's greatness, whose creation had involved some of the greatest artists of the Renaissance. Its construction, which did not come to an end until the following century after 176 years of activity and the succession of twenty-eight popes to the throne of Saint Peter, was regarded by Romans as a never-ending process. Ricci was not to witness the erection of Michelangelo's renowned dome, as it was not completed until 1588, four years after the death of its designer and ten after his own departure from the capital.

The atmosphere in Rome was steeped in the spirit of the Counter-Reformation. The Council of Trent (1545–1563) had ended just a few years earlier with an overall doctrinal and disciplinary reorganization of the Catholic Church after the rift in the Christian world caused by the Protestant Reformation. The pope's authority was being constantly strengthened, and his claims to supremacy over the temporal powers were being asserted with ever-greater determination. The creation of the Congregation of the Holy Office, or Inquisition, in Rome by Paul III in 1542 and the publication of the *Index Librorum Prohibitorum* by the order of Paul IV in 1559, with the ensuing repressive measures against nonorthodox authors and printers, made it possible to exercise rigid control over culture, thus stifling the lively growth of ideas that had characterized the previous century. The papal throne had been occupied for two years by Pius V, formerly the Dominican friar Antonio Michele Ghislieri, an inquisitor and future saint unswerving in the persecution of heresy and dissent, who excommunicated Elizabeth I of England in 1570.

At the time when Ricci entered the capital, Italy was a patchwork of states mostly subject to Spain, among which only Venice and, within certain limits, the Papal State retained any real independence from Madrid. Bitter religious disputes were interwoven in Europe with the struggle for supremacy among the nations. In the Near East, Suleiman the Magnificent had died two years earlier after bringing the Turkish Ottoman Empire to the peak of its power and threatening the eastern borders of Austria. Vying for supremacy over the world's oceans were the two Catholic maritime powers of Spain and Portugal, whose navigators were responsible for the most important exploits of the previous century, from the discovery of the New World to the first landings in India and the circumnavigation of the globe.[6] The image of our planet had changed, and expeditions in previously unknown seas and lands led to the redrawing of maps and the growth of trade, giving birth to a market that now embraced different continents. Missionaries traveled the routes opened up by explorers and merchants, Jesuits together with Franciscans, Dominicans, and Augustinians, eager to convert "the infidels" in every corner of the world and to regain in distant lands part of the power lost by the Catholic Church in Europe due to the Protestant Reformation.

In the previous century, while the boundaries of the known world widened, the Old World had undergone deep cultural change. Princes, military leaders, cardinals, courtiers, adventurers, merchants, and bankers, as well as artists, architects, writers, philosophers, astronomers, mathematicians, physicians, and magicians, all played their parts in a drama destined to transform the world. Now, however, halfway through the sixteenth century, the drive for innovation that had characterized the Renaissance period was forced to come to terms with the rigorous control over orthodoxy imposed by the religious authorities in Catholic countries like Italy and Spain. Despite the savage wars of religion that soaked Europe in blood and the intolerance that impeded the free expression of culture, evolution toward modernity did continue in knowledge and art as well as the gradual creation of nation-states. New ideas intermingled with old conceptions and philosophies on a complex and contradictory social and cultural scene. Age-old superstitions accompanied the first steps of modern science. Greater depth and specialization were achieved in every field of knowledge, and natural philosophy began to give way to the scientific disciplines fully established in the centuries to come. Mathematics took on a central role as an essential tool for the investigation and understanding of natural phenomena, and technology gained increasing power and importance.

We cannot know the dreams and aspirations of Matteo Ricci as he embarked on life in the Rome of the late Renaissance. The hagiographic accounts of Jesuit biographers[7] are rife with premonitory signs sent by divine providence to herald his destiny as a missionary and show no trace of the doubts, hesitations, and uncertainties he probably experienced, like most young people seeking their way in life. It can only be assumed on the basis of subsequent events that Matteo Ricci was soon convinced that a secular career was not for him. He began to attend the Marian congregation attached to the Roman College, the Jesuit university in Rome, in 1569 and made the decision to abandon law and enter the Jesuit order even before completing three years of university studies. He presented himself to the novitiate of Sant'Andrea al Quirinale on August 15, 1571, and was admitted to the Society of Jesus by Jeronimo Nadal, then vicar general. His spiritual guide in the house of probation was Alessandro Valignano, thirteen years his senior but admitted to the Jesuit order only four years earlier, a temporary replacement for the titular master of novices Fabio de Fabii. The register of the Society of Jesus, which still survives, includes a document drawn up by Valignano certifying the admittance of "Mattheo Ricci" from Macerata and attesting that the young person had signed the customary declaration of self-renunciation and complete obedience to the constitution of the order,[8] that he accepted "the way of life of the Society and was perfectly content to be admitted to whatever rank and office the Society might see fit to grant him and to perform obediently whatever he might be ordered."[9]

While it is possible that Alessandro Valignano sensed Ricci's qualities of character on their first meeting, he certainly had no way of knowing that the young man from Macerata would become one of his greatest allies in the missionary work in China and one of the wisest practitioners of the method he himself devised of spreading the faith. Valignano was appointed Visitor in the Indies shortly afterward, with the task of supervising the work of the missions in the Far East. He left Rome for Lisbon in September 1573 and set sail for the Indies from there the following year, together with forty young brethren.

The news of the radical decision taken by Matteo, now a novice in the Society of Jesus, was evidently a blow to his father, who immediately set off in a bid to persuade him to change his mind. Shortly after his departure, according to the Jesuit biographers, Giovanni Battista was struck down by a severe bout of fever and was forced to stop in Tolentino, about eleven miles southeast of Macerata. Perhaps seeing this as a sign from God, or simply having come to realize that his efforts would prove useless, he resigned himself to turning back and wrote to tell his son that he would respect his decision and make no attempt to stop him.

After his brief encounter with Valignano, Ricci's figure of reference was Fabio de Fabii, a Roman nobleman who had joined the order, like him, against the wishes of his family. In May 1572, shortly before his twentieth birthday, he took the simple vows that constituted the first step toward becoming a member of the Jesuit order.

The Society of Jesus and the
Roman College: *Ad maiorem Dei gloriam*

Joining the Society of Jesus, or Societas Jesu, meant belonging to a religious elite culturally in the avant-garde. Ignatius Loyola (1491–1556), the founder of the order and a scion of a noble Basque family, had abandoned a military career after being seriously wounded and had channeled his warrior's ardor into the religious struggle. It was while studying at the University of Paris that he created the Society of Jesus in 1534, together with six fellow students, including his compatriot Francis Xavier.[10] He conceived it as a rigidly hierarchical organization, a select militia at the service of the pope and the Counter-Reformation, with the task of defending the Church against heretics. Absolute obedience to the decisions of superiors was mandatory for Jesuits, as we read in the Constitution:

> Let holy obedience, in execution, in the will, and in the intellect, be always utterly perfect in us; let us obey with great promptness, spiritual joy, and perseverance whatever may be commanded of us.

Approved by Pope Paul III in 1540, six years after its foundation, the order had obtained a considerable degree of independence from the ecclesiastical hierarchy, and its members recognized the authority of no superior from outside the order other than the pope. In addition to the vows of poverty, chastity, and obedience, the members who completed the requisite series of studies and were judged spiritually fit also undertook to perform unhesitatingly whatever mission the pope might assign them by taking the specific vow *circa missiones*. The supreme head was the *Praepositus Generalis*, or Superior General, subject only to the regulations of the order and the pontiff. The long training before taking the vows and the techniques of self-control and asceticism developed by Loyola in the *Spiritual Exercises*, published in 1548, strengthened the gifts of discipline, energy, tenacity, and abnegation that made the order's members ideal instruments for the defense and propagation of the Catholic faith.[11]

Immediately after the creation of the Society of Jesus, Jesuit missionaries traveled the routes opened up by explorers to spread the Gospel among "infidels" in every corner of the world, making converts in Africa, South America, India, Malacca, Japan, and the Moluccas. The most difficult country to penetrate was China, whose coasts had been reached for the first time by the Portuguese in 1515 but where no priest had yet been able to settle.[12] The first missionary to seek entry into the Chinese empire during the Ming dynasty, after founding Jesuit missions in India, the Moluccas, and Japan, was Francis Xavier, who considered it necessary to focus the utmost attention on China due to the evident cultural influence exercised by the empire over the rest of Asia. Xavier was convinced that the missionary work in other Eastern countries, including Japan, would be much easier if China became Christian. Having left Japan and arrived at Goa in India at the beginning of 1552, the Jesuit took up residence a few months later on the small island of Shang-chuan, ten kilometers off the Chinese coast, and waited in vain for permission to enter the country. After a sudden illness, he died in December 1552, two months after Ricci's birth.

In Europe, the members of the Society of Jesus devoted themselves above all to education, considered the most effective form of missionary activity. Their cultural background was immensely rich, even though naturally bent to their religious ends, and many were confessors and advisers to princes and sovereigns. Their teaching took place in colleges, which included schools of every level and universities founded in many European countries and some where missions were operating. Renowned for their educational rigor and attended by members of the order and by the sons of the ruling class, the Jesuit colleges and houses scattered through the whole of Europe numbered over five hundred by the end of the sixteenth century.

The syllabuses followed the indications of the founder of the order, who envisioned a broad range of disciplines, albeit in line with the dictates of orthodoxy. "As regards letters . . . he wants everyone to be well-versed in grammar and the humanities, especially if aided in this by age and inclination. Then he rejects no kind of accepted culture, neither poetry and rhetoric nor logic and natural and moral philosophy, neither metaphysics nor mathematics . . . because the order must be endowed with every possible means of edification."[13] The method of teaching followed the instructions formulated by the founders of the order and subsequently laid down in the *Ratio studiorum*, promulgated in its definitive form in 1599 by Claudio Acquaviva, the heir to a noble Neapolitan family, who became the Superior General in 1581 and was to hold that position for over thirty years, covering the entire span of Ricci's life in China.

The Jesuits' allegiance in philosophy was to Aristotle and in theology to Saint Thomas Aquinas, the doctor of the Church who had succeeded in combining the Stagirite's teaching with Catholic doctrine in a rational system of thought. As we read in the *Ratio studiorum*, "Our brethren follow the doctrine of Saint Thomas absolutely and do everything possible to ensure that the students cherish it in their hearts."[14]

The most important Jesuit university, regarded as a model for all the others, was the Roman College, today the Pontifical Gregorian University. Organized on the same lines as the University of Paris, it received papal recognition as a center of higher education in 1556. According to a letter written by Loyola on the plans for the college in March 1553,[15] "most learned and assiduous" professors were to teach "intelligent and virtuous students of good background and education" and seek to turn out "eminent Jesuits." The order's teachers included experts in specialized disciplines like mathematics and astronomy.

Matteo Ricci was admitted to the Roman College on September 17, 1572, after a short period at its Florentine counterpart,[16] where he had been sent on taking his initial vows. Ugo Boncompagni, a convinced supporter of the Jesuit schools and missionary work, became Pope Gregory XIII in the same year.

The home of the Roman College, the fourth since its foundation and the last before its definitive move to the premises built by the order of Pope Gregory, was a solemn Renaissance palazzo built with funds donated by the Marquise of Tolfa, the widow of Paul IV's nephew Camillo Orsini. The complex consisted of two separate buildings "harmoniously laid out around two large arcaded quadrangles,"[17] one for the students and classrooms, the other for the religious community, beside which the church of the Annunziata stood. The Roman College taught over a thousand young people from all over Europe free of charge in that period.

The 130 of these who belonged to the order,[18] like Ricci, were offered an overall education but only on condition that they lived in the college and that their contacts with parents and relatives were kept to the bare minimum. For nearly five years, from the moment Ricci crossed the threshold of the building, his real family was to be the group made up of his fellow students and the teaching body. The Jesuit would always remember them with affection and nostalgia, as is clearly revealed on reading his letters from the East. In one of the first, written shortly after his departure for the missions and sent from Cochin, India, in November 1580 to Ludovico Maselli, rector of the Roman College in the years when Ricci attended it, we read as follows:

> I do not feel so much sadness . . . at being far away from my family *secundum carnem*, even though I am very attached to the flesh, as at being away from Your Reverence, whom I love more than my own father.[19]

The young Ricci set about the course of studies laid down for those belonging to the order: two years of rhetoric, three of philosophy, and three of theology. He studied Latin, the language in which the lessons were taught, as well as Greek and Hebrew in the first two years. The decision of the teachers at the college to present pagan authors of antiquity as models of style was influenced by humanism, the intellectual movement that had led to the rediscovery and reappraisal of Greek and Latin classical culture in the previous century. The texts studied were, however, vetted in advance by the ecclesiastical authorities, who took care to cut anything deemed inappropriate. Ricci's reading included the Latin authors Martial, Horace, Ovid, Virgil, and Quintilian, as well as Homer, Hesiod, Thucydides, and Demosthenes among the Greeks. The paradigm to be followed for Latin was Cicero, considered an unsurpassable example of Roman rhetoric. While rigid control was maintained over the content of the courses, the teachers' choices revealed a significant degree of independence with respect to the ecclesiastical authorities, as shown by the fact that Erasmus of Rotterdam was also read in the Jesuit colleges even though his works had been placed on the *Index*. Having completed the first two years, Ricci embarked on the three years of philosophy with in-depth study of Aristotelian logic, ethics, and metaphysics, as well as the ethics of the Stoics Epictetus and Seneca. In order to hone his dialectic skills, he took part in the customary monthly debates, during which students presented philosophical theses and defended them before an audience of teachers and students in accordance with previously established procedures.

Even though the philosophical exercises were carried out according to the rules of Aristotelian logic and in the name of reason, the end was theological. The Jesuits saw knowledge as a sword to be carefully honed and used to defend the Church. In no case was study to distract the novices from their religious mission, and still less to lead them onto paths incompatible with the strictest observance of doctrine.

Ricci attended the courses of rhetoric and philosophy, subjecting himself to what a Jesuit historian describes as "unflagging mental activity, constant practice and exercise, a sort of never-ending gymnastics of the mind."[20] He is also reported to have taken part in the "academies" or study groups made up of students particularly distinguished for learning, diligence, and piety. During the last year of philosophy, he attended the new course on controversies inaugurated by the young teacher of theology Roberto Bellarmino, a future cardinal and saint destined to become one of the most influential figures in the Society of Jesus.[21]

Christopher Clavius, Mathematics, and Astronomy

An integral part of the philosophical training imparted in the Jesuit colleges was the study of natural philosophy, understood as the sciences and especially mathematics, which at the time also included astronomy, music, geography, and applied disciplines like mechanics and architecture.

The second half of the sixteenth century saw mathematics taking on a significant and all-pervasive role in technology and the study of nature. Advanced arithmetical procedures were required in the then developing fields of trade and banking as well as in architecture, the manufacture of cannons, the study of the trajectory of projectiles, and numerous other technical and artisanal activities that called for precise measurement and calculation. Geometric skills were also indispensable in art in order to capture three-dimensional reality on canvas by means of perspective, a technique perfected in the previous century and based on principles that heralded the development of projective geometry. Mathematics was to take on a still more significant role in the following century, becoming the primary tool of the investigation of the physical world for Galileo. As the Pisan scientist wrote in a celebrated passage of his work *The Assayer,*

> Philosophy is written in that great book which ever lies before our eyes—I mean the universe—but we cannot understand it if we do not first learn the language and grasp the symbols, in which it is written. This book is written in the mathematical language.[22]

Mathematical knowledge was considered important also for theological purposes. According to the Church and its reworking of the Greek conception of nature, God designed and created the world in accordance with mathematical laws that man was capable of discovering and understanding by means of reason. The search for the laws governing the universe was therefore considered a religious quest, and the discovery of the mathematical relations underlying natural phenomena became a way to celebrate the greatness and glory of God's work. This philosophical vision was shared by scientists and found expression in the words of one of the great astronomers of the seventeenth century, namely Johannes Kepler (1571–1630), the discoverer of the laws governing the movements of the planets:

> The chief aim of all the investigations of the external world should be to discover the rational order and harmony which has been imposed on it by God and which He has revealed to us in the language of mathematics.[23]

Mathematics was held in great consideration at the Roman College, where the leading role in persuading colleagues to include arithmetic, algebra, and geometry in the syllabus was played by the German Christoph Klau (1537–1612), known by the humanistic name of Christophorus Clavius and in English as Christopher Clavius. An illustrious astronomer and mathematician, he taught at the Roman College from 1563 on and was one of the professors that most influenced Ricci's early development. Clavius was regarded as the Euclid of the sixteenth century, a reputation earned through the publication in 1574 of his annotated translation from the Greek of Euclid's *Elements*—the famous work on arithmetic and geometry written in the third century BC—considered one of the most complete versions produced during the Renaissance.[24] The German professor was also the author of treatises on astronomy, his best-loved subject, and education. The extent of the esteem he enjoyed among scholars can be gauged from his correspondence with some of the greatest scientists of the time, and above all his friendship with the young Galileo, who turned to him for advice on more than one occasion.

"I attach more importance to the opinion of Your Reverence than to any other."[25] It was in these terms that Galileo, then little over twenty, wrote to Clavius, who was twice his age, for advice on a problem of physics.

Clavius knew that most of the young novices showed little interest in science and that many professors thought it pointless to teach mathematics to future priests and missionaries. As he wrote,

> Professors of philosophy must have a knowledge of mathematics and . . . urge their students to devote themselves to the study of these sciences instead of neglecting them, as in the past. Students must understand that philosophy and mathematics are connected.[26]

Clavius undertook an authentic campaign to persuade his colleagues, maintaining not only that the decision to teach mathematics would enhance the prestige of the Society of Jesus, but also that the discipline of Pythagoras was a fundamental prerequisite for learning the other sciences and applied disciplines. Ricci shared his master's views and is reported to have derived great benefit from his teaching.

If mathematics was the foundation of science, then astronomy was its pinnacle. Father Clavius regularly observed the heavens from the terrace of the Roman College and witnessed in 1572 the appearance of a "new star," which remained visible for eighteen months in the constellation of Cassiopeia before disappearing into nothingness. Also observed by Chinese astronomers, it was actually a supernova, a star of great mass that explodes to shine very brightly for a certain period of time before burning out forever. A celestial phenomenon well known to science today, it was not understood at the time and was regarded rather as an odd meteorological event, it being inconceivable that anything new could appear in the perfect, incorruptible, immutable heavens.

Known halfway through the sixteenth century as "astrology," astronomy was divided into "meteorological astrology," the study of celestial bodies on the basis of observations and calculations, and "judicial astrology," the study of the influence of the stars on human life in order to draw up horoscopes, which is simply called astrology today. The latter was also taught in universities and was practiced even by great scientists like Kepler, who continued to take advantage of his reputation as an astrologer even in the seventeenth century in order to swell his income with commissions for horoscopes. Even though the belief that the celestial bodies influenced human life was commonly accepted, judicial astrology was banned in the Jesuit colleges because believing that the future was written in the stars was incompatible with the Christian idea of free will.

The description of the cosmos that Ricci studied at the Roman College and was later to teach to the Chinese dated back to Aristotle and had been presented in mathematical form by the astronomer and geographer Ptolemy (c. AD 138–180) in the *Almagest*[27] and was later reworked in the light of Christian doctrine by Aquinas. According to this model, the universe is finite and the earth immobile at its center. Rotating around it are eight spheres or "heavens" of the purest incorruptible crystalline material on which the moon, Mercury, Venus, the sun, Mars, Jupiter, and Saturn are set. Then come the fixed stars, so called in order to distinguish them from planets, which change their position in the sky. After the stars is the tenth and last sphere, called the *Primum Mobile*, beyond which Catholic doctrine located the empyrean, the dwelling place of God, the only unmoving sphere capable of setting all the others in motion.

Reinterpreted in the light of religion, the Ptolemaic system had been unchallenged for centuries as established fact and fully corresponded to the vision of a perfect universe created by God with the earth and man in the center, as described by Dante in the *Divine Comedy*. Scientists accepted it because it made possible fairly precise predictions of astronomical phenomena like solar and lunar eclipses and because it described the movement of planets by means of a mathematical system that, though complex,[28] proved sufficiently in line with observation.

When Ricci studied at the Roman College, the work of Polish astronomer Copernicus,[29] containing the new and more correct hypothesis of the structure of the universe with the sun at the center of the planetary system instead of the earth, had already been in print for thirty years, and the seeds of the Copernican revolution, one of the most shattering in the history of Western science, had begun to sprout, paving the way for the radical conceptual changes in the fields of cosmology, physics, philosophy, and religion that were brought about in the seventeenth century through the work of Galileo and Kepler. The conflict between the heliocentric system of Copernicus and the geocentric system of Ptolemy did not, however, affect Ricci, who died in China long before the dramatic events that led to the clash between Galileo, the defender of the Copernican theory, and the Church, which considered it a heretical doctrine.

Mathematical and astronomical knowledge had immediate application in drawing up the calendar, an essential tool for agriculture and social life. Given Ricci's particular flair for the scientific disciplines, it is reasonable to assume that he was one of the group attending a specialized course devoted to the construction of perpetual calendars, the study of the planetary tables, and higher-level astronomical calculations.[30] Promulgated by Julius Caesar in 46 BC, the Julian calendar was still in use in Ricci's day but was now out of step with the passing of the seasons. Its rectification was the task of a committee appointed by Pope Gregory XIII, with Clavius as one of its members. Even though Ricci had already left for the East by the time this reform was completed with the introduction of our present Gregorian calendar[31] in 1582, he was probably acquainted through his master with some of the problems of calculation to be addressed.

Ricci also studied geography and cartography, disciplines then in the full swing of development. The courses at the Roman College included not only Ptolemy's *Geography*, the compendium of the geographic knowledge of antiquity translated from the Greek in the previous century, but also the works of the most famous Renaissance cartographers, who described the newly explored world and used new techniques to represent the earth's surface. The innovations in cartography had proceeded in step with the new discoveries. While the map in which the name "America" appeared for the first time to indicate the New World had been drawn in 1507 by the German Martin Waldseemüller (1470–1521), the real progress was made sixty years later. It was in 1569 that the Flemish cartographer Gerhard Kremer (1512–1594), better known as Mercator, devised the "projection" that still bears his name, a geometric technique of map drawing in which the parallels, corresponding to degrees of latitude, became horizontal and the meridians, corresponding to degrees of longitude, became vertical, while the poles disappeared. On a navigation chart drawn in accordance with Mercator's method, the progress of a ship in a constant direction with respect to the needle of the compass could be represented as a straight line, thus making it much easier for navigators to plot the course and then follow it. His compatriot Abraham Oertel (1527–1598), known as Ortelius, brought out the first atlas in the modern sense of the term, namely the *Theatrum Orbis Terrarum*, a systematic collection of the most recent maps of the world developed with the collaboration of most of the leading geographers of the time. Published for the first time in 1570, it was regularly updated in subsequent editions.

The teaching imparted at the Roman College was not only theoretical but also included technical disciplines and the development of manual skills. The new scientific developments in the sixteenth century were in any case practically never the fruit of pure speculation but were matters of immediate application, and the theoretical capacities of natural philosophers were accompanied by practical skills that enabled them to construct the instruments they needed in order to explore nature.

Ricci also acquired technical understanding and developed his manual skills, learning among other things to construct globes that showed the heavenly vault and the earth's surface on a sphere and to draw maps using the most recent techniques. He studied the mechanisms of instruments of astronomical observation like the astrolabe, a device of ancient origin used to measure the apparent height of stars above the horizon and described by Clavius in an exhaustive treatise.[32] He became familiar with the working principles and construction of sundials, ancient instruments that were well known to Clavius and that used the shadow cast by a gnomon onto a marked surface to tell the time of day. He also learned the secrets of the mechanical clocks introduced in the fourteenth century that used chimes to ring the hours. Though still very imprecise, these were becoming rather popular both as table clocks and in miniature versions as watches to be hung around the neck.

Ricci could hardly have imagined just how much use he would make of this theoretical and practical knowledge in his missionary work. Much of it was to prove invaluable during his stay in China to communicate with a civilization that was different but eager to learn the knowledge produced by another culture.

It was while he was still studying and concentrated on his spiritual path that Matteo Ricci submitted a request to become a missionary. It is not known whether this was of his own volition or under the influence of his superiors. The young man had to wait for a long time before his application was accepted, as the selection process was very rigorous. Various students dreamed of setting off for the missions, but not all were deemed suitable. The "ardent longing for the Indies"[33] was in fact not always accompanied by any real ability to cope with the hardships involved in the missionary's life. Experience had shown that too many novices were unable to endure the rigors of ocean voyages and life in unhealthy climates, illness, and homesickness. After becoming Visitor of Missions in the Indies, Valignano himself had taken steps to ensure the selection of candidates with an intellectual and psychological profile in keeping with the demands of the undertaking, so as to avoid pointless suffering and failure.[34]

Ricci had all the right qualities, being thoroughly prepared and fired with great determination. While he was completing the third year of his philosophy course, at the end of 1576, Martino da Silva, the Portuguese Procurator of Missions in India, returned to Italy in order to select new missionaries for the East and accepted Ricci's request in agreement with Superior General Everard Mercurian.

The training and education received during the five years spent at the Roman College—repeatedly recalled by Matteo in his letters from China as a happy and intense period—provided him with the essential grounding for his life to come, a cultural background that was to prove invaluable in spreading the Gospel in the East.

Notes

Abbreviations

FR   Fonti Ricciane, Storia dell'Introduzione del Cristianesimo in Cina.
OS II   Matteo Ricci, Le lettere dalla Cina, in Opere storiche del P. Matteo Ricci S.I., 2 vols., II.

1. Harmonices Mundi (1618), translated as The Harmonies of Worlds or The Harmony of the World, book III, ch. 1; quoted in Judith V. Field, "Astrology in Kepler's Cosmology," in Astrology, Science, and Society: Historical Essays, ed. P. Curry (Woodbridge, Suffolk/Wolfeboro, NH: Boydell and Brewer, 1987), p. 154.

2. The figures for 1617 give a total of 13,889 inhabitants (FR, book V, ch. XXI, p. 549, no. 2).

3. FR, book V, ch. XXI, p. 549.

4. FR, book V, ch. XXI, p. 550.

5. The Jesuit Sabatino de Ursis (1575–1620), one of Ricci's companions on the China mission, was the author of his first biography, P. Matheus Ricci S.I. Relação escripta pelo seu companheiro (Rome, 1910).

6. The Portuguese navigator Bartolomeu Dias rounded the Cape of Good Hope near the southernmost tip of Africa in 1488. His compatriot Vasco da Gama landed in Calicut, India, in 1498.

7. For biographic details, see also FR, introduction, pp. ci ff, and book V, ch. XXI, pp. 549 ff.

8. Written by Ignatius Loyola between 1541 and 1550.

9. FR, book V, ch. XXI, p. 553.

10. Francisco de Jassu y Xavier (1506–1552). He founded the College of Saint Paul at Goa (India) in 1542 and was canonized in 1622 together with Ignatius Loyola.

11. Carlo Capra, *Età moderna* (Florence: Le Monnier, 1996), pp. 112 ff.

12. Franciscan friars entered China in the thirteenth and fourteenth centuries during the Mongol Yuan dynasty (see chapter 7, "China and the Cathay of Marco Polo").

13. From a letter written by Loyola's secretary Alfonso Polanco in 1551, in Riccardo G. Villostrada, *Storia del Collegio Romano* (Roma: Pontificia Università Gregoriana, 1954), p. 111.

14. Villostrada, *Storia del Collegio Romano*, pp. 112–13.

15. Villostrada, *Storia del Collegio Romano*, pp. 14–15.

16. FR, book V, ch. XXI, p. 556, no. 1.

17. Mario Fois, "Il Collegio Romano ai tempi degli studi del P. Matteo Ricci," in *Atti del convegno internazionale di Studi Ricciani, Macerata-Roma, 22–25 October 1982*, ed. Maria Cigliano (Macerata: Centro Studi Ricciani, 1984), p. 206.

18. M. Fois, "Il Collegio Romano ai tempi degli studi del P. Matteo Ricci," p. 207.

19. OS II, p. 12.

20. M. Fois, "Il Collegio Romano ai tempi degli studi del P. Matteo Ricci," cit., p. 215.

21. R. G. Villostrada, op. cit., p. 72.

22. Galileo Galilei, *The Assayer* (1623), translated by Thomas Salusbury (1661), p. 178, as quoted in *The Metaphysical Foundations of Modern Science* (2003), by Edwin Arthur Burtt (Mineola, NY: Dover Publications), p. 75.

23. Cit. in Morris Kline, *Mathematics: The Loss of Certainty* (New York: Oxford University Press, 1982), p. 31.

24. Christophorus Clavius, *Euclidis Elementorum libri* XV, Romae apud Vincentium Accoltum, 1574. Some editions of the *Elements*, originally in thirteen books, also contained two additional books that are considered apocryphal.

25. Pasquale D'Elia, "Echi delle scoperte galileiane in Cina vivente ancora Galileo (1612–1640)," in *Rendiconti dell'Accademia Nazionale dei Lincei. Classe di Scienze Morali, Storiche e Filosofiche* (Rome, I/5–6, 1946), pp. 131–32.

26. Henry Bernard, *L'apport scientifique du père Matthieu Ricci à la Chine* (Tientsin: Hautes Études, 1935), p. 28.

27. The Arab name of the *Megále mathematikè syntaxis tes astronomías*, known also by the Latin name *Syntaxis*.

28. The system was based on the geometric devices of the eccentric, epicycle, deferent, and equant.

29. Copernicus presented the heliocentric system in *De revolutionibus orbium coelestium*, which was published in 1543. The author was on his deathbed when he saw the first printed copy.

30. Jonathan Spence, *The Memory Palace of Matteo Ricci* (New York: Penguin Books, 1985), p. 143.

31. The Julian calendar divided every period of four years into three of 365 days and one of 366. As a result, a discrepancy of three days accumulated between the "tropic" or solar year and the Julian year every four hundred years, and the spring equinox fell on March 11 in the sixteenth century instead of March 21. The Gregorian calendar was introduced to solve this problem in 1582 with a decree whereby Thursday October 4, 1582, was followed by Friday October 15, and the cycle of leap years (of 366 days) was modified to comprise all of those exactly divisible by four but not centurial years unless divisible by four hundred. (The year 2000 is thus a leap year, for example, while 1900 and 2100 are not.) The difference in length with respect to the true solar year was reduced to 0.0003 of a day. The Gregorian calendar was subsequently adopted by nearly all nations, including non-Catholic peoples (Great Britain in 1752, the USSR in 1918, Greece in 1932, and China in 1911). It was introduced in Goa in 1583.

32. Christophorus Clavius, *Astrolabium* (Rome, 1593).

33. Gian Carlo Roscioni, *Il desiderio delle Indie* (Turin: Einaudi, 2001), p. 100.

34. Gian Carlo Roscioni, *Il desiderio delle Indie*, pp. 100 ff.

CHAPTER TWO

~

In the East

From Rome to Lisbon, Coimbra, Goa, Cochin, and Macao, 1577–1582

The Chinese cultivate letters seriously and hold learning in high regard but show little interest in arms.

The Chinese are alert, enterprising, and lively in their actions.
The Chinese have the best government imaginable and adhere rigidly to established customs.

—Alessandro Valignano[1]

Departure: "All Those Seas"

It was on May 18, 1577, that the group of Jesuits departing from Rome for the East received the customary blessing of Gregory XIII. Not yet twenty-five years of age, Ricci left the capital immediately after this meeting with the pope—together with his fellow student Francesco Pasio from Bologna—for Lisbon, the port of departure for eastward-bound vessels. Priests traveling to the area covered by the Portuguese *padroado*[2] (the protectorate over missions in the whole of Asia apart from the Philippines, which were under Spanish dominion) were required in that period to be Portuguese by birth or to obtain permission from the Portuguese authorities in order to embark in their ships. Spain and Portugal had vied for mastery of the oceans in the previous century until a precise boundary was established between the two empires with the Treaty of Tordesillas in 1494. The imaginary line of demarcation, known as the *raya* in Portuguese, ran 370 Spanish leagues west of the islands of Cape Verde,

dividing Brazil approximately along the 46th meridian west of Greenwich. The
Portuguese and Spanish had a free hand respectively east and west of the *raya*.
When the earth was later proved to be round and after Magellan's voyage of
discovery in the service of Spain to the Philippines, where he died in 1521,
it became essential to draw another line of demarcation antipodal to the first.
The Spanish and Portuguese met in 1529 and agreed that the new *raya* would
run along the 17th degree of longitude east of the Moluccas. What lay east of
this belonged to Spain, and what lay west belonged to Portugal. In practical
terms, the Portuguese had the whole of Asia apart from the Philippines, and
the Spanish crown all of the Americas except Brazil.[3]

Even though Ricci knew that he was unlikely ever to return from the missions, he did not make the trip to Macerata to see his loved ones again, which
shows just how radical his decision to detach himself from his family was. He
sailed from Genoa to Cartagena and then continued overland, arriving in
Lisbon at the end of June.

Since vessels bound for India set sail only in March and April in order to
take advantage of the favorable winds and the monsoon season in the Indian
Ocean, Ricci had a long wait and spent nearly a year in Coimbra learning
Portuguese, which he soon spoke better than Italian. He also began to attend
the courses in theology required for entry into the priesthood at the Jesuit
College, returning to Lisbon only when the ships were ready to set sail.

Ricci and the thirteen other missionaries who were to sail with him were
granted an audience with Sebastian I in the castle of Almeirim on March
20, 1578, and then were accompanied three days in a solemn procession to
the quay on the banks of the Tagus. Awaiting them were three carracks,
the *São Luis*, the *São Gregorio*, and the *Bom Jesus*, which they boarded on
the evening of March 23. These three-masted vessels armed with cannons,
broad-beamed, and riding high on the water, were still used halfway through
the sixteenth century both for war and for long trading voyages before
their definitive replacement with the faster and more manageable galleons.
Loaded with goods for sale in the Eastern markets, each ship carried a group
of Jesuits together with over a hundred sailors, soldiers, merchants, and adventurers of every type.

"Brother Ricci, student of theology," as he was listed in the ship's manifest, sailed on the *São Luis*, the flagship, together with the thirty-five-year-
old Michele Ruggieri from the Puglia region, who had entered the novitiate
a year before him after studying law in Naples. His real name, Pompilio, of
Latin origin, had been replaced with a Christian name as required for priests.

The priests traveling on the other ships included Francesco Pasio; Rodolfo
Acquaviva, son of the duke of Atri and nephew of Claudio Acquaviva; and

the Portuguese Duarte de Sande. None of them knew their final destination, only that they were initially bound for Goa, a Portuguese outpost in India where they would stay at the Jesuit College of Saint Paul until their superiors decided on their definitive posting.

The moving scene on the quayside as the vessels set sail at dawn on March 24 was described by one of the missionaries in a letter from the East:

> Fathers wept for their sons and sons for their fathers, women for the husbands they saw leaving them for such distant parts and such perilous seas, with little hope in most cases of ever seeing them again.[4]

The ships were to follow a route similar to the one taken by Vasco da Gama in 1498, when he reached Calicut in India for the first time by circumnavigating Africa and then crossing the Indian Ocean. If all went well, the voyage would take six months.

Travel by sea was hard, unhealthy, and very risky in that period, when it was calculated that one ship in four would go down on average during a long voyage such as the one to be made by the missionaries. The dangers were many and varied. While attack by pirates or other maritime powers to seize possession of the rich cargoes of merchandise was very frequent, more serious perils lay in the structural fragility of the vessels and the lack of adequate instruments to plot their course.

Direction was calculated with the aid of the compass, the most important instrument on board, and latitude by using the astrolabe and quadrant to observe the height of the North Star and the constellations above the horizon and judge from their position in the sky how far the ship was from the equator. Longitude was instead calculated roughly on the basis of the estimated distance traveled from a known port. The margin of error was enormous. In the absence of reliable equipment to determine longitude,[5] a ship faced the open sea with no precise points of reference, at the mercy of the elements, and in danger of colliding with reefs. In order to arrive safely at their destination, everyone trusted to luck and, above all, the Lord's help.

Other serious risks were run on board, where the passengers' accommodation and sanitary conditions were at the limit of human endurance. The already confined space was crammed to the bursting point with merchandise and supplies for the voyage, including barrels of salted meat and fish, rice, hardtack, flour, dried fruit, and casks of wine. The hundreds of passengers competed for the tiny area left free. As the small amounts of fresh food and drinkable water soon went bad and the diet became less varied, travelers fell prey to illnesses. The most frequent was the dreaded scurvy, which decimated crews on long voyages until the beginning of the nineteenth century, due to the prolonged shortage of the vitamin C contained in fresh fruit and vegetables, which it was impossible to keep on board.

The four-berth cabin allotted to the Jesuits was scarcely big enough for them to lie down close to one another and try to sleep, tormented by insect bites and the heat, which became unendurable near the equator. The terrible hardships, which the missionaries were scarcely able to bear, were described as follows by one of the Jesuits who traveled with Ricci in a letter to his superiors:

> Those desirous of traveling to India should not be too tied to life but ever ready to die, having great faith in Our Lord and a great desire for suffering, ready to mortify all their senses, for here one learns to know oneself by experience, not by theoretical reflection.[6]

The extreme conditions did not prevent the Jesuits from practicing their faith and from ensuring its respect by the sailors as well. The missionaries offered confession and celebrated the most important religious festivities with processions on deck. They confiscated playing cards, dice, and any publications they considered obscene, and they punished blasphemy with a system of fines, on agreement that the money thus obtained would be used for the common good. Their work for the sailors also involved caring for the sick with medicinal herbs received from the Portuguese sovereign, which were boiled in cauldrons on deck.

While Ricci did not describe the voyage—which can be reconstructed on the basis of documents and the correspondence of other passengers—in his letters from the East, he did make an indirect reference to it when he was threatened with expulsion from China in 1587 and begged the Chinese to let him stay, stating that he would never be able to travel back across "all those seas" between China and his native land.[7]

Once past Madeira and the Canary Islands, the carracks were threateningly accompanied for a short distance by two French ships, which then sailed away without taking hostile action as they headed for the Brazilian coast to take advantage of the favorable winds. They crossed the equator after a month of sailing and steered southeast toward the Cape of Good Hope.

When on deck, observing the sky by day and contemplating the stars by night, Ricci thought over what he had learned in the astronomy course at the Roman College. It was generally accepted that the earth was round at the end of the sixteenth century, and the Jesuit had the opportunity to see the proof—something which was self-evident to seafarers—for himself. A note in the margin of one of the maps drawn in China referred to his observation during the voyage that the north and south pole stars were the same height above the horizon.[8]

Leaving the islands of Cape Verde behind them, the ships arrived in June at the Cape of Good Hope, the southernmost tip of the African continent, lashed by gales and high seas. Bartolomeu Dias, the first to sail those perilous waters in 1488, called it *Cabo Tormentoso*, the Stormy Cape, a name that the king chose to change on his return to Portugal into *Cabo da Boa Esperança*, a reference to his hopes of discovering the long-sought sea route to India.

Having rounded the cape, the carracks entered the Indian Ocean and stopped for a stay of six weeks at Mozambique, where the Portuguese had a trading outpost, on the mainland facing the island of Madagascar. The sailors replenished the stores of food and water, and the merchants loaded a few hundred slaves for sale on the Eastern markets. The small fleet resumed its voyage in August, sailing around the Horn of Africa to head across the Indian Ocean for Goa. While the ship faced the last stretch of open sea, Ricci was unaware that Chinese navigators had made the same trip various times starting from the opposite direction nearly two centuries before on junks far more imposing than the Portuguese ships. By order of Yongle, the third emperor of the Ming dynasty, who reigned from 1403 to 1424, six voyages of exploration led by Zheng He, a Muslim eunuch remembered as the greatest admiral in Chinese history, arrived as far as the Persian Gulf, the Red Sea, and the coasts of Kenya. A seventh expedition was organized to the same lands during the reign of Xuande and was completed in 1433. The sailors caught zebras, leopards, and giraffes in Africa and brought them back to the court as weird and wonderful trophies, an event recorded in the dynastic chronicles. According to historical reconstructions, the Chinese fleets of the time were of a size inconceivable for Westerners and presented technical characteristics clearly superior to those of any other country. The expeditions commanded by Zheng He were in fact made up of hundreds of vessels and carried between twenty and thirty thousand passengers, including mounted troops, interpreters, government officials, and physicians. The ships were already fitted with watertight compartments and carried all possible provisions as well as fresh water in special tanks. The junks on which the dignitaries traveled were gigantic. While the length of one hundred meters suggested by some scholars has been challenged as excessive, it can reasonably be asserted that the largest vessels reached up to sixty meters and were equipped with three decks and four or five masts.[9] Even on the most conservative estimates, they were far more impressive than any Portuguese carrack or galleon of the late sixteenth century.[10] Moreover, the Chinese ships were also equipped with a rudimentary compass consisting of a magnetic needle on a floating support in a container filled with water, an instrument whose invention is regarded by many historians as yet another instance of Chinese superiority over Europe. The first description of the magnetic needle as an aid for navigation is in fact to be found in a Chinese document of the twelfth century, and even though this period coincides more or less with the first appearance of the device on ships in the West, its use on Chinese junks appears to have begun long before. One established fact is that the Chinese had known the properties of magnetite, the material used to make the compass needle, since the earliest times, as there are records of spoon-shaped instruments on bronze supports very similar to primitive compasses used by geomancers in magical and divinatory practices long before the Christian era.

Despite their considerable advantage over the West in the nautical field, the Chinese lost their maritime supremacy immediately after the last expedition and the death of Zheng He, when the emperor decided to dismantle the fleet and put an end to the great voyages of exploration. The serious threat of the Mongols from the North, which necessitated the mobilization of ever-greater military and economic resources while the imperial coffers were increasingly impoverished, and competition from private expeditions, which had taken control of the most lucrative branches of trade, had made maritime undertakings on such a scale unfeasible. No imperial fleet had since sailed west across the seas, and a century later it was Portuguese ships that set sail for the East in search of new markets.

In India

After the last month of uninterrupted sailing, the Portuguese carracks arrived on the western coasts of India to the great rejoicing of many passengers exhausted by their long voyage.[11] Ricci disembarked in Goa on September 13, 1578.

Standing on a site separated from the mainland by a series of lagoons, the city was the first outpost of Portugal's dominions in the East, conquered in 1510 by the Portuguese navigator and military leader Afonso de Albuquerque, one of the major architects of imperial expansion, who wrested it from the sultan of Bijapur after massacring nearly all of the native population. The hinterland was still under the control of the Muslim ruler, who mounted an unsuccessful siege to regain the city just a few years before Ricci's arrival.

Before creating the outpost of Goa, Albuquerque had occupied the island of Socotra in the Gulf of Aden in 1506, Ormuz at the mouth of the Persian Gulf the following year, and Malacca, a tributary of China now belonging to Malaysia, in 1511, after being appointed viceroy of the Indies in 1508. Despite their rapid expansion, the Portuguese did not seek to conquer territories in the interior of the countries reached by sea but only to control coastal cities serving as stopping points for their trading routes. Other Portuguese commanders built harbors and fortresses in Ceylon, Sumatra, and Japan, and first arrived in China in 1515, later establishing a permanent settlement at Macao near Canton.

From the East, merchants imported goods for which there was great demand in the West. Eagerly sought after to preserve and flavor food, spices such as pepper, cinnamon, nutmeg, cloves, and ginger were considered as precious as gold and silver. Then there were all the other exotic goods like rhubarb, ginseng, scented wood, pearls, jade and turquoise, tea, hides, and typical Chinese products, above all the porcelain, lacquer, and silk famed in the West since the time of the Roman Empire. Even though the secret of silk manufacturing had been prized out of the Chinese as early as the fifth century AD and silk was now produced by other Middle Eastern and European countries, the Chinese variety was the most coveted, especially if worked or embroidered.

Goa was a typical trading city, bustling and cosmopolitan, inhabited by three to four thousand Portuguese; merchants of various nationalities including Persians, Arabs, Turks, and some Venetians; and Jesuit, Franciscan, Dominican, and Augustinian missionaries, who arrived directly from Europe or from other places in the East. The local population, of the Muslim or Hindu persuasion, was over twice the size of the foreign contingent.

Alongside the markets—where goods of every kind from every part of India and the other Portuguese possessions were sold, including African slaves—stood numerous monasteries and fifty churches. The first was built by the order of Albuquerque and was dedicated to Catherine of Alexandria, the patron saint of the city.

Goa was governed by a viceroy appointed in Lisbon with a mandate for the Portuguese dominions in India, and by a council of Portuguese nobles and heads of the trading companies. Watch was kept over religious orthodoxy by the local tribunal of the Inquisition under the intransigent guidance of Bartolomeu da Fonseca, who boasted of having filled the soil with the bones of heretics. The year of Ricci's arrival alone saw seventeen burned at the stake after being forced to parade through the streets in macabre processions clad in tunics impregnated with sulfur. Many were "New Christians," members of Jewish families who were forced to embrace Christianity after the expulsion of the Jews from Portugal in 1497.[12]

Ricci was received into the Jesuit College of Saint Paul, founded forty years earlier by Saint Francis Xavier, whose remains lay in the adjoining church. He resumed his theological studies and taught Greek and Latin to the older pupils at the mission school, attended by over four hundred local children and adolescents. Many of these were orphans, entrusted to the Jesuits in accordance with customary practice and inculcated by them with Christian values.

Living in Goa, Ricci realized that the Hindu and Muslim populations were being forcibly coerced into conversion. The city's Hindu temples had been destroyed by the Portuguese soldiers in 1540, and a law prohibited Christians from having "infidel" servants, thus obliging whoever needed to work with the Portuguese to become Catholic. Moreover, all converts were required to abandon their caste and customs, take a Portuguese name, and adopt Western dress. The situation in which Ricci found himself in that world of blurred boundaries between the sacred and the secular, where religion was mixed up with trafficking, war, coercion, and death, was a far cry from any idea of a mission he may have formed during his years at the Roman College. The harrowing experience of having to adapt to such an extreme reality, as well as to the torrid climate, something still harder to bear for a physique already sorely tried by a long voyage, weakened him to the point where he fell seriously ill. In order to hasten his recovery, the Jesuit authorities transferred him to the town of Cochin on the Indian coast south of Goa, where he stayed for nearly a year, continuing to study theology and to teach Latin and Greek to pupils of the local Jesuit school. It was in Cochin that Ricci was ordained into the priesthood three months before his twenty-eighth birthday and celebrated his first mass on July 26, 1580, as he related in a letter to Ludovico Maselli a few months later: "And on the feast of Saint Ann I sang a solemn mass to the great rejoicing of the fathers and my pupils."[13]

In the same letter, written three years after his departure from Italy, Ricci spoke to the superior, whom he recalled with filial affection, of his nostalgia for the time he had spent in Rome:

> I cannot say what things I imagine at times and how they arouse in me a certain sort of melancholy . . . thinking that the fathers and brothers I loved and love so much at the college, where I was born and raised, might forget me while I hold them all so fresh in my memory. And so one of the good prayers I say with many tears in my misery is to remember you, Most Reverend Father, and the other fathers and brethren at the college.[14]

Ricci returned to Goa at the end of 1580 in order to attend the second- and third-year courses in theology while waiting to be assigned to a mission. Many changes had taken place in the meantime. In 1578, two years earlier, Sebastian I had been killed in the battle of Alcázarquivir against the Turks, and Portugal too had come under the rule of Philip II of Spain while Ricci was in Cochin. This dynastic change was to have no effect on trade or the life of the missions in the East, as it had been decided that the division into areas of Spanish and Portuguese influence would remain in force in accordance with prior agreements.

Ricci was also informed about the fate of the companions who had already left the college in Goa. The previous year, after a few months on the coast of Malabar, Michele Ruggieri had received orders to go to Macao and await a favorable opportunity to gain entry into China. Rodolfo Acquaviva was on a mission with two companions at the court of Akbar, the Muslim ruler of the immense Mughal empire[15] in the northern part of India, where he was to stay for three years in an attempt to open the way for Christianity. On his return, when Ricci had already left, the young Acquaviva, now head of the mission at Salcette near Goa, was to be killed, together with four other Jesuits, by natives. According to historical reconstructions of the event which took place in 1583, the cause of the attack was a hatred for priests due to the destruction of hundreds of Hindu temples by Portuguese soldiers and to ill-considered manifestations of contempt for the local religion on the part of one of the missionaries.[16]

"Chinese in China": Valignano's Policy of Cultural Accommodation

Ricci felt useless in Goa and longed for nothing more than to begin his missionary work. Despite the commitment he put into his work, he derived no satisfaction from the teaching of Latin and Greek grammar, a task that he could not get out of[17] and which he performed solely through a "spirit of obedience," as he confessed in a letter of November 25, 1581, to Claudio Acquaviva,[18] who had been appointed Superior General of the Company of Jesus just a few months earlier.[19] Writing to superiors was one of the duties that missionaries were required to perform on a regular basis in order to provide information about the countries in which they lived and to report on their activities, as well as to express doubts or ask for support. Of the fifty-four letters that have survived out of the unquestionably much larger number sent to Europe by Ricci, twelve are addressed to Superior General Acquaviva and cover the entire period of his mission. In the first letter from Goa, Ricci not only congratulated his superior on his recent appointment but also took the opportunity to express some views about a recent decision taken by his superiors with which he disagreed, a somewhat courageous step for a member of an order insisting on absolute and unquestioning obedience.

The Jesuit authorities had forbidden Indians who were studying for the priesthood from attending the courses on philosophy and theology so as to avoid them becoming "overly proud of their learning" and refusing to work among the poorer sections of the indigenous population. Ricci explained the grounds for his dissent in a number of points. If the reason given for denying access to the advanced courses were valid, he argued, then it would hold also for the novices educated in Europe, to whom the entire syllabus was instead open. Moreover, as he bluntly asserted, not all of the European brethren who had studied philosophy and theology put their knowledge to the best use. A staunch defender of the role of culture in the process of evangelization, Ricci maintained that the restrictions imposed on Indians would have the sole effect of "fostering ignorance in the ministers of the Church in a place where knowledge is so necessary." As he pointed out, the Indian novices were "in any case to become priests and to have souls in their keeping, and it hardly seems appropriate, among so many sorts of unbelievers, for priests to be so ignorant that they are unable to answer an argument or to put one forward in order to confirm themselves and others in our faith, unless we wish to hope for miracles where none are necessary." He concluded his plea with the point closest to his heart, namely that preventing the locals from studying "letters" lest they should become "swellheaded" only brought the risk of incurring hatred and obtaining insincere and short-lived conversions.[20]

These frankly expressed observations highlight the principles upon which Ricci intended to base his missionary work. His convictions with regard to the importance of "knowledge" formed during his years at the Roman College were certainly strengthened in Goa, where he saw for himself how the methods used by the Portuguese soldiers to conquer markets and the coercion imposed on the population to convert them caused distrust, fear, and hatred. The young Jesuit meant to adopt a different method of proselytism, one that would follow the guidelines laid down by the Visitor Alessandro Valignano after his arrival in the Far East. While Clavius had been the point of reference for Ricci's mathematical studies in Rome, Valignano was to become his mentor for his missionary work in China.

Born in Chieti in 1539, Alessandro Valignano graduated in law in Padua at the age of eighteen and entered the Society of Jesus at twenty-seven, four years after being imprisoned for wounding a courtier. Having held important posts such as rector of the College of Macerata, he assumed responsibility for the missions in the East at the age of thirty-four. Of imposing physique and feared for his fiery temper, he was a man of acknowledged ability and charisma. Valignano arrived in Goa four years before Ricci and traveled a great deal through India. He reached Macao in August 1578 and stayed there for nearly a year. It was on the basis of his appraisal of the situation in the East that the Visitor devised a long-term strategy to increase the number of conversions. He was convinced that the missionaries should learn the language of the country in which they were to work, study its way of life, adapt to the local customs, and respect the local traditions unless they proved repugnant to Christian morality. Generally referred to as cultural accommodation, this missionary policy was considered innovative at the time. The Jesuit sinologist Pasquale D'Elia describes it as follows:

> It was certainly not his intention to "Europeanize" the peoples of the Far East. What he wanted, and very strongly, was instead that in all things compatible with dogma and evangelical morality the missionaries should become Indian in India, Chinese in China, and Japanese in Japan. This held for food, clothing, and social customs; in short, for everything that was not sinful.[21]

During Valignano's stay in Macao, his attention focused on China, the empire impervious to all foreign penetration that had already closed its doors on Francis Xavier and to all the Jesuit, Franciscan, and Dominican missionaries seeking entry after him. Anecdotal evidence of how much China occupied the Visitor's thoughts is provided by the Jesuit historian and missionary Alvaro Semedo, who describes him as gazing from a window of the Macao College one day in the direction of the Chinese empire and murmuring, "Fortress, O Fortress, when will you finally open your gates?"[22]

Valignano knew that past failures had convinced most priests that the project of evangelizing China was impracticable, and that the bishop of Manila had reported to the Portuguese sovereign and the pope that only a miracle would make conversion of the Chinese possible.[23] Even though he was the only one to think otherwise, Valignano was determined to attempt the undertaking once again, not least because he was convinced on the basis of evidence gathered over a long period that China was "a great and noble" country inhabited by "people of lively intellect given to study" and governed "with peace and prudence."[24] If it was to be won over to the Christian faith, it would be necessary to find missionaries prepared to adapt to the local culture and become "Chinese in China."

On arriving in Macao at the end of July 1579, Ruggieri found detailed written notes recommending the study of Chinese that had been left by Valignano before setting off for Japan. It would be his task to open the way to China while Ricci was still in Cochin, as we have seen, reluctantly teaching Latin and Greek grammar.

Macao, the Gateway to China

The Portuguese colony of Macao on the Chinese border was situated on a peninsula in the midst of lush subtropical vegetation on the estuary of the Zhujiang, or Pearl River, in the Guangdong province on the South China Sea. The Portuguese name Amacao, from which Macao derives, was a compound of Ama, a local divinity, and gau, meaning "port." The Portuguese had built up a rich settlement of about ten thousand inhabitants with a large hospital and some churches. There were about five hundred families of Portuguese merchants married to Indian or Chinese women as well as missionaries of various nationalities and Indian slaves. The numerous Chinese residents were mainly small shopkeepers and craftsmen or were employed as interpreters for commercial transactions and relations with the local authorities. The pope had recently declared the city a diocese with jurisdiction over China, Japan, and Korea.

Relations between China and the Portuguese did not run smoothly, as attested by the wall built a few years earlier to separate the mainland from the area reserved for the colonialists, which the Chinese were allowed to enter only with permits twice a week. Portuguese ships had permission to sail up the estuary twice a year as far as neighboring Canton,[25] the capital of the Guangdong province and the most important commercial center in southern China, where they stopped for as long as was needed, from two weeks to a few months, to conclude their business. Every other contact between Westerners and the Chinese was discouraged.

The precarious balance of this peaceful coexistence was demonstrated by an incident that took place a few years earlier, when the Jesuit Cristoforo da Costa baptized a young Buddhist from Canton and took him to Macao. Whether justified or unjustified, the suspicion that the young man had been forced to convert triggered a reaction in a section of the local population, who stirred up a riot and even threatened to destroy Macao, until the local officials ordered the missionaries to send the young man back to his hometown.

Relations between the Chinese and Portuguese became strained immediately after the first Portuguese ships made a stop in southern China. An embassy led by Tomé Pires traveled all the way to Beijing in 1520 to request authorization to trade freely throughout imperial territory. Not only were the delegates denied an audience with the emperor, but the Chinese—having learned that Portugal was still occupying their protectorate of Malacca and fearing that it might wish to invade China—had them imprisoned on the way back to Macao and refused to release them. The Chinese government subsequently banned all trade with Portugal. However, economic interests ultimately prevailed, and the ban, which had never been respected, was officially lifted in 1554. The Chinese had since accepted the gradual colonization of Macao in practice, albeit without granting official authorization.

The fear of foreigners and the consequent hostility toward merchants and missionaries were particularly strong in the coastal provinces, as the local populations were exasperated by the recurrent attacks of Sino-Japanese pirates from time immemorial. The scourge of piracy was so dreaded that the Chinese government decided to prohibit all trade between China and Japan in 1560. While this ban was still officially in force, commercial transactions took place all the same through the Portuguese, who plied back and forth between the two countries with their ships. The merchants loaded Chinese products in Macao, especially silk, the commodity most prized in the land of the rising sun, and brought back Japanese silver, greatly in demand in China for use above all as money and in the production of ornamental objects and jewelry. As the precious metal was so coveted in China that it fetched nearly double what it would in the rest of the world, the Portuguese made a fortune by purchasing Chinese goods that they sold in Japan and Europe for practically twice the amount of silver they had invested. The ships loaded with merchandise usually left Macao in June for Japan and in January for India and Europe.

The transit of goods in Macao was controlled by three agents, often including a representative of the Society of Jesus, who ensured division of the goods purchased in Canton according to established quotas so as to allow all the merchants resident in the city to share in the profits. The Jesuits also invested in the sale of silk in accordance with the very favorable terms of an agreement secured by Valignano, which guaranteed them a set percentage of the product every year.[26] The direct involvement of priests in commerce, which served to finance the missions, was criticized by some members of the order but had already been sanctioned by Pope Gregory XIII and would be permitted also by Superior General Acquaviva, who was well aware that the donations of rich merchants were not enough to ensure the survival of the Jesuit residences. The system worked and business was booming despite the ever-present danger of shipwreck. The worst occurred in 1573, when a typhoon struck a vessel just out of Japan, causing one hundred deaths and the loss of eight hundred thousand ducats, a colossal sum for the time.

Immediately after his arrival in the Jesuit residence of Macao, a building of forty-eight rooms located on the outskirts of the city with an attached novitiate and a church dedicated to the Mother of God, later to become the College of Saint Paul, Michele Ruggieri devoted his energies to the study of Chinese. It was no easy matter to set about learning such a complex language, especially as it was almost impossible to find suitable teachers, most of the Chinese residents being uneducated, speaking only the local dialect, and being ignorant of Portuguese. The missionary had to make do for a certain period with a painter who did not speak his language but could at least draw the figures corresponding to the Chinese words on a sheet of paper.

As the months passed, Ruggieri realized that his progress was very limited and that his studies cost him what Ricci later described as "great toil." The Jesuit did not even have the support of the other missionaries, who were convinced of the futility of the China enterprise and were irked that their companion had been exempted from all tasks by order of Valignano in order to concentrate on his studies. Alone against everyone, having become, as Ricci put it, a sort of "martyr to the fathers and brothers here"[27]—that is, his fellow priests and superiors—Ruggieri wrote to Valignano repeatedly, asking to be teamed with Matteo Ricci, his traveling companion on the *São Luis* who had still to be assigned to a mission. The Visitor finally agreed and gave instruction to this effect to the authorities in India.

Meanwhile, in an effort to switch from study to action, Ruggieri decided to enter into China in the only possible way, namely by accompanying the merchants on their journey to Canton. He did this on three occasions, endeavoring each time to stay for as long as possible and to establish relations with the local officials, not least by offering them gifts in accordance with Chinese practice. He had been received by the *haidao*, the official responsible for the security of the coastal areas and for control over foreigners, and had made contact with a military commander, to whom he presented a mechanical clock. The amazed reaction to this gift led Ruggieri to believe that spring-powered devices capable of ringing the hours were unknown in China, where mainly water clocks and sundials were used to measure the passage of time. The missionary had no way of knowing that it was in fact the Chinese who had constructed the first mechanical clocks, the most famous of which being the astronomical tower of Su Song. Dating back to 1092, this clock of nine meters in height used hydraulic devices to indicate the position of the sun and the stars and to tell the time in hours and fractions of an hour. The mechanical clocks of Western design were a novelty, however, and the Chinese began to use the term "bells that ring by themselves" for those objects shown to them by the missionary that were capable of chiming suddenly, as though by magic. The success obtained showed the Jesuit that following the local custom of making gifts of rare objects and demonstrating knowledge of a few words of Mandarin Chinese was an excellent way to win the favor of dignitaries, and he began to think that the task of penetrating China would not prove so very difficult. In order to make suitable preparations for this enterprise, he obtained permission to build a new residence in Macao, the House of Saint Martin, complete with a small chapel situated behind the college, where he intended to lodge the future converts and to continue the study of Chinese together with Ricci. In the meantime, he wrote to the Superior General requesting precious objects and books for presentation as gifts to Chinese officials, including an illustrated Bible and two mechanical clocks, which he already dreamed of presenting to the emperor one day.[28]

Ruggieri visited Canton again in March 1582 after Valignano's return from Japan. Despite the delay due to the slowness of communications between Macao and Goa, Ricci had finally received instructions to proceed to the Portuguese outpost on the threshold of China. It was in April that the man destined to develop the plans sketched out by Valignano and commenced by Ruggieri hurriedly embarked on the first ship bound for Macao, where he arrived three months later after a stop in Malacca. He traveled together with Francesco Pasio, who was on his way to Japan via Macao. Shortly before boarding, Ricci added to his baggage a mechanical clock intended, in accordance with Ruggieri's suggestions, as a gift for the governor of Guangdong. The Jesuit fell so seriously ill during the voyage as to fear for his life, but he recovered immediately after disembarking in Macao on August 7, 1582.

Notes

1. Jonathan Spence, *Chinese Roundabout: Essays on History and Culture* [trad. it. Roma: Fazi, 1996, pp. 66–67].

2. From *padrão*, the stone cross erected by Portuguese navigators at every new landing place.

3. Gaetano Ricciardolo, *Oriente e Occidente negli scritti di Matteo Ricci* (Naples: Chirico, 2003), pp. 41 ff.

4. G. C. Roscioni, op. cit., p. 108.

5. It became possible to calculate longitude accurately on board vessels only in the second half of the eighteenth century with the introduction of the first efficient marine chronometers.

6. J. Spence, *The Memory Palace of Matteo Ricci*, cit., p. 68.

7. FR, book II, ch. IX, p. 238.

8. *Il Mappamondo cinese del Padre Matteo Ricci S.I.*, 3rd edition, Beijing, 1602, now in the Vatican Library, commentary, translation, and annotation by Pasquale D'Elia (Vatican City: Biblioteca Apostolica Vaticana, 1938), pls. 3 and 4.

9. *Dictionnaire d'histoire maritime* (Paris: Éditions Robert Laffont, 2002), pp. 344–46.

10. Joanna Waley-Cohen, *The Sextants of Beijing* (New York: Norton, 1999), p. 46.

11. J. Spence, *The Memory Palace of Matteo Ricci*, cit., p. 80.

12. J. Spence, *The Memory Palace of Matteo Ricci*, cit., p. 106.

13. Letter dated November 29, 1580; OS II, p. 13.

14. Letter dated November 29, 1580, p. 12.

15. The term "Mughal" or "Mogul" was used in the West for the sovereign of the Indian-Islamic dynasty and, by extension, his empire, the founder of which was Bubur or Baber (1483–1530) of Timurid-Turkic lineage, the fifth descendant of Timur or Tamerlane. The dynasty was strengthened by Akbar the Great (1542–1605).

16. G. C. Roscioni, op. cit., p. 82.

17. As he wrote from Cochin to Gian Pietro Maffei in November 30, 1580; OS II, p. 17.

18. Letter to Claudio Acquaviva, November 25, 1581; OS II, p. 19.

19. On February 19, 1581, at the age of 38.

20. Letter to Claudio Acquaviva, November 25, 1581; OS II, p. 20.

21. FR, introduction, p. XCIII.

22. FR, introduction, p. LXXXVII.

23. FR, introduction, p. LXXXVIII.

24. FR, introduction, book II, ch. I, p. 142.

25. Guangzhou in Mandarin Chinese. Canton is the Western name for the Guangdong province and is also used for its capital.

26. J. Spence, *The Memory Palace of Matteo Ricci*, cit., pp. 175–76.

27. Letter to Claudio Acquaviva, February 13, 1583; OS II, p. 32.

28. Letter from Michele Ruggieri to Everard Mercurian, November 12, 1581; ibid., appendix 3.

CHAPTER THREE

~

The Difficulty of Learning Chinese

From Macao to Zhaoqing, 1582–1583

If it cannot be said that philosophers are rulers in this land, it can at least be truthfully said that the rulers are guided by philosophers.[1]

My intention is nothing other than to go ahead with this enterprise, which I regard as one of the most important and useful to God in Christendom today. We consider it a very good thing to be responsible for as many souls as there are in this other world of China.[2]

—Matteo Ricci

The Name of China, Ideograms, and Brushes

The first direct contact between Ricci, who turned thirty on October 6, 1582, and the Chinese population came in the Portuguese colony. He was struck by their small build, their youthful appearance belying their actual age, their eyes which he described in his history of the mission[3] as "small, black, markedly oval, and protruding,"[4] their minute noses and ears, and their straight black hair worn long by both sexes, under a sort of cap for the men and held in place with valuable ornamental hairpins for the women of the upper classes. While most of the Chinese living in Macao belonged to the lower class, visiting officials clad in silk were sometimes seen in the streets. When it was very sunny, they walked in the shade of large paper parasols held by servants, as did the wealthy Portuguese traders.[5]

Having settled in at the Saint Martin residence and in the absence of Ruggieri, who had made another trip to Canton, Ricci set about following the Visitor's instructions by learning about the government, customs, and way of life of the great empire stretching out on the other side of the wall. In accordance with Valignano's orders, which he asked Superior General Acquaviva to confirm by letter, Ricci was to be assigned no other duties so as to avoid distracting him from the task he had been set. He was delighted to enjoy a considerable degree of freedom from the local clergy and their dogged incomprehension of the China mission. As he wrote to Acquaviva, "They are all very devout but the things of Christianity are understood only by those who actually deal with them."[6]

Ricci knew that the great Chinese empire was of ancient origin, was richly endowed with culture, and was proud in the conviction of its superiority to other peoples. It was commonly believed that the Chinese took no particular interest in discovering what was happening outside their borders. The Jesuit was only exaggerating a little when he described them as "convinced that all the knowledge in the world is contained in their kingdom and all the others are ignorant barbarians. Speaking in their books and writings of foreign kingdoms, they always assume them to be peoples slightly inferior to animals."[7]

Ricci remembered what he had learned in the courses of history and geography at the Roman College and compared his knowledge with what he read in Chinese books with the aid of interpreters. He knew that China was the country referred to as *Sinai* in Ptolemy's *Almagest* and that it corresponded to *Serica*, the term used in Greco-Roman antiquity to designate the eastern region from which silk came. He was surprised to discover that the name *Cina* or *China* used by Westerners was completely unknown to the Chinese, who referred to their country as the *Zhong-guo*, or "Middle Kingdom," an expression still in use today, or with the name of the reigning dynasty, the Ming at the time, often preceded by the adjective *da*, meaning "great," hence *Da Ming*. Matters were further complicated by the fact that not all of the Eastern countries used the same name for China. While the Japanese still referred to it by the name of the Tang dynasty, in power from the sixth to the ninth century of the Common Era, the inhabitants of Cochin China, a region of present-day Vietnam and Thailand, then called Siam, used the name of the Chin or Qin dynasty ruling in the second century BC, from which the name "China" is thought to have then derived. The capital was called *Beijing*, meaning "northern capital," which the Portuguese transformed into *Pequin* on the basis of its pronunciation in the Cantonese dialect, and which Ricci wrote as *Pachino, Pacchino, Pequinum,* or *Pequim*.

The absolute ruler was the emperor, or *huangdi*, referred to as "the Son of Heaven," who governed with the assistance of a bureaucratic structure of officials, *guan* in Chinese, recruited through a system of competitive examinations.[8] These officials were resident both in the capital Beijing and in the fifteen provinces of the empire, each administered by a governor[9] and a hierarchy of *guan* in charge of the prefectures, sub-prefectures, districts, and further territorial subdivisions.

The emperor ruled a country larger than the whole of Europe, where the distances, the size of the provinces, and the number of the inhabitants of cities, towns, and villages reached orders of magnitude inconceivable for Westerners. China had a population of approximately two hundred million at the end of the sixteenth century.[10] The Ming dynasty, a name meaning "light," had been in power since 1368, and the fourteenth emperor, Zhu Yijun, had been on the throne for nine years, his succession having taken place in 1573, before he reached the age of ten. He was known as Wanli, the "era name" he had chosen in accordance with custom on his accession,[11] at which point the numbering of the years started again from zero. As Ricci was informed, the year 1582 was therefore referred to as the "ninth year of Wanli" by the Chinese.

Now familiar with some basic facts about China, Ricci set about learning Chinese with the aid of teachers and devoted his energies above all to the study of Mandarin, the language spoken by the educated classes[12] and very different from the local dialects used in all the provinces. Although well trained in the learning of new languages, the Jesuit found Chinese completely different from any classical or contemporary language he had ever studied, including the hardest. He described it to Martino de Fornari,[13] his professor of rhetoric at the Roman College, as "nothing like either Greek or German" and went on to give lengthy explanations of its characteristics and its difficulties for the learner. One of the peculiarities of Chinese was the absence of declensions, declinations, conjugations, genders, forms, tenses, and modes. The meaning of a phrase depended on the order in which the words were placed, with the aid of a few particles. Another was the fact of consisting mostly of short words of one or two syllables, whose pronunciation was an authentic riddle, as practically every word changed its meaning when pronounced in different tones.[14] While pronunciation was a torment, writing proved still more complex. Ricci described the ideograms, elaborate characters made up of numerous minute strokes of ink, as "tangles of different letters" and the writing as something impossible for anyone to believe without seeing or attempting for himself. The language was made still more elusive by the fact that many Chinese words written with different characters were very similar in pronunciation. As a result, communication was often ambiguous, and writing from dictation was almost impossible. As if this were not enough, the pronunciation of the same words in the different dialects changed so much as to make conversation between the inhabitants of different provinces difficult. As the Jesuit complained to his former teacher, "It is the most ambiguous spoken and written language ever to be found." He noted on numerous occasions that in order to make themselves understood and clear up misunderstandings in oral communication, the Chinese would often use their fingers to draw the characters corresponding to their spoken words in the air or on the palm of their hand, thus showing that it was the written rather than the spoken language that unified the empire. Children learned to write by devoting their first few years of school to memorizing the basic characters, a demanding task that required constant practice. Ricci was not frightened by the scale of this undertaking, which was still more onerous for an adult, because he was naturally gifted with an excellent memory and knew how to increase its capacity by means of the ancient mnemonic techniques studied at the Roman College. His ability was indeed such that he is reported to have had perfect recall even of things he read only once.[15]

Ricci committed as many characters as possible to memory and did exercises every day in the correct use of the brush used by the Chinese for writing, which was held with the wrist at a precise angle to the paper. The Chinese brushes varied greatly in shape and size, and the bristles of different animals were used in accordance with their purpose. Those preferred for writing were the stiff, short hairs of weasels, martens, and skunks, especially suitable for the smaller characters, or hares, rabbits, deer, and wolves, while goat bristles were prized above all for painting.[16] Made of bamboo, ivory, wood, lacquer, porcelain, and precious metals, the handles could be sober or richly decorated. The technique Ricci learned during his daily exercises struck him as closer to painting, and his comment to De Fornari—"their writing is more like painting"—pinpointed the aesthetic and creative dimension of calligraphy, which had indeed become an art in its own right in China and was appreciated as much as the representation of landscapes or animals.

In his exercises and in writing letters to Rome, Ricci noted that Chinese paper was much flimsier than the type used in Europe and that only one side of the sheet could be used. Paper had been invented in China in the second century AD, if not earlier, and had come into general use there about a thousand years before Europe. It had been commonly used for centuries not only for writing but also to make hats, shoes, clothes, blankets, money, kites, and ornamental objects, as the missionary was amazed to discover.[17]

One year later, Ricci's progress was already greater than his friend Ruggieri had managed in three, and he was now able to remember and write a large number of characters: "I've got a good number of them into my head and can already write them all." It is hard to tell just how many characters Ricci learned in his first year of study and in the later course of his life, when he set about writing books in Chinese. He states in his history of the mission that Chinese has a total of seventy thousand characters, but knowledge of ten thousand is sufficient for everyday purposes. While this is an exaggeration, the total number is still very high—forty-nine thousand according to the dictionary published in 1716 during the reign of the emperor Kangxi.[18]

Books Galore

Having attained some familiarity with the writing, Ricci began to examine Chinese books and saw that they were produced in a different way from those in the West. He discovered that they were read in the opposite direction, turning the pages from left to right, which gave a European the impression of beginning at the end and ending at the beginning. Moreover, the writing on every page was vertical rather than horizontal, and the words and phrases were written one after the other with no breaks and no punctuation, thus leaving the reader the task of isolating the groups of characters constituting units of meaning.

In seeking out manuals to consult with the aid of interpreters in order to draw up the report on China requested by Valignano, Ricci became aware of the extraordinarily vast scale of book production. Printing was indeed widespread in the Ming era, including not only historical, philosophical, and ethical works published in literary Chinese, the written language that played a role comparable to Latin in Europe, but also a large number of books in the vernacular. Works for all tastes were to be found on the market, from romantic novels to all sorts of practical handbooks for everyday use, technical works on agriculture and handicrafts, dictionaries, glossaries, and guides for merchants.

This vast circulation of printed volumes surprised Ricci and confirmed his view of the Chinese as a literate people. The vast output of publications was made possible by the use of xylography, or wood-block printing, the most ancient technique known. This had become widespread in China as early as the sixth century AD, during the Tang dynasty, and long ahead of the West, where the use of an analogous procedure did not begin before the end of the thirteenth century. The characters and figures of a page of a book were carved in relief on a block of wood used as a matrix for printing, which was then coated with ink and pressed against sheets of paper so that the shapes in relief were printed as black characters on a white ground. Colored illustrations were also reproduced with the use of different inks. The method required considerable skill in carrying out the intaglio work but proved economical because the completed wooden matrices made it possible to run off as many copies of the book as might be required at any time. Ricci observed and admired the Chinese craftsmen and their mastery in carving the wooden blocks, and he realized that they worked much faster than the Western printers using the more recent technique of movable type: "As regards speed and facility, it seems to me that their engravers cut a block in the same time as it takes our printers to compose and emend a sheet, or slightly less."[19]

Printing with movable type had also been known in China long before in Europe, with wooden or ceramic type being used there in the eleventh century, whereas it was not until halfway through the fifteenth century that Johannes, or Henne, Gensfleisch (c. 1400–1468), known as Gutenberg after his family's hometown, brought it into large-scale employment in the West. Instead of wooden blocks engraved with entire pages, this technique used small blocks of lead, each bearing a letter of the alphabet in relief on one of its faces. This "type" was then arranged in a special container to compose the words for printing. Unlike wood-block printing, where the completed matrices were no longer susceptible of modification, the movable type could be used repeatedly for different publications. Because the very high number of Chinese characters involved the use of an equally high number of types, thus making the printing process too expensive, this technique was used in China only for works of particular importance, such as imperial publications.

Ricci studied all the books he could gather together and had some parts translated by his interpreters, impatiently awaiting the day when he would be able to read them unaided. He was impressed by the quantity and quality of the treatises on medicinal herbs, embellished with detailed illustrations, and probably consulted some of the texts later included in the most important pharmacological work of the Ming era, namely the *Bencao Gangmu* or *Compendium of Materia Medica* by Li Shizen, published in 1596 and containing the names of 1,892 plants, 11,000 recipes for cures, and 1,100 illustrations. The work also made the first mention of a method of immunization against smallpox, over two centuries before Western medicine. Ricci commented on the methods of Chinese medicine in his letters—"they do everything delicately with herbs"[20]—and reported admiringly that the physicians were able to treat dental problems by inserting "iron" into the teeth, by which he probably meant something similar to fillings or primitive dentures.

The Jesuit also found useful information in the numerous Chinese geographic treatises featuring the different provinces of the empire, which he studied carefully with the intention of using them to draw more accurate maps of the country than those commonly circulating in Europe. The maps of the East published in the West were in fact not only incomplete in their representation of largely unexplored countries but also contained misinformation due to the unscrupulous manipulation of data by the Spanish and Portuguese so as to enhance the importance of the territories whose trade they monopolized. Ricci warned De Fornari not to trust maps of the world because of the gross mistakes they made, "either through lack of knowledge or due to the disputes over borders between the kings of Portugal and Spain," and announced his resolve to correct the inaccuracies: "They will now cease." He set to work immediately by calculating the geographic coordinates of Macao and deciding to do likewise for each of the other Chinese cities he would visit.

The Charade of the Permit and the Letter from Wang Pan

Ricci hoped that his stay in Macao would be short and that he would soon be able to settle in China together with Ruggieri, not least because various signs seemed to indicate that the Chinese authorities were not as hostile as had been thought.

While he was still en route from Goa to Macao, the governor of the Guangdong province, Chen Rui, resident in Zhaoqing to the northwest of Canton, expressed his desire to receive Macao's two highest authorities, namely the bishop and the captain of the garrison, in an official audience. The invitation was significant, and the Portuguese decided to accept, albeit with the precautionary step of sending Michele Ruggieri and the judge Matthias de Panela, two figures of lesser official standing, in their place.[21]

Their meeting with the governor, described by Ricci in his subsequent account of these events as "shrewd and fond of money,"[22] proved most cordial. The official showed his appreciation of the mirrors and lengths of velvet and wool presented to him as gifts and entrusted the two visitors with silver to buy other goods in Macao, asking them to return with new Western objects for a further meeting, at which only the judge was present. Being obliged by illness to remain in Macao, the Jesuit took care to send a pair of reading glasses, articles still unknown in China and in great demand throughout the East, as a personal gift, together with the promise that he would deliver a mechanical clock in person as soon as he was better.

The effects of these attentions were beyond all expectations, as the governor was so pleased with the gifts that he gave the judge a permit authorizing Ruggieri and a fellow priest to reside in China. Given this unexpected opportunity, Valignano decided to act quickly. As Ricci had now arrived in Macao together with Francesco Pasio, the Visitor asked the latter to take up residence in China with Ruggieri instead of leaving for Japan, despite his awareness that neither of them had yet mastered the language. After settling in, the two missionaries would be able to submit a request to the authorities for Ricci to join them. Valignano authorized Ruggieri and Pasio to adopt the dress and appearance of Buddhist monks, exchanging their customary black apparel for the traditional gray robes and shaving their heads and chins. In view of the fact that bonzes enjoyed great respect in Japan, where a Jesuit mission had been successfully established, this step was intended to convey the idea to the Chinese that the two men were priests in the easiest and most immediately evident way.

Ruggieri and Pasio arrived in Zhaoqing at the end of December 1582[23] and soon obtained permission from the authorities for Ricci to join them. In the meantime, Valignano set off again on his constant travels throughout the East for the purpose of organizing the missions, heading this time for India.[24] Before Ricci was able to join his companions, however, the governor was removed from office by one of the *guan* responsible for ensuring the smooth functioning of the provincial administration—one of the dreaded censors known as "the emperor's eyes and ears"—and the missionaries' position in China became most precarious. Ruggieri and Pasio were ordered to return to Macao but managed to obtain a letter from the mandarin addressed to the *haidao* in Canton, who was in control of the entry of foreigners, asking him to grant the missionaries permission to reside in the provincial capital. While awaiting an audience with this official, the missionaries returned to Macao, and Pasio was authorized to continue on his way to Japan, abandoning the Chinese enterprise forever.

When the new governor, Guo Yingpin, took office in Zhaoqing, his subordinates found a copy of the letter delivered to the Jesuits by his predecessor in the records. Given the absence of any documentation of the steps that had been taken as a result, the officials feared punishment for failure to perform their duties and instructed the Portuguese authorities to return the original, which was lying unused and "sealed so that it could not be opened" in the Jesuit residence in Macao. Determined not to miss this opportunity for slipping through the meshes of the Chinese bureaucracy, the rector Francisco Cabral decided to ignore the order and to send Ruggieri and Ricci to present the letter to the *haidao*.

It was then that the missionaries entered the labyrinth of Chinese bureaucracy, discovering its complexities and its almost infinite procedural ramifications, and becoming aware that the strict laws safeguarding the territories of the empire were applied with the utmost rigor by some officials and with considerable elasticity by others. In order to be received by the *haidao*, authorization had to be obtained from the district official resident in Xiangshan, not far from the provincial capital, who made it known, however, that he regarded a document issued by a sacked governor as devoid of any validity. The missionaries then decided to leave without authorization, but nobody was prepared to take two foreigners without written permits by boat to Canton. Fortunately, the hostile official suddenly left Xiangshan, and his replacement, who knew nothing about the matter, granted the Jesuits permission to present themselves to the *haidao*. The latter, however, proved just as elusive as he was courteous, claiming that he lacked the power to grant a residence permit and advising the Jesuits to apply to the new governor, supposedly the only individual capable of doing so. After so much effort, they found themselves back at square one.

Not only were the Jesuits ordered to leave Canton posthaste, but the governor also had an edict posted on the walls of all the towns in the province forbidding anyone to grant foreigners residence permits and threatening anyone who taught Chinese to foreigners with severe punishment. Ricci and Ruggieri returned to Macao "with practically all hope now lost of ever being able to obtain entry . . . into China."[25]

In August 1583, less than a week after their return to Macao, Ricci and Ruggieri received a letter signed by Wang Pan, prefect of the region in which Zhaoqing was located and hence an administrative official of a certain importance, inviting them to take up residence in the town. This came as a great surprise. Nobody could imagine what had induced Wang Pan, an official famed for his integrity, to ignore the edict just issued by the governor, his superior. Some later reconstructions of the events suggest that Wang Pan was prompted by curiosity, having heard of the Jesuits' mechanical clock—the "bell that rang by itself"—and wishing to see it for himself; others that the mandarin had learned that Ricci and Ruggieri were experts in mathematics and astronomical calculations and wished to meet these two sages from far away.

Ricci saw Wang Pan's invitation as a sign "more likely to have come from heaven than through human agency," but he also thought more prosaically that the handsome gratuity bestowed by Ruggieri on some administrative officials during his first stay in Zhaoqing so as to secure their intercession on the Jesuits' behalf might have finally borne fruit.

Whatever the contingent reasons may have been, this development was one of great symbolic significance. After all the Jesuits' fruitless efforts to gain entry to China, it was a mandarin that took the initiative and invited them in. Events had taken a turn favorable to the missionaries through unfathomable subterranean processes.

Residence on Chinese Soil in Zhaoqing

Ricci and Ruggieri prepared to leave for Zhaoqing at the end of August. The first difficulty was raising the money to finance the opening of the new mission, since the eight thousand ducats assigned to the Jesuits of Macao had disappeared with the wreck of yet another Portuguese ship the year before. The Portuguese merchant Gaspar Viega came to their aid with an offer to cover their initial expenses pending the arrival of fresh funds by sea.

With shaven heads and chins and clad in gray robes, with the addition of a square cap similar to the biretta of Catholic clergy[26] being the only detail distinguishing them from Buddhist monks, the two Jesuits embarked at the beginning of September 1583, together with some servants and their Chinese interpreter, Filippo, a convert to Christianity born in Macao. They were to sail up the Pearl River to Canton, receive the permits needed to continue their journey from the *haidao*, and then proceed along the river to Zhaoqing with a military escort sent to protect and watch over them by order of Wang Pan.

Most of the transport in China took advantage of a network of rivers and canals enabling vessels of all shapes and sizes to proceed through the country. All the merchants in the south of China stopped in Canton, where the most important markets were located. Ricci's impression on leaving the provincial capital was that the port of the densely inhabited metropolis was more crowded than Venice or Lisbon and that the Pearl River, which he judged to be wider than the Po, was so congested as to constitute "one long harbor." When the Jesuit learned that the capital, Beijing, could also be reached by way of the river and canal system in approximately three months, he had the image of China as "an enormous Venice," as he wrote to Giambattista Román, the Spanish procurator resident in the Philippines, from Zhaoqing on September 13, 1584.[27]

Sailing alongside the Jesuits' medium-sized junk were all kinds of sampans, the flat-bottomed wooden boats used in the Far East for rivers and coastal waters; huge barges carrying materials or passengers; and the sumptuously equipped and decorated ships of eminent mandarins. Ricci found out that the Chinese distinguished all vessels in terms of their cruising speed, the fastest junks being called "wind boats" and the slowest craft "horse boats." In addition to the vessels in motion, he observed ramshackle sampans moored along the banks and used as dwellings for entire families together with a few ducks and chickens.

The two Jesuits saw the rich Chinese countryside opening up before their eyes, rice paddies and cultivated fields alternating with plantations of sugar cane, thick clumps of bamboo, orchards, and market gardens. Along the banks of the river, lined in the Chinese fashion with embankments covered in vegetation and "cool, shady" trees, they saw peasants carrying large wicker baskets hung at both ends of long bamboo canes resting on their shoulders. When the river came to one of the very numerous and thickly inhabited villages, they caught glimpses of enclosures full of pigs, ducks, geese, chickens, goats, and water buffalo. Ricci could see no flaw in the well-being of the inhabitants of the fertile land "full of trees and gardens" into which he was now venturing for the first time. On viewing the regular succession of villages and towns, he formed the unreal idea of China as a very orderly country. As he wrote to Román, "The whole of China looks as though it was constructed by a mathematician who went around, compasses in hand, putting all the inhabitants in their right place."

On September 10, 1583, after about ten days of travel, the Jesuits disembarked in Zhaoqing, a town of subtropical climate surrounded by wooded hills, cultivated fields, and orchards at the confluence of the Xi Jiang, a tributary of the Pearl River, and one of its lesser branches. They were taken with no delay to an audience with the man who had arranged their entry into China, the prefect Wang Pan, before whom they knelt down and asked for permission to remain and live in the town in order to worship their god, the Lord of Heaven and Earth. The official gave them a warm welcome and responded to their request for land on which to build a house by granting them permission to look for a suitable site. The missionaries found a spot meeting their requirements just outside the city walls and close to the point where the two rivers met, which Ricci described as "very cool due to the many trees and gardens all around it."[28] An octagonal nine-story pagoda called the "blossoming tower" or "tower of good fortune" was already under construction there to house the city's administrative offices. Traditionally erected with an odd number of floors gradually decreasing in size, towers were used throughout Chinese territory as religious or public buildings.

The Jesuits' choice was approved by Wang Pan and endorsed by the governor. The prefect arrived in the park on the day of the official granting of the site in order to celebrate this important event, borne by four grooms in a litter that struck Ricci as very similar to the one used by the pope, and accompanied by a procession of guards and lesser officials. Some carried large colored parasols or wooden tablets indicating the prefect's rank in the imperial bureaucracy. Some beat gongs to warn the populace that the procession was passing. Some held bamboo canes and iron chains, instruments commonly used to punish outlaws, which they beat on the ground to produce a sinister noise.[29] One guard marched in front with a sealed box containing the indispensable seal required to validate every document issued by the prefect. This precious object, from which Wang Pan never allowed himself to be separated, had been entrusted to him by the emperor during the official ceremony of appointment, when the *guan* had solemnly sworn to perform his duties faithfully and justly. Ricci knew that any official who lost his seal, the symbol of his power, would be stripped of office and severely punished. He was even told that some mandarins slept with the seal hidden under their beds for fear of being robbed.

While a crowd of people poured into the park to witness the unusual ceremony and to peer at the faces of the two Westerners, whose features were of a kind never previously beheld, the Jesuits kowtowed in the customary manner, kneeling three times and bowing their foreheads to the ground three times on each occasion, and thanked Wang Pan, promising to respect the Chinese laws and never to accommodate other foreigners in their dwelling.

The governor assumed that the Jesuits would wish to worship the same idols as the Buddhists, whose robes they wore, and was astonished when the two Westerners requested another small plot of land to build a chapel to their god, the Lord of Heaven. Even though the newcomers' religion was completely unknown to him, the mandarin granted their request with the typically detached Chinese attitude toward forms of religion, saying that it made little difference to him what deity his protégés might wish to worship.

Immediately after this exchange of promises, the Jesuits presented the mandarin with their gifts in accordance with ritual as the indispensable event crowning every meeting. The climax of the ceremony came when Ricci slowly opened a small wooden box and solemnly extracted a transparent object shaped like a pyramid. On direct exposure to the sun's rays, this mysterious entity emitted all the colors of the rainbow. Referred to by Ricci as "a triangular glass from Venice,"[30] this prism of glass with a three-cornered base made by Venetian craftsmen was capable of breaking down the light that struck one of its faces into the seven colors of the spectrum. Wang Pan's reaction to the object, which looked like a magical amulet, told the Jesuits that prisms and mechanical clocks would prove the most suitable gifts to ensure the favor of Chinese officials.

The mandarin also appreciated the other gifts of a more customary nature, a small painting of the Virgin Mary and some handkerchiefs embroidered by hand, which he sent home for his wife to see but then returned to the Jesuits together with the prism in order to avoid any suspicion of deriving personal gain from the priests' arrival.

Wang Pan's friendly and helpful attitude toward the missionaries contrasted with the evident hostility of another important mandarin, who had taken part in the ceremony with obvious reluctance, namely the official supervising the construction of the tower. The Jesuits gave little thought to this, as their safety was guaranteed by the protection of Wang Pan, the most important official resident in the city after the governor, but they were soon to realize that these feelings of aversion were shared by a large section of the local population.

Well aware of the great privilege granted them as the only foreigners resident in the Guangdong province, the Jesuits expressed a desire to pay their respects to the governor. Having issued the edict against foreigners and being certainly influenced by the very Chinese fear of losing face, the official made it known that the Jesuits were to content themselves with his permission to stay and not to request a meeting. He had no intention whatsoever of receiving them.

Notes

1. FR, book I, ch. V, p. 36.

2. Letter to Claudio Acquaviva, February 13, 1583; OS II, p. 35.

3. The work written by Ricci and published after his death with the title *Della entrata della Compagnia di Giesù e Christianità nella Cina* will be referred to in the text for brevity as his history of the mission.

4. FR, book I, ch. VIII, p. 88.

5. Nigel Cameron, *Barbarians and Mandarins* (Oxford: Oxford University Press, 1989), illustration p. 128.

6. Letter to Claudio Acquaviva, February 13, 1583; OS II, p. 35.

7. FR, book I, ch. IX, p. 102.

8. Established in the fifth century under the Sui dynasty, the system of examinations for the selection of state officials developed through Chinese history to become to backbone of the empire. Its abolition in 1905 was followed six years later by the collapse of the empire.

9. The term used by Ricci in his history of the mission is *viceré*, or viceroy, corresponding to "governor" in the current terminology.

10. Cf. Patricia Buckley Ebrey, *The Cambridge Illustrated History of China* (London: Cambridge University Press, 1996), p. 195.

11. At the beginning of their history, the Chinese numbered the years starting from the accession of each sovereign. A new system was introduced in 163 BC (the seventeenth year of the reign of Emperor Wen of the Han dynasty) whereby each emperor selected a *nianhao* or "era name" of particular significance, which could refer to his reign as a whole, and thus be retained until his death, or be changed at will to indicate different periods. This lasted for over fifteen centuries until the advent of the Ming dynasty, when each ruler adopted just one *nianhao*, thus leading to the practice in Europe and to some extent also in China of referring to an emperor by the name of his years on the throne. "Wanli" is the *nianhao* of Zhu Yijun (1563–1620). According to the dating accepted by most authors and adopted here too, Wanli took the throne in 1573. According to Ray Huang and others, he did so in 1572.

12. The term "Mandarin" is instead used today to refer to Putonghua, the official language of the People's Republic of China.

13. Letter dated February 13, 1583; OS II, pp. 27 ff.

14. Mandarin Chinese, the language spoken by the ruling class, had five tones in the south of the country but four in the north. Ricci thus speaks of five tones in his history of the mission. The fifth is the neutral tone.

15. See the section on the palace of memory in chapter 8.

16. Marina Battaglini, "Matteo Ricci e la tradizione libraria cinese," in *Padre Matteo Ricci. L'Europa alla corte dei Ming* (Milan: Mazzotta, 2003), p. 48.

17. Robert Temple, *The Genius of China* (London: Prion Books, 1998), p. 81.

18. Knowledge of between 2,000 and 3,000 characters is enough to read a newspaper in contemporary China.

19. FR, book I, ch. IV, p. 31.

20. Letter to Martino de Fornari, February 13, 1583; OS II, p. 30.

21. FR, book II, ch. II, p. 162, no. 3.

22. FR, book II, ch. II, p. 161.

23. The Gregorian calendar was not introduced in Goa until 1583, and the date therefore refers to the Julian system.

24. Valignano made regular visits to Macao and always kept in contact with the missionaries dependent upon him by letter.

25. FR, book II, ch. II, p. 175.

26. Letter to Girolamo Benci, October 7, 1595; OS II, p. 163.

27. Letter to Giambattista Roman, September 13, 1584, pp. 36–49.

28. FR, book II, ch. III, p. 185.

29. Letter to Martino de Fornari, February 13, 1583; OS II, p. 30.

30. FR, book II, ch. III, p. 188.

CHAPTER FOUR

~

The Man from the West

Zhaoqing, 1583–1584

Books arrive where the fathers cannot and our things are stated much better in writing than speech in this land due to the great power of letters here.[1]

—Matteo Ricci

Fan Chi inquired about wisdom. The Master replied, "To devote yourself to what is appropriate for the people, and to show respect for the ghosts and spirits while keeping them at a distance can be called wisdom."

—Confucius, *Analects* (6, 22)[2]

Chinese Life

On Chinese soil for the first time in the company of Ruggieri alone, Ricci was conscious of being observed with curiosity whenever he walked through the streets. The local inhabitants gazed at the strange man from far away and smiled in amazement at the shape of his eyes and face. The Jesuit in turn examined the new world surrounding him, eager to understand its diversity but also to discover reassuring similarities with life in Europe.

The missionaries intended to devote the first months of their stay to the construction of their residence. They planned a two-story brick building in the European style, quite unlike the one-story Chinese dwellings made of wood with no foundations. Just as the laborers were about to start, however, the official in charge of erecting the tower, who had already displayed a

hostile attitude, made it known that the day chosen was not considered pro-
pitious and that the commencement should be postponed. The interpreter
explained to the astonished Jesuits that nobody in China ever began any
enterprise, and certainly not the construction of a house, without consulting
the astrological almanac with its list of the days and times considered auspicious or inauspicious for undertaking every type of activity. Published every
year by the imperial astronomers together with the calendar and its astronomical predictions, this "book of fortune" was in such demand that stocks
soon ran out and a flourishing industry had developed for the production of
unauthorized copies. Opposed to every form of superstition and suspecting
duplicity on the part of the Chinese, Ricci refused to take the warning into
consideration, but as luck would have it, a sudden torrential downpour made
it effectively impossible for work to begin.

The Chinese took advantage of the delay to ask the Jesuits to move the
location of the building farther away from the entrance to the tower. Ricci
agreed, and his obliging attitude was rewarded with a gift of wood, bricks,
and other materials. The episode was an instructive lesson in local customs.
The missionaries realized that the Chinese preferred not to say directly what
they wanted, just as they would avoid flatly refusing by inventing obstacles,
possibly of an astrological nature, until it was dropped.

Even though work on the residence took up most of Ricci's time and energies, he resumed his study of Chinese in order to become independent of
interpreters as soon as possible, and he endeavored to improve his knowledge
of the local ways and customs so as to adapt fully to the new life.

His observation of the activities carried out in the town told him that
the Guangdong province was rich and abundantly provided with all the
requisites for prosperity and that trade and handicrafts were both thriving.
He thought Zhaoqing much more densely inhabited than an Italian town of
equivalent size and more orderly in appearance with its "well built, straight,
paved" streets,[3] and he was struck by some peculiar constructions on columns
similar to triumphal arches. Made of brightly colored wood on a stone base,
these monuments erected to commemorate important figures were a common feature in all Chinese cities.

The Jesuit observed the inhabitants and their constant activity as he
walked through the streets teeming with life. Men and women wore garments reaching down to the ground, very often made of silk and with long
sleeves "like our Venetians."[4] The men wore various kinds of round caps
made of horsehair or velvet, square hats being reserved exclusively for mandarins. He noted the presence of a great many elderly people in the streets
and deduced that the deadly epidemics well known in Europe were unusual

in China and that the life expectancy there was high. He was surprised to see that, unlike Europeans, none of the Chinese carried weapons, with the sole exception of the bodyguards of important *guan* or soldiers on duty, and that the brawls and disturbances commonly encountered in the streets of European cities, where violence was an everyday occurrence, were practically nonexistent. Noting also that the Chinese did not consider it dishonorable to turn and run when attacked, he regarded them as peaceful by nature and even effeminate in view of their attention to dress and their apparently submissive nature,[5] a hasty judgment that he revised when his understanding of Chinese society deepened.

His explorations led him to wander through the large and small markets, meeting places for the local population where products of every kind were on sale, from fruit, vegetables, and cereals to pork, poultry, and freshwater fish displayed on wooden tables or simply laid out on the ground. Some vendors offered boiled vegetables and rice ready for consumption, together with wine made from cereals. Onlookers gathered around people crouched on the ground between the stalls to play cards or dice, the common pastimes of the poor. Fortune-tellers, both men and women, and sometimes blind, were to be found offering their services for a few copper coins in front of every shop in every street and square. On seeing just how numerous they were, Ricci realized with dismay that horoscopes and all kinds of fortune-telling were even more popular than in Europe.

Intermingled with the people in the streets were priests of the two most important Chinese religions, Taoists[6] with long hair and square, black caps and Buddhists with shaven heads. The latter were mendicants and carried bowls for the morsels of boiled rice and vegetables they received as alms.

Women were seldom seen in the streets of Zhaoqing, as it was considered seemlier for them to stay at home out of sight, and it was only the female peasants who went out regularly to work in the fields. Polygamy was practiced in China, at least among the members of the upper classes wealthy enough to maintain one or more concubines. Deeply rooted in the traditional way of life, this practice stemmed from the need for male heirs to perpetuate the family name and perform the rites of the cult of ancestors, a duty incumbent on all Chinese. It was in connection with polygamy that Ricci referred to the emperor in a letter to Giulio Fuligatti as a "poor Sardanapalus shut up [in his palace] with more than forty women, who are his wives."[7]

On the few occasions when the Jesuit was able to see women as a guest in private homes, he noted that they had tiny feet and walked with a stiff and unnatural gait. He had already observed this in Macao, and he learned that it was the custom to bind the feet of female babies so as to stunt their growth, a cruel practice that transformed these extremities into deformed stumps on which the adult women could barely stand. It had begun during the Song era around the tenth century, originally reserved for women of the highest rank but subsequently extended to all social layers. Peasant women wore footgear of padded cotton, and the wives of government officials wore tiny pointed shoes adorned with embroidery even more precious than the work embellishing the garments of Renaissance ladies. The practice seemed inhuman to Westerners but was considered natural in China, where tiny feet, likened to "gilded lilies" or "new moons" by poets, were regarded as one of the most important female attributes. Though not cruel like the binding of feet, another thing that Westerners found odd and distasteful was the way the richer women as well as many mandarins let their finger nails grow disproportionately long and used precious tapering cases to protect them.

It was, however, not only the differences that struck Ricci. He was also surprised at the Chinese use of tables, chairs, and beds, practices in which "all the world differs from them and us . . . as all the other nations eat, sit, and sleep on the ground."[8]

The missionary soon realized that the town was a place not only of prosperity and abundance but also of widespread poverty leading to forms of social degradation, as in Europe. As he noted in his history of the mission, someone unable to buy a wife would agree to sell himself as a servant to a rich man in order to be wedded to one of the female domestics. Those able to afford a wife but not a family would even sell their male children with no concern about their fate and murder the females at birth. He also observed that prostitution was widespread.

Poor and rich mingled on the bustling streets, the former on foot and the latter with fitting means of transport. Since carriages were forbidden, merchants rode horses while important figures forced their way through the crowd in litters, covered for all except state officials. While the ownership of a palanquin with a large number of bearers, as many as eight for the most important mandarins, was considered a mark of social prestige, there were strict regulations governing the choice of color, red being forbidden and green allowed only for officials of the fifth rank and above.[9] The most demanding had their litters fitted with a shelf making it possible to read and write during journeys. Still more luxurious were the junks of state officials seen passing on the river, some of which were spacious enough to accommodate a crowded banquet. Ricci once saw one bound for Beijing that he described as bigger to him than the church of the Roman College.[10]

The months passed, and the Jesuits' home was finally completed. It was a comparatively small but cozy residence with four bedrooms and a verandah on the upper floor and the other rooms, including one used as a chapel, on the ground floor, as well as a large courtyard. In his rare moments of repose, Ricci could gaze from the windows upstairs at the junks on the river, enjoying "a beautiful view of the water, boats, mountains, and woods." He described the house with some satisfaction in a letter as "the most pleasant place in the town."[11]

Discovering Chinese Society

In order to safeguard the foreigners, Wang Pan sent them a permit authorizing them to visit Macao and to travel freely throughout the province, and he issued an edict proclaiming that the missionaries were living in China by permission of the authorities. It was with understandable satisfaction that the Jesuits exhibited this document over the entrance of their house.

Once the word had spread that the foreigners' stay was authorized, the residence became a magnet for curious citizens, all eager to see the interior of such an unusual building and above all the wonderful objects it contained, which were the talk of the town, especially the "priceless precious stone" or "glass containing a piece of the sky," as some Chinese called the prism that Ricci had presented to the prefect and that many officials had enjoyed the privilege of examining. When the Chinese saw the painting of the Virgin Mary hanging in the chapel, they were most surprised that the Westerners should worship a female god, and the missionaries hastily replaced it with an image of Christ so as to avoid misunderstandings.

Delighted to see his home visited by men of culture, Ricci placed his library of Western books on display together with the Chinese works he was studying with the aid of an interpreter. He wished to make it understood that he was the representative of a civilization as rich and as ancient as the Chinese, where "letters and sciences were held in esteem," and that he was interested in the cultural achievements of his host country. The Chinese officials examined the works on religion and science with great interest as well as those with the illustrations showing European cities. While many confined themselves to admiring the elegant bindings, others realized that those books in an unknown language contained knowledge from distant countries and asked questions about their content.

In receiving their numerous visitors, the Jesuits soon learned the characteristics of Chinese society and the forms of behavior to be adopted during these encounters. The economic elite was represented by the great landowners and the ruling class by the *guan*, officials of the state bureaucracy selected through an extremely rigorous system of competitive examinations. The two social categories largely overlapped. On the one hand, the sons of rich land-owners had the means to study and to sit the examinations offering access to the bureaucracy. On the other, officials appointed to positions of importance were able to purchase estates. The *guan* were cultured men whose studies focused primarily on Chinese history and the texts of Confucianism, the official state philosophy. Ricci realized that it was impossible to understand China without a knowledge of its most representative philosophy, and he vowed to study it in depth as soon as he had mastered the classical Chinese in which the ancient texts were written.

The official doctrine originated with Confucius (Kong Fuzi, or Master Kong, in Chinese), a thinker traditionally held to have been born in 551 BC in the small principality of Lu in the present-day eastern province of Shandong. A scion of a decayed aristocratic family, Confucius held a series of positions, including minister of justice. But he resigned every post in the state administration due to disagreements with his lord, and he began his travels through the numerous Chinese states in the hope that his teachings might have a positive influence on the political practice of their rulers. Dis-appointed by his failure to achieve the task he had set himself, he abandoned all hope of a political career and returned when over sixty to his hometown, where he devoted himself to private teaching and was surrounded by numer-ous pupils until his death at the age of seventy-two.

The philosopher left no writings, but his ideas were collected by disciples in the *Lunyu*, or *Analects*, a series of aphorisms beginning with the formula "The Master said," and fragmentary conversations between the philosopher and his pupils or between the philosopher and the rulers who came to him for advice on sound government. Ricci was repeatedly made aware that all educated Chinese knew this work by heart.

The Confucian philosophy consisted of a set of primarily ethical and political precepts and made no mention of metaphysics. It put forward a hi-erarchical and ritualistic conception of society and laid great stress on culture as a means of human improvement. The resulting ideology had a deep and lasting influence on Chinese culture and constituted the basis for the cre-ation and perpetuation of the form of centralized, bureaucratic government existing in China since the birth of the empire.

The bureaucracy consisted of about twenty thousand officials stationed in every part of the country during the late Ming era. While 10 percent of these worked in the capital, the others—governors, prefects, and magistrates, whose respective areas of jurisdiction were provinces, prefectures, and dis-tricts—were appointed in Beijing and were sent to serve in provinces other than those of their birth so as to prevent favoritism. As they did not know the dialect of the cities in which they served, they were assisted in their relations with the population by the local administrative staff, who represented the second level of the bureaucracy. The bureaucrats were divided into nine ranks, the ninth being the lowest and the first the highest, which were in turn subdivided into two levels. The duties and privileges of the *guan* were minutely codified according to their rank. The color of their robe was red for officials of the fourth rank and above, and blue for all the others. The style of accessories, such as headgear and boots, also changed according to hierarchical position. The most immediately obvious insignia of rank was the embroidered birds, as Ricci had noted on the mandarin square of Wang Pan, starting with quail for the lowest level and rising through oriole, mandarin duck, heron, silver pheasant, wild goose, and peacock, to golden pheasant and crane. The *xie zhai*, a mythological creature of menacing appearance with a scaly body and a horn to gore miscreants, was instead the embroidered badge of the dreaded censors.

While hierarchies were unquestionable, duties precise, priorities absolute, and procedures implacable within the framework of the state machinery, corruption and the abuse of power, as Ricci was to observe on various occasions, were as widespread as in Europe, and many officials were all too ready to supplement their low salaries by making decisions in favor of those able to offer valuable gifts.

Not all of the *shidafu*, meaning the literati who had passed the imperial examinations at one or more levels, held posts in the state administration and were therefore *guan*. Some failed to obtain employment, some fell into disgrace and were removed from office, and some were on leave for the three-year period of mourning customary on the loss of a parent. Those holding no position in the bureaucracy devoted their energies to teaching in the state schools and to giving private lessons to prepare candidates to sit the imperial examinations, for which there was great demand. Commissions to draw up documents, memorials, and letters in the styles appropriate to different circumstances were another lucrative source of income. Those with no need to worry about money could simply cultivate their knowledge, dabbling in calligraphy, writing poems, and taking part in the countless *shuyuan* or academies of the late Ming era, where intellectuals and men of culture would gather to discuss philosophical, ethical, and political subjects. Only a minority devoted themselves to the study of technical disciplines such as mathematics and medicine, which were considered sciences of an inferior level in China. As a pastime, the *shidafu* enjoyed playing *wuqi*, a "war game" in which they could display their talent for strategy at the purely theoretical level.

While scholars and landowners were at the top of the social ladder, merchants were held in much lower regard, rich and poor alike, being preceded in terms of priority also by farmers and artisans. Commerce and economic activities were in fact despised by the Confucian ideology but nevertheless underwent a phase of explosive expansion in the late Ming era, especially in the southeast of the country. The most prosperous entrepreneurs, who made their money through the manufacture and sale of silk, cotton, porcelain, valuable wood, and every other kind of merchandise, even took the liberty of wearing precious silk garments like high-ranking officials, although this was prohibited.

It was immediately clear to Ricci and Ruggieri that their primary contacts in the variegated panorama of Chinese society should be with literati and state officials, as these were the most cultured classes and were the most closely connected with the imperial power structure. Once the linguistic barrier had been overcome, the *shidafu* and *guan* would be able to hear and understand the Jesuits' message, grant them the indispensable permits required for residence on Chinese soil, and facilitate their relations with the local authorities. In order to communicate with them on an equal footing, Ricci studied Mandarin Chinese assiduously and practiced reading and writing the literary language every day. After nearly a year in Zhaoqing, he was already able to speak Chinese without an interpreter.

The Five Continents:
The First Edition of the Map of the World

Time passed. The two Jesuits had pawned the prism for the equivalent of twenty *scudi* to pay for the material needed to build their residence and were now in debt. Ruggieri decided to seek funds in Macao and left on a junk with thirty oarsmen placed at his disposal by the prefect Wang Pan, who asked him to bring back a clock, declaring his readiness to pay any price for one of the "bells that ring by themselves."

Ruggieri reached his destination only to find that the coffers of the Jesuit college were empty, and he was forced to stay there for a few months awaiting the arrival of ships from Japan with silver for the missions. As he had not even managed to find a clock for the prefect, he sent an expert craftsman of Indian origin to construct one in the Jesuits' residence in Zhaoqing. Ricci describes the man in his history of the mission as a very dark-skinned "*canarino*," the term used for the inhabitants of the Canary Islands, who were similar in complexion to Indians.

During the absence of his companion, Ricci realized the true extent of the hostility felt by a section of the population, who used injurious epithets like "foreign devils" to refer to the missionaries. Rumors had long been spread that the building of the tower was secretly financed by the Portuguese with the intention of entering China in the wake of the Jesuits, and the building was now known with contempt as "the foreigners' tower."

The mounting tension reached a climax when stones were thrown at the missionaries' house one night. A servant rushed out and caught the youngster responsible but wisely decided to let him go for fear of making matters worse. Sometime later, the boy's parents reported Ricci to the authorities for having used a magic potion to paralyze him and hold him captive for three days with the intention of selling him in Macao. The charges were immediately brought to the office of Wang Pan, who summoned Ricci to an audience. The interpreter spoke in his defense and showed the prefect the stones thrown at the house, which he had taken with him as evidence. Wang Pan ordered the Jesuits to send the clockmaker, whose presence was seen as a danger by the population, back to Macao and decided to hear the other witnesses. Three officials involved in the construction of the tower who were present at the time unexpectedly spoke up for the missionaries, and the short trial came to an end. The accuser was beaten "very cruelly" on the legs with wooden sticks, a traditional form of Chinese punishment that could be continued to the point of causing the death of the guilty party. The following day, the prefect presented the missionaries with a new edict to be hung in their entrance forbidding any further molestation.

Peace returned to the residence, and the local dignitaries resumed their regular visits. The objects that the mandarins observed with the most curiosity included a planispheric map of the known world[12] that Ricci had hung on the wall of the room in which he received guests in order to show them his country and to teach the Chinese some geography.[13] The Jesuit had in fact noted that the local maps presented a Sinocentric view of the world, with China shown as occupying practically all of the known lands. While Europe and America did not even appear, countries like Japan, Korea, the tributary states of Southeast Asia, the regions to the north of China, and India were so small that the surface they occupied all together was less than a single Chinese province. America and Europe were instead clearly marked on Ricci's map, and China was shown in its correct size.

In actual fact, not all of the Chinese maps totally ignored the rest of the world, as some drawn in the past included countries of Central Asia and the regions of Africa reached by the seafaring expeditions of the eunuch Zheng

He. It is, however, a fact that the existence of the five continents was not known to the Chinese in the Ming era.

Ricci was convinced that ignorance of geography was one of the causes of the hostility felt by the Chinese toward foreigners:

> Their conception of the greatness of their country and of the insignificance of all other lands made them so proud that the whole world seemed to them savage and barbarous compared with themselves; it was scarcely to be expected that they, while entertaining this idea, would heed foreign masters.[14]

While pleased to be able to show the Chinese something they did not know, the Jesuit noted that their reactions to the European map were by no means unanimous. Some took offense on seeing their country so diminished; some concealed their perplexity in laughter, a ploy the Chinese often used to cover up embarrassment; and some took the representation to be a sort of Taoist amulet. There were a few literati who believed that that map was accurate and who displayed an interest in discovering everything Ricci knew about the faraway countries shown there. One of these was the prefect, who was eager to learn everything the newcomers had to teach him and who was so impressed by the European map of the world that he asked the missionary to make him a copy with the Western names translated into Chinese.

Ricci thus realized that with the aid of an image—something far more effective than an explanation in his still-halting Chinese—the distant world from which he came had found a place in the scholars' imagination, and meaningful contact had been established between Chinese and European culture.

The Jesuit set to work in response to the prefect's request. Being obliged to cut China down to size but afraid of giving offence, he hit on a way of making his more realistic representation of the earth easier to accept. Diplomatically abandoning the Eurocentrism of Western maps of the world, he placed Asia in the center, with the Americas on the right and Europe and Africa on the left, thus granting China a privileged position while showing its true proportions with respect to the other countries. He also took care to include information from the Chinese sources he had been able to examine. The *Yudi shanhai quantu*, or "complete map of the mountains and seas," has not survived, even though Ricci also sent copies back to his superiors, but historians have managed to reconstruct it on the basis of reproductions and descriptions found in documents of the period.[15] The Jesuit indicated the five "zones" into which the world was divided with Chinese names—North and South America, Asia, Libya (Africa), and Magellanica, meaning the Antarctic area with its still indefinite boundaries—and did the same for the oceans, the major seas, the Nile and the Plate (the only two rivers shown), and China, with Beijing and all the provinces of the empire. He indicated the cardinal points and drew the lines of latitude and longitude and the equator but not the tropics.[16]

Engraved on wood blocks and printed in 1584, the map of the world drawn in Zhaoqing was the first Western-style map to appear in a Chinese version. Ricci subsequently made a number of increasingly detailed versions including new information from European and Chinese sources, but always with China in the central position. By a significant coincidence, the year in which Ricci's map of the world was printed in China also saw the first publication of a map of China in Europe. Drawn by the Portuguese Jesuit Luis Jorge de Barbuda, it appeared in an edition of Ortelius's atlas.[17]

While Wang Pan liked Ricci's map of the world so much that he had his own name added to it and numerous copies printed as gifts for friends, not all of the literati shared his enthusiasm. One furiously objected that China was drawn too close to the North Pole. Others mocked the author. "When they saw the world so great and China in one part of it, so small in their estimation, the more ignorant people began to make fun of the description."[18]

Those who instead tried to understand it were pleased to see that the Jesuits' homeland was too far away to constitute a threat. Nobody would send troops from such remote kingdoms to invade China.

Together with the map of the world, Ricci presented the mandarin with the clock that the craftsman had begun to construct and that he had completed himself. Wang Pan was very happy but gave it back a few months later, as he could not get it to work. In the meantime, having noted the great success of mechanical clocks, Ricci decided to place a very large one on the outside wall of his residence to ring the hours so loud that it could be heard all through the neighborhood. This was the first public mechanical clock of Western style to appear in China. Though greatly admired, it was not used to tell the time, not only because it was inaccurate, but also because the Chinese divisions of time were different from those in the West. The standard unit of time in China was twice as long as an hour, and the day was divided into one hundred quarters of an hour instead of the ninety-six of the West. Moreover, day and night were divided into periods of different length,[19] impossible to represent on a Western dial. It was easier for the inhabitants of Zhaoqing to tell the time by observing the sun and the stars, as country folk had always done all over the world. Despite their appreciation of Western technology, the scholars also found it more practical to follow the traditional divisions of time.

Ruggieri had returned from Macao in the meantime with sufficient silver to pay their debts and to keep the mission going for another six months at least. The money enabled the missionaries to enlarge their house with the addition of six rooms and a small chapel. Now there was room to accommodate twelve people, including servants, interpreters, and novices living with the Jesuits, and to receive visitors in suitable style. After the publication of the map of the world, which had made the Jesuits known all through the province, playing host had become a full-time job. The visitors now included *shidafu* and *guan* passing through Zhaoqing in order to pay their respects to the governor, as well as the ambassadors of Cochin China en route to Beijing who left some pieces of silver and sticks of incense as gift for those monks of a Western religion.

They all admired the two-story house built in the European style and examined the map, the paintings, and the books, including the new volumes full of pictures of Italian cities that Ruggieri had just brought from Macao. In order to entertain their guests, the Jesuits had to learn what Ricci called the "courtesies," the greater and lesser rituals required in order to receive figures of high rank in accordance with protocol. They learned that the most common form of greeting involved no physical contact and that Western customs like embracing or kissing the hand were wholly unacceptable. Respect was shown by joining the palms and the long sleeves of the robe at chest height as though in prayer and then raising and lowering them before the guest, who replied with the same gesture, while repeating the Chinese equivalent of "please," an expression Ricci transcribed as "*zin zin*."[20] It might also be necessary to bow or to kowtow, bending your forehead to the ground once or more times, depending on the circumstances. The Jesuits learned to offer their visitors tea, *cha* in Chinese, a beverage still unknown in Europe and mentioned by Ricci for the first time in his writings, calling it "*cià*" and describing it as a hot infusion made from dried leaves that the Chinese drank all the time and offered immediately to their guests. It was "conducive to a good disposition and digestion," and the Jesuits were soon in the habit of drinking it like the Chinese.

Mandarins calling at the residence would present a "book of visits" containing polite remarks or short poetic compositions as well as a list of the gifts for the host. Custom required every visit to be returned within three days, but it was sufficient to send your own book if this proved impossible. Appreciation for gifts was to be shown in the form of objects of equivalent value, but any considered excessively valuable could be given back.

The gifts that Ricci prepared for his calls on the most important figures were above all celestial and terrestrial globes of iron and copper that he constructed himself and copies of his map, objects that served to transmit Western culture and science and that helped him to initiate an invaluable form of communication. In showing the terrestrial globes to the Chinese, Ricci knew that he was revealing to them for the first time the fact that the earth was round, something accepted in the West but still unknown in China. In accordance with the most ancient cosmology (the *Gai Tian*, or theory of the "celestial hemisphere"), most Chinese were in fact still convinced that the earth was flat and square and was surrounded by the semispherical dome of the sky, in which the sun, the moon, and the planets were set. In actual fact, different cosmological hypotheses had been put forward in Chinese antiquity, and the idea that the earth was round had been developed in a theory dating back at least to the fourth century BC known as the *Hun Tian*, or the theory of the "celestial sphere," which described the heavens as "an egg, as round as a ball for an arbalest," and the earth as "the yolk of the egg."[21] Few men of learning were familiar with this theory in the Ming era, however, and of those who knew of it, few regarded it as better grounded than the others developed in the course of Chinese history.[22]

The reactions to his gifts provided Ricci with an easy way to assess the recipients' knowledge and discover how far science had developed in China. His initial contacts and learned conversations with scholars led him to believe that the country was lagging far behind Europe in the sciences, and he found it quite natural to teach some elementary astronomy and mathematics to those showing the most interest. His only regret was that he had few books to consult in case of necessity, but he drew consolation from the reflection that in such a particular situation, "even the little [remembered] is worth a lot."[23] Proceeding step by step, Ricci thus endeavored to explain to some literati the structure of the universe as described by Ptolemy, with the round earth in the center of the cosmos and the planets and stars set in the crystalline spheres. He was pleased to see that his first lessons aroused great curiosity, and his knowledge was much admired. With an understandable bias that led him to underestimate Chinese knowledge without having examined it in depth, he came to believe that he had earned the reputation of a great scientist.

"And with these things never before seen or heard in China, and with the account of the course of the stars and the planets and the earth in the middle of the universe, the fathers were given great credit and he was regarded as the greatest mathematician in all the world, due to how little they knew of all those things."[24]

Religion in China: Heaven, the Gods, and the Name of God

The question of the form of religion practiced by the Chinese was the first the Jesuits needed to address if they were to undertake their missionary work

in full awareness of the situation. The answer was neither simple nor un-
ambiguous, as numerous cults and doctrines with a varied pantheon of gods
coexisted in the Middle Kingdom. It was no easy matter for a foreigner to
identify the religions served by the monasteries, the large and small temples,
the pagodas, and the simple altars erected by the roadside and dedicated to
lesser divinities and the guardian spirits of places and towns.

Religion played a very different role in China from the West, and the
separation of spiritual and temporal power taken for granted by Europeans
did not exist. Chinese culture drew no distinction between the immanent
and the transcendent, so a creator of the universe and supreme lawgiver that
was distinct from the earthly world was therefore inconceivable. The only
permanent reality for Chinese thinkers was the Tao, or Way, an indefinable
mystical principle regarded ever since the earliest times as the origin of all
natural phenomena, together with qi—"flow" or "vital energy"—a combination of energy and matter that permeated and animated the entire universe.
The Chinese saw the heavens and the earth as closely connected and as
influencing one another, with earthly well-being dependent on man's ability
to achieve harmony with the heavens. This view was wholly alien to Aristotelian philosophy and Scholasticism, according to which heaven and earth
were separate and different in nature, one the natural home of God and the
other of man.

It was believed in China that the emperor, the supreme authority known
as the Son of Heaven, ruled by divine mandate, with the task of organizing
society so as to ensure harmony between the celestial and terrestrial worlds.
As a regulator of society and the universe, the emperor was responsible for
promulgating the calendar drawn up every year by the imperial astronomers[25]
and for celebrating propitiatory rites in accordance with the dictates of
the established schedule and ceremonial protocol. Month after month, he
performed an elaborate liturgy in the Palace of Light, a pavilion inside the
imperial palace, following a path that symbolized the movements of the sun
in the course of the seasons and entering a different room every new moon
to call for good harvests and to lay down rules of conduct guiding agricultural
activities. Twice a year, at the winter solstice on December 23 and at the
spring equinox on March 21, he went to the Temple of Heaven in a solemn
procession with offerings to the heavens, the earth, the moon, and other
lesser divinities.

If the worship of heaven was an exclusive prerogative of the emperor and
was forbidden to anyone else on pain of death, the guan and shidafu practiced
rites dedicated to a variegated pantheon of national and local divinities recognized by the state. These forms of worship, together with those practiced

by the peasants to other minor divinities, constituted a widespread "popular religion." Every town was protected by a divinity to which new officials paid homage on taking up their posts in the local administration, and every region had its own specific divinities, often associated with rivers, mountains, and natural phenomena, or with the spirits of eminent figures of the past who were venerated by the people and in whose honor celebrations were organized on special occasions by the literati and wealthy merchants. For scholars, religion was above all intertwined with the observance of rites and had nothing to do with devotion to a unique and personal deity like the god of Christianity. For the common people, as in the West, religion consisted above all in seeking the protection of divinities and patron saints.

In addition to the rituals codified by the state, other forms of devotion were widely practiced in China, where family ancestors were worshiped by every member of the population regardless of class. Ricci observed that there was a small altar in every home with small tablets of wood bearing the names of forebears, upon which members of the family, especially the eldest son, would place offerings of food and would burn scented incense on special anniversaries. Dating back to very ancient times, the cult of ancestors was the form of devotion most deeply rooted in Chinese culture. It had coexisted with all the forms of religion developed throughout the empire's long history and reflected the importance always attached to the past in Chinese thinking. Ricci did not regard it as a form of superstition or idolatry but indeed as performing the positive function of teaching "children and the ignorant"[26] respect for their ancestors and filial devotion.

Peculiar to the literati was the cult of Confucius, considered the protector of the bureaucratic class and the model of a good official. In the simple and evocative temples dedicated to Master Kong, his statue as an authoritative elder with a long beard and serene smile welcomed visitors in the middle of the main courtyard. The *shidafu* would go there on particular occasions, including the anniversary of the master's birth, September 28, as well as every full moon and new moon, to bring offerings of food, burn incense, and listen to celebratory music.

Ricci considered the rites dedicated to Confucius to be secular ceremonies, and Confucianism, which he described as the "sect of literati," to be not incompatible with the Christian doctrine. It was in fact not a religion and had no priests. It was a philosophy focusing on ethics and social life, which found its source of inspiration in the ancient world but ignored the supernatural and took no particular interest in a life after death.

The need for spirituality and the yearning for a transcendental world found expression in the two most important religions practiced in China, namely Buddhism and Taoism. Better organized and more authoritative, the former dated back to the Indian master Siddhartha, who lived in the fifth century BC and became known as the Buddha, or "enlightened one." Imported from India, Buddhism had spread from the first century AD on, assuming typically Chinese characteristics over the years. It was deeply rooted in the social fabric, and Buddhist temples were to be found throughout the empire, together with the typical pagodas housing relics of Buddha, a Chinese variant of the original Indian stupa.

Buddhist doctrine was not monolithic but ramified in a variety of schools that differed from one another but shared some fundamental conceptions, such as the idea of life as suffering, the origin of suffering as desire, and the end to suffering and final salvation, or nirvana, as attainable by leading a righteous life and renouncing the satisfaction of worldly desires. Some schools envisaged the existence in the afterlife of a paradise and a place of punishment comparable to the Christian purgatory, from which release could be obtained after the purging of guilt. Buddhists believed in the transmigration of the spirit after death and the reincarnation of every individual in another living being, whose animal or human form would depend on one's conduct in the previous life. Ricci described the Buddhist doctrines as "a Babylon so intricate that none can truly understand or explain it." He made no effort from the very outset to conceal his disdain for a religion that worshipped not only the Buddha but also a series of lesser divinities, and he condemned it implacably as a "sect of idols." It was, however, precisely Buddhism that constituted a potential obstacle to the spreading of the Christian message by virtue of the complexity of its doctrine and its deeply rooted and widespread presence in China, as well as certain similarities it had to the Catholic religion.

As Ricci learned from Chinese texts, the country's three million Buddhist monks took vows of chastity, sincerity, poverty, nonviolence, and abstinence from fermented beverages. However, in much the same way as the Catholic clergy in the Middle Ages and early Renaissance, few of them actually obeyed these precepts. Many had wives and children and led corrupt lives. Nearly all of them came from poor families, had entered the priesthood as children driven by need, and were mostly devoid of culture. Ricci described the bonzes as "the lowest and most depraved people in China," and his judgment was shared by the literati, who regarded Buddhist and Taoist monks as occupying the lowest rungs of the social ladder, even though the wives and concubines of dignitaries would often turn to them in search of comfort and favors from the deities. Ricci's negative judgments and generalizations about bonzes and the Buddhist culture were largely preconceived, as the Jesuit had not studied this doctrine of Indian origin and its canonical writings in depth and had no direct acquaintance with any of its more authoritative followers. As we shall see, he was to meet very learned and open-minded Buddhist monks and believers during his long stay on Chinese soil and to engage in peaceable discussions with them. On the other hand, there were also bitter clashes with certain other monks and scholars.

Firsthand knowledge of China made the Jesuits aware that their decision to adopt the dress of Buddhist monks in order to obtain the respect of the Chinese had been an error. Even though the missionaries wore their "square cap in memory of the cross" to distinguish themselves from bonzes, they were nearly always mistaken for followers of Buddha and found it very difficult to make it understood that their religious message was different. Deciding that it would be impossible to effect a change in dress for the moment, the Jesuits hoped to demonstrate that they had nothing whatsoever to do with Buddhism through the concrete fact and example of a life devoted to knowledge and the practice of virtue.

The other form of religion strongly rooted in the Chinese culture was Taoism, whose origin lay in the teaching of the "Old Master" Lao-tzu, one of the great Chinese thinkers and a near contemporary of Confucius, born already old according to legend after eighty-one years in the womb. This was expressed in the *Tao Te Ching*, or "Book of the Way and of Virtue," which presented an ideal existence lived in accordance with the Tao. Unlike Confucianists, who found fulfillment in political life and social action, Taoists did not aspire to public positions but withdrew into solitude in order to meditate on the natural order, and they practiced "non-action." The Taoist philosophy, which had deeply influenced Chinese culture in its various offshoots, gave rise in the second century to an organized religion with its own sacred writings, monasteries, and priests, who worshipped a varied pantheon of divinities, with Lao-tzu and the Jade Emperor at the top. The Taoist monks practiced celibacy, lived on the alms they received, and were involved in certain rituals, such as calling for rain in periods of drought and freeing homes from evil spirits. It was instead only Buddhist monks that took part in funeral ceremonies.

As Ricci learned, life in the Taoist and Buddhist monasteries followed the rules laid down by the respective doctrines but was subjected to the rigorous overriding control of the Chinese state through the ministry of rites. In no case was a religious cult allowed to operate in China outside or above the framework of imperial power and challenge the primacy of the Confucian doctrine.

In spite of the differences between the various forms of worship, no religion was regarded as the absolute truth in the Middle Kingdom, and the boundaries between doctrines were very blurred. While the peasants made no substantial distinctions between the divinities of popular worship and those of Buddhism and Taoism, the literati and officials with their Confucian training also included followers of Buddhism and Taoism and others sympathetic to both doctrines. And even though the most cultured individuals despised all forms of popular superstition, they did not hesitate to kneel down before effigies of the various patron saints when they needed to ask for their intercession and request favors.

As a first step toward spreading their religion, the Jesuits had the Ten Commandments translated into Chinese (*Zuchuan Tianzhu shijie*) together with the Lord's Prayer, the Hail Mary, and the Creed. This was followed immediately by the translation, with the aid of a scholar from Fujian who had moved into their residence, of a catechism prepared by Ruggieri two years earlier (entitled *Tianzhu shilu*, "The Veritable Record of the Lord of Heaven"). The missionaries decided to have this published because they realized that the written word counted for far more than any oral dissertation in China and that a printed work could easily reach a great many people, especially as they still lacked sufficient mastery of the language to convince anyone by preaching alone.

Printed in November 1584, the catechism was the first work to be published by Europeans in China. Written in the form of a dialogue between master and pupil, it presented a short history of Christianity, some reflections on the immortality of the soul, and the Ten Commandments. It was also a Chinese book in terms of appearance, with a cover of blue fabric bearing the imprint of a seal in accordance with local practice, made up in this case of the letters IHS—standing for *Iesus Hominum Salvator*—beneath a cross, the emblem of the Society of Jesus.

The task of preparing the edition of the prayers and the catechism brought Ricci for the first time up against the problem of what to call the Christian god in Chinese. As he was aware, the missionaries in Japan had used a word similar in sound to *deus*, namely *deusu*. This was impossible in Chinese because the letter *D* was pronounced *T*. Moreover, Ricci preferred to use a term capable of conveying a sense similar to what the word "God" meant for Christians. He was helped in making this difficult choice by a merchant who had manifested his readiness to adopt the Catholic faith to Ruggieri during his stay in Zhaoqing with Pasio. In order to pray as the Jesuits taught him, the man had constructed a sort of altar in his home and had placed upon it a small wooden tablet bearing the painted word *Tianzhu*, meaning Lord of Heaven. By agreement with Ruggieri, Ricci chose to use this Chinese name for the Christian god, and a term equivalent to "Our Lady the Mother of the Lord of Heaven" for the Virgin Mary.

The decision seemed right and natural, as Ricci explained in his reports to his superiors, because the Chinese regarded the heavens as a higher entity of sacred character. He was unaware that *Tianzhu* had already been used to indicate Buddhist and Taoist divinities, and he did not realize that the adoption of a term already endowed with a meaning in Chinese culture might create confusion. He went no further into the question for the moment and felt satisfied with his choice.

The catechism was printed in over a thousand copies and enjoyed wide circulation. The first to receive one was Wang Pan, who in turn presented the Jesuits with two wooden plaques to hang over the doors of the house and the church. Carved with the inscriptions "People from the Holy Land of the West" and "The Church of the Flower of the Saints," they were a token of great respect for the foreigners.

The preparation of the religious writings was accompanied by initial attempts to win converts. The first to receive baptism was an old man on his deathbed, to whom the Jesuits had given assistance. He was followed by a few more peasants as well as artisans and small shopkeepers. While contenting himself for the moment with reaping the first fruits of his work among people incapable of understanding the doctrinal aspects of the religion, Ricci was determined to make the ruling class the target of his missionary efforts as soon as his mastery of Chinese and his standing in the local society proved satisfactory. He would seek to address scholars and officials, the cultural and political elite of the country, and show them that the Christian doctrine was based on reason.

Notes

1. FR, book II, ch. IV, p. 198.

2. The source used for all quotations from the Analects of Confucius is Roger T. Ames and Henry Rosemont Jr., *The Analects of Confucius: A Philosophical Translation* (New York: Ballantine Books, 1999).

3. Letter to Giambattista Roman, September 13, 1584; OS II, p. 2.

4. FR, book I, ch. VIII, p. 89.

5. Letter to Giambattista Roman, September 13, 1584; OS II, p. 48.

6. While the Pinyin system of romanization is used systematically in the text, the terms Taoism, Taoist, Tao, and Tao Te Ching have been left in the older Wade-Giles form of transcription due to the extent to which they are already established in the English language.

7. Letter dated November 24, 1585; OS II, p. 70.

8. FR, book I, ch. IV, p. 35.

9. Timothy Brook, *The Confusions of Pleasure* (Berkeley: University of California Press, 1998), p. 51.

10. Letter to Giulio Fuligatti, November 24, 1585; OS II, p. 66.

11. FR, book II, ch. V, p. 212.

12. Ricci's map of the world was a projection of the earth's surface onto a plane divided into two hemispheres.

13. This was probably a plate from the atlas of Ortelius or a Portuguese map printed in Goa or Macao. See P. D'Elia, *Il Mappamondo cinese del Padre Matteo Ricci*, cit., pp. 21–22.

14. FR, book II, ch. V, p. 209.

15. Richard Smith, *Chinese Maps* (Hong Kong: Oxford University Press, 1996), p. 43.

16. I. Iannaccone, "Matteo Ricci e l'introduzione delle scienze occidentali in Cina," in *Le Marche e l'Oriente, Atti del convegno internazionale di Studi Ricciani, Macerata, 23–26 ottobre 1996*, ed. Francesco D'Arelli (Roma: Istituto Italiano per l'Africa e l'Oriente, 1998), p. 208.

17. Translations of Chinese maps had already been printed in Portugal in 1563.

18. FR, book II, ch. V, pp. 209–10.

19. Isaia Iannaccone, *Misurare il cielo: l'antica astronomia cinese* (Naples: Opera universitaria, Dipartimento di studi asiatici, Istituto Universitario Orientale, 1991), pp. 12 ff.

20. "Qing, qing" in the Pinyin system (cf. FR, book I, ch. VII).

21. I. Iannaccone, *Misurare il cielo*, cit., p. 35.

22. See chapter 8 ("The 'Absurdities' and Achievements of Chinese Astronomy") for another Chinese cosmological theory.

23. Letter to Giulio Fuligatti, November 24, 1585; OS II, p. 66.

24. FR, book II, ch. V, p. 212.

25. See chapter 8 ("Astronomy and the Emperor") for Chinese astronomy and the calendar in relation to imperial power.

26. See FR, book I, ch. X, pp. 108 ff, for Ricci's description of the Chinese religions.

~

CHAPTER FIVE

The Pride of Li Madou

Zhaoqing, 1585–1589

The upper classes get on with us very well and are losing their fear of foreigners. Many say that we are almost like them, which is no small thing in such a proud and inward-looking nation.[1]

—Matteo Ricci

The Master thought under four categories: culture, proper conduct, doing one's utmost, and making good on one's word.

—Confucius, *Analects* (7, 25)

"We Have Become Chinese": Ricci Turns into Li Madou, Xitai

It was a calm November evening. Silence reigned in the residence, and the missionaries had withdrawn to their rooms. Ricci sat at the table reading a Chinese text, now satisfied with his ability to recognize and write the characters easily and to converse with the locals and confess converts without the aid of an interpreter. He would have liked to practice writing with the brush a little longer but was too weary. It was now 1585, little more than two years since his arrival in Zhaoqing with Ruggieri, and he felt a wave of homesickness at the thought that he would never see Europe again. Missionary work was a definitive and irrevocable choice for him. He sought comfort in his loneliness by thinking back to the happy years spent at the Roman College and began a letter to the Jesuit Giulio Fuligatti, a fellow student in Rome, feeling sure that dialogue with distant friends would help him through this moment of melancholy. While writing the sentences on the paper, he realized that he was finding it increasingly difficult to use his mother tongue and made excuses for his inelegant style. Italian words were mixed up with Portuguese and Spanish expressions, with the addition every so often of epithets translated from the Chinese, as when he referred to rice, the basis of the staple diet, as "great rice," after the local fashion. Ricci realized that his effort to adapt to Chinese customs was slowly eroding not only his ability to speak Italian correctly but also his typical Western appearance and wrote of his transformation: "As you will already know, we have become Chinese in dress, mien, ceremony, and all outward appearances."[2] The change was also accelerated when Ricci and Ruggieri took the decisive step of adopting Chinese honorifics. The locals already used a sort of phonetic transcription of their Christian names in which, as the sound of the letter R was unknown in China, Ricci became "Li" and Matteo "Madou." Placing the surname before the given name in accordance with Chinese custom, they called the Jesuit Li Madou, the name by which he is still remembered today in China and Japan. Ruggieri in turn had become Luo Mingjian. The acceptance of these names was, however, not enough. As Wang Pan himself explained to the missionaries, it was also necessary to adopt a *hao*, or honorific, which Ricci called a "great name," something indispensable in relations with literati and officials. Ricci thus took the honorific *Xitai*, meaning "from the Far West," and Ruggieri *Fuchu*, meaning "restorer."

While two names were sufficient for the missionaries, the upper-class Chinese adopted many more in the course of their lives. Only the surname, represented by a single character, was unchangeable, and there were fewer than one thousand of these in the entire country, all dating back to ancient times and never altered. The other names of a person, which were nearly always represented by two characters, could instead be numerous, and their choice depended on age and the circumstances in which they were used. A male baby received a "small name"[3] and was also called by the number designating his position with respect to his brothers in order of birth. At the age of three months, he received the name that he would use as an adult together with the surname to sign the book of visits. Then came the "school name" used by masters and fellow pupils. Another name was received on coming of age at twenty-one,[4] and those achieving a high social position would then assume a *hao* to be used by everyone other than their superiors. Scholars also adopted further names alluding to moral or intellectual qualities or written in rare characters, and "religious names" were taken by monks. There were fewer names for women, who were inferior in terms of social condition. In the family, they were always called by their "small name" or number in the sisters' order of birth until they married, while outsiders could address them by their father's surname. Once married, they received names referring to their husband's status. Only women of high social position could receive other names to be used within the family circle.

Ricci adapted to local custom and grew used to being called Li Madou or Xitai in different social circumstances and to addressing his visitors in a manner appropriate to their rank.

Thinking back over all the changes he had undergone, he confessed to Fuligatti that he felt as though he had "become a barbarian for the love of God" in that remote and inhospitable land, which he referred to bitterly as "this sterility here." The pain of distance was, however, accompanied by hope, and Ricci, when not overcome by homesickness, felt that he was beginning to love the country in which he now lived: "I am adapting to the land and growing as fond of it as I can."[5] The missionaries now seemed to arouse less distrust and to have been accepted by the local population. Confirmation of this came when he heard some officials say that the foreigners were not so different from them, a success in that "closed and arrogant" land of which he hastened to inform Superior General Acquaviva in a letter written in October 1585.[6]

The course of events during his stay in Zhaoqing gave Ricci further grounds for satisfaction. Wang Pan had been promoted to the position of superintendant of the provinces of Guangdong and Guangxi, but without being obliged to leave Zhaoqing, where he continued to protect the Jesuits. The mandarin's wife, who had already had a daughter, finally succeeded in giving birth to the longed-for son, and Wang Pan declared that the foreigners had brought him good fortune. The final piece of good news was the appointment of the new prefect Zheng Yilin, who had let it be known that he was as well disposed toward the Jesuits as his predecessor.

In this situation of comparative peace and tranquility, the Jesuits were able to devote much of the day to their missionary work. They developed the habit of crossing the river on a sampan to visit the homes of the small shopkeepers and merchants on the other side and preach the principles of the Catholic religion. For the time being, the missionaries preferred to work among the poorer classes, where polygamy was not widespread. The less affluent, who could not afford to keep more than one wife, were monogamous by necessity and were therefore not obliged to make painful sacrifices in order to adopt a faith that would not tolerate what it regarded as an immoral practice. The preaching proved moderately successful in this sphere, even though it is hard to believe that the peasants and small shopkeepers could ever fulfill Ricci's hopes and truly understand the underlying doctrinal principles of

Catholicism, something that did not happen even in Europe. In the Jesuit's opinion, the new converts simply believed that they would obtain more comfort and understanding from the righteous and generous Jesuits than from Buddhist or Taoist monks. One day the missionary was invited into the home of an elderly recent convert and was asked to baptize his wife and daughter, a request that surprised him, as the women had always remained hidden in their rooms during his repeated visits. The old man demonstrated his gratitude by consigning some books on Buddhist doctrine and some statuettes of divinities he kept in the house to Ricci for destruction. The previous year had brought twenty new converts[7]—not a great number, but enough to convince the religious and political authorities on whom the missionaries depended that it was possible to spread the Gospel in China.

The Failure of the Idea of a
Spanish Embassy to the Chinese Emperor

In view of the initial successes, the Spanish authorities in the Philippines reported to their government that the Chinese empire had opened its borders to the Jesuit missions and that the situation looked promising. This gave rise in 1584 to the idea of organizing an embassy from Philip II of Spain to the emperor to request that missionaries be granted free access to the whole of Chinese territory. The governor of the Philippines and the archbishop of Manila sent an emissary to Macao with new funds for the China mission and letters asking the Jesuits to obtain the necessary permits for the entry of the Spanish ambassadors. There was already talk of the gifts planned for the Son of Heaven: horses, gold, precious fabrics, swords, oil paintings, mirrors, crystal prisms, clocks, and jars of wine made from grapes, for a total value of at least seventy thousand ducats.[8]

Francisco Cabral, the Jesuit rector in Macao and superior of the China mission, wrote to Ricci and Ruggieri, already chosen as official interpreters of the embassy, asking them to have the governor of Guangdong issue the indispensable permits required for the entrance of the Spanish embassy. Wang Pan raised no objections and thought indeed that it was an excellent idea, as he himself would no longer have anything to fear for allowing foreigners to stay on Chinese soil if the emperor received a Spanish delegation.

The request that Ricci and Ruggieri submitted to the governor was approved and forwarded to the *haidao*, but the Portuguese authorities in Macao opposed the initiative, suspecting that the offer to help the Jesuits masked the aim of seizing control of the immense Chinese market. Spain was indeed already planning to establish a commercial outpost in the Guangdong province, and the Portuguese knew that an influx of Spanish silver from South America into the markets of Canton would lead to a rise in the prices of Chinese products, with disastrous consequences for their trade.

In light of these considerations, the authorities in Macao were resolutely opposed to the embassy and claimed that Spain's initiative violated the still valid agreements, codified in the papal bull of 1514, reached on the succession of the Spanish sovereign to the throne of Portugal, which retained its exclusive rights to trade with China. While the question was under discussion, the *haidao* resolved matters by refusing to allow the Spanish delegation into the country. The presence of missionaries in Zhaoqing was already more than enough, and no other foreigner would be permitted to enter the Da Ming empire, not even as an ambassador.

Now that there was no more hope of intervention on the part of the Spanish crown, the Jesuit authorities addressed the problem of how to foster the growth of the China mission. Francisco Cabral visited Zhaoqing to see the progress for himself and report on it to Superior General Acquaviva and the Visitor of Missions Valignano. He ascertained that the missionaries maintained good relations with the authorities and the local population, and gave a positive assessment of their work, even though the results seemed modest in comparison with those obtained thirty years earlier through the mission led by Francis Xavier in Japan, where two thousand people had been baptized in the space of two years.

Given the sound foundations laid and taking the objective difficulties into account, Alessandro Valignano set about ensuring the economic independence of the Jesuits in China and secured an annuity from the viceroy of India sufficient to cover all their expenses. It was agreed that the missionaries were to receive part of the proceeds of the customs duties paid by the merchant ships stopping in Malacca. The sum would be sent to Macao twice a year, and each priest would receive an annual stipend of one hundred ducats, together with a certain number of casks of wine to celebrate Mass.[9] The Visitor also decided to assign two more missionaries to China. One was Duarte de Sande, described by Ricci as "virtuous, scholarly, and prudent," who had sailed from Lisbon to India with Ruggieri and Ricci but had remained in Goa. The other was Antonio de Almeida, a young missionary "of rare virtue and religious fervor," who had just arrived in India from Portugal. They arrived in Macao in July 1585 and stayed there while awaiting the indispensable entry permits.

The first to reach Zhaoqing was Duarte de Sande, brought back by Ruggieri on his junk after a trip to buy some goods in Macao for the governor. Despite his lack of an official residence permit, De Sande stayed on in the

Zhaoqing mission with temporary authorization from the providential Wang Pan, now rightly considered the Jesuits' guardian angel on Chinese soil.

The missionaries' footing in the Guangdong province seemed to be firmly established, and the new prefect even promised to take them to Beijing with him on the occasion of the customary gathering of imperial officials to be held the following year, in 1586. The most important *guan* were required to present themselves in the capital every three years in order to pay homage to the emperor and to be assessed on the basis of reports on their activities drawn up by their superiors and by the censors. Those guilty of crimes, of accepting bribes in return for favors, or of displaying excessive cruelty or weakness in the performance of their functions were liable to a range of punishments including loss of rank, expulsion from the bureaucracy, imprisonment, and exile.

Informed of the possibility of a trip to Beijing, Valignano decided that Ruggieri and Almeida would be the ones to visit the capital while Ricci remained in Zhaoqing with De Sande, who was appointed superior of the China mission by the Visitor in August 1585. Ruggieri went to Canton to prepare for the possible trip to the capital and found time to help Wang Pan's brother obtain a good price from the Portuguese merchants for the silk he had come to sell.

It was now 1586. The ecclesiastical authorities were delighted to hear of the progress achieved by the China mission, and Pope Sixtus V granted a plenary jubilee to celebrate the Jesuits' success. Superior General Acquaviva wrote a letter of encouragement to the missionaries in China and had a painting of Jesus sent to Macao, together with three mechanical watches to be worn around the neck and a table clock of precious workmanship. Further religious paintings were sent from Japan and the Philippines. While the valuable objects were meant to serve as gifts for the emperor and officials in the capital, the paintings were for future missions in the Middle Kingdom.

Despite the Jesuits' optimism regarding the possible benefits to be gained from a trip to Beijing, the idea was soon abandoned because Wang Pan considered it very dangerous, feeling sure that a journey by foreign missionaries inside the empire, and especially one bound for the capital, could trigger unforeseeable reactions on the part of the authorities. Though advised to be prudent and not to move away from Zhaoqing, Ruggieri attempted to found a new mission in the eastern coastal province of Zhejiang, south of Shanghai, where he traveled with Antonio de Almeida. Realizing the impossibility of carrying out his plans, Ruggieri returned to Zhaoqing while Almeida continued to Macao, where he stayed for a few months. The two missionaries' fruitless attempt to penetrate another province was, however, a cause of great concern for Wang Pan, who began to fear that his friendship with the foreigners might have negative repercussions on his career.

Superstitions, Wondrous Potions, and False Accusations: Wang Pan's Volte-face and Ruggieri's Departure

Time passed. It was now 1587, and the missionaries devoted themselves zealously to their small community of 37 converts. Ricci continued to study written Chinese with a new tutor and made great strides in his understanding of classical works. Meanwhile, in order to take advantage of his skills and to help the new missionaries in the study of Mandarin, he, together with Ruggieri, compiled a Portuguese-Chinese dictionary, the first ever from a European language into Mandarin. The manuscript, a document of great historical interest, is still preserved in the Roman archives of the Society of Jesus.

News of the Jesuits' presence had spread, and the circulation of Ricci's map of the world made them known throughout the Guangdong province. Driven by curiosity to meet Li Madou, mandarins visiting Zhaoqing to confer with the governor seized the opportunity to call at the missionaries' residence and examine the clocks, prisms, books, and paintings. Ricci was able to establish good relations with *shidafu* and *guan* thanks to his mastery of Chinese, his capacity for learned conversation, and his knowledge of the local rules of conduct, as well as his personal gifts of affability, modesty, and discretion, which were well suited to the Confucian mentality.

Every so often, however, someone would come knocking at the doors of the mission in the belief that the Jesuits were wizards and practiced alchemy, the complex interweaving of philosophical doctrines, magic, and investigations of nature aimed at discovering the secrets of life and the principles making it possible to transmute base metals into gold and silver. A discipline of ancient origin also practiced in Europe, alchemy was an authentic and widespread obsession in China. Many believed that it was possible to transform the red mineral cinnabar (mercuric sulfide) into silver by means of amber, which had only been known in China for a few decades and was considered a precious material with magical properties. The Chinese were convinced that the Portuguese possessed huge amounts of amber and used it to produce silver, finding no other explanation for the fact that merchants bought vast quantities of cinnabar in China, transported it to India and Japan, and returned from those countries with their ships loaded with silver.

The same suspicion extended to the Jesuits, who never seemed to want for silver and had no need to ask for alms like the other monks. While many Chinese alchemists concentrated on the transmutation of base metals, others were obsessed with the search for an elixir of eternal youth, an illusory goal pursued also by practicing the physical and respiratory exercises suggested by various monks. One of the most sought after ingredients for the potion of immortality was the yellowish residue derived from the process of separating cinnabar into its components—mercury and sulfur—which was erroneously held to be pure gold. Two self-styled wizards called on the missionaries one day claiming to have used this and to be over two hundred years old, despite their youthful appearance. Many believed Ricci to be an alchemist with secret formulas in his keeping and begged him constantly to reveal them. The more strenuously the irritated Jesuit denied any knowledge of transmutation, the more convinced they were to the contrary.

Ricci deeply disapproved of the passion for alchemy and of the practice of geomancy or *feng shui*, literally "wind-water," the typically Chinese art of interpreting the characteristics of a place to see whether it was suitable for the erection of a building. Nobody in China, starting from the emperor, constructed or ordered the construction of any edifice whatsoever without consulting a geomancer, as it was believed that a mistake in the positioning of the entrance and rooms, or in the location of the structure with respect to surrounding elements such as hills, rivers, and lakes, could unleash negative energies that would bring perennial misfortune upon whoever lived there. The Chinese also consulted geomancers in order to decide where to place their tombs, one of the decisions with the most influence on family fortunes. Ricci was irritated by talk of more or less magical beliefs, spells and curses, horoscopes, and various forms of divination offered by those he referred to with contempt as "astrologers, geomancers, augurs, fortunetellers, and frauds."[10] Whenever he had the opportunity, he tried to convince his Chinese friends of the fallacious nature of all forms of the superstition. Many consulted fortune-tellers and were so influenced that, as Ricci observed to his horror, they ended up really falling ill if an illness was predicted. Others saw sorcery behind every innocent action. When Ricci officiated at his first baptism, converting an old man on his deathbed, some neighbors spread the rumor that the Jesuit's real intention was to steal a gem that the peasant kept hidden in the back of his head, a claim that echoed the custom of setting precious stones in that part of statues of Buddha.

Wang Pan was also superstitious and had begun to think that his friendliness toward the Jesuits was a source of misfortune, as the promotion he had awaited for three years, which would involve a higher rank and his transfer to another province, was late in arriving. Regardless of superstition, the mandarin was also well aware of how easy it was for a bureaucrat to fall into disgrace and began to fear that the hospitality he had granted to the foreigners had provided his enemies with dangerous ammunition and had shown him in a bad light to his superiors. As time passed, Wang Pan's benevolence toward the Jesuits turned into hostility, and the *guan* even demanded to have his name erased from the plaques he had given them and from the matrix on which Ricci's map of the world was engraved. He soon dispensed the missionaries from the obligation of paying homage to him on ritual occasions, and finally he ordered them to leave the city in November 1587.

De Sande, who had never obtained an official permit to reside in Zhaoqing, returned to Macao immediately, but Ricci was ready to fight in order to remain with Ruggieri. The Jesuit drew up a memorial defending the missionaries and went to present it in person to Wang Pan, asking him not to send them back to Macao and above all not to have them expelled from China, as they would never survive the long voyage back to Europe.[11] Apparently moved to compassion, the prefect granted Ricci permission to remain in the city and issued a new edict in favor of the missionaries, whose position, however, remained precarious. The rumor that the building of the tower was financed by the Portuguese continued to circulate, and further episodes threw discredit on the Jesuits.

A young Chinese convert christened Martin who lived in Canton visited the missionaries in Zhaoqing and stole the prism from their house with the intention of selling it. He also boasted that they had taught him the secrets of alchemy, thus confirming the suspicions that they were wizards and cast evil spells. Not content with the serious damage already done by his words, he went so far as to accuse Ruggieri of having an adulterous relationship with a married woman. The Jesuit was acquitted of these ignominious and groundless accusations, and Martin, finally found guilty of theft and slander, was imprisoned and beaten so severely that he died in his cell. The restored atmosphere of peace was to be short lived. Wang Pan finally obtained his longed-for promotion and was assigned to the administrative offices of the central Huguang province, part of the present-day provinces of Hunan and Hubei. His now inevitable departure would deprive the Jesuits of the support that had never been wanting in time of need.

In order to honor the mandarin, who had governed the town with wisdom and rectitude, the inhabitants of Zhaoqing erected a pagoda with his statue and the traditional brazier for burning incense. In accordance with custom, they presented the official with a pair of boots and placed the old ones in a receptacle in the middle of the pagoda beneath an inscription listing the meritorious actions performed in the city by the former prefect. Once the celebrations were over, Wang Pan left Zhaoqing and disappeared from the missionaries' lives forever.

Ruggieri spent some time in Macao waiting to see Valignano on his way through from Japan, and De Sande returned to Zhaoqing in his place. The times had changed, however, and the new prefect's pronouncements in favor of the missionaries' continued presence in the city were now no longer enough to prevent new episodes of intolerance. The most serious took place when the river was in full spate due to excessive rain. The population feared a repetition of the flooding that had struck the countryside the previous year, causing the deaths of dozens of people, the loss of thousands of acres of cultivated land, and the destruction of hundreds of homes. Built of masonry on two stories, the Jesuits' house was the only one to survive unscathed, while nearly all of those living close to the river had lost most of their belongings.

Thrown into a state of panic by the rising waters of the river, the peasants began to cut down trees and bushes and to collect all kinds of materials to build makeshift protective barriers in front of their houses. A group of peasants entered the Jesuits' residence on the pretext of looking for material in the courtyard and attacked the building, breaking down its doors and windows. Ricci kept a cool head, met the attackers face to face, offered them wood, and told them to take whatever they wanted as long as they did not destroy the house. His prompt action nipped the violence in the bud.

De Sande chose to return to Macao again, and Ricci, afraid to think what might happen in the event of another similar episode, asked the prefect to issue yet another edict forbidding acts of violence against the Jesuits. By now, however, the missionaries were wondering how long the authorities would be able to defend them from the growing hostility of the local population. News of the serious problems regarding the safety of the mission in Zhaoqing reached Valignano, who thought it essential to request the protection of the country's highest authority, namely the emperor. The only way the Visitor could see of doing this was by organizing a papal embassy to request the Son of Heaven to grant the Jesuits permission to live in China and preach the Christian doctrine freely. To this end, he instructed Michele Ruggieri to leave China as soon as possible and to provide the king of Spain and the pope with firsthand testimony of the difficulties encountered in missionary work in the Middle Kingdom, highlighting the potential benefits to be obtained from converting that immense empire and asking that an embassy be dispatched. Ricci was instead to prepare the terrain by applying to the authorities for permits and providing the requisite documentation.

Ricci's account of his companion's sudden departure—"Because Father Ruggero [sic] was already old and unable to learn the Chinese language, [Valignano] took advantage of this opportunity to send him to Europe"[12]— seems to suggest that the organization of the journey was a pretext to remove

Ruggieri, who could hardly be considered old at the age of forty-five, from China. Some historians have indeed suggested that the decision to send the Jesuit back to Europe was not due to his known difficulty in learning Chinese but rather to his failure to see eye to eye with the Visitor on how the Gospel was to be spread.[13] Whatever the real reasons may have been, Ruggieri certainly derived no luster from comparison with the charismatic personality of his young companion from Macerata, with whom Valignano had established a perfect understanding.

Michele Ruggieri left Macao at the end of November 1588 after five years of life in Zhaoqing with Ricci. He set sail with a consignment of gifts for the pope and the king of Spain, including a screen decorated with a painted map of China. The ship taking him to Europe was wrecked in the Azores, and the gifts were lost, but Ruggieri succeeded in reaching Spain and obtained a promise of assistance in dispatching a papal embassy to China from Philip II. The Jesuit then arrived in Rome but was prevented from obtaining an audience by the deaths of four popes shortly after they succeeded to the throne of Saint Peter, Sixtus V and Urban VII in 1590 and Gregory XIV and Innocent IX the following year. These unforeseeable events made all discussion of the Chinese question impossible and forced the Jesuit authorities to abandon their plans. Ruggieri was then sent to Salerno, where he died at the age of sixty-four. Ricci spent a few months on his own in Zhaoqing before finally being joined by the young Antonio de Almeida.

Expulsion from Zhaoqing

The missionaries' position became increasingly awkward. At the end of 1588, on completion of the fifth year of their stay in Zhaoqing, some retired mandarins resident in Canton presented a report attacking the Jesuits to the censor of Guangdong. In China, where age was honored and experience respected, it was not unusual for groups of authoritative elders to make suggestions on important issues in social life, which were taken very seriously by the authorities.

The document expressed Chinese fears with regard to the Westerners and the possibility that the Portuguese might be seeking to conquer the whole of China after their progressive colonization of Macao. The "foreigners from strange kingdoms"[14] were described as spies determined to discover the secrets of the empire, enemies ready "to scatter our people in the sea like fish and whales," and "thorns and nettles" that had planted their roots in the good Chinese earth. If the settlement in Macao was the manifestation of a disease threatening the empire at its borders, the presence of the Jesuits in

Zhaoqing was a plague in the heart of the country. The elderly officials called for the missionaries to be rooted out as soon as possible and for all foreigners to be expelled from China.

While the impact of this memorial was not to be underestimated, Ricci was determined not to lose heart and drew up a defense of the missionaries for presentation to the censor and the *haidao*. Matters reached a head with the arrival in Zhaoqing of the new governor Liu Jiezhai, who took a hostile attitude and decided to confiscate the Jesuits' residence and expel them from the city.

Ricci rushed to Macao to consult with Valignano, who advised him to ask the governor for permission to move the mission to another Chinese city and to return to Macao if this request was refused.

On Ricci's return to Zhaoqing, the prefect's lieutenant called and presented the governor's sealed decree, where the compensation for the requisition of the house was set at a sum equivalent to 60 *scudi*, less than a tenth of its real value.

The Jesuit sent word to the governor that he had no intention of accepting the money, as he knew that doing so would preclude any possibility of returning to Zhaoqing at a later date and regaining possession of the house. When his request for an audience was refused, Ricci sent memorials in his defense to the more influential figures in the city and the province, feeling confident of obtaining the support of a good many *guan*. Passing through Zhaoqing to discuss matters with the governor, the imperial censor of the Guangdong province called on the Jesuits one day to pay his respects with a group of dignitaries from his retinue. The official wished to see the clocks he had heard so much about, the prisms that glowed in the sunlight, the paintings, the maps, and the globes. On entering Ricci's room, he was surprised to find an entire library of European and Chinese works. What possible danger could there be in that bizarre man from the West, so enamored of culture as to have a study as full of books as a scholar? Ricci hoped that the censor's apparent sympathy might help him overcome the hostility of the governor. He proved unyielding, however. The Jesuits were informed at the beginning of August 1589 that they had three days to leave the city and that they were to accept the compensation for the confiscation of their house.

When the lieutenant asked Ricci to hand over the keys and held out the money, the Jesuit had the courage to answer that he was grateful for the offer but found himself obliged to decline. He followed this immediately by asking the lieutenant for a permit to move to another locality in the province. The official refused categorically but was unable to persuade Ricci to accept the money, which he was forced to take back to the government offices.

On August 15, 1589, as Ricci and Almeida were about to sail for Macao and a small group of converts and friends had gathered to bid them farewell, the lieutenant offered the money once again, and Ricci once again refused. Moreover, he succeeded in obtaining a written statement attesting that the Jesuits had not accepted the money and that they had left without ever breaking the law.

On reaching the provincial capital, Canton, the missionaries' junk had to wait in the harbor while the permits for Macao were being drawn up. Without even setting foot on land, the Jesuits abandoned their gray Buddhist robes for their customary garments, resigned by now to the idea of returning to the life they had left behind them six years earlier. Ricci was deeply embittered to see that his efforts to create the first mission on Chinese soil had all been in vain. He felt exhausted and compared his labors to those of Sisyphus, condemned by the gods to push a heavy boulder to the top of a hill only to have it roll back down again for all eternity. As he was abandoning himself to the most melancholy thoughts, however, he saw a fast vessel arrive with some provincial officials sent by the governor with astonishing instructions to take him back to Zhaoqing immediately, together with his companion.

Having changed their dress once again, the missionaries were escorted into the town they had just left and were summoned to an audience with the governor, who was furious because they had not accepted the money offered. His insistence was not a matter of principle but was born of the knowledge that if he could not show that he had paid for the Jesuits' house, even a symbolic sum, he would be open to the accusation of having appropriated a dwelling for his personal gain. No civil employee, no matter how powerful, could risk such a serious charge.

Ricci looked hurriedly for an interpreter, an indispensable intermediary in any meeting between a foreigner and an official of high degree, but the only one prepared to help had a very limited grasp of Portuguese. On arriving before the *guan*, Ricci was handed the money by the governor in person, and he refused it once again. The official explained that refusing the offer was a serious breach of etiquette, and Ricci replied that he was unable to accept a gift from someone who chose to expel him for no crime from the city in which had lived a peaceable life. The mandarin lost his temper and berated the interpreter for mistranslating Ricci's words, as he could not believe that the Jesuit would choose to disobey his orders. Ricci spoke up in the interpreter's defense and asked the governor for permission to move to another city where he could live in peace for the rest of his days.

The mandarin gave way in the face of such stubbornness. In order to avoid losing face, he declared that it had always been his intention to grant the Jesuits a new residence, and he suggested either the great Buddhist monastery of Nanhua in the northeast near the borders of the Guangdong and Jiangxi provinces, which could be reached by junk in ten days, or the town of Shaozhou, thirty kilometers farther north, two localities falling within his jurisdiction. He then handed Ricci the money again, and the Jesuit accepted it.

Visibly pleased at having brought these exhausting negotiations to a satisfactory conclusion, the governor presented the Jesuits with some works relating his feats during the victorious military campaigns against pirates on the island of Hainan and asked the lieutenant of the prefect of Shaozhou, who was present at the audience, to take care of the missionaries.

Some officials who had remained Ricci's friends paid their respects as he left the room and was immediately escorted to the junks with Almeida. They had barely enough time to get the indispensable luggage on board, to distribute all the rest among the converts, and to entrust a letter informing Valignano of their decision to move to another locality to the pilot of the vessel on which they had traveled, which was returning to Canton.

Seen off by the group of converts who had gathered for the last farewell, Ricci and Almeida set sail on August 15, 1589. They left the city that had been their home for six years with sorrow but with their heads held high, bound for another unknown region in the Chinese interior.

Notes

1. Letter to Claudio Acquaviva, October 20, 1585; OS II, p. 57.

2. Letter to Giulio Fuligatti, November 24, 1585; OS II, p. 72.

3. FR, book I, ch. VIII, p. 90. See also Endymion Wilkinson, *Chinese History: A Manual, Revised and Enlarged* (Cambridge and London: Harvard University, Asia Center, 2000), pp. 98 ff.

4. FR, book I, ch. VIII, p. 90.

5. Letter to Ludovico Maselli, November 10, 1585; OS II, p. 65.

6. Letter to Claudio Acquaviva, October 20, 1585; OS II, p. 57.

7. Ricci provided converts with handwritten copies of his own translation of the Gregorian calendar to indicate the feast days (FR, book II, ch. XIII, p. 270, no. 6).

8. FR, book II, ch. VI, p. 216, no. 1.

9. FR, book II, ch. VI, p. 224, no. 2.

10. FR, book I, ch. IX, p. 97.

11. See chapter 2 ("Departure: 'All Those Seas'").

12. FR, book II, ch. XI, p. 250. See also nos. 1 and 2.

13. Paul Rule, *K'ung-tzu or Confucius? The Jesuit Interpretation of Confucianism* (London: Allen & Unwin, 1986), pp. 3 ff.

14. FR, book II, ch. XI, p. 253.

CHAPTER SIX

~

The Meeting of Confucius and Euclid

From Nanhua to Shaozhou, 1589–1592

The Master said, "I have never failed to instruct students who, using their own resources, could only afford a gift of dried meat."

The Master said, "I do not open the way for students who are not driven with eagerness; I do not supply a vocabulary for students who are not trying desperately to find the language for their ideas. If on showing students one corner they do not come back to me with the other three, I will not repeat myself."

—Confucius, *Analects* (7, 7–8)

Of these sciences, the gate and key is mathematics.

—Roger Bacon[1]

The Buddhist Monastery and the Mummy of Liuzu

The junks carrying Ricci and Almeida followed the course of broad Xi Jiang River east to the point where it was joined by a tributary from the northeast. In order to enter and sail back up this river, the Jesuits had to transfer to a lighter but sturdier vessel more suitable for sailing upstream. When the current made progress impossible, the junk was hauled by teams of men waiting on the bank to catch ropes thrown from craft in difficulty.

The landscape gradually altered as they penetrated the interior of the province at the slow pace of river navigation. The plain gave way to mountainous uplands; rice paddies and clumps of light green bamboo alternated with the more intense hues of dense oak forests. The boundless expanse of fields stretching away as far as the eye could see conveyed a sense of vastness, and Ricci, aware that he was only traveling through a short stretch of the Guang-dong province, realized for the first time just how huge China really was.

Eight days of travel brought them to the river port of Shunyao, a short distance from Shaozhou, the first stopping point arranged by the authorities supervising the missionaries' journey on behalf of the governor. They were met on the quay by a servant of the lieutenant of Shaozhou with instructions to accompany them to the Buddhist monastery of Nanhua, one of the largest and most important in the region, where the missionaries would be allowed to stay with official authorization. Not understanding that the Jesuits had noth-ing to do with Buddhists despite their similarity in dress and appearance, the authorities thought that living in a temple together with the monks would be the best possible arrangement for them. Having no wish to refuse a courtesy visit, Ricci and Almeida agreed to continue on horseback to the sanctuary, but not to having their luggage unloaded from the junks. They would make it clear as soon as possible that they had no intention of living with the monks.

Buddhist monasteries were important centers of social aggregation, en-dowed, like their European counterparts, with landed properties and tenant farmers. Their economic activities, which supported the community together with the alms received, included letting accommodation to pilgrims and way-farers, as well as the sale of religious articles such as incense and devotional statues and paintings. The prosperity of the nearby villages also depended on the monasteries, as their inhabitants earned a living by selling agricultural produce to the monks and pilgrims or by setting up small artisanal companies to produce ceremonial objects.

The monastery of Nanhua,[2] the "Temple of the Flower of the South," was situated in the broad, green valley of a river surrounded by wooded moun-tains. The immense complex consisted of twelve buildings providing accom-modation for about a thousand monks and laid out around a pagoda on the top of a hill. There was a small village at the foot of the steep climb up to the monastery, and the surrounding plain was an unbroken expanse of orchards and fields growing rice, cereals, and vegetables. Ricci was again struck by the abundance of the produce offered by Chinese soil.

The monks were followers of the "school of meditation," or *Chan*, a Chi-nese variant of Buddhism better known in the West by the Japanese term *Zen*. According to legend, its founder, Bodhidharma, attained enlightenment after sitting immobile for nine years. The temple was dedicated to Huineng, better known as Liuzu, the "sixth patriarch" or "sixth ancestor" of the Chan school, a monk who lived in the seventh century AD. According to the widely known legend, as a baby he was fed by a spirit with dewdrops instead of his mother's milk, and he entered the monastery when still very young as a servant responsible for cleaning the rice. Having become a monk, he led an exemplary life of penance and came to be regarded as a spiritual guide by the pilgrims who flocked from all the towns in the surrounding area to see him. During the last few years of his life, Liuzu had himself bound in chains and left the resulting sores to fester and fill with worms as an extreme act of penance. After his death, his mummified body was displayed in a niche to the adoration of the faithful.

Deeply prejudiced against Buddhists, Ricci was already in a state of some irritation when he entered the monastery and was received by a group of monks led by the prior, who courteously showed him into the rooms reserved for figures of great prestige. Li Madou had no intention of being fooled by a friendly welcome that he regarded as a sham, believing that the monks were concerned and afraid that the wiser and more virtuous Jesuits might remain in the temple and seek to impose their iron discipline. Recorded in an account of the visit in Ricci's history of the mission, this interpretation reflects the author's biased hostility toward the followers of a rival religion.

After a short pause for refreshment, the missionaries were taken into the temple, which was made up of several rectangular rooms separated by courtyards. It was the first time that Ricci had found himself in the heart of a Buddhist place of worship, and he was astonished at the abundance of statues of Buddha, reckoning that the main hall held as many as five hundred, made of wood, bronze, white or gilded plaster, stone, and marble, in all sizes, from small to "disproportionately large." Votive offerings of fruit, bowls of food, and incense were placed in front of them. There was a huge bronze bell, the biggest he had ever seen, hanging from an imposing wooden structure inside a tower of stone in the main courtyard.

After their visit to the dark rooms heavily scented with incense, the Jesuits were taken to a cavern to pay their respects to the mummy of Liuzu, preserved in a coat of lacquer and illuminated by the light of a hundred candles above an elevated altar accessible by means of a staircase.[3] All the monks knelt down in silence with great solemnity, but the missionaries remained standing, to the consternation of their hosts. Ricci was convinced that a non-Buddhist Chinese visitor in his place would have genuflected with the others out of courtesy, but he had no intention of bowing down to a pagan idol, even at the risk of being impolite.

On leaving the rooms of the temple, the Jesuits walked along the narrow paths through the poor and unhealthy living quarters. The monks were shabbily dressed, and the presence of many women and children showed their disregard for the vow of celibacy. Observing the bonzes in their own environment did nothing to change the opinion that Ricci had already formed on meeting them in the streets of Zhaoqing. He thought them uncultivated, dishonest, and immoral, and he felt renewed aversion for them.

Regardless of whether Ricci was right to suspect the prior of hoping in his heart that the Westerners would not find the accommodation at the temple to their liking, the Jesuit could not wait to be on his way and was determined to stay in the village at the foot of the hill rather than accept the Buddhists' hospitality. When he expressed his intention not to remain, the prior was evidently relieved and even offered to accompany Ricci as far as Shaozhou and to help him buy a piece of land for the new residence. Almeida returned to the junk and continued along the river while Ricci spent the night in the village before setting off with the prior on horseback the following day.

Having arrived in Shaozhou on August 26, 1589, Li Madou was granted an audience with the lieutenant and had to explain why he had declined accommodation at Nanhua. The Jesuit took advantage of this opportunity to criticize the monks, claiming that his good reputation would have been damaged if he had stayed at the temple. He said that he wished to settle in Shaozhou, where he would be able to honor the Lord of Heaven and delight in the scholarly company he found congenial. The lieutenant was very surprised at these words, as he had thought that the priests were Buddhists and had no idea that they worshiped a god called the Lord of Heaven. The prior also had his say and criticized Ricci in turn for his failure to kneel before the monk Liuzu. According to Ricci, however, the mandarin had little fondness for the monks and took the missionaries' side, saying that fetishes like the mummy of the patriarch were not revered in China in the ancient times held in such consideration by Confucianists. The prior replied that it was indispensable to offer idols for adoration in order to win people over to the faith. At the end of this peaceable skirmish between the mandarin, the missionary, and the monk, Ricci obtained permission to reside in the city.

Life in Shaozhou and the Meeting with the Would-be Alchemist Qu Taisu

Located slightly south of present-day Shaoguan, Shaozhou[4] was a rich commercial town of some five thousand households surrounded by lush and fertile land. It stood at the confluence of two navigable rivers, the Wu Shui flowing from the west and the Zhen Shui from the east. Twice as big as Zhaoqing in terms of size and population, the city occupied an area stretching out on both banks of the Zhen Shui, which were connected by a pontoon bridge. Situated a short distance to the northeast on the same river was the major port of Nanxiong, a point of transit for goods from Europe and India bound for the interior and for products from the Chinese provinces bound for Canton. The area produced a cheap and delicious sweet wine made from grapes, which was sold in great quantities to the Portuguese, and had an abundance of river pearls, a commodity in great demand on the European markets. It also manufactured a valuable type of velvet, a material that the Chinese had imported from Europe in the past but then had learned to produce at lower cost and now sold to Western merchants.

On settling in, the Jesuits realized that the climate was torrid and stifling. They also learned that malaria was endemic and was more likely to strike those unaccustomed to living in a subtropical environment. Since another move was out of the question, the missionaries set about looking for a suitable site to build their new residence and found one in the western part of the town just outside the walls, a large uninhabited field very close to a Buddhist temple, where the missionaries took lodgings while awaiting the indispensable authorization from the governor. The land belonged to the monks, and Ricci offered to buy it on the lieutenant's advice. Eager to conclude a profitable transaction at the foreigners' expense, the bonzes asked an exorbitant price, at least ten times what would have been reasonable. Ricci refused to pay and waited to hear the governor's decision. The Jesuit now conducted the negotiations by himself, as he knew enough Chinese to do so and no longer trusted interpreters.

Sorely tried by the climate, Almeida and Ricci fell seriously ill while awaiting a reply and were confined to bed for a long time in the care of a local physician. They were still convalescent when the good news arrived in October that the governor, whose jurisdiction extended to the monasteries, would grant them the land free of charge, along with the essential residence permits.

Ricci decided that it would be better to build a single-story house in the Chinese style, having no wish to repeat the mistake made in Zhaoqing of arousing envy with a Western-style building. He also decided to design a more spacious chapel, however, in the hope of making many converts in the new town.

Meanwhile, the letter sent by Ricci through the pilot in Zhaoqing finally made its eventful way to Macao, and the superiors, left without news for so long and very concerned about the fate of their brethren, learned that Ricci and Almeida had moved. Greatly relieved, Valignano wrote letters of encouragement and sent two young Chinese novices educated at the Jesuit school in Macao to Shaozhou. One was Zhong Mingren, christened with the Portuguese name of Sebastião Fernandes in accordance with customary practice, and the other was Huang Mingsha, now called Francisco Martines. He appointed Duarte de Sande, already superior of the Chinese mission, as rector of the college in Macao and arranged for the Portuguese Jesuits João Soerio and João da Rocha to be sent to Macao and to study Mandarin Chinese with a view to entering China later on. The Visitor had no time to make any further decisions, as he had to leave again immediately for Japan in aid of the flourishing local mission, whose survival was seriously endangered now that General Toyotomi Hideyoshi had unleashed a persecution of Christians.

When the house was completed, the small religious community resumed its customary life of study and prayer and devoted its energies to patiently and gradually building up the friendly social relations indispensable to the work of spreading the Gospel. Here, too, the Jesuits' residence was soon visited by a whole procession of literati and officials eager to meet the man from the West skilled in the construction of extraordinary objects, the author of the map of the world and the catechism, whose reputation had spread all the way from Zhaoqing. Ricci began to make the acquaintance of the local dignitaries, a group of *guan* and *shidafu* who seemed friendlier and better disposed on first sight than the officials and scholars he had met in Zhaoqing. The impression that the dignitaries of Shaozhou were more responsive may have been related, however, to the change in Ricci's behavior. After seven years in China, he had now attained such a mastery of the language and customs that he was perfectly at ease in social intercourse, following the ritual as though he had lived in the Middle Kingdom all his life.

In Shaozhou too, however, false rumors were spread to discredit the missionaries. It was said that they were alchemists expelled from Zhaoqing because they refused to teach the governor their secrets. Ricci was concerned about this slanderous gossip, but it was precisely his reputation as an alchemist that led to an important meeting the year after his arrival.

One day in 1590, he received a visit from a *shidafu* named Qu Rukui but better known as Qu Taisu, who had already called at the Jesuits' residence in Zhaoqing the previous year and had been greatly impressed by Ricci's wisdom and charisma. Obsessed with alchemy and convinced that the missionary was a great adept capable of teaching him its secrets, he decided to travel to Shaozhou on learning that the Jesuit had moved there. Three years younger than Ricci, Qu Taisu was the son of the eminent mandarin and illustrious scholar Qu Jingchun, who had held the very important post of minister of rites and had died at an early age. Qu Taisu had studied for a long time and passed the imperial examinations but held no position in the bureaucracy.

Ricci was now familiar with the system of examinations that opened the way to a career in the bureaucracy. Selection took place in three stages. Held annually in the most important cities of every province, the first examination earned successful candidates the title of *xiucai*, or "budding talent," which Ricci regarded as equivalent to "bachelor," the first academic degree in medieval universities. This qualification brought a number of privileges, including exemption from certain duties obligatory for the rest of the population and permission to wear a special gown with a black hat and boots. The "budding talents" were a sort of reservoir of excellent students, about one hundred thousand in the country as a whole at the time, the best of whom were subsequently selected for participation in the second-level examinations held every three years in the provincial capitals. Successful candidates, about 10 percent of the total, became *juren*—provincial graduates or "literati recommended [to the court]" (translated by Ricci as *licenziato* or "licentiate")—who were qualified to hold positions on the lower rungs of the bureaucratic ladder. Held again every three years but this time in Beijing, the third and highest examination conferred the qualification of *jinshi*—metropolitan graduate or "literatus presented [to the court]," which Ricci equated with "doctor"—and permitted access to the upper echelons of the bureaucracy.

Even though admission to the Confucian schools and the examinations was open to all in principle, it was in practice only wealthy families such as those of great landowners that could afford to support their sons for all the years required to obtain an official post. Young men often sat the examinations repeatedly, willing to invest many years of their lives in the enterprise. The stakes were very high and the competition correspondingly fierce, as some of the privileges enjoyed by those obtaining good positions in the bureaucracy were extended to members of their immediate family, whose well-being thus also depended on the candidate's success. When a son passed an examination, the family celebrated on a lavish scale and erected a wooden arch before their front door. The young man's name and those of all the other successful candidates were then carved on massive stone tablets in the courtyards of the Confucian temples.

Qu Taisu passed the first two levels of examinations with flying colors and became a *juren*. But then, finding himself alone with no authoritative guidance after his father's sudden death, he abandoned any ambition for a career in the bureaucracy and ceased his studies. He devoted his energies to pursuing the impossible dream of alchemy and spent years traveling in search of experts capable of teaching him how to transmute base elements, accommodated everywhere with all the respect due to the son of an important *guan*. Having squandered practically all of his inheritance over the years and being heavily in debt, he was now living in Nanxiong with his concubine, who had stayed with him after the death of his wife.

In accordance with custom, Qu Taisu visited Ricci bearing gifts. After prostrating himself three times as required, he invited the Jesuit to a solemn banquet and asked him to become his master. The young scholar's social position made this a sign of great respect, especially as the master-pupil relationship was understood to last for the rest of one's life. Ricci presented Qu Taisu with valuable gifts in turn to show him that Jesuits did not teach for gain but solely for the love of wisdom. He then agreed to become his master but surprised him by declaring that he would not teach him the secrets of transmutation but rather a discipline that would help him to cultivate his mind, namely mathematics. Qu Taisu accepted with great curiosity.

Doing Sums with Brush and Paper

Ricci had noted that the Chinese used the abacus,[5] a rectangular frame of wood with beads that could be slid along wires, in order to make arithmetical calculations. Merchants, shopkeepers, literati, and officials used this with great skill to add, subtract, and multiply but found it much harder to divide and extract square and cube roots. Commonly used in China from the eleventh century on, the abacus was a descendant of the tablets employed for calculation in antiquity by the Chinese and even earlier by the Babylonians, followed by the Greeks, Indians, and Romans, which had evolved with different characteristics in the various countries over the centuries.

In its form as a counting board,[6] the abacus had long been supplanted in Europe by the more flexible and effective method of written calculations using Hindu-Arabic numerals. Commonly used today, this base ten positional numeral system[7] was invented in India and was introduced into Europe by the Arabs sometime around the tenth century. It made it possible to perform arithmetical operations, including multiplication and division, more easily than with the abacus and the outmoded Roman numerals. The disputes between "abacists" and "algorists"—advocates respectively of the old systems of calculation and the new methods,[8] soon established as an invaluable tool for merchants, bankers, architects, and everyone required to keep systematic accounts—were now a thing of the past.

Written calculation was not used in China despite the existence of a decimal positional numeral system conceptually similar to ours and originating long before the analogous system was adopted in India.[9] The symbols representing the numbers from one to nine were made up of vertical or horizontal dashes, and zero was an empty circle, as in the West. This acquired the new name of *ling*—meaning "dew drop" in ancient Chinese—during the Ming era.[10]

When Ricci saw Qu Taisu using the antiquated abacus—"that device of threaded beads"[11]—to do sums, he said he would teach him a new system of calculation and set about doing so with brush and paper. The scholar discovered that the new written method was effectively an improvement, especially as a record remained of the various operations required to arrive at the final result, thus making it much easier to check the calculation performed. Moreover, written calculation made it possible to carry out more complex arithmetical operations than the abacus.

The value of the Western method in the eyes of Qu Taisu and the other literati wishing to learn it from Ricci was, however, not only practical. The ability to perform "calculations with the brush," as the new method soon came to be called by the Chinese, enabled mandarins to acquire another cultural advantage with respect to the other social classes in the field of mathematics, where they had never enjoyed supremacy. All merchants were skilled in reckoning, more so indeed than the mandarins, but none of them knew the Western art of written calculation.

Teaching Qu Taisu confirmed Ricci's suspicion that the scholars' cultural background was deep but almost exclusively humanistic. Even though arithmetic was part of the basic school syllabus in China and the literati studied some aspects of it in greater depth during their later education, mathematics was regarded in the Ming era as an inferior branch of knowledge with respect to literary studies, and it was not one of the set subjects in the imperial examinations. While technical questions on astronomical calculations and the calendar were occasionally included,[12] this was not standard practice.

As a result of this situation, the numerous mathematicians of the Ming era mostly belonged to the lower classes. For example, the author of one of the most important mathematical works of the period—namely the *Suanfa Tongzong*, or *Systematic Treatise on Arithmetic*, published in 1592 and including a detailed description of how the Chinese abacus worked—was Cheng Dawei, born into a family of merchants and employed as a clerk in local administration. The only government official to become a skilled mathematician was Gu Yingxiang,[13] appointed governor of Yunnan halfway through the sixteenth century and subsequently minister of justice.

Ricci believed that mathematics was not only little studied in China but was also very backward with respect to developments in Europe. The reality was very different from the image formed by the Jesuit, who had only limited knowledge of his hosts' culture, was influenced by his preconceptions, and knew nothing of the history of Chinese science. There were in fact many important mathematicians in China during the period when Ricci lived there, and the scientific discoveries achieved can be considered significant, as contemporary historians of mathematics have pointed out. Peter Engelfriet, who has studied the influence of the work of Ricci and the other Jesuits on the development of mathematics in China, observes for example that Cheng Dawei described a method of solving systems of equations with many unknowns that would have been something new to Ricci if the missionaries had shown any interest in Chinese mathematics.[14]

It is, however, true that mathematics, and science in general, was going through a phase of decline with respect to the past during the Ming era,[15] and there was no scientific community comparable to the one existing in the West at the time.[16] Scholars taking an interest in mathematics in China were comparatively isolated and had great difficulty obtaining specialized texts because the classical works of Chinese mathematics had disappeared from the libraries.[17] Even the most famous work, namely the *Jiuzhang suanshu*, or "Nine Chapters on the Mathematical Art"—which dated back to the early centuries of the Christian era, boasted countless commentators, and had been printed for the first time in 1084, four centuries before the first printed version of Euclid's *Elements* was published in Latin in Venice in 1482—was no longer available in its complete version. Scholars sometimes even embarked on great journeys in the hope of finding copies of long-out-of-print treatises on algebra and arithmetic in remote libraries. Cheng Dawei himself had collected the books for his studies by traveling through China for more than twenty years, clear proof that those who studied mathematics in China were spurred by passion rather than by any hope of institutional recognition. The only exceptions were the imperial mathematicians and astronomers responsible for performing the calculations necessary for drawing up the calendar, who enjoyed positions of great prestige but were in many cases devoid of intellectual curiosity or any real skill, as Ricci was to see for himself.[18]

Euclidean Geometry and the Achievements of Chinese Mathematics

Ricci was unaware of China's mathematical achievements in previous ages, when Chinese scholars had made many breakthroughs long in advance of their Western colleagues. One of the many instances of this regarded pi, the ratio of the circumference of a circle to its diameter, for which the sixth-century Chinese mathematician Zu Chongzhi succeeded, with the help of his son, in calculating an approximate value down to the tenth decimal place with a precision that no one in the West was to surpass for eleven centuries.

This result was so significant that a region of the moon was named after this Chinese mathematician.

Other important achievements were made in algebra in the Song era between the tenth and thirteenth centuries, regarded as the "Chinese Renaissance," and in the immediately subsequent Yuan era. Rather than the abacus, the Chinese of the time used counting rods of bamboo, ivory, or iron, with black for negative numbers and red for positive, in more advanced calculations. Placed on a tabletop divided into squares, they were used to perform complex operations such as extracting square and cube roots and solving algebraic equations and systems of equations.[19] All officials of the period carried a bag of rods with them ready for use and were so quick in manipulating them that, according to a writer of the ninth century, it was impossible to follow the movements of their hands.[20] The works of algebra printed in those years also contained highly advanced results. The *Shushu jiuzhang* ("Mathematical Treatise in Nine Chapters") published in 1245 by the mathematician and imperial official Qin Jiushao—whose passion for numbers did not save him from having repeated charges of corruption lodged with the censors—included numerical equations higher than the third order and a method for calculating the square roots of large numbers that was not discovered in the West until six centuries later.

The *Siyuan yujian* ("Precious Mirror of Four Elements") of 1303, considered the highest expression of Chinese algebra of the period, included equations up to the fourteenth order and presented an approximate way of calculating solutions that appeared in the West as Horner's method only five centuries later. The "four elements" mentioned in the title were the heavens, the earth, man, and matter, the names used to designate the four unknowns in an equation. Another feature of this volume was the representation on its cover in Chinese characters of a set of numbers arranged in triangular form and showing the coefficients of the successive binomial powers up to eight, which appears to have been discovered two hundred years earlier. Also known as Pascal's triangle, this was introduced in Europe by Niccolò Tartaglia in the sixteenth century, and the typical image presenting the binomial coefficients in triangular form appeared for the first time on the cover of a book by the German Peter Bienewitz, in Latin Petrus Apianus, in 1527.

Apart from these instances of primacy, the comparison of Chinese and Western mathematics is both difficult and completely meaningless, according to many scholars, as the two disciplines developed with different characteristics. Even if Ricci had had the opportunity to read the Chinese treatises on mathematics, he would have found it hard to understand their value. The Chinese approach was in fact more concrete than that of the Greeks, who laid the foundations of mathematics in the West. Described as possessing practical and empirical genius by Joseph Needham, a scholar of Chinese science, the Chinese were oriented toward algebra rather than geometry, were more interested in calculation than hypothetical-deductive procedure, and preferred analogical reasoning to a succession of logical steps.[21] While Greek treatises provided a systematic and logically organized exposition of the subject under examination, Chinese works tended to present and solve specific problems.[22]

These cultural differences did nothing to deter Qu Taisu, who forgot all about alchemy and developed a keen interest in Western mathematics. On being asked to continue the lessons, Ricci decided that the time had come to teach him Euclid's *Elements* in the Latin translation by Clavius that he had brought from Italy. Having made a thorough study of the work at the Roman College, he agreed with the German Jesuit in regarding it as the most important text for anyone beginning mathematics. The value of the *Elements* lay not only in its content but also in the hypothetical-deductive method in terms of which the results were organized and presented. Starting from a list of definitions of the key elements, such as the point and the straight line, and a series of postulates or nondemonstrable assertions, Euclid proved over five hundred theorems and provided the greatest example of logical rigor achieved by Greek mathematics.

The style of the text was something completely new for Qu Taisu, who thought of numbers and geometric figures as concrete objects rather than Euclid's abstract idealizations. As noted above, while methods of reasoning and written proofs had been developed in China,[23] a concept of hypothetical-deductive geometric demonstration comparable to the Greek had not, and mathematical assertions were often proved in a very concrete way.[24] For example, the Pythagorean theorem that the square on the hypotenuse of a right triangle is equal to the sum of the squares on the two adjacent sides can be proved either on the basis of geometric properties deduced from axioms and other theorems or by means of the procedure presented in an ancient Chinese text, which involves constructing a right triangle and the squares on the hypotenuse and the other two sides and showing concretely by cutting out and arranging the relevant pieces of the figures that the surfaces in question match precisely as asserted by the theorem.[25]

Exposed for the first time to the style of Euclid's demonstrations, Qu Taisu developed a passion for geometry and devoted himself to his studies. Ricci was pleased to see that the scholar "never tired of learning" and spent "day and night over his books." Under Ricci's guidance, he translated the first of the fifteen books of the *Elements* in the Clavius edition into Chinese. The manuscript, which has not survived, is generally considered the first attempt to introduce Euclidean geometry into China, even though historians of science suggest that a translation was made during the Yuan era into the Mongolian language, no trace of which now remains.[26] Qu Taisu stayed in Shaozhou a whole year to attend Ricci's lessons, and he also learned the basics of astronomy from a commentary by Clavius on Johannes de Sacrobosco's *De Sphaera mundi*, the renowned exposition of the Ptolemaic geocentric conception of the universe written in 1233 but still studied in the sixteenth century. The young Chinese scholar copied its illustrations and verified the calculations with ever-increasing assurance.

Now convinced of the value of Western science, Qu Taisu went so far—at least according to Ricci—as to assert that after studying with the Jesuit, Chinese books were like "men with no brain" by comparison with those of the West.[27] The master followed up this crash course in theory with practice, explaining the working principles of mechanical clocks and scientific instruments like quadrants and astrolabes to Qu Taisu and teaching him how to construct rudimentary celestial globes of wood, brass, and silver. The Jesuit devoted his energies to his enthusiastic student nearly all day and moved seamlessly back and forth between scientific and religious instruction. Qu Taisu proved an attentive student also of the foundations of the Christian doctrine and used a small book to make note of queries regarding catechism to be submitted to Ricci.

The Jesuit was pleased with his pupil's progress and believed that he was now ripe for conversion to Catholicism, in this case as a carefully considered decision based on rational conviction. There was, however, one obstacle that the Jesuit had underestimated. In order to join the Christian religion, Qu Taisu would be obliged either to marry or to repudiate his concubine, as the missionaries explained clearly. Marriage with a woman of lower social class was a violation of the rules governing Chinese society and hence was out of the question. At the same time, the scholar had no intention of leaving the woman who, he hoped, would provide the son his wife had been unable to give him. Faced with this dilemma, Ricci's first Chinese friend preferred to forgo baptism, and the missionary was obliged to resign himself to this decision.

Social Relations and Popular Hostility

Ricci's friendship with a *shidafu* with excellent connections in Chinese society enabled him to make the acquaintance of many influential figures. The *guanxi*, or network of personal relations, was indispensable to establishing social position in China, and Ricci was received with the utmost consideration when introduced as the friend and master of Qu Taisu. Through his contacts with personages in the civilian and military worlds, the Jesuit began to form a deeper understanding of Chinese society and realized that the military authorities, while enjoying privileges, were devoid of political influence and were inferior in status to government officials. While access to military positions was also through a system of highly selective examinations, the designated examiners were *shidafu* with no experience in the martial field, thus providing further proof that the knowledge of Confucian literati was considered superior to any specialized skill. Like the bureaucracy, the military hierarchy was divided into nine levels, each of which was represented by the emblem of a ferocious animal embroidered on ceremonial garments: lions for the ninth and eighth levels; tigers, leopards, and bears down to the fifth; panthers for the fourth and third; and rhinoceroses for the second. The seahorse was the far less intimidating badge of the first level.[28]

The more Ricci established his position in the local society, the more visits he received from dignitaries passing through the town on the river who were curious to make his acquaintance. The Jesuit was able to hold conversations with ever-increasing naturalness and now also understood the local dialect, an indispensable means of communication with peasants and shopkeepers. One of the visitors was a son of the governor who had expelled the Jesuits from Zhaoqing, who showed the missionaries all the respect and consideration his father had denied them. The most frequent callers included Su Dayong, the district magistrate of nearby Yingde, who invited Ricci to his home to meet his aged father. The Jesuit accepted the invitation together with Qu Taisu, and his visit to Yingde was a major event in the calm life of that small town. The magistrate held a sumptuous banquet, with music in his honor, at which all the local dignitaries were present. The mandarin's father had a long conversation with Ricci and was so impressed by his personality as to remain in contact by letter for the rest of his life.

On his return to Shaozhou, Ricci was relieved to learn that the new prefect Xie Tianqing was a good friend of Qu Taisu. Proof of the mandarin's goodwill soon arrived in the form of an edict to be displayed at the residence as a deterrent to any hostile action.

Even though everything seemed to be going smoothly, the Jesuit was concerned about Almeida. The younger missionary suffered from poor health, he found the climate practically unbearable, and he had a tormented relationship with his faith that led to the self-infliction of such corporal penances that Ricci was obliged to keep watch over him so as to avoid useless excesses. Having fallen seriously ill, Ricci's young companion left for Macao to be treated by the Portuguese doctors there and did not return until a few months later, still convalescent and severely weakened. A relapse soon proved fatal, and Almeida passed away on October 17, 1591. Ricci was not alone for long, being joined before the end of the year by Francesco de Petris, aged twenty-nine, from the town of Rieti in Italy, who seemed to adapt to the climate much better than his ill-fated predecessor. Meanwhile, Qu Taisu, having completed his fruitful period of study, had returned to Nanxiong to take care of his affairs, but he kept in contact with his master by letter, assuring him that he had not abandoned mathematics and providing him detailed reports of discussions he had about Euclid's geometry with his scholarly friends.[29]

A rich merchant with Buddhist leanings from the same town as Qu Taisu had stayed at the missionaries' house for a month during a visit to Shaozhou and had been converted. Now baptized a Christian with the name of Joseph, he invited Ricci to spend a few days in Nanxiong. The Jesuit accepted and was the guest of his friend Qu Taisu for a week in February 1592. When he saw Joseph again, he discovered that after his conversion the merchant had abandoned his family and his thriving business and was living as a hermit in the mistaken belief that the new religion he had joined required the renunciation of all worldly goods. Ricci was dismayed, as he intended to seek new converts during his stay in Nanxiong, and he was afraid that this example might discourage others from following his teaching. His fears proved groundless, however, as his preaching aroused great interest.

Ricci met many of the local dignitaries in the town on the river and was forced into a very active social life. He used a closed litter to speed his progress through the crowded streets by avoiding curiosity and attempts to stop him, but the stratagem did not always work and the doors were often opened by people suspecting his presence inside and intent on viewing him in the flesh. Without a moment's respite, Ricci often spent the entire day and much of the night discussing religious or cultural themes, barely finding the time to eat, say his prayers, and celebrate Mass. Individual visits were combined with the inevitable banquets held in his honor, sometimes even four or five in the same day. The missionary rushed from one to another, tasting each of the numerous dishes every time so as to avoid giving offence. All this hard work was rewarded, as many inhabitants of Nanxiong asked Ricci to initiate them into the new Western religion and were to receive baptism. Despite his best efforts not to accept converts with no more than a superficial indoctrination, he was obviously forced to do so on occasion. On his return to Shaozhou, well pleased with the success of his trip out of town, he learned that the governor of the Guangdong province, the hated *guan* responsible for expelling the missionaries from Zhaoqing, had been accused of corruption by the imperial censor and sentenced to pay a fine but had died suddenly before settling his debt with justice. While his death freed the Jesuits from an adversary who could still have done them harm, new enemies were busy preparing hostile actions against the missionaries in Shaozhou too.

The first episode of intolerance took place the previous year, in January 1591, when Ricci exhibited an image of the Virgin, which he had received as a gift from the Spanish authorities, in the chapel in concomitance with the celebrations of the Chinese New Year. A small crowd of local inhabitants rushed to see the painting, but some young men took advantage of the confusion to throw stones at the residence and attack the servants. The prefect issued an edict deploring the event, and having identified the guilty parties as the sons of local dignitaries, he declared his readiness to put them on trial. But Ricci decided against pressing charges to show his capacity for forgiveness. A year and a half went by, but then, one night in July 1592, the residence was attacked by a group of over twenty armed men who tried to break down the doors with axes, wounding De Petris in the head and Ricci in the hand. The missionaries were forced to barricade themselves in their rooms. Ricci jumped out of the window to seek help, but he tripped in the darkness and severely twisted his ankle. Even though no one came to the Jesuits' aid, the servants' strenuous defense of the house finally put the attackers to flight. It was an easy matter to discover that they were also the ones responsible for the incident the previous year. The prefect was again ready to try them, but Ricci preferred to forgive them once more. When Valignano, on returning from Japan, was informed of the attack and of Ricci's injury, he summoned him to Macao for treatment by the Portuguese doctors, but nothing could be done for the Jesuit's ankle. Even though the pain subsided over the years, Ricci was no longer able to travel long distances on foot.

On his return to Shaozhou, Ricci discovered that his benevolence toward the attackers had been interpreted as weakness and that relatives of the accused were plotting to have the Jesuits expelled from the city. He decided to scare his enemies by threatening to ask the prefect to punish the guilty parties, whereupon the false accusations were promptly withdrawn.

Three years had now gone by since the move to Shaozhou, and Ricci was able to draw up an initial balance sheet of missionary work in the second Chinese residence, where twenty-two converts had been baptized. Determined as he was to seek quality rather than quantity, and keenly aware that China was a difficult country to conquer, the Jesuit was not overly concerned about the smallness of the number. As he wrote to Superior General Acquaviva on November 15, 1592,[30] in an "uncultivated wilderness" like China, it was still necessary to break open the crust of the land before sowing could commence.

Notes

1. Roger Bacon, *Opus Majus* (1266–1268), part IV, distinction I, chapter I, trans. R. B. Burke, *The Opus Majus of Roger Bacon* (Philadelphia: University of Pennsylvania Press, 1928), vol. 1, p. 116.

2. Little now survives of this great monastery. An enormous kitchen utensil called the "frying pan of a thousand monks" was found in its ruins in 1934. See FR, book III, ch. I, pp. 280–81.

3. Letter to Alessandro Valignano, September 9, 1589; OS II, p. 78.

4. Ricci writes that the city's name was Qujiang, but it was called Shaozhou, meaning prefecture, because the prefect had his residence there.

5. Called a *suanpan* in Chinese and still used for arithmetical calculations in China. For further information about numbering and systems of calculation, see Georges Ifrah, *Histoire universelle des chiffres* (Paris: Seghers, 1981) [trad. it. *Storia universale dei numeri*, Milano, Mondadori, 1989, p. 120, 383, 431].

6. Boards divided into parallel rows and columns on which pebbles and other objects could be used as counters to represent numbers and perform arithmetical operations. See Georges Ifrah, op. cit. pp. 120.

7. This decimal positional system uses the ten digits from zero to nine to write all numbers, the value of each digit in the number being multiplied by ten in relation to its position starting from the right.

8. See Georges Ifrah, op. cit., p. 131.

9. See Carl B. Boyer, *A History of Mathematics* (1968), [trad. it. *Storia della matematica*, Milano: Mondadori, p. 233].

10. Joseph Needham, *Science and Civilisation in China*, vol. 3, *Mathematics and the Sciences of the Heavens and Earth* [trad. it. *Scienza e civiltà in Cina*, vol. 3, *Matematica e Astronomia*, Torino: Einaudi, 1985, p. 21].

11. FR, book III, ch. III, p. 297.

12. A. Benjamin Elman, *A Cultural History of Civil Examinations in Late Imperial China* (Berkeley: University of California Press, 2000), p. 466.

13. Peter M. Engelfriet, *Euclid in China* (Leiden: Brill, 1998), p. 101.

14. Peter M. Engelfriet, Siu Man-Keung, *Xu Guangqi's Attempts to Integrate Western and Chinese Mathematics in Statecraft and Intellectual Renewal in Late Ming China* (Leiden: Brill, 2001), p. 290.

15. Jean-Claude Martzloff, *A History of Chinese Mathematics* (New York: Springer-Verlag, 1987), p. 19. This view is not shared by all historians of science and is the subject of lively debate. See for example Roger Hart, "Quantifying Ritual: Political Cosmology, Courtly Music and Precision Mathematics in Seventeenth-Century China," and other articles by the same author: http://uts.cc.utexas.edu/~rhart.

16. Even though most European mathematicians were also nonprofessionals in the sixteenth and seventeenth centuries (François Viète was a lawyer and Gerolamo Cardano a physician, for example), they did form a fairly homogeneous community. For mathematics in the Ming era, see P. M. Engelfriet, *Euclid in China*, cit., pp. 98 ff.

17. Engelfriet, *Euclid in China*, cit., p. 99.

18. See chapter 8 ("Astronomy and the Emperor") and chapter 10 ("The Forgotten Astronomical Observatory").

19. C. B. Boyer, op. cit., p. 233, and G. Ifrah, op. cit., p. 135. The latter devotes parts of chapters 8, 26, and 28 to China.

20. C. B. Boyer, op. cit., p. 233.

21. J. Needham, op. cit., p. 191.

22. For the characteristics of Chinese mathematics, see J.-C. Martzloff, op. cit., pp. 69 ff.

23. J.-C. Martzloff, op. cit., p. 273.

24. For further discussion of the use of logical deduction in ancient Chinese thinking, see Angus Graham, *Later Mohist Logic, Ethics and Science* (Hong Kong: Chinese University, 1978).

25. J.-C. Martzloff, op. cit., p. 297.

26. P. M. Engelfriet, *Euclid in China*, cit., p. 136.

27. FR, book III, ch. III, p. 298.

28. Valery M. Garret, *Chinese Clothing* (Hong Kong: Oxford University Press, 1994), p. 15.

29. P. M. Engelfriet, *Euclid in China*, cit., p. 61.

30. OS II, p. 106.

~

CHAPTER SEVEN

Metamorphosis into Mandarin

From Shaozhou to Nanchang, 1593–1595

The Master said, "Having studied, to then repeatedly apply what you have learned—is this not a source of pleasure? To have friends come from distant quarters—is this not a source of enjoyment? To go unacknowledged by others without harboring frustration—is this not the mark of an exemplary person?"

—Confucius, *Analects* (1, 1)

The Master was always gracious yet serious, commanding yet not severe, deferential yet at ease.

—Confucius, *Analects* (7, 38)

Do not impose on others what you yourself do not want.

—Confucius, *Analects* (15, 24)

Distance and Nostalgia

The mission was plunged into mourning once more in November 1593. Having made substantial progress with Chinese in just two years and being already able to provide real support, Francesco de Petris fell seriously ill with malaria and died in the space of a few days. Ricci had become accustomed to the presence of his fellow countryman and to relying on his help, but he now found himself alone again. In sending the news to Superior General Acquaviva and Girolamo Costa, he spoke of losing a "dearly beloved"[1] brother, his "only companion and refuge in this wilderness."[2] Now aged forty-two, Ricci had been living in China for ten years and realized that time had passed quickly. On thinking back over past events, he felt only limited satisfaction with the results achieved. The "passions," as he liked to put it, had alternated with consolations. While he considered himself fortunate to have escaped the illnesses that had befallen his brethren, he had also suffered hardship and loss and had to fight against hostility and prejudice. There were only a few dozen converts, not many by comparison with the expectations of early years. In a moment of fatigue, he had even wished for "a happy death" such as the martyrdom his companion Rodolfo Acquaviva had found in India.[3]

Echoes of the bitter reflections and moments of sadness to which the Jesuit gave way every so often are to be found in his letters, even though he seldom allowed his emotions to show in the reports of events he sent to his superiors and brethren. It was not customary for Jesuits to succumb to sentiment, revealing their human weaknesses and forgetting their higher mission. In any case, it can hardly have been easy to entrust one's most private thoughts to letters written to family in the knowledge that it would take at least three years for them to reach their destination and as long to receive a reply. In the least favorable circumstances, the period of six or seven years between sending a message and receiving an answer could increase considerably, as in the exceptional case of a letter sent by Valignano from Japan in 1589 via Macao, which took seventeen years to arrive in Rome.[4] As correspondence was also lost all too often in the frequent shipwrecks, the missionaries sought to increase the probability of their messages reaching their destination by sending at least two copies, one entrusted to the Portuguese carracks taking the western route from Macao via India and the other to the Spanish galleons taking the eastern route from Manila to Mexico, where it would be transported overland across the isthmus of Tehuantepec to another ship bound for Europe.

As the letters made their long journey, events and states of mind changed, and all immediacy was lost. In the saddest cases, the messages arrived when the intended recipient had already passed away. In a letter to Fabio de Fabii dated November 12, 1594, Ricci enjoined him to continue writing despite the precarious nature of their correspondence because it was such "a great consolation" to receive mail, and he confessed his own discouragement: "Many times, remembering how many long letters I have written to the dead over there, I lose the strength and will to write." Ricci wrote to his father Giovanni Battista every year and to his brothers less frequently,[5] but he seldom received a reply. In the second of the two surviving letters sent to his father from Shaozhou, he complained of having no news: "It would comfort me to know how they are and whether they are all alive."[6] This silence on the part of Ricci's family suggests that Giovanni Battista still harbored a grudge for his son's choice of career and his abrupt decision to leave for the missions without returning to Macerata for a last farewell. Ricci heard of the death of his grandmother Laria not from the family but from a fellow Jesuit, and spoke of this in a letter to his father,[7] expressing sorrow at their separation, a distance for which he found consolation in the thought that earthly life was short and they would all soon meet again in heaven. The letter ended with this plea: "For pity's sake, keep writing to me."

Ricci did not fail to inform his father in his letters about the progress he had achieved in spreading the Gospel, but he also tried to introduce other subjects in the hope of interesting his father and perhaps making the remote, alien world in which his son was living feel a little closer. He told him, for example, about the Chinese products bound for Europe that he saw in transit along the river to the port of Canton. One of the most common of these products in Shaozhou, where it was collected in great amounts, was rhubarb, whose reddish bark was used in China above all to dye fabrics and whose root was in great demand in the West for the preparation of medicines, as Ricci's father, being an apothecary, was well aware. Although the Chinese production was very abundant, the plant was considered rare and expensive on the European markets because most of the rhubarb sent from the East by land and sea was poorly preserved and deteriorated en route.

A very different subject was the Japanese invasion of Korea, China's most faithful tributary kingdom. After the troops of the Rising Sun, led by the shogun Toyotomi Hideyoshi, conquered Seoul and Pyongyang in the months of May and June 1592, the Chinese government was forced to mobilize the army and prepare for a war to expel the invaders. This obligatory decision was discussed with mounting concern because conflict would worsen the already precarious financial situation of the Chinese state, whose accounts were chronically in the red during the late Ming era.

The echoes of the fighting were, however, somewhat faint by the time they reached Shaozhou in the heart of the Guangdong province. Ricci continued his missionary work with a great deal of effort and little to show for it while awaiting the support of a new companion. This did not take long. About halfway through 1594, a few months after the death of De Petris, he was joined by a fellow Italian named Lazzaro Cattaneo from Sarzana, previously assigned to the Japan mission but then diverted to China by Valignano.

Minister Wang and the Reform of the Calendar

Cattaneo arrived with important news that was to mark a turning point for the mission. Ricci had always disliked being mistaken for a Buddhist monk, and his embarrassment only grew with the passage of time, as he informed Valignano repeatedly. His friend Qu Taisu had also made it clear to the missionaries that the robe of a bonze was not in keeping with the position they had established for themselves in Chinese society, and he suggested that they should dress in silk like the literati and introduce themselves with titles emphasizing their status as men of culture.

Cattaneo met Valignano in Macao before leaving for Shaozhou and discussed the problem with him at some length before obtaining the long awaited authorization. The missionaries were now permitted to grow their hair and beards, to wear silk garments similar to those of the *shidafu* on official occasions, and to present themselves as *daoren*, or "masters of the Way."[8]

Ricci was greatly relieved. The missionaries immediately stopped shaving and cutting their hair and had new garments made with a view to adopting them in the future when a suitable opportunity arose. The decision to alter the image and title with which the missionaries presented themselves to the Chinese could not have been timelier. Now enjoying a reputation for wisdom and learning that clashed with his shabby monklike appearance, Ricci was called upon to receive ever greater numbers of visitors desiring to see his scientific instruments and demonstrations of his skill as a mathematician. Even a *guan* of high rank like Wang Zhongming, who had just resigned his post as minister of rites in Nanjing for reasons of health, stopped in Shaozhou on his way to his hometown on the island of Hainan in order to meet Xitai, Li Madou, of whom he had heard a great deal. Nanjing in the Jiangsu province was the second city in China after Beijing. Its name means "capital of the South," and it had in fact been the capital of the empire for five dynasties and during the reign of the first two Ming emperors. The city enjoyed the privilege of retaining the same government structure as Beijing and hosted six ministries (of rites, punishments, finance, war, public works, and personnel) identical in name to those in the capital. The ministers were considered very important dignitaries, albeit of less political influence than their colleagues in Beijing.

Wang spent an entire day in conversation with the Jesuit and was greatly impressed by his mathematical and astronomical knowledge. According to Ricci's own account, the minister even suggested the possibility of his help being requested in the reform of the Chinese calendar,[9] explaining that the system had been in need of radical correction for a long time but the decision to commence was constantly postponed because the imperial astronomers were not capable of performing the task. The Chinese calendar was of the lunisolar type, and the year was divided into twelve months each roughly corresponding to a lunation, the period of a complete revolution of the moon around the earth. There was also a further division of the year into twenty-four solar periods of approximately a fortnight, each of which was divided in turn into three periods of five or six days. The beginning of spring, for example, was spread over the three periods named "the wind melts the ice," "the animals awaken from hibernation," and "the fish swims beneath the ice," short descriptions of the phenomena of nature in that part of the season.

As the period formed by the twelve lunar months did not coincide exactly with the solar year, it was necessary to include an entire intercalary thirteenth month every so often. The Chinese calendar still in use had been drawn up by the astronomer Guo Shoujing for the emperor Kublai Khan in 1281 during the Yuan era and had been adopted with the name of *Datong* but no substantial modification by the subsequent Ming dynasty. Albeit very advanced for the period in which it was conceived, it had become obsolete due to lack of revision and was now out of step with the seasons and was imprecise in the prediction of astronomical phenomena like eclipses.

When the time came to set off again, the minister had Ricci accompany him to his junk and kept him on board talking until late in the night, probably with further reference to the problem of the calendar. The Jesuit was aware of the difficulties to be encountered in devising a perpetual calendar system and remembered what he had learned at the Roman College from Christopher Clavius, one of the creators of the Gregorian calendar. Ricci unquestionably realized that the reform of the Chinese calendar could offer the Jesuits an extraordinary opportunity, and it was probably then that he began to make plans to have brethren sent to China who were more expert than he was in the complex astronomical calculations required to correct the system.[10] He was in fact becoming convinced that success would confer immense prestige on the missionaries at the imperial court and would pave the way for the work of spreading the Gospel. Hope may have been kindled in Ricci's breast that night, but he could scarcely have imagined how many years would have to pass and how many trials and tribulations the Jesuits would have to go through before one of their order was finally appointed with imperial approval to reform the Chinese calendar.[11]

Confucius, "Another Seneca":
The Translation of the Confucian Classics

In accordance with Valignano's recommendations, Ricci never ceased study-ing Mandarin and reading works of history and philosophy in an effort to understand the culture of the Confucian literati. Only if he succeeded in sharing the knowledge of the *shidafu* would he be able to converse with them on an equal footing, present the Christian doctrine with real authority, and find the best arguments to convince them of the validity of his religious message. Deeper study of Chinese philosophy was also prompted by plans to write a new catechism to replace the one published in Zhaoqing on the basis of Michele Ruggieri's text, which Valignano found unsatisfactory because it had been prepared without an adequate understanding of Confucianism.

Ricci devoted himself from 1591, if not earlier, to the study of the most im-portant canonical works that Chinese scholars were required to know perfectly in order to pass the imperial examinations. In addition to the *Analects* of Con-fucius, the Four Books of Confucianism traditionally comprised the *Doctrine of the Mean* and the *Great Learning*, works devoted to the rules governing the society in the master's day, and the *Mencius*, an exposition of the thought of the philosopher of that name,[12] who lived two centuries after Confucius and is considered his most important heir.[13] They did not contain a systematic expo-sition of a developed body of doctrine but rather provided precepts for correct moral and social conduct and recommendations for sound government.

The Jesuit began to study them together with Almeida and continued with De Petris in the conviction that the knotty texts would be a good way for his companions to improve their knowledge of classical Chinese. After their deaths, he went on alone and decided in accordance with Valignano's wishes to translate the four Chinese works into Latin in order to acquaint the brethren in Europe with the thinking of the Middle Kingdom's greatest phi-losopher. Michele Ruggieri had embarked on a similar project but had been dissuaded from continuing by Valignano, who regarded his grasp of Chinese as inadequate for the task and preferred to wait for Ricci to carry it out.[14]

The assignment was most demanding, and Ricci thought the help of a "very learned" master indispensable. He accordingly resumed lessons in clas-sical Chinese, becoming a pupil again at the age of over forty, as he wrote to Claudio Acquaviva on December 10, 1593 ("I am going to become a school-boy in my old age"),[15] confirming that he had been at work on the difficult translation for at least a year.

Ricci completed his task at the end of 1594 by producing the first Latin paraphrase of the Confucian works accompanied by numerous comments.

During the years of the mission's activity, the manuscript was used for study by Jesuits arriving in China and served as a text of reference for the compilation of the celebrated *Confucius Sinarum Philosophus*, the first complete presentation of the life and work of Confucius in the West, published in Paris in 1687 by a group of Jesuits under the supervision of Philippe Couplet from the Spanish Netherlands.[16]

The Four Books of Confucianism aroused the same interest in Ricci as the Greek and Latin works studied at the Roman College, and he found remarkable similarities between Confucian morality and the principles of Western ethics, as well as a particular affinity between the Chinese philosophy and Stoicism. He described them in a letter to Superior General Acquaviva as "sound moral documents"[17] and Confucius as "another Seneca," appreciating him as he had the great classical thinkers of the West: "In his sound way of living in harmony with nature, he is not inferior to our ancient philosophers and indeed superior to many."[18] Ricci was unquestionably struck by the fact that Confucianism identified man's primary duty as the practice of two fundamental virtues, namely rectitude and benevolence or humanity, *ren* in Chinese, and encouraged citizens to cultivate solidarity, respect, courtesy, and trust. Moreover, the Chinese philosophy saw the family as the basis of society and the state as a great family, the emperor being described as the "mother and father" of his subjects. According to Confucius, the foundations of society were the five key relations between ruler and subject, father and son, husband and wife, elder and younger brother, and friends.

Another cornerstone of Confucian philosophy that Ricci could not fail to appreciate as a humanist was veneration for the past and the most ancient traditions. To quote one of the master's best-known dicta, "Following the proper way, I do not forge new paths; with confidence I cherish the ancients."[19] In developing his studies, the Jesuit was pleasantly surprised to note that some of the Chinese master's pithy utterances bore obvious similarities to sayings of Western classicism now part of the legacy of European culture. The Confucian view of the virtue of the just and constant mean as the supreme requirement[20] recalled Aristotle's view of virtue lying at the mean in the Nicomachean Ethics, just as the Chinese injunction not to impose on others what you do not wish for yourself[21] is echoed in the well-known principle enunciated in the New Testament.

Ricci knew that the Confucian philosophy had been reworked over the centuries and was studied during the Ming era in the interpretation developed in the eleventh century by Zhu Xi, a member of the school known in the West in modern terms as Neo-Confucianism. Zhu Xi inserted the great master's teaching into a more organic and complex philosophical system that took up elements of the Buddhist and Taoist doctrines in a highly demanding work of synthesis that has given rise to comparisons with Aquinas. His interpretation had become established dogma over the centuries, and no scholar failing to embrace Neo-Confucianism completely could ever pass the state examinations in the Ming era. Ricci did not accept Zhu Xi's version, not least because of his discovery that ancient Confucianism spoke of *Shangdi*, the "Lord on High," a sacral figure he regarded as possessing the same characteristics as the Christian god, whereas Zhu Xi referred rather to a supreme culmination or principle, *taiji*, the origin and foundation of all things, a concept far removed from the idea of a personal god. On reading the Confucian classics, Ricci formed the conviction that the catechism he had already begun to draft[22] would be able to show Chinese scholars that Christian thinking and morality were perfectly compatible with ancient Confucianism before its Neo-Confucian reinterpretation. There would, however, be time for lengthy reflection on all these matters, as the Jesuit was determined that the writing of his religious text would take just as long as was necessary to ensure that it was an important and lasting work.

The study and translation of the Four Books enabled Ricci to take a further step toward integration into Chinese society. He now enjoyed the admiration of literati, as they had never known of a "barbarian" capable of quoting Confucius and discussing philosophy and ethics like a candidate for the imperial examinations. Li Madou, as his friends observed, was turning into a *shidafu*.

Despite the social and cultural successes, little progress was made in spreading the Gospel, and Ricci, for all his patience, began to feel some alarm. He had already expressed his concern to Acquaviva two years earlier—"so much time and so little fruit"[23]—and the situation had not improved, as shown by the total of just under forty converts in the space of nearly four years. It was now clear that the decision to remain in Shaozhou had proved unfruitful, not least because the persistent hostility of a section of the population toward the Jesuits, along with the widespread malaria, gave rise to constant concern. In his role from afar as supervisor of the China mission, Valignano suggested to Ricci that given this state of affairs, he and his companions should try to move to a less hostile province with a healthier climate as soon as possible. The opportunity to do so presented itself far sooner than expected.

The Attempt to Reach Beijing:
Shipwreck and the Abandonment of Buddhist Robes

Recently summoned to Beijing as vice minister of war responsible for leading the Chinese army in the offensive against Japan, Shi Xing[24] passed through Shaozhou at the beginning of May 1595. The *guan* was traveling with his eldest son, aged twenty-one, who was in a state of severe depression after failing the first-level imperial examinations. As Ricci was well aware, failure to meet the set standards constituted a humiliating setback for the candidate and a disgrace for the family, who expected to improve their social position on his entry into the state bureaucracy. Since the selection process was extremely rigorous and only a small percentage of students succeeded in passing, the competing candidates were under great psychological pressure, and the most fragile broke down beneath the weight of the responsibility they felt. Ricci's friends who had been through this experience told him about the sheer toil of preparation, the fear of failure, and the obsession with auspicious signs portending success.

The Chinese believed in the prophetic value of dreams, which they interpreted as messages from the world of spirits, and all the candidates endeavored to discover good omens in their nightly visions before the examinations. To this end, they consulted the various books on sale devoted to the interpretation of dreams, publications full of illustrations showing young students asleep at their desks with their heads resting on their books and their dreams represented in great white clouds. If the image in the cloud was of a victorious warrior or a conquering hero on horseback, success was guaranteed. The abundance of such publications showed the extent to which the examinations constituted a collective nightmare.[25]

The disappointment of failure had shattered Shi Xing's firstborn son and brought him to the brink of madness. Not knowing how to help, the mandarin sent Ricci gifts and a pressing invitation to visit him on his junk in the hope that the Westerner's wisdom might suggest some remedy. The Jesuit realized that he was being presented with a golden opportunity to leave the town and reach Beijing. He asked the vice minister to take him to the capital so that they could discuss his son's problems during the long journey by river. The mandarin agreed, the indispensable permit was obtained from the governor, and Ricci prepared to leave together with two servants and the two young catechists João Barradas and Domingos Fernandes, the sons of Christian families in Macao, who were in Shaozhou for the preparatory training required for entry into the Society of Jesus.

The journey to Beijing along the system of rivers and canals connecting the south of China with the capital took at least two months. The small fleet of junks left on May 18, 1595.[26] The first carried Shi Xing, the second his wife, concubines, children, and domestic servants, along with the others his retinue, now including the missionaries, together with a huge amount of baggage. The vice minister's vessels enjoyed right of way with respect to all commercial craft and cleared their path when the canals and rivers were very crowded by beating drums during the day and illuminating the decks with red lanterns at night. There were supply stations along the way at which the convoy was provided with food, meat, fish, rice, fruit, vegetables, wine, and water at the expense of the provincial authorities. When the wind was not sufficient to swell the sails, the boats were hauled by the teams of men always waiting on the banks to offer their services.

After a short stop in the city of Nanxiong, Ricci was accommodated on the mandarin's junk and finally had the opportunity to travel in one of the richly decorated floating palaces he had seen passing on the river so often from the windows of his house in Zhaoqing. There were numerous bedrooms equipped with every comfort as well as a galley, a storeroom, and even a large hall for banquets containing about ten tables.[27]

Shi Xing was kept busy at every stop by receiving the requisite courtesy visits of local dignitaries. As the vice minister was so occupied with his social commitments that he never found the time to discuss his son's problems, Ricci preferred to hire a junk all for himself and to travel on it together with his companions.

On proceeding northward, the vessels entered a tributary where navigation was made difficult by the presence of rapids and hidden rocks, particularly in a stretch known as "eighteen currents." Before undertaking this risky passage, the *guan* stopped to burn sticks of incense in a Buddhist temple, thus showing that mandarins also became devout believers when faced with danger. The flagship managed to negotiate the rapids unharmed, but the smaller vessel carrying the women and children struck the rocks and started shipping water. On hearing the desperate cries of the passengers, Ricci ordered his helmsman to steer alongside and managed to get the women and children on board safe and sound by means of a daring maneuver. Having immediately moved to another junk in accordance with etiquette, he took the good news of the rescue to the vice minister who was waiting anxiously some distance upriver.

They all set off again the following morning, with Ricci and João Barradas now on one of the vessels carrying the retinue. A strong wind started blowing as soon as they got underway and threatened to capsize the junks, which were flat-bottomed like all river craft, with comparatively tall masts and sails of matted rushes instead of the canvas traditionally employed in the West. Ricci's boat overturned on being caught by a violent gust, and the Jesuit found himself in the water. Being unable to swim, he commended his soul to God and struggled to keep afloat. He managed to grasp a rope and catch his breath before clambering onto a spar and clinging to it as well as to a piece of wood tossed up by the waves. With the aid of a servant, he finally found refuge on the overturned hull. All the passengers had survived the peril except João, who knew how to swim but had disappeared beneath the water. Ricci did not give up hope. Tied to a rope and helped by some of the servants, he dived repeatedly in search of his companion but with no success.

The death of Barradas was a serious blow for the Jesuit, who would have given up at that point if he had not felt that it was his duty to carry out his mission in the capital. The mandarin tried to comfort him and provided silver to pay for the funeral, which was very generous of him, as another vessel had been wrecked in the meantime, with the loss of nearly all the baggage.

On arriving at the town of Ji'an, the junks were met by a gale, and the vice minister began to see these events as bad omens. Frightened and intent only on reaching Beijing as soon as possible, he decided to continue overland with the women and part of his retinue, leaving some servants to resume the journey by river with the rest of the surviving baggage when the weather improved. Changing means of transport was no problem for a *guan* of his rank, who was entitled to provisions, fresh horses, and bearers at the expense of the local authorities at every stage of his journey. This privilege did not, however, extend to Ricci, who did not have sufficient money with him to pay for further transport. Given this state of affairs and his growing conviction that taking foreigners to Beijing had not been such a good idea, Shi Xing advised Ricci to turn back.

The Jesuit had no intention of giving up. His thirteen years in China had taught him to insist in order to obtain what he wanted. He offered the mandarin's secretary a prism in return for securing a permit for him to continue at least as far as Nanjing, but the gift was declined with the explanation that the vice minister had yet to receive the indispensable seal of office, without which such documents had no validity. Ricci then went straight to Shi Xing and, finding him still greatly upset at the loss of his baggage, tried to console him by explaining that misfortunes were sent by the Lord of Heaven to test the strength of one's faith, a concept that the mandarin, being wholly unacquainted with Christian morality, unquestionably found it hard to understand. He refused Ricci's request for a permit but suggested in view of the Jesuit's determination not to return to Shaozhou that he should stay in Nanchang, the capital of the Jiangxi province, a peaceful city where he had friends to whom he could write letters of recommendation. He advised him most earnestly against going to Nanjing, a city too strongly connected with the imperial court, where a foreigner would be very unlikely to find a warm welcome due to the suspicion aroused by the war with Japan. Ricci was not to be convinced, however, and left the prism as a gift in order to make the *guan* feel indebted. This move proved effective, and the vice minister finally helped him to obtain a permit to proceed to Nanjing from the local authorities. Shi Xing left the following morning in a convoy of at least thirty litters with mounted guards and servants. Ricci resumed the journey by river with part of the retinue.

During a stop for supplies in a small port, Ricci discovered that the magistrate Liu Wenfang, an acquaintance from Shaozhou, was stopping there on his way back from Beijing after the customary journey made every three years to pay homage to the emperor. Having arranged to make a formal visit of courtesy, the Jesuit decided that this would be a good opportunity to show off his new garments of silk made for him shortly before leaving, which had been stored in a leather trunk. Now sporting a long beard and flowing locks, Ricci donned for the first time the robe of dark red silk with blue borders and the customary long, wide sleeves; a belt in the same colors; new embroidered slippers of black silk; and a tall, stiff, black square hat that reminded him so much of a bishop's miter. As he wrote a few months later to his fellow Jesuit Girolamo Benci, "We had all adopted Chinese dress, retaining the square biretta in memory of the cross, but this year I have even dispensed with that for an outlandish hat, pointed like a bishop's, so as to become totally Chinese."[28] He also prepared the indispensable book of visits, entrusted it to the servant who was to accompany him, and had himself borne in a litter to the door of the magistrate's temporary residence, where he waited for the master of the house to greet him on the threshold in accordance with ceremonial etiquette.

While not surprised by the change in dress, this acquaintance displayed greater respect for Ricci than he had on their previous meetings, when the Jesuit was dressed as a monk. He bowed with his hands and sleeves joined in the customary greeting and repeated the phrase qing qing, ("please, please"). Ricci returned this greeting with the same gestures but remained standing instead of kneeling down. The mandarin then took a chair, positioned it in the place of honor facing north, dusted the seat symbolically, and invited his guest to be seated. The missionary took a chair in turn and placed it before Liu Wenfang with the same gestures. During the learned conversation that followed, Ricci spoke in Chinese with no difficulty whatsoever, quoting various passages from Confucius and Mencius from memory. It was a duet performed on an equal footing by a Confucian scholar and a missionary who acted just like a Confucian scholar.

When the time came for Ricci to take his leave, the master of the house accompanied him to the door insisting that he should stay, in accordance with ritual. After a series of bows, Liu Wenfang withdrew and appeared to have gone back definitively into the house before reappearing on the threshold for the last farewell, as custom required, just when Ricci was about to enter his litter.

Expulsion from Nanjing

The party encountered no further obstacles as they continued along the river. The Jesuit wrote down the latitudes of the towns they passed through, using a small astrolabe to make rough calculations of the position of the sun and the stars with respect to the horizon. He took note of the mountains, lakes, and rivers, as well as of changes in the landscape and crops, with the intention of drawing a detailed map of the vast territory he was discovering little by little, well aware that he was the first European to penetrate into the heart of the China of the Ming dynasty.

The convoy made a brief stop in Nanchang, where news of the presence of a foreigner soon spread and a crowd gathered. Ricci decided to stay on board in order to avoid incidents. After setting off again, the party stopped to visit a Taoist temple in front of which a market had been set up with an abundance of local produce. Prompted by curiosity, Ricci entered the picturesque building full of believers, but his presence soon attracted attention. When it was clear that the Jesuit displayed no reverence before the statue of the saint, a group of the faithful insisted on his kneeling down and resorted to force when he refused. One of the vice minister's servants intervened to extricate him from this awkward situation and took him back to the junk with no further incident. Ricci decided that he would never again enter a temple without previously declaring his religious convictions.

The junks continued on their way and entered Lake Boyang, an immense river basin more than one hundred kilometers in length. A short distance from the northwest shore was Mount Lushan, its peak always hidden by stormy clouds and whose slopes were said to be dotted with over three hundred Buddhist temples visited by thousands of pilgrims. On reaching the town of Jiujiang on the far side of the lake, the junks entered a bend of the mighty Yangtze, or Yangzijiang, the longest and most important river in the empire. Called the "Blue River" or "Long River" (Changjiang) by the Chinese and actually the fourth longest in the world, the Yangtze starts at the foot of the Tibetan plateau in the western province of Qinghai and runs a distance of 5,800 kilometers before flowing into a majestic estuary on the Yellow Sea north of present-day Shanghai in the Jiangsu province. A great and pulsating artery of the empire, the Yangtze runs the entire width of China and constituted for centuries the only channel of communication between the innermost regions of the country and the eastern coast.

Ricci was struck by the width[29] and depth of the river as well as by the countless junks of all sizes crowding its waters. He saw four-masted vessels with the customary sails of rush matting and noted that groups of smaller junks traveled side by side in small fleets for protection against the frequent attacks of pirates lurking in ambush along the banks. He observed strange groups of two-story bamboo rafts and realized that they were houseboats moored to the bank and used as temporary dwellings by the merchants who stopped there to conduct their transactions. Proceeding northeast along the Yangtze and generally sailing close to the strong north wind, the junks cut diagonally across the southern part of the present-day province of Anhui.

The Jesuit admired the towns and houses erected along the banks of the river, and the small temples built on the peaks of rocky islands, from which the monks emerged to ask the passing vessels for offerings, and he observed how the vegetation and climate changed before his eyes. With the Guangdong province now behind them, the rice paddies had begun to give way to fields of grain with rows of windmills alongside them. Isolated willows and pines grew in place of the luxuriant bushes and trees that lined the banks to the south. Ricci was glad of a break from the rice-based diet and enjoyed the oatcakes bought very cheaply from sellers along the banks, together with an abundance of freshly caught fish.

The Jesuit realized during stops that firewood was a rare commodity in that part of China and was sold at high prices by those who built up stocks for the winter. He was told that for heating during the coldest months, the peasants burned the canes that grew along the banks or a fuel that he had never seen before, a dark substance that he described as "a sort of bitumen-like mineral or stone that they extract from mountains, which produces heat for a long time but no flame and has a smell similar to sulfur."[30] It was coal, widely used in China at the time but practically unknown in Europe.

Marco Polo, the Venetian merchant who had traveled to Cathay three centuries before Ricci, also spoke with wonder in his *Travels* of the "black stones" burned in winter for heat. Ricci was well acquainted with Polo's work, which had enjoyed very large circulation in Europe, and he began to think over what he had read there during the long journey along the river, noting many similarities with what he was now discovering. He remembered that Marco Polo had also described a great river flowing from east to west and separating the nine kingdoms in the south of Cathay from the six in the north, as wide as a sea and used by a quantity of vessels of such size as to cause amazement. Polo called this the *Chian, Chiansui,* or *Quian,* but Ricci began to think it might actually be the Yangtze. The Jesuit was greatly struck by these similarities because everyone in sixteenth-century Europe was convinced that the Cathay where Marco Polo had lived and the China that traded with the Portuguese and where Ricci was now living were two different countries, the former shown on all the maps of the time as located in an unspecified area northwest of the latter.

It was nearly a month since the beginning of the journey and eleven days since the departure from Ji'an when the group of junks entered the province of Jiangsu. They reached Nanjing on the western bank of the Yangtze on May 31. Ricci was most curious to see the second capital, which the Chinese considered the most beautiful city in the world, and he resolved to settle there.

Nanjing covered a very large area, it had a population of one million inhabitants, and it was protected by three rings of city walls. The outermost, which ran for a distance of sixty kilometers, enclosed the village in which Ricci took temporary lodgings. The second,[31] thirty kilometers in length, encircled the city proper and had thirteen gates. The third, situated in the heart of the metropolis, protected the Imperial City, the location of the palace where the Son of Heaven had lived when Nanjing was the capital. This was subsequently used as a model for the Forbidden City, the imperial residence in Beijing. China's second city was guarded by a contingent of fifty thousand soldiers.

As soon as he had settled in, Ricci entered the city for a short exploratory visit. On observing the system of rivers and canals with stone bridges running through the center, he was reminded of the description in Marco Polo's *Travels* of a beautiful town called Chinsai (or Quinsai) full of canals crossed by "twelve thousand bridges." The city mentioned by Polo was in fact almost certainly Hangzhou in the Zhejiang province, which had even more canals than Nanjing, but Ricci, who had no way of knowing this, confined himself to noting the surprising similarities between what he saw and Polo's words.

Nanjing was richly provided with vegetable gardens, lakes, parks, and wooded hills. The open-air markets offered an extraordinary abundance of meat, apricots, and all kinds of fruit, as well as peanuts, pine nuts, and vegetables at very economical prices. Ricci admired the sumptuous palaces, the great mansions, the towers, and the innumerable pagodas, but he judged the architectural style of the edifices as somewhat austere due to the absence of the triumphal arches of colored wood and stone that embellished the other towns he had visited, such elements being forbidden in an imperial city. Although the urban landscape was charming, Ricci noted a "vigilant and suspicious" atmosphere in the streets and thought it safer to continue his explorations in a covered litter. It did not take long for the Jesuit to find mandarins who had heard of him through friends that had made his acquaintance during their travels to Zhaoqing and Shaozhou. The *guanxi*, or network of social contacts based on common acquaintances, also worked in Nanjing, and the Jesuit was invited to numerous banquets where he presented himself dressed in silk as a *daoren* or "master of the Way."

The basis for his stay in the second capital was very fragile, however. Without the intercession of an authoritative mandarin willing to vouch for him, it was impossible to obtain permission from the authorities to reside in the city. On the advice of friends, Ricci turned to Xu Daren, undersecretary at the ministry of public works. They had met when the mandarin was military supervisor in Zhaoqing, and he recalled making him the gift of a terrestrial globe and an hourglass and receiving an informal invitation to visit Nanjing.

The dignitary received Ricci with every honor but became hostile on learning of his desire to settle in Nanjing, as he had no wish to be accused of favoring the entry of foreigners into the city. Determined not to jeopardize his career, he cut their meeting short, promised another, and immediately ordered information to be gathered about the missionaries. When Ricci was admitted to the second audience, Xu Daren announced that he had been informed of the missionary's expulsion from the town of Zhaoqing on charges of conspiring against China. He decreed that the missionaries could not stay in Nanjing and sent his men to threaten their landlord, forcing him on pain of torture to sign a document undertaking to hire a junk at his own expense and to make sure in person that they boarded it the following morning and left the city forever. The Jesuit had no choice but to obey and decided to fall back on Nanchang, as advised by the farsighted vice minister of war with whom he had left Shaozhou.

After the failure of his attempt to reach Beijing, this expulsion from Nanjing dampened Ricci's customary optimism, and he succumbed to dejection during his journey to Nanchang. He tells us, however, that one night Christ appeared in a dream bringing consolation and assurances that his plans would eventually succeed, and he saw himself walking freely in a splendid imperial city. The memory of this vision made him feel stronger and more hopeful on awakening. Having regained his combative spirit, he succeeded in making friends with a dignitary from Nanchang that he met during one of his stops, who promised to help him find accommodation in the city through acquaintances.

China and the Cathay of Marco Polo

On his way back along the river, Ricci thought over the extraordinary similarities between Marco Polo's descriptions and the cities and countryside of the provinces he was traveling through, and he began to wonder whether Cathay, which he called "*Cataio*," and China were not in fact the same country. He knew that the kingdom visited by the Venetian merchant was considered a mysterious and mythical place whose immense riches fired many with the desire to travel there. He also knew that its exact geographic location was still unknown, as no one had since been able to retrace Polo's journey to the outermost frontiers of Asia. Ideas about Cathay were still as confused in the sixteenth century as they had been in the fifteenth, when Columbus had attempted to reach the Indies by sailing westward on the celebrated expedition that led to his landing in the Americas in 1492. Well acquainted with the *Travels*, the Genoese navigator took with him a letter addressed to the Great Khan, or "*Gran Cane*," as Marco Polo called the emperor of Cathay, and expected to be able to meet him on arrival at his destination. The search for Cathay was continued in the sixteenth century, particularly by the English, who were prevented from using the routes to the eastern markets that circumnavigated Africa, which were monopolized by the Portuguese, and who hence were eager to find new routes to the north of Europe. At the end of the century, however, Holland was also engaged in unsuccessful expeditions in search of a northeast passage to the East, above all with Willem Barents.

The origin of the mistaken belief in the existence of two different countries called China and Cathay is easy to reconstruct on the basis of the historical and geographic knowledge now available in a brief outline of the course of events from the time of Marco Polo to the Jesuits' China mission.

Marco Polo left Venice with his father Niccolò and his uncle Matteo in 1271 and arrived in Cathay by way of the Silk Road in 1275. Having spent sixteen years at the imperial court of Kublai Khan[32] in the capital Khanbalik, he returned by sea to Italy, where he was imprisoned by the Genoese three years later during the war between Genoa and Venice, and he dictated the account of his travels to his cell mate Rustichello da Pisa.

In Marco Polo's day, Cathay was part of the immense Mongol or Tartar (from *Tatar*, the Turkish name for a Mongol tribe) empire, created from 1209 on by Genghis Khan and his successors, one of the most extensive empires in history, stretching west as far as Poland and Hungary and east through Russia and Central Asia to Korea. It was precisely the *pax mongolica*, the only form of control possible over such a vast territory, that made possible the interminable journeys along the silk roads traveled by the Polo family all the way into Asia. The Mongol empire had been divided up among Genghis Khan's heirs, and it was Kublai who finally completed the annexation of China begun in his grandfather's day. Kublai adopted the name Yuan—meaning "origin"—for the new imperial dynasty established in the Middle

Kingdom and destined to reign there from 1271 to 1368. He also transferred the capital from Karakorum, the ancient heart of the Mongol empire, to Khanbalik, located on the plain where Beijing stood in the Ming era. After the Mongol conquest, the country was called Cathay, a name first introduced into the West by Marco Polo and deriving from the Kitan, a nomadic people of stockbreeders from southern Manchuria who founded the Liao dynasty in northern China.

While the Mongols had undergone partial sinization through contact with the conquered civilization and their haste to adopt the occupied country's form of government, their rule had also changed the character of the Chinese empire, at least on the surface. They had transformed China into a multinational country that allowed people of different races from the countries under their rule to become state officials and had indeed appointed Marco Polo to perform imperial assignments. The court of the Mongol sovereign was a melting pot of ideas, civilizations, and religions in which the millennial Chinese culture enjoyed no primacy, as shown by the fact that no government official used Mandarin Chinese, nor was its use required of imperial guests like Marco Polo, who never even mentioned the typical characters of Chinese writing in his *Travels*.

Christian missionaries also presented themselves at the Mongol court in the shape of Franciscan friars or Minorites on papal missions to seek an alliance against the Muslims. Pope Innocent IV sent Giovanni da Pian del Carpine, the author of the *Historia Mongolorum*, to Karakorum in 1245; Willem van Ruysbroeck from Flanders arrived in Mongolia a few years later; and Giovanni da Montecorvino reached Khanbalik in 1294. Made a bishop in 1307, he remained in the capital until his death. Another Franciscan missionary was Odorico da Pordenone, who returned in 1330. Temur, the last Mongol emperor, received the papal legate Giovanni dei Marignolli, an emissary of Benedict XII, in 1342.

As the papal legates learned only the Mongol language and were in contact primarily with non-Chinese figures, their missionary work had no impact on the native population.[33] Like Marco Polo, the Franciscan missionaries described Cathay on their return to Europe as a multiethnic Mongol country, which seemed to have little in common with China. While the Franciscans' manuscript reports had very limited circulation, and Ricci himself was almost certainly unacquainted with them, Marco Polo's book was very well known indeed, but the information it contained proved insufficient to clarify the precise identity and geographic location of the country where he had lived. Moreover, Polo failed to mention not only the Chinese writing and many typical customs such as drinking tea, but also and quite inexplicably some of the most important technological developments like printing, which was already widespread in thirteenth-century China. Legend has it that he exclaimed on his deathbed, "I have told you only half of what I have seen." Even so, the gaps in his account were so evident as to make some later historians doubt whether he had actually been to China at all.

The missing elements in the *Travels* were not, however, the primary cause of the persistent confusion about the identity of Cathay and China. The mystery had lasted through the ages because relations between China and the West came to an end when the Chinese Ming dynasty drove the Mongols out in 1368, after a rule of under a century, and regained control of the empire. The Franciscan mission was swept away after nearly a hundred years, and no trace of Christianity remained in the Middle Kingdom. Having reasserted its strength and national identity, and sure of its self-sufficiency and cultural and material superiority, the Chinese empire erased all traces of the recent past, withdrew into isolation, and forgot the outside cultural influences to which it had been exposed in the Yuan era. The Muslim world seized control of Central Asia and established a monopoly over trade between the East and the West. The silk roads became impracticable and China inaccessible and impenetrable. The cessation of direct communications and the lack of interest in the world outside shown by nearly all of the Ming emperors—with the exception of Yongle and Xuande, who sent out the expeditionary fleets led by the eunuch Zheng He in the first half of the fifteenth century—had prevented exploration and the transmission of knowledge. The only way left to arrive in China, the country of silk and porcelain, was by sea, a route that was not opened up until early in the sixteenth century, when the Portuguese sailed around Africa and across the Indian Ocean. Ideas in the West were further confused by the fact that the name Cathay, now forgotten in some countries of South Asia, was instead still used in Central Asia and by the Muslim peoples.[34]

Wholly unaware of events in the Middle Kingdom subsequent to Marco Polo's visit, Ricci traveled through the heart of China with the spirit of an explorer, believing himself the first Christian missionary to penetrate so far and certain that his observations would prove invaluable for Westerners. Reflections on the similarities between China and Cathay did not, however, distract him from planning his journey back along the river, which was at the center of his thoughts as the junk approached Nanchang. The Jesuit was determined to stay in the town for only as long as it took to obtain the indispensable backing for residence in Nanjing, after which he would again seek to reach Beijing, the heart of the empire. On disembarking in Nanchang at the end of June, he discovered that the *shidafu* he had met during the trip had kept his word. Some of the dignitary's servants were waiting to deal with his baggage and take him in a litter to a house prepared for his accommodation.

Notes

1. Letter to Claudio Acquaviva, December 10, 1593; OS II, p. 116.
2. Letter to Girolamo Costa, October 12, 1594; OS II, p. 120.
3. Letter to Fabio de Fabii, November 12, 1592; OS II, p. 95.
4. FR, book III, ch. II, pp. 289–90, no. 3.
5. Three letters written to Ricci's father Giovanni Battista have survived, and four of those sent to his brothers, two to Orazio and two to Antonio Maria.
6. Letter dated December 10, 1593; OS II, p. 113.
7. Letter dated November 12, 1592; ibid., p. 96.
8. The missionaries were to present themselves as *shenfu*, "spiritual fathers," after 1605 (FR, book III, ch. IX, p. 335, no. 2).
9. FR, book III, ch. VII, p. 327.
10. For the idea of reforming the Chinese calendar, see the letter to João Alvares (or Giovanni Alvarez) dated May 12, 1605; OS II, p. 285.
11. See chapter 8 ("Astronomy and the Emperor") and chapter 18.
12. His name in Chinese is Meng Ke (c. 372–289 BC). "Mencius" is derived from Mengzi, meaning "Master Meng."
13. Confucius is traditionally accredited with the authorship of the *Annals of the State of Lu* (*Chunqiu*) and the editing and publication of the *Book of Documents* (*Shujing*), the *Book of Songs* (*Shijing*), the *Book of Rites* (*Liji*), and the *Book of Music* (*Yuejing*). He is also thought to have written the appendices to the *Book of Changes* (*Yijing* or *I Ching*). The *Book of Music* was lost during the Han era, and the others subsequently became known as the Five Classics. It was during the Song era that the Neo-Confucian school selected the Four Classics regarded as the primary sources of Confucian doctrine, namely the *Analects* (*Lunyu*) of Confucius and the *Mencius* (*Mengzi*) together with the *Doctrine of the Mean* (*Zhongyong*) and the *Great Learning* (*Daxue*), both drawn from the *Book of Rites*.
14. FR, book II, ch. XI, p. 250, no. 1. Cf. also P. Rule, op. cit., p. 7.
15. OS II, p. 118.
16. Lionel M. Jensen, *Manufacturing Confucianism* (Durham and London: Duke University Press, 1977, pp. 114, 121).
17. Letter to Claudio Acquaviva, December 10, 1593; OS II, p. 117.
18. FR, book I, ch. V, p. 39.
19. Confucius, *Analects*, 7, 1
20. Confucius, *Analects*, 6, 27.
21. Confucius, *Analects*, 15, 24.
22. Cf. the letter to Girolamo Costa of October 12, 1594; OS II, p. 122.
23. Letter dated November 15, 1592; OS II, p. 105.

24. There is some dispute over the identification of this figure. See FR, book III, ch. IX, p. 339, no. 1.

25. For dreams regarding the imperial examinations, see A. B. Elman, op. cit., pp. 326–45.

26. For an account of the journey, see the letter to Duarte de Sande of August 29, 1595, OS II, p. 126.

27. Letter to Claudio Acquaviva, November 4, 1595; OS II, p. 191.

28. In a letter dated October 7, 1595; OS II, p. 163.

29. Roughly 1,500 meters across at the point where Ricci entered it but narrowing to about 60 meters in the gorges.

30. Letter to Duarte de Sande, August 29, 1595; OS II, p. 141.

31. Now largely restored, these are the longest city walls surviving from ancient times.

32. For the original terminology used by Polo, see the editions of Il Milione, the Italian title of the Travels, published by Einaudi (1954) and Mondadori (1990).

33. Cf. FR, introduction.

34. Still used for China today in the Slav languages and many others.

CHAPTER EIGHT

~

The Strength of Friendship
Nanchang, 1595–1596

Robbing life of friendship is like robbing the world of the sun.

—Cicero, *Laelius de amicitia* (Laelius on Friendship) (45–47)

The Master said, "Governing with excellence can be compared to being the North Star: the North Star dwells in its place, and the multitude of stars pay it tribute."

—Confucius, *Analects* (2, 1)

A Courteous Welcome to Nanchang

Ricci spent his first few days in Nanchang at home thinking over his unsuccessful attempt to settle in the second capital. He was bitterly disappointed, as he would never have expected such an abrupt volte-face from Xu Daren, a dignitary he had considered his friend. As he wrote in a letter the following August to his superior Duarte de Sande, "This, Father, was how our great friendship with this mandarin came to an end."[1]

The Jesuit reconsidered his relationships with the Chinese literati. With the exception of Qu Taisu, whose support and affection he believed to be sincere, the dignitaries that Ricci called friends were in reality superficial acquaintances eager to meet him because they were attracted by his gifts and curious about his learning, but they were ready to ditch the "foreign devil" rather than stand by him in adversity. None of them could take the place of his companions at the Roman College, who were constantly in his thoughts and to whom most of his melancholy letters were addressed. These were the sentiments expressed during that period to Girolamo Benci: "How far apart we are now, brother, and how little hope there is of meeting again in this life. But the love within me increases with the distance between countries and I trust in God, so that the less hope I have of seeing my beloved friends again in this world, the greater my certainty of seeing them in glory in the next."[2]

On recovering from his initial dejection, Ricci decided to explore the town and look for people capable of helping him obtain a residence permit. Once again, it was essential to establish good relations with the local dignitaries, and he had to do this on his own, as his young traveling companion Domingos Fernandes was somewhat lacking in the social graces. Ricci did not fail to point this out to De Sande: "But since Domingos Fernandes, who I brought here with me, did not possess the talent required . . . ."[3] Facilitated as he was in personal relations by his sociable character and mastery of Chinese, Ricci certainly had no lack of this aptitude.

He judged Nanchang to be twice the size of Florence and found it much more beautiful than Canton, the other provincial capital he knew so well. It was orderly and elegant with wide streets and a large number of brightly colored celebratory arches carved in wood. Its wealthier inhabitants were not predominantly merchants, as in Canton, but were mostly literati and officials. Ricci divided these into four main groups.

The first comprised the large number of *guan* and army officers of high rank serving in the provincial capital. Then there were the young *xiucai*, or "budding talents," particularly numerous in Nanchang due to the presence of three schools offering courses of preparation for the imperial examinations. Proof that these institutes deserved their excellent reputation was provided by the fact that no fewer than eight of the successful candidates graduating as *jinshi*, or metropolitan graduates, at the most recent imperial examinations held in Beijing were from Nanchang, as against only five from the populous province of Guangdong. The city took great pride in this distinction, of which Ricci was soon informed, and in being the birthplace of one of the grand secretaries, the *guan* of the highest rank in the state bureaucracy. Between two and six of these secretaries were appointed at any one time to take responsibility for supervising government activities. The third group comprised the feared and respected relatives and friends of the grand secretaries, together with the relatives of other important officials and temporarily unemployed mandarins awaiting positions. The fourth social class of great prestige was the numerous and exclusive group of princes of the imperial family. With the sole exception of the designated heir, all of the emperor's sons were obliged to leave the capital on reaching puberty and take up residence in provinces far away from Beijing. They all received large allowances from the state that enabled them to live in luxury as long as they complied with the laws forbidding them to hold positions in the state bureaucracy and the army or to travel inside the country without special permission from the emperor.

The law exiling the relatives of the Son of Heaven from the capital was introduced by Yongle, the third Ming emperor, who usurped the throne from his nephew in 1402. The new ruler deemed it prudent to exile his own heirs by decree and prohibit them from holding any position so as to prevent any future threat to his authority. Adopted by all of the following eleven emperors, including Wanli, over a span of nearly two centuries, this practice served to eliminate infighting, but it had serious repercussions on the empire's finances. As the princely title and associated income were inherited by the firstborn son and all the other descendants were entitled to allowances and privileges, the number of relatives of the emperor living at the government's expense increased over the years to become an intolerable burden. In Nanchang alone, by Ricci's perhaps excessive estimate, they accounted for a fifth of the local population.

Needless to say, Ricci felt very much at home in the select milieu of a town apparently devoid of the xenophobic tensions that existed in the two capitals and the coastal provinces, just as the vice minister Shi Xing had foreseen when he advised him to stay there. It was indeed in Nanchang that Ricci came to change his mind about the readiness of the Chinese to become his true friends. He soon met with "courteous and friendly" people, including his landlord, who advised him to begin his series of formal visits with the wealthy physician Wang Jilou, an influential figure and close friend of Shi Xing.

Ricci dressed as a scholar, requiring his servants to wear long robes too, and hired a litter, determined to act "with as much authority as possible" and follow the dictates of etiquette to the letter. No one in his new home had ever seen him dressed as a Buddhist monk, and they would all know him only as Li Madou, Xitai, the learned preacher well versed in the local "courtesies." The meeting with the physician went very smoothly indeed, not least because Shi Xing had kept the promise he made before leaving for Beijing and had written to inform his friends of the Jesuit's impending arrival. A member of the city's most exclusive circles and on very good terms with the governor general of the Jiangxi province, whose son was one of his patients, the physician was more than willing to act as host and held a banquet in Ricci's honor to which he invited the city's dignitaries, including their imperial highnesses Kang Yi, prince of Jian'an, and Duo Geng, prince of Le'an.

I Cannot Tell a Lie

Ricci had already attended numerous banquets and was familiar with the etiquette. The homes of the wealthy mandarins in which they were held were richly decorated with valuable objects and antiques. The Chinese appreciated vases of bronze, objects of terracotta and jade, seals carved in semiprecious stones, tiny bottles of scent, and works of calligraphy on paper or canvas. They collected plates, vases of all shapes and sizes, bowls, boxes, and small water jugs of porcelain. While this material had been used in China since the first centuries of the Christian era, the secret of its manufacture was still unknown in Europe, where it was not introduced until the eighteenth century. Ricci was particularly enamored of its gleaming perfection and called it "the most beautiful and crystalline thing in the world."[4] Even though excellent china was produced in the Ming era, above all in the factories of Jingdezhen, which worked nonstop for the imperial court and the homes of the richest Chinese, ancient porcelain was greatly prized, especially pieces from the Song dynasty. The great interest in antique objects fostered the commerce of fakes produced with the utmost skill and sold either as copies to those unable to afford originals or as authentic works at very high prices to unwary collectors. Another product that Ricci greatly admired, used in Chinese furnishing since ancient times but wholly unknown in Europe, was lacquer. The Chinese used this varnish derived from plants to give wooden furniture and boxes a smooth and shiny finish that was easy to clean. The coat of lacquer on banqueting tables made the use of tablecloths quite superfluous, as the Jesuit noted in his precise description of Chinese ways.

The banquet took place in accordance with customary practice. The guests were received in an atrium, where they were served tea and engaged in conversation before being invited into the dining room. The host went out into the courtyard with a goblet of wine, poured its contents onto the ground, and bowed toward the south in honor of heaven. He then took his seat together with all the guests at a long rectangular table, placing the guest of honor in the center and taking his place alongside him. Each place was laid with a bowl of warm wine and the customary chopsticks—made of ebony or ivory, and with gilded or silver-plated tips for the most important occasions—with which the food, served in small pieces, was lifted to the mouth. Since the use of chopsticks and china spoons for soups avoided direct contact with the food, no one washed their hands either before or after dining, as Ricci did not fail to note in pointing out the differences with respect to practice at Western tables. In response to a gesture of invitation from the host, the guests took their bowls in both hands and sipped the wine while awaiting the first dish. It was only when the host had lifted the first piece of food to his mouth that the others followed suit and the banquet began in an atmosphere of general merriment.

Such occasions sometimes included discussions on philosophical subjects, or forms of entertainment that ended up in repeated libations of not particularly strong wine made from rice and other cereals, which Ricci found vaguely similar to beer. There were at least twenty dishes, which always included meat, fish, vegetables of every type, and soup; and the alternation of foods and tastes—savory, sweet and sour, spicy, and bitter—was based on the effect of the various substances on the organism in accordance with the precepts of Chinese medicine. The appearance of enormous trays of fruit on the table marked the definitive end of the succession of courses. Even though he preferred the simple rice and vegetables of the everyday diet to the elaborate dishes of the banquets, which were served in excessive amounts, Ricci loved the local cuisine and was now accustomed to sampling each delicacy in moderation, well aware that guests in China were under no obligation to finish everything on their plates.

After Ricci's participation at a banquet together with two imperial princes, word of Xitai, the sage from a distant land, began to spread, and he soon came to the attention of the governor, Lu Wan'gai, who gave orders to discover the foreigner's real intentions. Under threat of eviction from his terrified landlord, Ricci was summoned to an audience. The *guan* proved well disposed, however, expressing his appreciation for the Jesuit's gift of a prism, which he then returned for the sake of propriety, and readily granting him permission to take up residence in the city. He also commissioned the construction of an astrolabe and a sundial, which the Jesuit delivered some days later with the addition of a celestial globe. The prefect Wang Zuo proved less obliging and showed some reluctance to sanction the foreigner's stay in the city but finally bowed to the wishes of his superior.

Having received authorization, Ricci began his search for a house and made the requisite round of calls on the local authorities and the most important literati and men of culture. One of these was the elderly philosopher Zhang Doujin, considered one of the four most authoritative figures in the province and head of the White Deer Grotto Academy, whose members— formerly including the Neo-Confucian philosopher Zhu Xi—gathered regularly to discuss moral and philosophical subjects. The scholar was already familiar with Ricci's map of the world and intended to publish a reproduction in the astronomical and geographic encyclopedia entitled *Tushupian*, on which he was then working. He asked Ricci for clarification on aspects of European science and in turn provided advice enabling Ricci to understand Chinese society more deeply. He also invited Ricci to take part in the academy's discussions. The debates held in public and in the *shuyuan*, or academies, ensured lively intellectual contact between scholars and fostered the circulation of new ideas. It is therefore hardly surprising that a learned foreigner should be invited and his opinions listened to with great interest.

Ricci took part in these amicable disputes, speaking in Chinese and astonishing those present with his ability to quote Confucius like a scholar. He felt fully at ease in his role as a *daoren* while illustrating the principles of Christian doctrine to that select audience. This was an invaluable opportunity to gauge the reactions of Chinese literati to the idea of an immortal god, the supreme legislator who rewards or punishes, and to descriptions of the heaven or hell awaiting men in the next life. Ricci became aware during these discussions just how alien his beliefs were to the Chinese mentality, which had no place for or understanding of the concept of sin. For Chinese ethics, it made no sense to speak of waiting for happiness to be received after death. Importance was attached instead to practicing the moral virtues and improving oneself so as to obtain well-being and serenity during this life, observing the rites, respecting the hierarchies, and fostering fulfillment of the cosmic order on earth. Buddhist doctrine did possess an elaborate concept of hell, corresponding rather to the Christian purgatory, where the deceased remained only until complete atonement had been attained, avoiding the eternal and irrevocable damnation described by Ricci. During one of the discussions, not knowing how to respond to the missionary's talk of divine judgment in the afterlife, Zhang Doujin quoted the observation by a scholar of the Song era intended to demonstrate the uselessness of the Buddhist belief in a heaven and a hell similar to those of Christianity: "If there is a heaven, it is right that the good should ascend to it . . . if there is a hell, the evil will go there. Let us try to be good and not evil."[5] The exchange of views came to an end without one opinion prevailing over the others.

Despite the diversity of viewpoints, Ricci was convinced that it would be easy to prove the validity of his teachings to the literati. Astonished at the inadequacy of their arguments, which appeared to violate the most elementary rules of dialectics, he was certain of being able to persuade them on the terrain of rationality, where he felt best equipped. In actual fact, what Ricci saw as an incapacity for logical reasoning was rather a way of thinking based on different mental categories and parameters from those to which he was accustomed. The very originality of Chinese culture made communication between the Jesuit and the literati rather like a dialogue of the deaf.[6] Despite his optimism, it would be no easy matter to bring Chinese scholars to recognize the supposed superiority of Western philosophy and religion, as he and especially his Jesuit successors in the mission were to learn. When Chinese intellectuals formed a deeper understanding of the Christian religion after Ricci's death—and of the philosophical, social, and political repercussions that the spread of Catholicism in China would involve—they were able to produce what they saw as valid and perfectly logical arguments against it.

Ricci's social success grew over time, and with it the number of people eager to make his acquaintance. His understanding in the fields of science, philosophy, and ethics aroused wonder, as did his physical appearance, above all the thick beard reaching "almost down to his belt," something quite exceptional for the Chinese. The missionary was obliged by etiquette to return every invitation and to attend countless banquets, a way of life that led him to fast by day so as to do justice to the cuisine in the evening. Ricci also endeavored to eat only fish on Friday, but he soon noted that this strange habit gave rise to mockery, whereupon he adopted an alternative diet of vegetables and pulses, which he succeeded in maintaining also when dining out.

After two months of intense social life, he was so tired that he complained to his friend Zhang Doujin. The philosopher suggested a remedy. When yet another visitor turned up at the door, it would be enough to have the servants say that the master was out. The Jesuit replied that he could not do this, as it would be a lie. The philosopher burst into laughter and retorted that the Chinese lied all the time. Ricci then explained that it was considered wrong in his country not to tell the truth, above all for a priest wishing to teach the moral virtues to others. Moreover, he thought it his duty to open the door to whoever came looking for him. The explanation came as a great surprise to Zhang Doujin, who did not regard falsehood as a sin. Ricci was known in the city henceforth as a man who never told lies.

The "Treatise on Friendship," a Moral Essay in Chinese

Now accepted into the most exclusive circles, Li Madou was a frequent guest at the home of Prince Kang Yi, a palace as sumptuous as the residence of a European prince, with great courtyards and pavilions set in grounds scattered with ponds full of water lilies and lotus flowers, where the prince engaged his guests in conversation.

The Jesuit brought the customary gifts of prisms, terrestrial and celestial globes, sundials, and copies of his map of the world, which had become an effective means of cultural exchange, receiving lengths of silk and silver ingots in exchange. Particular appreciation was shown for an oil painting on copper of Saint Lawrence, which the prince had framed in ebony and jade. He in turn gave Ricci a fan decorated by his own hand. Fans were widely used in China both to combat the heat and as accessories, performing a role comparable to that of gloves in Europe. Rigid or folding, they could be round, square, or oval in shape and were made of a whole range of materials, including bamboo, perfumed sandalwood, ebony, ivory, paper, silk, and thin gauze. Those most in fashion as gifts for important personages were folding fans of dark wood, with white or gilded paper upon which it was customary to write sonnets and greetings or to paint flowers and animals, as the imperial prince had done.

Having come to know Xitai, Prince Kang Yi invited him to move into his palace. Ricci preferred to decline the offer but was very flattered. After twelve years in China, he now felt satisfied with his social standing. As he reported to De Sande, "We are gaining more and more credit and respect among the Chinese." He explained that securing the consideration of the most important mandarins was "extremely necessary" to the success of the mission, the aim being not "to seek honors" for their own sake but to prepare the terrain for the spreading of the Christian doctrine. "In this land where the law of Our Lord is not known," he argued in defense of his decision to adopt mandarin dress, "the reputation of that law depends to a certain degree on the credit and reputation of its preachers, for which reason it is necessary that we should adapt externally to the local ways and customs." He added that there was no danger of his success leading him into the sin of pride, as this would be prevented by the still vivid memories of the suffering, humiliation, disgrace, and persecution endured in Zhaoqing and Shaozhou, a period during which, as he put it, "we were treated and regarded as the scum of the earth."[7]

The situation now seemed to have undergone a radical change, and Ricci felt so at ease among the literati of Nanchang and so sure of his mastery of the language that he decided to attempt the writing of a treatise in praise of friendship in Mandarin Chinese. What subject could be more suitable to celebrate the start of a dialogue on an equal footing with the Chinese in the city where he had been received with such a kind welcome? Ricci knew that friendship was considered one of the fundamental relationships for Confucian society and was regarded as equally important by the authors of the Western world, who had sung its praises since antiquity. Inspired by his love for the classics, he set vigorously to work on the *Jiaoyou lun*.[8] He dedicated this "Treatise on Friendship" to Prince Kang Yi and made him a gift of the manuscript at the end of 1595.

The introduction employs a typical device of rhetoric to set the scene. Having been welcomed and treated to a sumptuous banquet, Li Madou is asked by the prince to explain what they think of friendship in Europe, a land where—as Ricci puts it, insisting on the concepts to which he attaches such importance—"discourse is based on reason." In reply, as befits a learned humanist, he offers seventy-six maxims drawn from Greek and Latin authors and fathers of the Church, carefully selected to demonstrate the affinity between the moral principles of the Chinese and European cultures.

The authors included Horace ("My friend is nothing other than half of me, and so I must treat him as I treat myself"); Cicero ("The world without friendship would be like the sky with no sun"); Aristotle ("If there were no friendship in the world, there would be no joy"); Saint Augustine ("He to whom I can show my heart completely becomes my intimate friend"); Martial on the vulnerability of those who open their hearts to feelings ("If I have few friends, I have little joy, but also little sadness"); Erasmus on the need for honesty ("The fulsome praise of friends does me more harm than the undue criticism of enemies"); and Seneca ("If you cannot be a friend to yourself, how can you be a friend to others?").[9] Other maxims reworked by Ricci on the basis of memory invited reflection on affection, fellow feeling, solidarity, loyalty, and understanding. In order to explain that friendship meant the communion of two people in the Chinese culture as well, Ricci pointed out that in ancient Chinese, the character for "friendship" contained the stylized drawing of two hands. Finally, to make his treatise more entertaining, he accompanied some of the Chinese versions with phonetic transcriptions of the original Latin so that the scholars could read them aloud as though in that language.[10]

Having completed the work, the first written in Chinese by a Westerner, he circulated it in manuscript form among his friends and acquaintances.[11] Its success was far beyond Ricci's most optimistic expectations. It seemed as though everyone in town was dying to read Li Madou's maxims, and many delighted in quoting them during banquets. Ricci had to draft some copies to keep in his house, as visitors passing through were always begging to read the work and copy out passages. The Jesuit would have been glad to have the treatise printed in order to facilitate its circulation, but he could not obtain the indispensable imprimatur from the ecclesiastical authorities in Goa. He was to encounter the same problem in the years to come every time he wished to publish a moral or scientific work in Chinese, and he complained of this in a letter to Superior General Acquaviva,[12] asking to be allowed to dispense with the authorization of inquisitors who were resident in India and were called upon to judge his works without any knowledge of Chinese. This dispensation was never forthcoming.

The problem was solved by the Chinese, who printed and circulated various editions of the treatise without even asking the author's permission. The work was to retain its popularity in later years, and Ricci prepared a new expanded version that met with the same success.

The Jesuit now felt ready to found a new mission and asked Duarte de Sande to send funds from Macao and brethren to live with him in Nanchang, as Cattaneo had remained in Shaozhou. His requests were granted, and he was joined in December 1595 by the Portuguese Jesuit João Soerio, fourteen years his junior, before whom he solemnly professed the fourth vow, *circa missiones*, in January 1596, a step making him eligible for the highest positions in the Society of Jesus.

In the space of a few months, Ricci managed to buy a house within the walls of the city not too far from the governor's mansion, and he settled in with Soerio; the Chinese Jesuit Huang Mingsha, christened Francisco Martines, who arrived from Shaozhou; two young probationers from Macao; and five servants.[13]

An Extraordinary Gift: The "Treatise on Mnemonic Arts"

Even though Ricci encountered a higher level of culture in Nanchang than in the other Chinese cities, rumors spread there too that he was a sort of wizard skilled in alchemy, and he often found himself in the embarrassing position of having to deny any knowledge of secret formulas. Fortunately, he was aided in avoiding questions about the transmutation of base metals by the great interest his other talents aroused in that city full of scholars. One of these was his exceptional memory that helped him not only in the study of Mandarin and the classics of Chinese philosophy but also to recall what he had learned at the Roman College so many years ago. During a meeting with a group of *xiucai*, perhaps prompted by the remarks of these young literati on how hard it was to learn by heart the countless Confucian quotations required in order to pass the examinations, Ricci demonstrated his extraordinary memory by asking one of them to write down a succession of Chinese characters chosen at random. After reading them just once, he was able to repeat them all faultlessly from beginning to end, and he then added to the general amazement by repeating them backward, from end to beginning, with no mistakes and no hesitations.

News of this astonishing feat soon spread through the city, and everyone was convinced that Ricci had some secret, miraculous technique, a "divine rule" of memory, that they all begged him to reveal. The governor Lu Wan'gai asked him to teach it to his sons, who were then studying for the imperial examinations.

A good memory was vital for Chinese scholars and students, who took years as children to learn the elaborate characters of the written language, and then as adults had to memorize thousands and thousands of passages from the Confucian classics for the state examinations. In the West, a good memory was instead regarded as an indispensable tool of rhetoric, the art of persuasion. Orators such as Cicero, who was reportedly able to speak for days in the Senate without once referring to written notes, had to be able to store enormous amounts of data and concepts in their mind for use in their disquisitions.

Ricci had an extraordinary memory. As he stated in a letter to Girolamo Costa dated October 28, 1595, he was able to remember as many as five hundred Chinese characters after reading them through just once.[14] He was, however, also able to draw on the mnemonic techniques devised by the ancient Greeks, which had been revived in the Middle Ages and had become extremely popular in the fifteenth and sixteenth centuries.[15] According to a legend recounted by Cicero in his De Oratore ("On the Orator"), their invention dated back to the Greek poet Simonides, who lived in the fifth century BC.[16]

Tradition has it that the noble Scopas commissioned Simonides to recite a poem in his honor at a banquet in Thessaly but took offense because the poet introduced the exploits of Castor and Pollux into the composition. He refused to pay more than half the agreed sum and said that the Dioscuri would doubtless come up with the rest. Shortly after this unpleasant incident, the poet was told by a servant that two young men were asking for him at the door. He went outside but found nobody there. In the meantime, however, the roof of the banqueting hall collapsed, killing Scopas and all of the guests. Needless to say, it was Castor and Pollux that saved Simonides as a reward for honoring them.

According to the legend, the corpses were mangled beyond recognition, but Simonides was able to help the families find the remains of their dear ones by remembering the exact places in which the guests had been seated. The idea of developing a mnemonic technique arose out of this episode. It involved arranging the objects in question in a precise order and associating them with specific places so as to harness the resources of visual memory.

Ricci knew the treatises on mnemonic techniques by Cicero and other Latin and Greek authors, and he had himself written a short work as a student on the method of "loci," or places, which he decided to revise and translate into Chinese in response to the pressing requests. The Xiguo jifa, or "Treatise on Mnemonic Arts," opened with the legend of Simonides and Scopas and then went on to provide a concrete example of how to apply the method.

This involved creating an imaginary building in the mind[17] proportionate in size to the amount of information to be stored there. A small house, temple, or pavilion could be used for just a few elements, whereas a series of constructions, each with various rooms, would be needed to contain hundreds. The next step was to create images associated with the items to be memorized and place them inside the building. Any item could then be recalled by entering the building mentally and seeing the images stored there.

As Ricci went on to explain in greater detail, the concepts to be memorized had to be associated with images capable of arousing strong emotions, like human figures in motion performing precise actions, wearing clothes indicative of their occupation and social status, and with facial expressions showing their frame of mind. As an example, he showed how to memorize the four Chinese characters meaning "war," "to want," "profit," and "goodness." He started by drawing a building with just one room and the entrance facing south and constructed four images by breaking down the Chinese characters representing those concepts. Since the character "war" was composed of two ideograms, one meaning "spear" and the other "to stop," Ricci associated it with the image of two warriors in combat—one holding a spear and the other clutching him by the wrist—and drew it in the first corner. The character "to want," formed by the components "woman" and "West," was associated with the image of a woman from a western tribe and was drawn in the second corner. As a combination of "corn" and "blade," "profit" was associated with the image of a peasant cutting corn, and "goodness," composed of "mother" and "child," was associated with a woman holding a child in her arms. These two images were placed respectively in the third and fourth corners.

Ricci pointed out that while this prototype "palace of memory" was very simple, a trained mind could expand and furnish it to memorize further concepts in a crescendo of mental associations and symbolic representations.

The Jesuit gave a copy of his work to the governor, who passed it on to his firstborn son with exhortations to make good use of it. His friends were quick to have it printed for circulation among the eagerly awaiting *shidafu*. The scholars appreciated the treatise as a display of learning but found the technique described far too complicated and less practical than the method they had learned in childhood, which consisted of repeating and copying characters and phrases over and over again until they were imprinted in the mind, possibly with the aid of rhymes or mental associations.

The Chinese friends, hoping to see the secret of Ricci's memory revealed so that they could take advantage of it, were therefore disappointed. For those not as naturally gifted as the Jesuit, who had managed to learn Chinese as an adult in just ten years, the path of study was above all one of hard work and commitment, with no shortcuts, as the governor's son was quick to realize. Having read Ricci's treaty, he told the author that the technique would be no good to him, as only someone already endowed with an exceptional memory would be able to use it successfully.

The "Absurdities" and Achievements of Chinese Astronomy

Ricci took care to maintain a ready supply of gifts for dignitaries by constructing the small scientific and astronomical instruments that had now become his calling cards. The sundials that he made on the basis of what he had learned at the Roman College proved very popular in Nanchang. The Chinese also produced these devices in a range of sizes, including a portable variety fitted with a magnetic compass for orientation and an adjustable dial for use in different latitudes. The Chinese sundial differed in conception from the Western one, however, as it reflected the polar and equatorial character of Chinese astronomy. In studying the variations of the celestial vault during the seasons, the astronomers of the Middle Kingdom attached greater importance to observation of the pole and the circumpolar stars,[18] whereas their Western colleagues concentrated above all on the stars in the zodiac. Moreover, the Chinese referred the position of the celestial bodies to the equator rather than to the ecliptic, as in the West.[19] Ricci's failure to perceive the radical differences between Chinese and Western astronomy led him to underestimate the former. He did, however, sometimes note real errors in the local instruments used for the measurement of time, as in the case of some sundials in Nanchang that were not correctly calibrated for the city's latitude.[20]

The Jesuit constructed sundials of various sizes and had the finest of these, made in black agate for the governor, inscribed in Chinese with the names of the constellations of the zodiac, the duration of the days and nights in the various months of the year, the hour at which the sun rose and set, and the date of entry into the different constellations. The decorated sundial was such a success that the missionary constructed many others of the same type by request. The happy few who received them as gifts allowed their friends to make copies on paper by means of the xylographic procedure for making inscriptions on stone in the temples.

Ricci noted that many of the *shidafu* whom he presented with instruments were keen to understand how they worked and took an interest in his descriptions of the structure of the universe. Encouraged by their curiosity about Western astronomy, he explained the Ptolemaic system to the more intelligent among them, as well as the use of the astrolabe, showing them how to calculate the altitude of stars above the horizon. The latter task was made much easier by reference to the drawings in the *Astrolabium* of Christopher Clavius, which he had asked his old professor of mathematics to send and had just received.[21]

The Jesuit's increasingly close relations with his circle of friends and acquaintances confirmed him in his belief that Chinese intellectuals had only a primitive grasp of scientific knowledge, and he went so far in a letter to a still unidentified addressee[22] dated October 28, 1595, as to give a list of the erroneous ideas he heard in conversation as "absurdities" of Chinese astronomy. According to Ricci, the Chinese were still convinced that the earth was flat and were unaware of the existence of the antipodes. Moreover, many of them accepted explanations of natural phenomena based on bizarre beliefs and had no idea of the real size of heavenly bodies. For example, they believed that the sun was not much bigger than "the bottom of a barrel" and that it was hidden behind a mountain that blocked its beams at night. Solar eclipses, considered as unlucky in China as comets were in the West, also gave rise to fanciful explanations. The Chinese character for an eclipse meant "to eat" and reflected the ancient belief that the sun disappeared from view because it was swallowed by a dragon. The extent to which this idea lingered on in the Ming era is shown by the fact that when the phenomenon took place, the imperial astronomers would perform the ancient ritual of beating drums and playing bronze instruments in the public squares in an attempt to "rescue the sun" by scaring the dragon away.

Ricci was not surprised that the common folk accepted such rudimentary explanations of natural phenomena, since ignorance of the laws governing them was just as widespread in Europe as in China. He was surprised, however, that such farfetched ideas should be shared by the cultural elite of the country. In a letter to Superior General Acquaviva dated November 4, 1595,[23] he commented that the scholars knew little of science and devoted too much attention to "morality and elegance in speaking or rather writing." The same letter mentioned another Chinese conception of the universe that he considered a glaring error: "They think that the sky is a void and that the stars move in the void." The Jesuit had evidently heard of the *Xuauye*, or "dark night," cosmology dating back at least to the fourth century, according to which the universe is infinite, boundless, and empty, and the celestial bodies floating within it evolve in a process of constant transformation of indefinite duration. Ricci considered this simply absurd by comparison with the Aristotelian-Ptolemaic conception of the universe as born out of an act of divine creation, motionless, limited in space and time, and precluding any possibility of a vacuum.

Though devoid of any theoretical framework, this Chinese vision of the universe is closer to contemporary cosmological hypotheses than Ricci's, and the void, as described by the physics of our day, is a basic concept encompassing the secrets of the constant transformation of matter and energy. The theory put forward by the missionary was indeed backward, even for his day, and was on the verge of being superseded by developments in European astronomy. At the very time when he was talking about these subjects to the Chinese, broader-minded European scientists were in fact becoming convinced of the validity of the heliocentric theory developed by Copernicus and were abandoning the geocentric system of Aristotle and Ptolemy. The clash between Galileo and the Church over the Copernican system was less than twenty years away. Despite the Pisan scientist's forced recantation in 1633, the more accurate description of the universe was to become established in the following decades, and the conception of the universe in which Ricci firmly believed was to be jettisoned forever.[24]

Sure of himself and unaware of the course that scientific progress was to take, the Aristotelian Jesuit was convinced of the overwhelming superiority of his knowledge, not least because his reputation as an astronomer was borne out by the facts when he predicted the timing and duration of the solar eclipse of September 22, 1596, with greater accuracy than the Chinese astronomers by consulting the tables he had brought with him.[25] This was a small personal triumph. From that moment on, as he wrote with just a touch of overemphasis to Acquaviva,[26] the inhabitants of Nanchang began to consider him "the greatest mathematician and natural philosopher," a view that he admitted he would have shared if the whole world had been reduced to China. In a letter to Girolamo Costa, he spoke of being "another Ptolemy" in the estimation of the Middle Kingdom's inhabitants.[27]

In actual fact, even if we disregard their cosmological views about the structure of the universe, Chinese astronomy was by no means as backward as it may have appeared, and it had certainly not been so in the past. Historians of science have established that the Chinese astronomers of antiquity were well in advance of their Western colleagues in many fields, especially observations. The Chinese had studied the heavens meticulously since the dawn of time, listing the stars and recording every celestial event with far greater tenacity and precision than any other people. It is to them that we owe, among other things, the earliest and most detailed star catalogues. While Ptolemy listed 1,028 stars and 48 constellations in the third century BC, an almost coeval Chinese catalogue included 1,464 stars and 284 constellations, and one compiled two centuries later had 10,000 stars, the highest number ever recorded.

China also produced maps of the heavens long before the West. The most renowned of these is the planisphere drawn by the geographer and astronomer Suzhou—tutor to the heir to the throne Huang Sheng—in 1193 and subsequently carved in stone. It presents a typical Chinese division of the celestial vault into twenty-eight segments of different widths, each characterized by a particular constellation serving as a point of reference.

In addition to a description of a solar eclipse discovered on a fragment of animal bone used for casting oracles and written over one thousand years before the Christian era, China can also boast the earliest records of sunspots, the dark, irregular shapes that appear and disappear cyclically on the sun's surface as a result of magnetic disruption of the solar magma. Indicated in the ancient language with a character meaning "crow" or "dark," their appearance was regularly recorded in China back in the pre-Christian era, together with details of their shape, size, and duration.[28] Sunspots were instead still unknown in the West during the late sixteenth century and would remain so until first observed by Galileo with his telescope in 1610, nearly two thousand years later.[29]

The appearance of supernovas was also documented in China long before the West. As is known, the Chinese records for 1054 included the most famous event of this kind ever observed, an explosion in the Taurus constellation that shone so brightly as to be visible also by day for three consecutive weeks.

Ricci was naturally inclined to underestimate Chinese astronomy, as he had no way of knowing its history and primacy with respect to the West. As historians of science have pointed out, his assumption of superiority was not always justified. In any case, Western and Chinese astronomy were the products of worldviews and methods of investigating nature so far removed from one another as to make direct comparison very difficult. Moreover, as the Jesuit was only just beginning to understand, the role of astronomy in Chinese society was very different from the one it performed in Europe. In China it was a state science, and astronomers were government officials working in conditions of semisecrecy and reporting directly to the emperor.

Astronomy and the Emperor

The role of astronomy as a science at the service of the imperial regime went back to the dawn of Chinese thinking and influenced the development of the discipline from the very outset. Chinese philosophy saw the heavens and the earth as intimately and indivisibly interwoven, and the universe as an immense organism in which the various parts communicated with and were influenced by one another in the same way as the organs of the human body. The entire universe evolved in accordance with the Tao and underwent constant change driven by *qi*, or vital energy, endlessly circulating in the infinite variety of its manifest forms. This vision was incompatible with the description of the universe accepted by practically all of the European scientists of the time, whereby the heavens and the earth were radically different in nature. The former, the realm of God, were eternal, incorruptible, and perfect, whereas the latter, man's dwelling place, was exposed to the variability of natural phenomena and was subject to decline, decay, and death.

The Chinese saw the bond between the heavens and the earth as mediated by the Son of Heaven, whose task it was to ensure harmony between the two worlds in accordance with the Tao. The emperor was considered the link upon which earthly order depended and was compared to the pole star, the fulcrum around which the heavenly vault seemed to revolve.

The emperor celebrated the imperial rites dedicated to the heavens[30] and was responsible for presenting to his subjects the calendar drawn up by the court astronomers and made public during one of the most splendid ceremonies of the year. This "Book of the Laws of Time" showed the division of the year into twelve or thirteen lunar months and twenty-four solar periods, and it supplied the dates of the major festivities, the most important of which was the New Year, falling on the first day of the first lunar month and followed a fortnight later by the Feast of Lanterns. The moon was celebrated in midautumn and the ancestors in the third lunar month. The calendar also supplied the most important astronomical data, such as the positions of the sun, the moon, and the five known planets (Mercury, Venus, Mars, Jupiter, and Saturn) in the various periods of the year and the dates and duration of solar and lunar eclipses. An integral part of the publication was the astrological almanac listing auspicious and inauspicious dates.

With its wealth of social, religious, and political implications, the "Book of the Laws of Time" was the most important imperial document, and its compilation was considered so crucial to the state that the production of any other calendar was punishable by death. No one was allowed to perform astronomical calculations or possess books of astronomy without government authorization.

The importance attributed to the astronomers' task of predicting and classifying celestial phenomena was such that the occurrence of an inexplicable event such as a comet or a supernova in the heavens, or a natural disaster like an earthquake or a flood on the earth, was interpreted as a sign that the Son of Heaven had failed to perform his duties correctly. This was the reason for the painstaking precision of the observations carried out over the centuries by Chinese astronomers, who were required to record, or rather predict, every phenomenon departing from the normal run of events. When Wanli took the throne, the supernova that exploded at the end of 1572—the same dying star that Clavius observed from the terrace of the Roman College—was still visible in the sky. Slowly diminishing in intensity and to disappear the following year, this celestial phenomenon was a cause of great apprehension to the Chinese astronomers. The chronicles tell us that the grand secretary Zhang Juzheng, tutor to the child emperor, urged Wanli to examine his conduct so as to avoid any further disruption of the heavenly balance.[31]

When an evident mistake was made in the astronomical calculations, the emperor punished those responsible and sometimes ordered the imperial mathematicians to rewrite the calendar. Discrepancies were very frequent in the Ming era because the astronomical tables in use were archaic and inaccurate, and because the general framework of the old *Datong* calendar was now out of date. Particularly severe punishments were visited on those who failed to predict solar eclipses, as accuracy in this was believed to be the only way of neutralizing their ill effects. Fear of making mistakes had made the imperial astronomers highly skilled in excogitating imaginative excuses for their ignorance and in devising stratagems to safeguard their reputation. One expedient frequently used was to announce a larger number of solar eclipses than actually expected[32] and then to claim credit for averting them by means of propitiatory rites when they failed to occur, with no fear of being found out.

Celestial observations and calculations were performed by the office of astronomical observations, a complex bureaucratic structure employing hundreds of officials of every degree and level. A document dating from the end of the first millennium indicates a workforce of 500: 63 responsible for drawing up the calendar, 147 for astronomical observations, 90 for the measurement of time, and 200 for sounding the hours with bells and drums. There were at least twice as many in Ricci's time. Moreover, two different astronomical observatories had been operating in Beijing ever since the Song era, one manned by Chinese astronomers inside the walls of the imperial palace and the other manned by Muslims outside. The personnel of both institutions were required to develop predictions of celestial phenomena and then to compare their results. History tells us that the officials in charge were punished by the emperor in 1070, when the censors established that for years the two groups of astronomers had confined themselves to copying one another's results without bothering to make any independent calculations.[33] As Ricci realized on checking the predictions of the Chinese calendar, the imperial astronomers of the Ming era had evidently made little progress in terms of accuracy and diligence.

Now having a clearer idea of how important astronomy was to the empire and having ascertained that the literati were very interested in acquiring his skills, Ricci decided that if he stayed in Nanchang long enough, he would teach mathematics and astronomy more systematically than he had in the past. He was in fact convinced that science would prove the best way to establish credibility with the dignitaries and would thus facilitate the work of spreading the Christian doctrine. At the same time, however, he was aware that he was neither a mathematician nor an astronomer and that he lacked the books he needed to take on tasks as demanding as that of assisting the astronomers in revising the calendar, a possibility suggested by Minister Wang in Shaozhou. Realizing that he would need the help of a team of specialists if anything was ever to come of this, Ricci began to bombard the Jesuit authorities with requests to send out brethren skilled in astronomy to assist him in his plans to convert the Chinese, a project that placed science at the service of religion.

Notes

1. Letter dated August 29, 1595; OS II, p. 148.
2. Letter dated October 7, 1595; OS II, p. 163.
3. Letter dated August 29, 1595; OS II, p. 151.
4. FR, book I, ch. III, p. 15.
5. Letter to Duarte de Sande, August 29, 1595; OS II, p. 157. Cf. also Jacques Gernet, *Chine et christianisme, action et réaction* (Paris: Gallimard, 1982), p. 225.
6. On the misunderstandings and incomprehension between the Jesuits and the Chinese seen from the latter's standpoint, see Jacques Gernet, *Chine et christianisme*, cit., pp. 191 ff.
7. Letter to Duarte de Sande, August 29, 1595; OS II, pp. 160–61.
8. Cf. Pasquale M. D'Elia, "Il trattato sull'amicizia: primo libro scritto in cinese da Matteo Ricci S.I., traduzione antica (Ricci) e moderna (D'Elia)," in *Studia Missionaria* 7 (1952): pp. 449–515.
9. The quotations are taken from Pasquale M. D'Elia, "Il trattato sull'amicizia: primo libro scritto in cinese da Matteo Ricci S.I., traduzione antica (Ricci) e moderna (D'Elia)," in *Studia Missionaria* 7 (1952): cit.
10. According to D'Elia, Ricci followed the Buddhist practice of making phonetic Chinese transcriptions of prayers in Sanskrit. See FR, book III, ch. XII, p. 369, no. 1.
11. Ricci sent a copy of his work to Rome on August 14, 1599 (FR, book III, ch. XII, pp. 368–69, no. 1).
12. Letter dated August 15, 1606; OS II, p. 304.
13. Letter to Girolamo Costa, October 15, 1596; ibid., p. 230. João da Rocha was sent to Shaozhou first for a short period and then Nicolò Longobardo, who stayed with Lazzaro Cattaneo (FR, book III, ch. XIV, p. 385).
14. OS II, p. 184. See also FR, book III, ch. XI, p. 360.

15. Cf. Frances A. Yates, *The Art of Memory* (London: Pimlico, 1992), esp. chapter 1, and J. Spence, *The Memory Palace of Matteo Ricci*, cit., pp. 2–5.

16. Cicero's work contains the first written exposition of the method. See Steven Rose, *The Making of Memory: From Molecules to Mind* [trad. it. *La fabbrica della memoria*, Milano, Garzanti, 1994, p. 84].

17. See J. Spence, *The Memory Palace of Matteo Ricci*, cit., for a detailed description.

18. See J. Needham, op. cit., pp. 211 ff, for a description of the Chinese astronomical system.

19. See chapter 10 ("The Forgotten Astronomical Observatory").

20. As the position of the sun and its height above the horizon—and hence the length and direction of the shadow cast by the gnomon—vary with movement north or south along a meridian, every solar clock has to be calibrated for the latitude of the locality in which it is used.

21. Ricci thanked Clavius in a letter written in Nanchang on Christmas Day 1597, which is the only letter addressed to the professor to have survived (OS II, p. 241).

22. OS II, p. 166.

23. OS II, p. 207.

24. Kepler was to complete the theoretical and mathematical framework of the Copernican system by formulating the laws that govern the movement of the planets around the earth on elliptical orbits.

25. Ricci knew that the visibility of a solar eclipse and its degree depended on the part of the earth from which it was observed, and he had no difficulty predicting the duration of the phenomenon by taking into account the latitude of Nanchang.

26. Letter dated November 4, 1595; OS II, p. 207.

27. Letter dated October 28, 1595; OS II, p. 184.

28. See I. Iannaccone, *Misurare il cielo: l'antica astronomia cinese*, cit., pp. 16 ff.

29. Galileo spoke of this in his *Istoria e dimostrazioni intorno alle macchie solari*, printed by the Accademia dei Lincei in 1613. Attention should also be drawn to the dispute between Galileo and Father Christoph Scheiner over the paternity of the discovery of sunspots; see Ludovico Geymonat, *Galileo* (Turin: Einaudi, 1969), pp. 71 ff.

30. See chapter 4 ("Religion in China: Heaven, the Gods, and the Name of God").

31. Cf. Ray Huang, *1587, A Year of No Significance* (New Haven and London: Yale University Press, 1991), p. 11.

32. I. Iannaccone, *Misurare il cielo: l'antica astronomia cinese*, cit., p. 17.

33. I. Iannaccone, *Misurare il cielo: l'antica astronomia cinese*, cit., pp. 7 ff.

~

CHAPTER NINE

To Beijing!

From Nanchang to Beijing and Nanjing, 1596–1598

And so, in my view, Cathay is none other than China.

—Matteo Ricci[1]

The emperor is as distant as the heavens are high.

—Chinese saying

The Conjecture about Cathay, the Order to Reach Beijing, and the Gifts for the Emperor

Ricci led an intense and industrious life in Nanchang and earned a reputation for his knowledge in the fields of culture, ethics, and astronomy. Many *shidafu* were prompted by a reading of the Jesuit's treatises on friendship and memory and by admiration for his European-style sundials to hold banquets in his honor. Ricci never declined an invitation and rushed from one house to another, "with no time to catch his breath,"[2] in the hope that success in the local society would foster his missionary work. His companion, João Soerio, had adapted well to life in the mission and studied the Confucian classics under his guidance with great commitment. Despite the considerable degree of integration achieved, however, few conversions were made. After fourteen years of missionary work in China, the total number of baptized converts for all the residences was little over a hundred,[3] a modest figure that seemed unlikely to increase substantially in the immediate future.

Ricci was still convinced that it was better to eschew the facile, immediate success that could be obtained by baptizing large numbers of people regardless of the quality of their newfound faith and to aim instead at long-term achievement built on solid foundations and deeply considered conversion. Knowing the peculiarities of Chinese society, so rich in established traditions and loath to give the exclusive commitment to a new religion required by the Jesuits, Ricci preferred to proceed "on leaden feet," as he wrote to Superior General Acquaviva[4] to justify the delay in achieving the results expected of him by the ecclesiastical authorities. He had no intention of abandoning the more difficult and ambitious goal he had set for himself of persuading the literati to convert by showing them the superiority of European science and culture and by emphasizing the compatibility of Confucianism and Christianity. Whenever an exchange of views with an intellectual offered fresh food for thought, the Jesuit took note of the subjects addressed so as to develop them in greater depth in his catechism.

The missionary always managed to find time for study and reflection without neglecting his correspondence. The amount of mail he received had increased over the years, and he found himself obliged to reply to as many as twenty letters at the same time and to repeat the same account of life in the mission over and over. With the passing of the years, his customary European correspondents had been joined by new friends among the *shidafu*, who sent letters from other provinces that Ricci answered in Chinese, thus adding considerably to the burden of writing.

One day, the post included a letter from Girolamo Costa informing him that both of his parents had passed away. On October 13, 1596, a few days later, Ricci sought comfort in writing to his brother, the canon Antonio Maria. They had been out of touch for a long time, and the Jesuit, who had just turned forty-four, asked for detailed information about all the other members of the family. "The news about me is that I am already old and very busy here in China, where I have spent so many years and expect to end my life."[5] In actual fact, Giovanni Battista Ricci was certainly still alive in 1596, but the Jesuit was to go on believing Costa's erroneous information for a long time,[6] as rectification did not arrive until a few years later, by which time his father really had passed away. The delay in receiving news of loved ones far away and the uncertainty attendant on sending correspondence by sea were among the torments that plagued the missionaries. Moreover, the customary risk of shipwreck had been combined for some years now with the danger of attack by English and above all Dutch pirates. While expeditions were still being sent out on unsuccessful attempts to reach the Spice Islands and Cathay by a northern route from Europe, the fleets of the new sea powers had also begun to sail the waters of the Indian Ocean with the aim of ending the Portuguese monopoly of trade with China.

Ricci often thought about the identity of Cathay, his journey to Nanjing the previous year, and the possibility that the country where Marco Polo had lived was in fact China, a conjecture he had communicated to no one so far, at least as far as we can tell on the basis of surviving letters. It was finally mentioned as "a curiosity that I think Your Reverence and others will be interested to hear" at the end of the periodical report sent to Superior General Acquaviva in October 1596. Ricci explained that he had been struck by the similarity between the Yangtze and the "*Chian*" described by Polo, and he noted the presence of many bridges in Nanjing, albeit not the thousands counted by the Venetian merchant in "*Chinsai.*" He then suggested that Cathay was the name used by the "Tartars" for China, and he ended with no hesitation: "In my opinion, Cathay is none other than China . . . few can know it better than we do."[7]

While there is no record of any reply from Rome, Ricci was determined to collect fresh evidence to support his conjecture and to return to the question when he finally managed to reach Beijing, the city which would, if he were proved correct, correspond to the "*Cambalù*" (Khanbalik) where Polo had lived at the court of the "*Gran Cane*" (Great Khan).

The idea of moving to Beijing was always with him, and Valignano had also stressed repeatedly that the founding of a mission in the capital remained the most important goal for progress in the work of evangelization. Their hope was to obtain permission from the Son of Heaven to preach the Gospel throughout the territories of the empire. Only then, with the emperor's endorsement, would it be possible to make thousands or even millions of converts, as Ricci sometimes dreamed.

The idea of sending a papal embassy to the emperor, which Ruggieri had left to prepare nearly ten years earlier, was now definitively abandoned, even by Superior General Acquaviva. Having considered the situation, Valignano decided to wait no longer for help from Rome and Europe but rather to assign Ricci the task of traveling to Beijing and pleading the cause of Christianity before Wanli. Who indeed would be better able than Li Madou to obtain the permits, overcome the difficulties, cope with the unexpected, and negotiate with officials to achieve this goal?

In order to provide Ricci with greater autonomy in decision making with a view to this undertaking, Valignano appointed him superior of the China mission in 1597 as successor to Duarte de Sande and immediately sent him the gifts for the emperor that had been stored in Macao. In his history of the mission, Ricci describes a mechanical table clock sent by Superior General

Acquaviva that rang the hours and quarter hours in three different tones, a clock from the bishop of Manila, a Spanish painting of the Virgin, and a painting of Christ from the Italian school. It is probable that the gifts also already included[8] the two glass prisms and the *manicordio* (a portable table harpsichord) that were to appear in the complete list of the gifts presented by the Jesuits to the emperor in Beijing.[9]

Having taken delivery of these items, Ricci resolved to prepare the journey to Beijing in every detail so as to avoid a second failure. Recalling the Chinese saying "The emperor is as distant as the heavens are high," which he had often heard officials repeat in the provinces, he hoped in his heart to reach the heavens this time.

The Imperial Examinations for Entry into the Bureaucracy

Nanchang suddenly filled up with people in 1597 in the month known as the eighth moon in the Chinese calendar and September in the Gregorian. As happened every three years in all the provincial capitals, candidates for the imperial examinations arrived in the company of friends and relatives. The streets were so full of men dressed in silk that it was difficult to make any headway through the crowd. It was the first time since his arrival in China that Ricci had witnessed this sort of collective delirium of hopes, dreams, and disappointments lasting all month and culminating in the week of examinations. The Jesuit was the first Westerner to give Europeans an eyewitness account, in his letters and in his history of the mission, of the rituals and mechanisms of the periodical renewal of the ruling class.[10]

The squares were teeming with life. Peddlers poured in from nearby towns with produce from the country, markets sprouted everywhere, the shops filled up with goods, and fortune-tellers were to be found on every street corner ready to predict the results. There were four thousand candidates selected from the cream of the "budding talents" in the province, and only ninety-five, the quota set by law for the Jiangxi province, would graduate as *juren* or provincial graduate. Beginning on the nineteenth of the month and ending ten days later, the examinations were held in a huge prisonlike building surrounded by walls and four watchtowers. After being thoroughly searched, the candidates were locked in the four thousand tiny cells, furnished with a table and a bench for sleeping, to take the three written exams, each lasting two days. Kept in total isolation, they were allowed only two brushes, ink, and sheets of paper to write on. The frugal meals were served in the cells by the proctors. Any candidate falling seriously ill during the examinations was let out of the building through a gate in the outer walls and was taken home, as physicians were not allowed to enter. Conditions in the small rooms were particularly unpleasant when the weather was bad, as the openings made in the doors so that the proctors could ensure compliance with the rules exposed the candidates to wind and rain with no possibility of shelter. There was no way of copying from other candidates, and concealing notes was practically impossible, even though some highly imaginative stratagems were devised, as shown by the white undershirt covered all over with Confucian quotations now in the Gest Oriental Library at Princeton.[11] Anyone caught cheating was expelled and punished, but numerous attempts were nevertheless made to break the rules and pass the examinations by dishonest means.

As it was rumored that bribery had proved successful in the past, the members of the boards of examiners were now appointed by the ministry of rites and were sent directly from the capital so as to avoid any repetition of such occurrences. The case giving rise to the most talk had taken place twenty years earlier in 1574, when the grand secretary Zhang Juzheng was accused of persuading the examiners to pass his previously eliminated son. This was never proved, however, and many suspected that the episode was just part of a smear campaign launched against the powerful and controversial *guan* by his political adversaries.

The candidates were required to comment on passages from the Confucian classics in accordance with set and unchangeable criteria. Written in black ink, the compositions were handed in together with the names and surnames of the candidates and their parents under personal seal. They were then copied in anonymous form in red ink by an army of scribes. A selection process involving three different groups of examiners whittled the number down to 2,000, then 1,000, and finally 190, twice the number of places available. Finally, on the 29th of the month, a fourth group of examiners chose the best 95 compositions and published the list of successful candidates in order of merit. It was a great occasion for all of them and a real triumph for the first on the list. The family of every new *juren* enjoyed the moment of "glory and paradise," as Ricci put it.

The procedures for the third-level examinations held in Beijing were much the same, but the honor awaiting the three hundred *jinshi* or metropolitan graduates was still greater, and the first in order of merit became a sort of national hero. Li Madou took an interest in the examinations, as many members of the candidates' families took advantage of their stay in the city to visit the "sage from the West."

Once the excitement of the examinations was over, the city slipped back into its customary routine, and Ricci resumed his plans for the journey to Beijing. The most important thing was to make contact with authoritative *guan* capable of advising him on how to approach the imperial court. The Jesuit discarded the idea of seeking the aid of one of the imperial princes on learning that the emperor's relatives were regarded with suspicion at court and their intercession would only prove counterproductive. The Jesuit then recalled Wang Zhongming, the important official he had met in Shaozhou a few years earlier. The mandarin had just been recalled to Nanjing for a second term of office as minister of rites and would certainly have contacts at the court in Beijing. Aware that Wang Zhongming might well have occasion to pass through Shaozhou and to visit the residence during one of his journeys to the island of Hainan, Ricci asked the Jesuits there—namely Lazzaro Cattaneo, assisted at the time by the Portuguese João da Rocha, the Sicilian Niccolò Longobardo, and the Chinese novice Francisco Martines—to request his help. Their situation in Shaozhou was somewhat precarious, as the hostility of the local population was now so great that they had been forced to demolish the chapel in which they gathered to pray, but the mission was still operating.

It was well into 1598 by the time Minister Wang passed through Shaozhou and was informed of the missionaries' intentions. He promised his aid and decided to leave immediately for Nanchang, accompanied by Cattaneo and Da Rocha, to discuss the undertaking with Ricci in person. Relieved to hear that Li Madou intended to pay all the expenses of the journey to Beijing himself, the *guan* ascertained that the gifts for the Son of Heaven were appropriate and pronounced the project of obtaining an audience with the emperor feasible. In order to help his friends, he suggested that Ricci and Cattaneo should follow him to Nanjing, where it would be possible to seek the right contacts and secure admittance to the presence of Wanli. Without further ado, the two Jesuits; their Chinese brethren Zhong Mingren and You Wenhui, respectively christened Sebastião Fernandes and Manuel Pereira; and some servants embarked with Minister Wang on June 25, 1598, leaving João da Rocha and João Soerio to hold the fort in Nanchang.

Along the "Grand Canal" to the Capital

Ricci returned to Nanjing, the city from which he had been expelled three years earlier, after a journey of two weeks. On entering the city, he realized that the distrust of foreigners perceived on the first occasion had not diminished but had indeed worsened due to developments in Korea, where fighting had started again after a truce. Despite China's reconquest of Pyongyang and the peace negotiations already underway, the Japanese had launched a new offensive that was now in full swing, and the fear of invasion was spreading all through China. All foreigners were regarded indiscriminately as enemies, and nobody would offer the Jesuits accommodation for as long as the war lasted. To ensure his safety, Ricci stayed on the minister's junk and traveled in a covered litter when visiting local dignitaries to ask for advice on how to obtain an audience with the emperor. The mandarins he approached explained that it was indispensable to have the relevant authorities send a memorial to the court stating the reasons for the request, but when Ricci had one drawn up by a specialist scholar and submitted it to the official responsible for forwarding it to Beijing, the *guan* refused to accept the document of a foreigner.

Wang then suggested that Ricci should follow him to Beijing, where he had to go for the month of celebrations organized to mark Emperor Wanli's thirty-fifth birthday on 17 September. The mandarin would travel overland and the Jesuits on the junks carrying his baggage. This was the best opportunity Ricci could have hoped for, so they prepared for departure.

From Nanjing, a short stretch of the Yangtze led east to the Imperial or Grand Canal, running almost parallel with the coast through the provinces on the eastern seaboard to connect the south and north of China. It comprised a series of canals, each about forty meters wide, and stretches of river linked by a system of locks to create an entirely navigable waterway of 2,500 kilometers.

One of the most impressive works ever accomplished by man, the Grand Canal is a masterpiece of hydraulic engineering, a field in which the Chinese have excelled ever since ancient times due to the need for good channels of communication and efficient irrigation systems in a vast territory subject to long periods of drought. Work on the great project began between the sixth and seventh centuries AD during the Sui dynasty and continued through the following eras with the construction of new stretches and the rebuilding of older ones. It was entirely restructured from 1411 on in the Ming era, with a view to the transition of the capital to Beijing, so as to facilitate the transport of provisions for the court and the tributes of grain and rice from the southern provinces. The investment was colossal, and the improvements were radical and huge in scale. A workforce of 165,000 people was employed in the Shandong province to build the four reservoirs, fifteen locks, and one dam needed to channel water from the rivers into the Grand Canal and regulate the water levels in each of the stretches. Work was carried out farther south to free some stretches of the rapids that were responsible for at least one shipwreck a day according to the chronicles of the time.

The Imperial Canal was an endless construction project teeming with activity. Nearly fifty thousand men worked full time on its maintenance, and the transport of the tributes of agricultural produce alone required more than one hundred thousand people with over ten thousand vessels.[12] Even though most of the expense for transport and maintenance was borne by the local authorities, the costs of the great waterway were a burden on the empire's finances, and the duties paid by private merchant vessels at the stations along the way did little to offset the losses.

Ricci was fascinated by his journey through the economic and commercial heart of the empire, even though he failed to understand why the Chinese preferred this far slower and more laborious way to a short, quick voyage by sea along the coast for fear of pirates. Swift progress was in fact prevented not only by intense traffic but also by long waits at the locks to enable the transit of vessels from one stretch of river or canal to another with differing water levels. The junks were forced to line up and wait their turn at these bottlenecks for days at a time. Even though important mandarins like Wang had the right of way over merchants, delays were inevitable.

Ricci continued his journey of discovery northward through China with ever-growing interest, watching the countryside full of densely populated villages and fields of grain, rice, and millet unfold before his eyes. He never tired of recording distances and place names, making approximate calculations of the latitudes of the more important localities and noting the positions of major lakes, rivers, and mountains. He was amazed at the hundreds of vessels passing close to his at every hour of the day and night, and he observed the junks carrying perishable materials such as fruit and vegetables stop at the supply depots to stock up with ice. At one stage in the journey, his junk overtook an immensely long line of timber-carrying barges hauled by thousands of laborers on the bank. One barge after another, the line stretched along the river for nearly three kilometers by his calculations. The sailors told him that the wood was from the central-southern province of Sichuan and would be used to rebuild some pavilions of the Forbidden City destroyed in a fire two years earlier. Weighed down by their cargo, the barges would take at least a year to reach the capital.

After a month of travel and a long stretch through the Shandong province, the junks crossed the Huang He, the second-longest Chinese river (after the Yangtze), known as the Yellow River due to the deposits of loess that colored the water and kept it cloudy. Ricci recalled the Chinese phrase "when the Yellow River runs clear"—an event traditionally supposed to take place only once every thousand years—being used to indicate that something would never happen. The deposits that built up in the river along its course of 5,400 kilometers raised the level of its bed and led in the rainy seasons to the terrible floods for which it had always been known as "China's Sorrow."

Another month of travel brought Ricci to Tianjin, the "port of Beijing," one day away from the walls of the capital, where it was obligatory to leave the vessels and continue overland, as the last stretch of the Grand Canal was reserved exclusively for junks carrying goods for the court.

The First Time in Beijing, the City of Dust

Ricci entered the capital of the empire for the first time on September 7, 1598, fifteen years after arriving in China and 323 years after Marco Polo reached Khanbalik, the capital of Cathay, located on the same plain not far from Beijing.

He encountered two stretches of walls on entering from the southern part of the city, the first built in 1553 to delimit the "outer city" of houses developed over the centuries in the southern section of the original city, and the second controlling access to the "inner city," its most ancient nucleus. Consisting of a stone base and a superstructure of brick filled with beaten earth, the walls were the most imposing Ricci had ever seen, far taller and thicker than those encircling European cities. He estimated that twelve horses could have run abreast along the walkway on the top. Soldiers and eunuchs responsible for collecting excise duties were stationed at the city gates, which were closed at night and were kept under military guard. The city was built like a series of nested boxes, with the inner city surrounding the walled citadel of the Imperial City, the residence of the court and off limits to common mortals, and in the center of this the Forbidden City with the imperial palaces and the apartments of the reigning family, the true heart of the empire.

Cattaneo and Ricci were put up by Minister Wang, who had arrived before them, while the two Chinese novices and the servants stayed in rented accommodations. The *guan* had just heard that he would shortly be promoted to the post of minister of rites in Beijing and thought that it would be very easy to help his friends obtain an audience with the emperor once the appointment had been officially confirmed.

Ricci began to explore the city. He found it more austere than Nanjing, but its inhabitants initially appeared friendlier than in the south of the country. The produce on sale in the markets proved very expensive, as it was mostly imported from other provinces. He noted on walking through the streets that the curse of prostitution was even more widespread than in the other Chinese cities, and he was informed that there were as many as forty thousand whores.

Ricci soon noticed that Beijing, where it seldom rained, was enveloped in a cloud of dust that rose from the unpaved streets and mixed with a fine brown sand from the Gobi desert. The inhabitants wrapped their heads in black veils as protection against this almost imperceptible but omnipresent dust, which penetrated houses, closets, and trunks, worked its way between the pages of books, and clouded the delicate porcelain on display in the wealthier homes with a light patina. Ricci adopted the practice of covering his head, which also performed the useful function of concealing his foreign appearance.

He used the available means of public transport to explore the city, which offered the visitor a range of litters of various sizes or a horse or mule with a guide familiar with the streets and the addresses of public offices and officials. If no means of transport were obtainable for hire, it was possible to find one's way with the aid of the guidebook that all outsiders bought on entering the city, even though it was easy to get lost in the maze of *hutong*, or alleys, running through the most densely populated districts. Ricci noted on entering the homes of some dignitaries and minor officials that they had the same architectural structure as the poorer dwellings. They were low buildings surrounded by walls that concealed everything inside with a wooden door and a high step to keep evil spirits out. The houses of dignitaries had decorated front doors, and pairs of stone lions symbolizing power flanked the palaces of the most important *guan*. The entrance provided access to a square courtyard lined with trees and wooden arcades onto which the pavilions and rooms opened, a structure recalling the peristyle houses of ancient Rome. In a mansion owned by a wealthy mandarin, there would be another door in the side of the courtyard opposite the entrance providing access to another courtyard surrounded by rooms, and so on, in a reiteration of the same elementary structure directly proportional to the owner's wealth.

The climate in Beijing was much drier and harsher than in Nanjing, and the inhabitants used coal for heating as well as cooking, the bedroom being nearly always located beside the kitchen so as to take advantage of the heat produced during the preparation of meals. The model of the brick *kang*, or sleeping platform, connected to masonry conduits channeling hot air from the kitchen was widespread throughout the north of China.

The more Ricci explored the city, the more similarities he noticed between his own observations and his memories of Marco Polo's *Travels*, which prompted him to seek further evidence that Beijing and Khanbalik were one and the same. If Cathay really was a large and powerful country situated east of Persia, as it was believed in Europe, why had Ricci never heard it mentioned by the Chinese during all his years in China? Additional support for his conjecture was provided by two elderly Turks resident in Beijing for forty years. Having arrived as members of an embassy to the Son of Heaven, they had never been granted permission to return to their native land for fear that it might organize a military expedition against China, and they were forced to live as prisoners at the government's expense. They told Ricci that China was still called Cathay in Muslim countries and that that capital was known as Khanbalik, or "*Cambalù*" as he wrote it. This information was borne out by some Persian merchants. Ricci probably discovered also that during the Mongol dynasty, the Chinese used the term *Dadu*, meaning "Great Capital," instead of Khanbalik.

The confusion of the Mongol, Chinese, and subsequently Portuguese names used for China and Beijing had caused "our cosmographers to make two kingdoms out of one . . . with no possibility of finding out the truth until today."[13]

Certain that he had now cleared up all doubts and taking it as established fact that China and Cathay were one and the same, Ricci wrote again to his superiors in India and Italy but failed to convince them. The idea of Cathay was so deeply rooted in Western culture that it could not be dislodged very easily, and as we shall see, the Jesuit would have to try and try again before his brethren began to think that he might be right.

After his first superficial explorations of the city, Ricci tried to obtain an audience with the emperor. Since Wang had still to take office as minister of rites and was therefore powerless to help, the Jesuit was obliged to seek the support of other officials. He thus found out that in order to arrive at the imperial court, it was indispensable to negotiate with the *taijian*, or eunuchs, who operated a power structure parallel to that of the *guan* as a sort of private bureaucracy serving the emperor and controlling access to the Imperial City.

Ricci met a eunuch supposedly willing to act as an intermediary and showed him the gifts for the emperor. Having heard that the Jesuit was an expert alchemist, the *taijian* said that he would only help in exchange for his secret formulas for making silver. Ricci denied any such knowledge and was unceremoniously dismissed with the information that the war in Korea had made foreigners unwelcome and there was no possibility of being received at the court until it was over.

Meanwhile, the celebrations for the emperor's birthday had come to an end, and Wang, whose appointment was still awaiting ratification, was obliged to leave Beijing, having no grounds for prolonging his stay in the capital. The mandarin could do nothing more for his friends at present and advised them to return to Nanjing with him. The missionaries decided to remain in the hope of finding support elsewhere. Manuel Dias, who had taken over as superior of the Jesuit College in Macao after the death of Duarte de Sande the previous year, sent a bill of exchange to finance the missionaries' stay in the capital, but they were unable to cash it, and the same thing happened with another sent from Japan. Now devoid of sufficient funds and treated with growing hostility by the *guan* to whom they applied for assistance, they finally resolved to leave Beijing and await a "better time and better opportunity" to return. Ricci was bitterly disappointed and described the capital as a "Babylon of confusion rife with every kind of sin."[14]

Withdrawal to the South

The missionaries left Beijing on November 5, 1598. Their journey south was slow because their junk was not as fast as the minister's, and they had no right of way at the locks.

Unable to remain idle for long, Ricci decided to occupy the time by preparing a new version of the Chinese-Portuguese dictionary. In order to make it more complete than the one compiled in Zhaoqing with Ruggieri, he added phonetic transcriptions of the Chinese words and specified the rules for the correct pronunciation of the five tones with the aid of Cattaneo, who knew music and had good ear, and Sebastião, who spoke excellent Mandarin. Ricci hoped that the new dictionary would help missionaries avoid the "great confusion" initially encountered in the study of Mandarin.

They reached Linqing, on the border of the Shandong and Hebei provinces, after a month. It was now December, and the temperatures had fallen dramatically. The Grand Canal was beginning to freeze over, and it would soon be impossible to sail any farther. Ricci decided to continue alone by horse, leaving Cattaneo and the others in the town to wait for the thaw and take care of the gifts for the emperor, which it would have been imprudent to transport overland.

Ricci traveled with the sole aim of finding a safe place to stay in the south for as long as it took to plan his return to Beijing. He felt that this was a temporary withdrawal and that the goal was finally within his reach. His books had enjoyed an unexpectedly large circulation and had earned him a solid reputation, and his friends in high places at the imperial court would help when the time was ripe. After many years in China, he had learned that nothing was as simple as it appeared to be. Known causes did not always produce the effects envisaged, and the direct approach was not always the most effective way to attain an objective. It was sometimes necessary to take one step back and then perhaps to wait. Ricci had to behave like a Chinese sage seeking to accomplish a difficult project. The way was to set out in the desired direction and then allow events to take their course, making no attempt to bend reality to his own wishes but instead benefitting from the natural evolution of things. Still more patience was required.

Preferring not to return to Nanchang and realizing that it would be dangerous to stay in Nanjing on his own, he decided to head for Qu Taisu's hometown of Suzhou, situated in the southern part of the Jiangsu province southeast of Nanjing and slightly west of present-day Shanghai. This would enable him to remain in the vicinity of Nanjing, which he considered the best starting point for Beijing, and to benefit from his friend's help and protection.

He traveled for a long time in very bad weather with an icy wind sweeping down from Mongolia across the rough country roads. In order to proceed more quickly, he alternated the use of a horse and a sort of "one-wheeled wagon" carrying one or two passengers and pushed by bearers, which proved very comfortable. This strange vehicle was one of the many forms taken by the Chinese wheelbarrow, a device unknown in Europe before the eleventh century but widely used in China from the first century in different shapes and sizes and for a whole variety of military and civilian purposes.[15]

The climate improved as he left the province of Shandong for Jiangsu and continued south. The landscape also changed. Tea plantations alternated with rice paddies, and water became the dominant element with the system of lakes, canals, and rivers crisscrossing the vast Yangtze delta. Ricci took little notice of this, having fallen ill as a result of the cold and fatigue he suffered farther north, but he decided to press on to his destination in his feverish state. One month after leaving Linqing, he finally arrived in Suzhou, called *"Sugiu"* by Marco Polo and described in his *Travels* as the "city of six thousand stone bridges." Situated on the banks of Lake Tai Hu and also known as the "Venice of the East" by virtue of its system of canals, it was regarded as an earthly paradise along with Hangzhou: "Paradise is in the sky, Hangzhou and Suzhou are on the earth." This ancient saying, where the word "paradise" refers to the Buddhist and Taoist realm of bliss in the next world, is still used in China today. In the Ming era, the city was a flourishing commercial center enjoying a strategic position at the mouth of the Imperial Canal and famed as a holiday resort for officials of high rank. Ricci did not even spend one day there, however. On being informed that Qu Taisu had moved temporarily to the neighboring town of Danyang, slightly southeast of Nanjing, he summoned up his last reserves of strength and succeeded in making his way there. Deeply concerned about his master's desperate condition, Qu Taisu received him with great hospitality, giving up his own bed for him to sleep in and looking after him like a father until he had completely recovered. Having received one of Ricci's precious prisms as a token of gratitude, he had a special silver case made so that he could wear it around his neck. Qu Taisu also thought of selling it in order to pay off the debts he had run up at the time of his obsession with alchemy, but he changed his mind on hearing that Ricci intended to give an identical prism to the emperor, as it would hardly be fitting for something presented to Wanli as an object of exceptional rarity to be in the possession of another. He therefore kept the prism until Ricci had delivered his gifts to the Son of Heaven and then sold it for a sum equivalent to five hundred *scudi*, which he used to pay some of his debts.

When the Jesuit was able to resume his activities, he set off with Qu Taisu for Nanjing to ask the most influential dignitaries for the indispensable letters of permission to stay in Suzhou. He entered the second capital of China for the third time in January 1599 together with his friend.

The two men took temporary lodgings in a temple situated in the center of the city and went to visit Wang Zhongming, with whom Qu Taisu was also well acquainted. The minister had returned to his palace after the fruitless trip to Beijing and was still waiting to be recalled to the capital.

Notes

1. Letter to Claudio Acquaviva, October 13, 1596; OS II, p. 228.
2. Letter to Giulio Fuligatti, October 12, 1596; OS II, p. 217.
3. Letter to Girolamo Costa, October 15, 1596; OS II, p. 231.
4. Letter to Claudio Acquaviva, October 13, 1596; OS II, p. 225.
5. Letter to Antonio Maria Ricci, October 13, 1596; OS II, p. 219.
6. OS II, p. 218, no. 1.
7. Letter to Claudio Acquaviva, October 13, 1596; OS II, p. 228.
8. As attested, for example, by the Jesuit Sabatino de Ursis, who joined Ricci in Beijing in 1607 (FR, book IV, ch. I, p. 5, no. 3).
9. See chapter 12 ("The Solemn Entrance into Beijing").
10. Letter to Lelio Passionei, September 9, 1597; OS II, pp. 234 ff.
11. See P. Buckley Ebrey, op. cit., p. 198.
12. T. Brook, op. cit., p. 48.
13. FR, book IV, ch. II, p. 28.
14. FR, book IV, ch. II, p. 30.
15. R. Temple, op. cit., p. 85.

CHAPTER TEN

~

Heated Disputes and Science Lessons

Nanjing, 1599

The Tao produced One; One produced Two; Two produced Three; Three produced All things. All things leave behind them the Obscurity (out of which they have come), and go forward to embrace the Brightness (into which they have emerged), while they are harmonized by the Breath of Vacancy.

—*Tao Te Ching*, (42)[1]

There are men from a foreign land . . . who have invented the doctrine of the Lord of Heaven. . . . They say the Lord of Heaven has no body, no color and no voice. . . . How can he govern ministers and peoples, give orders, grant rewards, and inflict punishment? Even though these people are intelligent, they have not read the Buddhist sutras. It is therefore hardly surprising that their reasoning should be faulty.

—Zhu Hong, *Tianshuo* ("Explanation of Heaven")[2]

Social Life in Nanjing

Ricci was relieved to note on walking through the streets of Nanjing that the suspicion of foreigners encountered during his two previous visits had come to an end with the war in Korea. The death of the shogun Toyotomi Hideyoshi, supreme commander of the Japanese army, in September 1598 was followed by the withdrawal of the invaders from the occupied territories, and fear gave way to a lively atmosphere.

154

The minister received Ricci and Qu Taisu with the greatest respect and insisted on their staying in his palace for the New Year celebrations coinciding with the appearance of the first new moon of the lunar year on January 27, 1599. Marking the beginning of the Spring Festivity, this event was deeply felt and celebrated with all the splendor of which the Chinese were capable. All work ceased for a fortnight, and people poured into the temples and the parks, where fairs and shows were organized for adults and children.

Ricci was thus able to witness the celebrations from the privileged vantage point of the home of an important dignitary. Together with the mandarin's family, he enjoyed the customary firework display, regarded as indispensable in accordance with age-old beliefs of driving away evil spirits with explosions. The Chinese were true masters of the art of pyrotechnics, and Ricci was impressed by their extraordinary skill. On beholding the fantastic spectacle of multicolored Catherine wheels, glittering cascades, flowers, and fruit repeated at a frenzied pace night after night for many hours, he estimated that the Chinese consumed as much saltpeter in a fortnight as the Europeans in two years of war. Completely unknown in Europe before the Middle Ages, saltpeter, or potassium nitrate, had been well known in China, where it was found in abundance, since the third century if not earlier, and the invention of gunpowder, obtained by mixing saltpeter with sulfur and charcoal, was yet another instance of Chinese primacy with respect to Europe.

The long period of festivities came to its customary end with the picturesque Feast of Lanterns, when all the streets and buildings were hung with red lanterns of paper or silk in all shapes and sizes. Used in China since ancient times, lanterns were considered a symbol of fertility, and women sought good fortune by walking in their glow, which was also believed to help the spirits of ancestors find their way to the next world.

Spending the New Year celebrations with the minister gave Ricci an opportunity to meet many of Wang's colleagues, who were also his guests, and to see how animated social life was in the most exclusive circles. He realized from the deference he was shown that the minister had already spoken of him to the officials as a man of culture and had told them about the gifts for the emperor, which he had enjoyed the privilege of seeing in advance.

Noting that the presence of Li Madou added to the city's luster and that his friends were impressed by the Jesuit's learning, the minister endeavored to persuade him to move to Nanjing and ordered his secretaries to inquire whether there was any property for sale. The news that the minister's foreign friend was looking for a house spread very quickly, and many offers were made in the space of just a few days. Paradoxically enough, at the very time when he no longer had any intention of doing so, everyone was urging Ricci

to stay in Nanjing, the city from which he had been expelled four years earlier. On weighing up the situation, the Jesuit decided that his warm welcome
was a sign of God's will and that he should not let slip such a favorable opportunity. When asked for his advice, Qu Taisu encouraged him to stay in Nanjing and promised to help him meet the most important people there. The
minister of rites was delighted to hear that Xitai was going to stay and offered
him temporary accommodation in one of his own mansions. Ricci declined
the offer and rented a house, but he accepted some items of furniture from
Wang. He preferred to postpone the purchase of a residence for the mission
until he was joined by Cattaneo, who was still in Linqing awaiting the thaw.

As soon as he had settled in, the Jesuit embarked with Qu Taisu on a series
of courtesy visits to dignitaries capable of facilitating his stay in the city and
helping him obtain an audience with the emperor. Even though he already
had some experience dealing with the *guan*, he preferred to follow his friend's
advice and guidance. The higher the social level, the greater the subtlety
required in the art of *guanxi*.

Qu Taisu took Ricci to visit the *juren* Li Xinzhai, greatly respected as the
son of a governor and well known in the city as a tutor and a writer commissioned to produce literary compositions for weddings, funerals, promotions,
and transfers. As Qu Taisu also enjoyed a certain reputation as an author
for hire and Ricci was now known as a man of culture, Li Xinzhai saw them
as possible competitors and took a dim view of their presence in Nanjing.
Qu Taisu assured him that neither of them were in search of employment
and asked him to take Li Madou under his wing. This shrewd move had the
desired effect, and Li Xinzhai became a good friend.

The visit to one official of very great power, the author of philosophical
works and a speaker at the cultural debates then in fashion among literati,
was very cordial indeed. The mandarin, who had read the treatise on friendship, was delighted to hear that Ricci intended to stay in Nanjing and observed that there were already so many Muslims in the city that he could see
no objection to the presence of someone representing another foreign form
of worship. He evidently felt no distrust toward an unknown religion. In his
initial contacts with these high officials, Ricci had in any case taken care to
make only the vaguest of references to any characteristics of Christianity that
the Chinese might not readily understand and preferred to present himself
above all as a scientist, a moral thinker, and a man of culture. Ricci made the
best possible use of the strategy of cultural accommodation so as to avoid giving offense to scholars and win them over to his religion by indirect means,
interpreting the approach to missionary work developed by Valignano with
real insight and a deep understanding of Chinese society.

The Jesuit was aware that the dignitaries treated him with respect because he was a friend of the minister of rites, but he was also convinced that the good impression he managed to make during the visits served in turn to reinforce the minister's regard for him. This mechanism worked so well that Ricci saw it as a divine stratagem to further his religious mission: "God chose to make use of a splendid subterfuge . . . to make matters go more smoothly."[3]

As a friend of the minister of rites, Ricci was invited to a number of official ceremonies, where he mixed with the *shidafu* and *guan* as though he were one of them. The minister's sons took him to the Temple of Heaven at the beginning of March to hear the rehearsals for the concert to be held there shortly, on the occasion of the rites in honor of Confucius.

The Temple of Heaven, the most important place of worship in the city, was a complex of buildings representing the universe surrounded by walls and a moat. The component edifices, all sharing the same basic structure but differing in size, were set in vast courtyards with century-old trees that no one was ever allowed to prune. Reached by climbing flights of marble steps, the main building was a circular temple embellished with red, dark blue, and gold decorations and representing the celestial sphere. Like all the others, it was adorned with cosmological symbols, and its columns, steps, pillars, and stone slabs were all in multiples of nine, a number thought to play a key role in the organization of the world and hence recurrent in the Chinese tradition.

During the period when Nanjing was the capital, the emperor went to the temple twice a year to celebrate the rites ensuring harmony between the heavens and the earth and good harvests. After fasting for three days, the Son of Heaven would leave the imperial palace clad in yellow ceremonial robes adorned with dragons. Accompanied by a procession of dignitaries, elephants, eunuchs, musicians, and soldiers with banners representing the constellations of the zodiac, the planets, the holy mountains, and the rivers, he then proceeded solemnly along a route running from north to south. All the houses on the way were required to keep their doors and windows closed. Once inside the precincts of the temple, the emperor entered the Palace of Abstinence, where he spent the whole night purifying his body before performing the propitiatory rites. The following morning he proceeded to the circular altar to kneel down and make offerings before the empty throne of the Supreme Lord of the August Heaven placed beside his own. After the capital moved to Beijing, where a second and still more imposing Temple of Heaven was built, the imperial ceremonies were also transferred, and those in Nanjing were toned down.

Ricci went to the temple to listen to the music, an indispensable ingredient of all the most important ceremonies, which was performed as usual by

Taoist monks. Music played a very important role in Chinese rites, being regarded by Confucius as endowed with moral value and capable of establishing peace and harmony among people. Different instruments were used for different types of events. The range included percussion, wind, and stringed instruments made of materials like bronze, leather, wood, stone, bamboo, and silk. Some had vaguely similar Western counterparts, such as drums of wood and leather, flutes, harmonicas, lutes, and psalteries. Others were typically Chinese, like the imposing carillon of bronze bells of different notes and sizes set in a wooden frame and played by percussion. This instrument of ancient origin was first produced in the fourth century BC, if not earlier, when the Chinese were already capable of casting bells of particular notes with a perfection that would have been considered extraordinary in the West at the time. Other characteristically Chinese instruments included the lithophone, consisting of slabs of stone hung on a wooden frame, and tiger-shaped percussion devices.

Ricci observed the more original instruments with great interest but found "no consonance" in the way they were played together and derived no pleasure from the concert. Unable to appreciate the music of another tradition,[4] he was convinced that the "art of harmony" had been lost forever in China.

An Argument with a Buddhist

Ricci's success in scholarly circles was due to the fame of his writings, his scientific expertise, and his knowledge of Confucian philosophy, something "unheard of in China" that never failed to astonish his listeners. This responsiveness to the culture of his intellectual friends stopped at Confucianism, however, and included no aspect of the Buddhist and Taoist doctrines, despite his awareness that a good many Confucian literati had sympathies with both. Some *shidafu* even professed a kind of religion combining elements of Confucianism, Buddhism, and Taoism[5] that had enjoyed considerable popularity in Nanjing and the Jiangsu province. Referred to disapprovingly by Ricci as followers of the "three sects," its believers worshipped statues of Confucius, Buddha, and Lao-tzu placed side by side, an authentic abomination in the Jesuit's eyes.

Despite his aversion for religious syncretism, the Jesuit was involved in friendly discussions with followers of the "three sects," such as Jiao Hong, a high-ranking official temporarily suspended from office and living in Nanjing. It was through him that Ricci met the famous and highly controversial character Li Zhi, a *guan* who had left the bureaucracy and his position as prefect to devote himself to the study of Buddhism. This renowned scholar and intellectual paid Ricci a visit, complimented him on his treatise on friendship, and made him the gift of a fan decorated with verses in his honor. There was a widespread tradition of paying respects in the form of verses, normally written in books of visits. The slender volumes containing such poems were kept by their recipients as evidence of their social success, and Ricci had collected so many that, as he wrote with great satisfaction in his history of the mission, they would have made a bigger book than the *Aeneid* if he had put them all together.[6]

Li Zhi was greatly impressed by the personality of the Western sage and described him as follows: "While his extraordinary refinement is innate, his outward manner is of the simplest. I have never met his equal. [Unlike Ricci] people err through undue rigidity or obligingness; they make a show of their learning or are of limited intelligence." Despite his great admiration for the man, the philosopher expressed misgivings as to the reasons for Ricci's presence in China: "I do not really understand what he has come to do in this country. . . . I think that it would be more than foolish if his aim were to replace the teachings of the Duke of Zhou and Confucius with his own."[7]

Meetings between leading figures in Chinese culture and Li Madou, the sage putting forward a new worldview and a new religion, inevitably involved the risk of heated discussions, and the Jesuit did in fact find himself reluctantly drawn into a particularly bitter argument. Together with Qu Taisu, he had made the acquaintance of Li Ruzhen, a *shidafu* with Buddhist sympathies, and had engaged in some friendly exchange of views. In the course of one of the customary philosophical debates held in the city, Li Ruzhen clashed with the orthodox Confucianist Liu Douxu, who accused him of not holding the Chinese state philosophy in due consideration and cited Li Madou, Xitai, in public as an example of a wise man in favor of Confucianism and hostile to Buddhism. The echoes of this had yet to die down when Li Ruzhen invited the Jesuit to a banquet. Unwilling to get embroiled in some inopportune dispute, Ricci declined at first on the grounds that he was fasting, but he felt obliged to accept when Li Ruzhen assured him that he would be served special dishes in accordance with his diet.

Ricci arrived at the banquet and took part in the customary ritual of greeting with the other guests, about twenty in all, taking tea together before going in to dine. It was then that the Buddhist monk Huang Hong'en—better known as Sanhuai and renowned for his books and poems as well as his expert knowledge of the three Chinese religions—asked him about the faith practiced by the missionaries.

According to Ricci's account, he replied with a question: "What do you think of the Lord of Heaven, creator of all things?"

Sanhuai answered that he believed in the existence of the Lord of Heaven but, unlike the Jesuit, did not consider him a being superior to man.

Shocked by the monk's words, Ricci asked if he too was capable, like God, of creating everything that existed in the heavens and on the earth.

"Certainly," he replied. "I too would be capable of creating the heavens and the earth."

Ricci challenged him to prove this by producing a bronze brazier like the one burning in the room in front of all those present. This gave rise to a heated exchange, with Sanhuai dismissing the challenge as absurd and Ricci accusing him of having lied. Their curiosity aroused, the other guests gathered around to listen, some taking the Jesuit's side and some the monk's.

Sanhuai tried another approach: "You have the reputation of being a great astronomer and expert mathematician. Is this true?"

"I have a certain knowledge of these sciences."

"So, when you speak about the sun and the moon, do you go up into the heavens where these celestial bodies are or do they come down to you?"

"Neither of these happens. When we see an object, we form an image of it in the mind, and when we speak about that object later on, even though we no longer have it in front of us, we refer to its mental image."

Sanhuai replied: "In that case, you, who are a man, have created a new sun and a new moon, and therefore, just as I said, you can create whatever you want. I have proved that I am right."

Ricci countered as follows: "The images I have formed within me are not the real sun and the real moon but only mental copies, and if I had never looked at the sun and the moon in the sky, I could never have recreated their images in my mind." He went on to give an example: "If you see the sun and the moon reflected in a mirror, will you be so foolish as to believe that these celestial bodies are really contained in the mirror?"

Some of the guests—again according to Ricci's account—shook their heads and acknowledged that the Jesuit was right, at which point the monk lost his temper, and the host had to step in and separate the two adversaries so as to avoid the discussion degenerating into a real argument. Li Ruzhen asked the guests to step into the dining room. Ricci was seated in the place of honor with the host beside him to begin the banquet after the customary rituals.

In the interval between one course and another, when a great many dishes had piled up on the table and numerous toasts had been drunk, some of the guests put forward a philosophical issue for amicable discussion, as was customary on such occasions. This time it was the classic question of the goodness of human nature, dating back to the earliest traditions and addressed by all the great Chinese philosophers. According to Mencius, every man is naturally good. According to the philosopher Xun Qing, who lived in the third century BC and is accredited with the authorship of the *Xunzi*, human nature is intrinsically wicked and man has a spontaneous tendency toward evil. Those taking the middle ground maintain that behavior is determined by external influences. The debate continued at the banquet in more or less the same terms as when it had begun many centuries before. If man's nature is good, where does evil come from? If it is bad, where does good come from? If it is neither good nor bad, who can guide it toward goodness and how?

Ricci listened in silence, but when the host asked him to give his opinion, he seized the opportunity to resume the discussion with the monk Sanhuai. "We all agree that the Lord of Heaven is supremely good. Well then, if man is so weak that he does not know whether his nature is good or bad, how can Master Sanhuai claim that man is the equal of the Lord of Heaven? If he were truly the equal of the Lord of Heaven, how could he not know that he too is supremely good?"

Urged to answer by another guest, Sanhuai illustrated the Buddhist doctrine on this point to conclude that the Lord of Heaven is neither good nor bad. The argument finally came to an end with Ricci determined to say no more even if asked to continue, being now convinced that it was impossible to make the Chinese monk listen to reason. The latter was most probably also convinced that it was impossible to make a Western missionary listen to reason. It was in fact a debate of the deaf, as each of the adversaries was accustomed to reasoning solely in accordance with the postulates of his own philosophy. There was certainly no common ground between a Buddhist who believed that the world we perceive is not real and an Aristotelian convinced of the exact opposite, namely that the world is real and that the human mind can understand it by means of reason.

For a Buddhist, the absolute is beyond any determination and is innate in all beings, each of which possesses the nature of Buddha in the deepest recesses of its spirit. For Ricci, confusing the individual with God was simply heresy. The dispute was talked about for a long time in the city, and the Jesuit claims in his history of the mission that he was judged the moral victor.[8] While we do not know whether this was so, many intellectuals with a passion for philosophical arguments visited the missionaries' house to hear all about the clash and to spend the afternoon in discussion with Li Madou. He was flattered by their attention and decided to devote a chapter of his catechism to the subject of the goodness of human nature.

A Universe of Crystalline Spheres:
The "Treatise on the Four Elements"

Ricci ran up against the same old difficulties of mutual comprehension every time he talked to the Chinese, and he tried to point out what he considered the absurdity of their conceptions in order to guide them to the revelation of the Christian doctrine. The Jesuit was astonished to find that they did not reason in accordance with Western logic and did not distinguish, for example, the Aristotelian concepts of form, matter, substance, and accident. The Chinese conception of the universe as a great evolving organism with all of its parts interconnecting was in fact such as to preclude clear-cut distinctions like those between matter and spirit, between the world of the senses and the transcendental world, which were so fundamental for Western culture. What was obvious to Ricci was by no means so to the Chinese, and vice versa. For the latter, the only constant principle was the Tao, spontaneous order, the dynamic principle inherent in every natural process. According to Chinese cosmology, the universe was in a state of constant change and evolution due to the alternation of the two complementary and contrasting forces of yin—the female principle connected with shadow, the earth, passivity, and dissolution—and yang, the male principle connected with light, the sun, activity, and creation. These two forces gave birth to the five "agents" or elements of water, earth, fire, wood, and metal, seen as the dynamic processes forming the Whole through never-ending transformation into one another.

Certain that he knew the truth about the structure of the universe, Ricci was determined to demonstrate the erroneous nature of the vision of the world rooted in Chinese culture since the earliest times, and he hoped to do so by exploiting the evident curiosity of some intellectuals about his scientific knowledge. In Nanjing too, he had no difficulty finding scholars eager to learn about Western mathematics and astronomy and how to construct sundials, mechanical clocks, and rudimentary instruments for observation of the heavens. He was delighted to share his knowledge with them, feeling sure that they would embrace the Christian religion much more readily once they had realized that Western science was superior to theirs and understood and accepted the system of knowledge put forward by the Jesuits. Science had proved excellent "bait," as Ricci put it, in the case of Qu Taisu, leading him on to follow the religious teachings too, even though he had not yet made up his mind to convert. Would others follow his example in Nanjing? Ricci intended to guide Chinese intellectuals by the hand up the steps of knowledge starting at the bottom. Having taught them to reason in accordance with the principles of mathematical logic, he would help them to comprehend the description of the Ptolemaic universe and finally to understand that God was the supreme lawgiver, creator of the world and of the laws governing it. He would proceed from mathematics to theology.

His first pupil in Nanjing was Zhang Yangmo, a young man from Beijing sent by Wang Kentang, a mandarin in the capital who studied mathematics out of personal interest with a group of pupils. Wang Kentang was a member of the illustrious Hanlin Academy made up of the most influential bureaucrats, who were responsible for writing dynastic histories, drafting the most important government documents, and serving as tutors to the crown prince. According to Ricci, the academician wrote to say that he was aware of the lack of method in Chinese mathematics and wished to learn everything the Jesuit had to teach him. Since he could not leave the capital, he took the liberty of sending the pupil Zhang Yangmo in his place.

Zhang Yangmo learned "to do sums with the brush" and then read the first book of Euclid's *Elements* in Qu Taisu's translation, which impressed him so much that "he would only listen to arguments developed in the Euclidean way."[7] Noting once again that Confucian literati were fascinated by Greek mathematics, Ricci began to think that his plans to implant Western reason in the Chinese might actually work. Zhang Yangmo was so happy about learning Western science that he wanted to give Ricci some advice on the best way to refute the Buddhist beliefs before returning to Beijing. In his opinion, Ricci should simply go on teaching mathematics and astronomy until he convinced his adversaries of the validity of his knowledge. If he proved that his scientific doctrines described the world with greater accuracy, the Buddhists would be convinced that his explanation of the supernatural world was also more correct. While appreciating the advice, Ricci doubted that it would prove effective, and in any case he had no intention of devoting his energies to convincing Buddhists, preferring to concentrate on the attempt to win over the Confucian scholars.

In the meantime, a small group of literati had begun to gather regularly at the Jesuits' house in Nanjing. For Ricci, it was like running a sort of school of Western studies with arithmetic, astronomy, geometry, and cosmology on the syllabus. Prompted by a desire to correct what he regarded as the completely wrongheaded ideas of Chinese natural philosophy, he based his "lessons" on what he had learned at the Roman College. While it was believed in China that the universe was made up of various combinations of the five "agents" of water, earth, fire, wood, and metal, it was an established fact in the West that the sublunary world was composed of the four elements of water, air, earth, and fire. Both theories were of course to disappear with the progress of science, but Ricci, a true child of his time, was convinced of the validity of his knowledge and wrote a short treatise on the four elements in Chinese entitled *Si yuanxing lun* in order to convince his Chinese friends too.[9]

Having elucidated the composition of the universe, Ricci went on to demonstrate that the earth was round by exhibiting his terrestrial globes.[10] He then outlined the Ptolemaic system without going into the more difficult theoretical and mathematical aspects regarding the movement of planets, which he meant to explain only to those with sufficient aptitude for complex calculations. As had already happened in Nanchang, he was astonished at how hard it was for his "students" to accept the vision of a universe made up of crystalline spheres with the heavens and the earth rigidly separate.

Having presented the structure of the cosmos, Ricci spoke one day about comets. His explanation that these peculiar celestial bodies were formed out of the fire located beneath the sphere of the moon echoed the classic Aristotelian view of comets as meteorological phenomena belonging to the sublunary world rather than celestial bodies. His listeners were spellbound. No one in China had ever formulated a hypothesis as to how the comets might be formed, even though Chinese astronomers had observed "broom stars" since antiquity, keeping accurate records of their passing and being the first to note that the tail always points away from the sun. In the West, the first systematic observations of comets were the work of Paolo dal Pozzo Toscanelli[11] in the fifteenth century, and the discovery about their tail was first made in 1532 by the Italian scientist Girolamo Fracastoro[12] and Petrus Apianus.

The Chinese were also the first, in 421 BC, to observe Halley's Comet, the brightest of all comets, which reappears regularly in the sky every 76 years, when its orbit brings it closest to the sun. Their records of its periodical transits proved so accurate that Western astronomers were to use them in the twentieth century as the basis for calculating the exact cycle of its appearances.

Ricci did not confine himself to presenting the theoretical aspects of astronomy but also explained how to construct equipment for the measurement and observation of the heavens, such as spheres, globes, quadrants, and astrolabes. Even though he could not call himself a specialist, he was convinced that the Chinese had a great deal to learn in that field too. His certainty was, however, soon to be shaken by an unexpected discovery.

The Forgotten Astronomical Observatory

Ricci's reputation reached the ears of the officials on the Nanjing board of mathematicians responsible for making the calculations for the calendar in collaboration with their more authoritative colleagues in Beijing. The Jesuit often noted that he was able to obtain more accurate results by using the astronomical tables he had brought from Italy, and he regarded the local astronomers as possessing "little talent and knowledge." He also suspected that the *guan* mathematicians feared him as an expert scientist enjoying the friendship of Minister Wang and as perhaps capable of usurping their position one day. According to Ricci's account of events, it was made known through friends of the missionaries that Li Madou occupied a position of such importance in his native land as to have no need of any appointment in China, whereupon the delighted officials invited him to visit their observatory.

The tower was situated on the Hill of the Purple Mountains near the center of the city, surrounded by luxuriant woods and not far from the tomb of Hongwu, the first Ming emperor. The astronomers kept watch every night from a large terrace known as the Pavilion of the Pole Star to record celestial movements and report on any unusual phenomena to the court. On being taken to the top of the building, the Jesuit was astonished to discover a number of large instruments that were not only expertly cast in bronze but were also technologically advanced and unquestionably the work of highly skilled astronomers.[13]

Ricci saw a huge globe designed to represent the celestial sphere, so big that "three people could not have embraced it."[14] This was mounted on a hollow cube of bronze fitted with machinery to make it rotate. There was a massive armillary sphere—from the Latin *armilla*, meaning "bracelet"—supported by columns with a relief decoration of dragons swooping through clouds. Known ever since ancient times both in China and in the West, and consisting of concentric rings of wood or metal representing the great circles on the celestial sphere,[15] this device was used to observe the stars and record their coordinates by means of the graduated scale on the ring taken as reference. The armillary spheres produced in the West and China were similar in conception but differed in terms of the ring used to calculate the position of the celestial bodies, as Europeans used the ecliptic and the Chinese the equator. Moreover, the sphere representing the earth usually placed at the center of Western instruments was traditionally replaced in China with a sighting tube that could be rotated to point at the star whose position in the sky was to be determined.

Ricci also saw a gnomon, a metal rod of about twelve meters mounted vertically on a long, graduated slab of marble laid horizontally to point north, so that the shadow cast on the slab indicated the height of the sun above the horizon. This was used to measure the passing of time and to determine latitude.

What most impressed Ricci, however, was an enormous piece of equipment with a rectangular base of four meters by five that looked like a set of juxtaposed astrolabes. This was in fact an instrument quite similar to the one called a "torquetum" in the West, an instrument consisting of several interconnecting armillary spheres that was used to observe stars and give their position. Developed by the Arabs and then adapted by the Chinese to their equatorial astronomical system, this device can be considered the ancestor of modern telescopes with equatorial mounts. The bronze again bore a finely chased decoration of enormous dragons and clouds. Like the other instruments, the torquetum had grooves in the base that could be filled with water to make sure that it was dead level.

Ricci admired the beauty of the instruments and the decorations, which indicated an uncommon mastery of the technique of casting in bronze, an art in which the Chinese already excelled in the seventeenth century BC.[16] Above all, however, he marveled at the evident astronomical expertise of their designer. Closer examination then revealed that the instruments were not calibrated for the latitude of Nanjing,[17] which seemed inexplicable. Who could have made them? And where? The astronomers told him very vaguely that the equipment was very ancient, and its origin was lost in the mists of time. Ricci was convinced that they were the work of some foreigner deeply versed in Western science, finding it impossible to believe that such peaks of technological mastery and astronomical knowledge were possible in China.

In actual fact, however, the instruments had been made in China three hundred years earlier, in the Yuan era, by the great astronomer, engineer, and mathematician Guo Shoujing, appointed by Kublai Khan to reform the calendar and the inventor in 1281 of the division of the year that was still used, with few variations, in the Ming era.[18] It was precisely in order to make the calculations necessary for drawing up the new calendar that the scientist had had numerous astronomical instruments made, including those that so impressed Ricci. They were, however, calibrated for localities other than Nanjing, and the modifications required for their correct use were not carried out when the equipment was subsequently transported to the capital of the Jiangsu province. This had no practical consequences, as the officials at the observatory had no idea how they worked and had never tried to use them, as they confessed to Ricci's increasing amazement.

The Jesuit paid tribute to the high degree of scientific and technological expertise displayed by the Chinese equipment in his history of the mission: "These instruments are all cast in bronze with a great deal of work and decoration, so large and fine that the father had seen nothing better in Europe, and had been there for about two hundred and fifty years in the rain and snow without being ruined."[19]

Ricci's wonder and admiration were completely justified. Though dating back to the thirteenth century, Guo's instruments had hitherto remained the most advanced devices for astronomical observation in the world. It was precisely during Ricci's years in Nanjing that their precision was surpassed for the first time in the West by the instruments produced in the Uraniborg observatory by Danish astronomer Tycho Brahe, the most meticulous observer of the heavens in that era.[20] Brahe also adopted the equatorial system of reference used in China[21] for the first time in his equipment, thus attesting indirectly to the validity of ancient Chinese astronomy.

Notes

1. *Tao Te Ching*, 42, trans. James Legge, in The Sacred Books of the East, vol. 39 (Oxford: Oxford University Press, 1891).

2. Cit. in Jacques Gernet, *Chine et christianisme*, pp. 294–95.

3. FR, book IV, ch. IV, p. 47.

4. Chinese music does not follow the Western rules of harmony and therefore proves difficult for the unaccustomed listener to understand and appreciate.

5. A form of worship developed by Lin Zhaoen. See Jacques Gernet, *Chine et christianisme*, pp. 106 ff.

6. FR, book IV, ch. VI, p. 69.

7. See Jacques Gernet, *Chine et christianisme*, p. 30. The Duke of Zhou is a figure of the ancient Chinese tradition regarded as the founder, together with the sovereigns Wen and Wu, of the Zhou dynasty of the first millennium BC.

8. FR, book IV, ch. V, p. 55.

9. Printed in Nanjing (1599–1600) and then Beijing (1601). See FR, book IV, ch. V, p. 52.

10. Globes of excellent workmanship had also been made in China since ancient times but were used to represent the heavenly vault and the major constellations rather than the earth.

11. Paolo Dal Pozzo Toscanelli (1397–1482), mathematician, astronomer, and cartographer, responsible together with Brunelleschi for the calculations for the construction of the dome of Santa Maria del Fiore in Florence. His fame also rests on a letter to Columbus arguing that the shortest route to the East was across the Atlantic.

12. Born into a patrician family in Verona, Girolamo Fracastoro (1478–1553) was a physician and poet as well as a botanist, geologist, paleontologist, cartographer, and astronomer. He taught at the University of Padua and is considered the father of epidemiology.

13. Copies of these instruments can still be seen today in the ancient observatory of Nanjing.

14. See FR, book IV, ch. V, pp. 56 ff, for a description of the visit.

15. Including the meridian, which runs between the poles of the celestial sphere, the equator resulting from the intersection of the plane of the terrestrial equator with the celestial vault, the horizon, which forms a right angle with the vertical running through the point where the observer is located, and the ecliptic, the line that follows the apparent path of the sun in the sky during the year.

16. The Chinese were also the first to cast iron, a process developed in the fourth century BC, if not earlier.

17. They were calibrated for a latitude of 36°, whereas Nanjing was located at 32°15'.

18. See chapter 7 ("Minister Wang and the Reform of the Calendar").

19. FR, book IV, ch. V, p. 56.

20. The Danish astronomer Tycho Brahe (1546–1601) made the most precise astronomical observations with the naked eye before the introduction of the telescope. He built the Uraniborg observatory on the island of Hven, which he received as a gift from Frederick II of Denmark in 1576, and developed a geocentric model of the planetary system that was more advanced than the Ptolemaic and found support among many seventeenth-century astronomers until the definitive acceptance of the Copernican system.

21. The equatorial system of reference was subsequently adopted in the West too.

CHAPTER ELEVEN

~

Prisoner of the Eunuch

From Nanjing to Tianjin, 1599–1600

Li Madou has lived in the Middle Kingdom for a long time. He is no
longer a foreigner but Chinese, as he belongs to China.

—Guo Qingluo[1]

The Master said, "Exemplary persons learn broadly of culture, discipline
this learning through observing ritual propriety, and moreover, in so doing, can remain on course without straying from it."

—Confucius, *Analects* (6, 27)

No one has ever heard of a Lord of Heaven nailed to scaffolding in the
shape of ideogram number ten.

—Lifa Lun[2]

The Eunuchs, the Emperor's Private Bureaucracy

It was the month of April 1599. The heat and humidity in Nanjing were
already stifling. Flowers bloomed in the gardens, and the branches of the
trees were covered with the first bright green leaves. The ice blocking the
rivers and canals had melted in the north, and Ricci anxiously awaited the
arrival of Lazzaro Cattaneo from Linqing with the baggage and the gifts for
the emperor. He knew that it was dangerous to travel back along the Imperial Canal to Nanjing without an escort because the social situation had
become unstable after the end of the war in Korea. The expense of six years

169

of fighting (1592–1598) with the mobilization of over two hundred thousand soldiers had drained the state coffers, and the emperor had levied a new tax on commerce in all the provinces that weighed upon merchants and above all small shopkeepers. This created widespread discontent and fears of revolt in an age already plagued by popular uprisings.

In order to increase its revenues, the government also ordered the reopening of silver and gold mines, previously closed to prevent pillaging by bandits, and entrusted their management to the *taijian*, or eunuchs, who were also responsible for collecting taxes. The eunuchs were well known to be unscrupulous and to abuse their power for purposes of extortion. Some worked in cahoots with common criminals, claiming that the homes of wealthy merchants were built on top of silver mines and threatening demolition unless the owners agreed to hand over huge sums of money. Everyone submitted out of fear, but hatred of the eunuchs grew, together with terror at the idea of having anything to do with them. Scholars and officials loathed them but had no effective defense against their oppression, because the *taijian* constituted a structure parallel to the state bureaucracy, many of whose functions they had usurped, and answered only to the emperor. Ricci also despised them and described them as "idiotic, barbaric, arrogant people with no shame or conscience."[3] While trying to avoid them as much as possible, he was beginning to realize that the closer you got to the imperial court, the more you had to come to terms with them.

The most powerful of the thousands of eunuchs living in Nanjing was Feng Bao, who allowed himself the luxury of a litter with eight bearers, like the most authoritative mandarins. Ricci's friends advised him to go and pay his respects, as Feng Bao's favor was an essential prerequisite for a peaceful existence in Nanjing. The Jesuit reluctantly agreed but confined himself on entering the potentate's presence to pronouncing the customary conventional phrases rather than kneeling down and wishing him "one thousand years of life," as was customary for the most influential figures.[4] Fortunately, the eunuch was hard of hearing, and his secretaries, when called upon to repeat Ricci's words in a loud voice, took advantage of this to insert the greeting on their own initiative. Feng Bao felt that he had been treated with due respect, and Ricci had the satisfaction of sticking to his guns, even refusing the secretaries' request to leave a prism as a gift for their master. Feng Bao had been in close contact with Wanli many years earlier, acting as a sort of minder when the emperor was still a child and reigned under the tutelage of the grand secretary Zhang Juzheng.

The Son of Heaven had become attached to the eunuch, affectionately calling him "great companion" and often climbing onto his knee like a child.

Thanks to the emperor's protection, Feng Bao, who had no education but was an excellent chess player and a competent amateur musician, had been appointed master of ceremonies and was thus in charge of the court personnel and the secret police. Wanli had always considered him a faithful ally until he was discovered some ten years earlier to have amassed a fortune in exchange for granting favors to corrupt officials, whereupon he had fallen into disgrace and had his property confiscated. Banished from Beijing, Feng Bao had succeeded in establishing a predominant position in the second capital over the years.[5]

A constant factor in the history of the Chinese empire from the earliest times, eunuchs were initially employed as domestic servants in the imperial palace, above all to serve the concubines, but their functions were gradually extended to being a sort of private bureaucracy for the emperor. Their numbers and influence reached unprecedented levels in the Ming era, and in Ricci's day there were seventy thousand in the whole of China, twenty thousand of whom lived in the Imperial City as its dreaded custodians. Their numbers were to grow still further and reach a total of one hundred thousand by the end of the dynasty, with seventy thousand resident in the capital. The great majority were from poor families that decided to have one of their sons castrated and present him to the court as a servant, thus ensuring him safe and permanent employment. The families of those with successful careers in the imperial palace enjoyed privileges comparable to those of the wealthiest classes.

Realization that the growing influence of the *taijian* threatened to undermine the stability of the state prompted the first Ming emperor, Hongwu, to prohibit their education and to make any interference on their part in government affairs punishable by beheading. His orders were disregarded, however, and a palace school reserved exclusively for eunuchs was founded in 1426. The best students were allowed to continue their studies to levels of learning on a par with the Confucian literati, and those who reached the highest positions were capable of drafting notes for the emperor in an impeccable style fully comparable with the unsurpassable productions of the grand secretaries and the members of the Hanlin Academy.

The niche that the eunuchs had carved out for themselves constituted a contradiction within the state, whose official Confucian ideology envisaged no role for them other than that of palace servants. In actual fact, they now held key positions in the court, the provincial administration, the army, and the secret police. They were in charge of collecting duties and taxes, they managed state industries and controlled entire sectors of commerce, and they were employed as envoys on missions of foreign policy. They had also become the only channel for the transmission of memorials to the court, which gave them enormous power over even the most important government officials. Without drastic intervention on the part of the emperor, which was highly unlikely, it was now impossible to curb their ambitions, especially as they were not subject to investigation by the censors, as state officials were.

The history of the Ming dynasty was full of examples of powerful and corrupt eunuchs manipulating emperors of weak character, and everyone knew that Wanli was more of a puppet than any previous ruler. As Ricci learned, isolated officials had endeavored to rebel against the eunuch's excesses many times in the history of the dynasty, even at the cost of their lives, but their efforts always ended in failure. The unchallenged power of the emperor's private bureaucracy constituted one of the greatest political problems of the Chinese empire in the late Ming era.

A Chinese Name for Europe: The Second Edition of the Map of the World

Lazzaro Cattaneo and his companions arrived in Nanjing without incident in May 1599, and Ricci set about finding a house for sale. The search proved harder than expected, but then, as luck would have it, a somewhat unusual transaction was proposed by Liu Douxu, the orthodox Confucian scholar who had clashed with Li Ruzhen. Having built himself a large house three years earlier in strict accordance with the geomancers' indications, he nevertheless found that it was haunted by evil spirits. Exorcism by Taoist monks, who endeavored to dislodge the unwelcome guests by slashing the walls with sharp swords, proved completely ineffective. The ghosts were still there, and everyone attempting to stay even one night in the house ended up fleeing in terror. Liu Douxu offered Ricci the property at half price, pointing out that the virtuous Xitai could certainly count on the aid of his god, the Lord of Heaven, to defeat the forces of evil.

This excellent piece of business was transacted in just three days. The building was spacious, located on a hill offering protection from the recurrent floods, and had enough rooms to accommodate Ricci, Lazzaro Cattaneo, Sebastião Fernandes, Manuel Pereira, the servants, and the new converts. The Jesuits took the precaution of sprinkling all the rooms with holy water on moving in, but no hostile spirit came to trouble them that night or any other. Pleased to show that the missionaries were immune to local demonic influences, Ricci had the governor's edict confirming the Jesuits' permission to reside in Nanjing and ownership of the property hung in the entrance.

After taking up residence, the missionaries allowed themselves to be persuaded to place the gifts for the emperor on display to the local dignitaries in one room. The influx of visitors was far greater than expected and soon swelled to the proportions of an authentic invasion, with people pouring in at every hour of the day to admire the products of another culture, entranced by the prisms emitting beams of colored light and the magic of the mechanical clocks. The "bells that rang by themselves" so captivated the Chinese imagination that Ricci became a sort of patron saint of clockmakers after his death and was remembered in this role as a minor divinity at least until the early years of the twentieth century, when some clock sellers still hung his portrait in their shops.

The paintings also caused astonishment for their use of oil paints, the extraordinary realism of the faces, and the sense of depth obtained through the technique of perspective. This wonder was justified because ink was used for most of the painting in China, the techniques were different from those in Europe, and the art of portraiture had developed above all in the context of the cult of the ancestors to produce images of the deceased for display on altars. Moreover, various types of perspective were used in the same painting rather than the single linear perspective of Europe. Little importance was attached to showing the direction of the light or reducing the size of distant objects with respect to those in the foreground. In some typically Chinese paintings, where the painter was capable of capturing minute details of nature such as the beating of a bird's wings or the darting of a fish in a pond, rendering the idea of movement in a few delicate strokes, the background was omitted entirely. Ricci was insensitive to the peculiar beauty of Chinese painting: "They do not know how to paint in oils or to give shadows to the things they paint, and so all their pictures are dull and lifeless."[6]

Worn out after days of constant visits going on until late in the evening, Ricci decided to move the gifts to the house of the censor Zhu Shilin and to send the two clocks to Nanchang until it was time to take them to Beijing. Even in the absence of these objects, however, the visitors continued to pour in. The exhausted Jesuit wrote to Girolamo Costa in the only surviving letter of the Nanjing period, dated August 14, 1599, complaining that he often found no time to eat because of all the people he had to receive: "They flock to see me like lunatics."[7] Some wanted to ask Li Madou for mathematical explanations, and others to discuss moral questions. Wizards came knocking every so often to talk about alchemy. Many who had read or heard about the treatise on friendship asked Ricci about the customs and way of life in the "Far West," and he took advantage of this to paint an idyllic picture of Europe as a peaceful country free of conflict, where the Christian religion was practiced, the poor and needy were taken care of, and the moral virtues were practiced, and where it was the custom to take just one wife and remain together all through life.

The missionary's carefully edited account omitted all mention of the wars that soaked the European continent in blood, the plagues and famines that decimated nations, the rift between Catholics and Protestants, the widespread violence and injustice at all levels of society, and the ruthless crushing of all those who dared to challenge the dominant culture, such as Giordano Bruno, burned at the stake in 1600 for refusing to recant his beliefs. When Ricci talked about the pope, how he was elected by the assembly of cardinals, the role he played, and how he was honored by the faithful, his listeners were astonished. They could not understand how it was possible for the authority of a sovereign other than the emperor to be recognized or for a religion independent of the temporal power to exist. In China, the Son of Heaven was the absolute authority in both the political and the spiritual field, and he supervised the rituals of popular worship. Even a structured and organized religion like Buddhism was only tolerated because it was integrated into the social and political structure and was strictly subordinate to state control. Great importance was attached throughout Chinese history to combating the proliferation of uncontrolled cults and unorthodox sects, which were regarded as a threat to the established order.

Some of the visitors were familiar with Ricci's planisphere because they had been able to examine copies or because they had seen it cited and reproduced in works by Chinese authors. One of the most famous of these was the "universal map of the countless countries of the world, with an outline of past and present events" produced in 1593 by the well-known *shidafu* Liang Zhou, who presented Ricci's work with these flattering words: "I recently saw the map of Li Madou with his notes . . . and became aware for the first time of the immensity of the heavens and the earth."[8] Those impressed by the Jesuit's knowledge of geography included an important official at the Nanjing ministry of personnel named Wu Zhongming but better known as Wu Zuohai, who suggested that he should produce a new and expanded version of the map and asked for permission to use the engraved wood blocks to make copies for friends.

Ricci gladly agreed and drew a new map of the world divided into panels, which was printed in 1600[9] with a preface by Wu Zuohai as the *Shanhai yudi quantu* ("Complete Map of the Mountains and Seas"), the same title as the previous edition. Twice the size of the one drawn in Zhaoqing in 1584, it contained various new toponyms. For the first time, there was a name for Europe (*Ou-lo-ba*) and one for France, but still no Chinese name for Italy.

As mentioned above, the value of Ricci's map lay in its presentation of the five continents. From a strictly technical standpoint, however, not all of the characteristics of his geographic works were innovations for the Chinese, who had themselves produced many of excellent quality. Good maps indicating the level of the terrain with respect to a horizontal plane were already in use in China as early as the Tang era in the eighth century, when the measurement of degrees of latitude was also known. The earliest surviving examples of Chinese cartography are two maps carved on a stone in 1136, during the Song era, and now in the Shaanxi Provincial Museum, Xi'an, namely the *Yujitu* ("Map of the Tracks of Yu") and the *Huayitu* ("Map of China and the Barbarian Countries"), a very detailed map of the world showing over five hundred named localities, thirteen rivers with their tributaries, and four mountain ranges.

The two works, in which China is represented graphically while other countries are only indicated with captions, use a grid system to pinpoint the different localities and are regarded by experts as far more technically advanced than European maps of the same period.[10] The most famous Chinese cartographer was Zhu Siben, who lived in the Yuan era and produced the *Yutu* ("Terrestrial Map"). As reconstructed by historians on the basis of later reproductions, this atlas was influenced by Muslim, Persian, and Arabic cartographers, employed the grid system, and included maps of the Chinese provinces with the major rivers and sea lanes as well as some regions of Central Asia. Reprinted in 1555 as the *Guangyutu* ("Enlarged Atlas"), it appeared in successive revised editions until the nineteenth century.

It is, however, misleading to compare Chinese and European cartography solely on the basis of the techniques employed or the amount of data given, as they differed in terms of overall conception. While Europeans strove for the highest possible degree of topographical accuracy, describing the conformation of the terrain and the level of the land with respect to the horizontal plane and giving the altitudes of mountains, the Chinese concentrated above all on describing the appearance of the territory and devoted a great deal of space to written notes of a geographic, naturalistic, ethnographic, and geomantic character, as well as information of use for administrative purposes. Moreover, even though the earliest Chinese maps printed with wood blocks date back to the twelfth century, most of those from the Ming era were still drawn with the brush, were sometimes embellished with short poems and exercises in calligraphy, and displayed great attention to aesthetic considerations instead of the contemporary European focus on technical and quantitative aspects.

After careful examination of Chinese maps, Ricci decided in accordance with the strategy of cultural accommodation to adapt to the local style in order to present his message in the way most likely to please its intended targets. From the second edition on, he therefore included numerous annotations in the margins. In addition to disseminating elements of cosmography and geography, the written part also provided information about the duration of the day and night in the course of the year, the distance between the earth and the planets of the nine heavens, and descriptions of the climatic characteristics of different parts of the world.

The Nanjing edition enjoyed enormous success and circulation far beyond all expectations, numerous copies even being sent to Japan. Guo Qingluo, the governor of the central-southern province of Guizhou, produced a reduced version four years later with a preface celebrating Ricci's complete integration into Chinese society: "Li Madou has lived in the Middle Kingdom for many years. He is no longer a foreigner but Chinese, because he belongs to China."

The Journey to Beijing:
The Meeting with the Fearsome Ma Tang

While Ricci continued his intense social life and cultural exchanges with the *shidafu* without managing to make any converts among them, proselytism began to prove moderately successful in other social classes. The first to adopt the faith in Nanjing were a 70-year-old retired soldier that Ricci called Chin, who was baptized with the name of Paul and was known as Chin Paul by the missionaries, his firstborn son Martin, and other members of their family. Shortly after his conversion, Chin Paul handed over to Li Madou for burning baskets full of Buddhist and Taoist wooden idols that he had kept at home to protect the family. Instead of destroying them, the Jesuit sent them to Manuel Dias, the rector of the College of the Mother of God in Macao. As he wrote in his history of the mission, using one of the military metaphors of which the Society of Jesus was so fond, he considered them the "spoils of the first battle"[11] won in Nanjing.

Even though the prospects for evangelization looked promising, Ricci knew that it was impossible to achieve the great numbers of converts obtained in a short time by Jesuit missions in various other parts of the world and expected of him by the religious authorities. As he wrote to Girolamo Costa, "There [in Rome] they would like news of some great conversion in China. You must know that I and all the others here dream of nothing else day and night. It is for this that we have left our native land, those dear to us and our friends, that we wear Chinese clothing and footgear, and that we do not speak or eat or drink or live at home other than after the Chinese fashion."[12] Ricci knew he would have to wait: "The time of our stay in China is not the time of harvest or even sowing but of clearing wild forests and fighting with the beasts and poisonous snakes that live in them." Thinking of the future, he foresaw that his pioneering work would enable the missionaries following in his footsteps to obtain better results and claimed the recognition he felt was his due: "Others will come by God's grace and write of conversions and the fervor of the Christians, but it must be known that it was first necessary to do what we are doing now and that we are entitled to most of the merit. . . . China is very different from other lands, and the people, being judicious and more inclined to learning than to warfare, are very intelligent. . . . There is no memory of any foreigner ever living here as we are now."

Now forty-seven years old, Ricci was well aware of the difficulties still to be faced. Despite his exceptional energy that never ceased to surprise his companions, he felt sudden waves of fatigue at times, the ankle injured many years before was becoming more painful than usual, and it took more effort to carry out his normal obligations: "The trials of this arduous undertaking are such that I can hardly look forward to a long old age." Every time he feared he might succumb to fatigue, however, he managed to pull himself together and continue his preparations for the journey to Beijing. It was becoming urgent to set off for the capital and secure delivery of the memorial drawn up in Nanchang, as there was some risk of the emperor being informed that a foreigner had gifts for him and ordering them to be delivered without granting the missionaries an audience.

Since the funds at his disposal were insufficient to finish paying for the house and cover the expense of the journey, Lazzaro Cattaneo was sent to Macao to ask for help, but he found the coffers of the Jesuit college empty when he got there. The silver earmarked for the missionaries in China had gone down with the ship bringing it from Japan. Well aware that the journey to Beijing constituted the climax of seventeen years of work in China, Father Dias dispatched a courier to Nanjing with a bill of exchange and set about soliciting donations from the Portuguese merchants. Having taken delivery of another clock and a religious painting for the emperor, together with prisms, hourglasses, silk brocade, and precious books as gifts for the officials of the imperial court, Cattaneo returned to Nanjing in March 1600 with a 28-year-old Spanish Jesuit named Diego de Pantoja, initially assigned to the Japan mission but diverted to China with a view to the important mission in the capital.

It proved impossible to cash the bill of exchange, but the amount of silver raised in Macao was sufficient to cover expenses, and the missionaries concentrated on their preparations. Ricci decided to leave for Beijing with Pantoja and the Chinese lay brothers Sebastião Fernandes and Manuel Pereira. Cattaneo was to remain in Nanjing, where he would be joined by João da Rocha, while João Soerio was to move to Nanchang.

Knowing that the gifts for Wanli were his strongest card, Ricci decided to have the large clock, the showpiece of the collection, embellished by a team of local craftsmen highly skilled in wood carving and decoration. The results were perfection itself. The case of the clock now rested on a base supported by four columns, and the bells that struck the hours and quarter hours were placed in a dome on top of it. The wood was adorned with a pattern of dragons in relief against a background of yellow, red, blue, green, and gold. The dial had new hands in the shape of an eagle's beak, and the hours were written in Chinese characters. It was a small masterpiece that would have aroused the admiration of Renaissance craftsmen.

While the preparations were in full swing, news of the missionaries' imminent departure for Beijing reached Nanchang, and the imperial prince of Jian'an persuaded the eunuch tax collector to use his influence to secure an audience with Wanli. He also sent a servant bearing gifts to Nanjing to inform his friends of this, but the man was robbed and killed by bandits on the way. Despite the prince's kind intentions, Ricci was determined to accept no help from the *taijian* and managed to obtain a permit to travel to Beijing from the censor Zhu Shilin. In his haste to set off, however, he then rashly accepted the offer of passage on the northbound junk of a eunuch with a cargo of silk to deliver to the imperial court, who hoped to derive some profit from the presence on board of important figures bearing gifts for the emperor. They embarked on May 19, 1600, and Zhu Shilin came to see them off, wishing them every success and holding the prism that Ricci had left him as a gift.

The eunuch treated the Jesuits with great respect during the first part of the journey because they were friends of the censor and because their presence on board did prove advantageous. During the stops at the lock gates, as soon as it became known that the junk was carrying passengers with gifts for Wanli, many asked to see the wonderful objects intended for the Son of Heaven, and the eunuch allowed the masters of the vessels in front of his to do so in return for letting him go first. Many days ahead of schedule, the junk arrived at Jining in the Shandong province, where it was to stop for some time in order to take on fresh provisions and complete the mandatory bureaucratic procedures for continuation of the journey as far as Beijing.

Ricci informed the provincial governor Liu Dongxing that he would be paying the customary visit of courtesy, and the *guan*, who was aware of his reputation, sent a litter to bring him and received him with great cordiality.

It was in his house that Ricci had his second meeting with the philosopher Li Zhi, who was passing through the town. On hearing of the missionaries' intentions, the two dignitaries inspected the gifts for Wanli and read the memorial. Finding it unsuitable, they had a new one written in a more elegant style, which the governor presented to the Jesuit free of charge.

It was early in July 1600 when they reached Linqing, an obligatory stopping point for merchants sailing along the Great Canal and the location of a tax-gathering office whose director Ma Tang was the eunuch most feared in the whole of China. Sick and tired of his unjust demands, the local merchants had rebelled the previous year and set fire to the mansion where he lived, killing many of his assistants. The eunuch managed to escape in disguise, however, and returned to exercise his powers as before once the storm had passed.

The eunuch transporting the Jesuits went to pay the required homage to Ma Tang but was refused admittance. Irritated and determined to use any means whatsoever to attract the tax collector's attention, he informed him that his passengers were bearing articles for the emperor and invited him to inspect them. Ricci realized that he was in danger and rushed to ask for help from the military intendant Zhong Wanlu, an acquaintance from his period in Zhaoqing. Even though no state official or army officer could give orders to Ma Tang, the intendant did possess sufficient authority to try and curb his excesses. Zhong Wanlu counseled great prudence and promised to help as much as possible. In the middle of this conversation, however, the Jesuit was informed that Ma Tang was on his way to the junk to inspect the gifts. When he finally got back to his companions, he found a richly decorated vessel "as big as a palace" already moored alongside. The eunuch inspected the gifts and took delivery of the memorial, which he promised to dispatch to Beijing himself. When Ricci objected that he would prefer to rely on the help of his influential mandarin friends, Ma Tang laughed at his naïveté and asserted that no one had more power than he did at the court of Wanli. Ricci realized he had fallen into a trap. It was clear that the eunuch would hold the missionaries hostage until he found some way to take advantage of their presence, even by simply appropriating the gifts. The only guarantee of their safety was the protection of the military intendant Zhong Wanlu, with whom Ma Tang preferred not to cross swords, at least for the time being.

The missionaries' fate was now in the hands of the most feared of the *taijian*, and they transferred to another boat while the eunuch responsible for their plight was authorized to continue to Beijing and was granted exemption from customs duties in exchange for his precious information.

Imprisonment and Liberation

All too predictably, Ma Tang offered to safeguard the gifts for the emperor, whereupon Ricci strenuously objected that the clocks required winding and the religious paintings were used by the missionaries to say their prayers. The eunuch did not insist and sought to demonstrate his good intentions by inviting them to a splendid banquet followed by entertainment. It was an evening worthy of a European court with a rich and elaborate show of jugglers, acrobats, and mimes.

Ma Tang forced the missionaries to remain in Linqing for nearly a month under the constant surveillance of his guards and then decided to take them to Tianjin, where he had to go to deposit the revenues he had collected. Before leaving, the *taijian* thought it prudent to send a memorial to the emperor and notify him that the missionaries and their gifts were in his safekeeping. Like every other administrative transaction, the preparation and dispatch of a document to the court had to comply with the established procedures in every detail. The eunuch spent a few days in his palace drafting a preliminary version, during which time he received no visitors, and then had two copies made in the requisite calligraphic style by a specialist scholar. He then placed the memorials between two yellow panels of wood covered with a cloth of the same color, entrusted them to a courier, and accompanied the same all the way to the outermost gate of the palace. If he had wished to accord the maximum prominence to the event, Ma Tang would also have been entitled by protocol to have a bombard fired to mark the messenger's departure for Beijing.

When a memorial reached the Imperial City, together with the thousands and thousands of other documents that poured in every day from all the provinces of the empire, it was subjected to a long process of sorting through all the relevant offices before reaching the Son of Heaven, if judged worthy of attention. The documents that reached the Forbidden City differed in style and length and were examined by specific offices in accordance with the content and the type of request addressed to the emperor. Petitions, reports from provincial officials, and memorials such as the one from Ma Tang were sent to the office of transmission, which then forwarded a duplicate to the supervisors of the South Gate, an office that took its name from one of the entrances to the imperial palace.

The procedure was slightly different for documents submitted in a personal rather than official capacity to draw the emperor's attention to various matters, which had to be delivered by the author himself into the hands of the eunuchs in the offices of the Gate of Polar Convergence. Few documents of either kind actually reached the emperor, and none in the form in which it had been received. Most were subjected to numerous readings and revisions before being finally rewritten in the Pavilion of Literary Profundity by the grand secretaries or the eunuchs closest to the Son of Heaven. Needless to say, many documents were caused to disappear somewhere along the way, deliberately manipulated to further some palace intrigue, or made public before delivery to Wanli in order to discredit their authors. The reigning emperor was known to detest all bureaucratic tasks, even though he could not get out of examining the dozens of documents brought to his attention every day. The salient parts were often summarized by the secretaries or eunuchs, and the emperor confined himself to approving or refusing requests with a sign in vermilion ink. The use of this shade of red ink for annotations on documents was reserved exclusively for the Son of Heaven, and the orders in this case were so binding that anyone writing on a document in ink of that color without authorization would be put to death.

At the beginning of August, having sent the document that deliberately omitted a detailed list of the gifts for the emperor, Ma Tang moved to Tianjin with the missionaries and his retinue. Ricci felt imperiled and was very concerned about the possible reaction to the eunuch's intercession at the imperial court, as he knew that by law, and with no exceptions, all cases regarding the presentation of gifts to the Son of Heaven by foreigners were to be handled through the ministry of rites. Ma Tang's unorthodox initiative could have unforeseeable consequences. The reply to the eunuch's memorial arrived just over a month later with the foreseeable request for a detailed list of the Jesuits' gifts. The eunuch summoned Ricci, who was required to show his submission by presenting himself in clothes of ordinary cloth and kneeling. After yet another painstaking inspection of the gifts, Ma Tang decided that it would be appropriate to add the copy of Ortelius's *Theatrum Orbis Terrarum* that he had found in the missionaries' baggage. He dispatched the list as required and immediately had the Jesuits locked up in a military fortress, as was customary for all those who requested an audience with the emperor, until such time as permission was granted.

Time passed, and no reply was forthcoming. It was now November 1600, and the cold was already making itself felt in the missionaries' incommodious lodgings inside the fortress. Ma Tang began to fear punishment from the emperor for flouting customary procedures and became openly hostile to the missionaries, seeing them by now as nothing other than a source of trouble. Determined to derive at least some benefit from their presence, he burst into their rooms one day with a captain and a squad of soldiers and ordered a search on the pretext of having received information that the Jesuits were concealing precious jewels. The discovery of a wooden crucifix showing the blood dripping from Christ's wounds frightened the soldiers, and Ma Tang was convinced that it was a fetish constructed in order to cast an evil spell on the emperor.

Ricci promptly explained that the image was of a holy man who had suffered in order to defend his faith and that its realism served to imprint his sacrifice in the memory. The captain only believed him on being shown other crucifixes of the same kind kept in the trunks, but commented that it was not a good idea to keep a sculpture of a wounded man in the house. The eunuch confiscated everything that had been found, including the reliquaries and the silver chalices for the Mass, but not the silver ingots, as he could hardly commit blatant theft in front of the captain. Ricci asked for the chalices to be returned on the grounds that they were religious objects, and Ma Tang agreed, contenting himself with seizing all the other articles of value and nearly all the gifts for the emperor. The soldiers stole as much as possible and locked up the Jesuits' remaining possessions in wooden crates, including their books. Ma Tang returned to Linqing immediately afterward.

Confined to the fortress together with his companions, Ricci was afraid for the first time of seeing everything he had built up over his seventeen years in China destroyed. December arrived, and he wrote to Ma Tang, urging him to request a reply to the memorial, and also to his military friend Zhong Wanlu in Linqing, asking for advice on what to do. The intendant sent a servant with an answer, but the man was beaten and refused admittance when he turned up at the prison gate. Zhong Wanlu succeeded in having another letter delivered secretly to inform his friends that Ma Tang wanted to have them expelled from China in chains. His advice was to escape, make for the Guangdong province, and return to Europe as fast as possible. The situation was so serious that Ricci sent Sebastião to Beijing to seek assistance from all the mandarins they knew, but not one of them had the courage to stick his neck out by coming to their aid.

In January 1601, more than six months since Ricci had fallen into the hands of Ma Tang, the reply to the memorial arrived unexpectedly in Tianjin when all hope had been lost. By order of the emperor, the prisoners were to be taken to Beijing with their gifts immediately, and the ministry of rites was to take charge of them in accordance with the customary procedure for ambassadors from foreign kingdoms.

Nobody ever found out how the situation changed in favor of the missionaries after so long. According to the explanation Ricci subsequently heard from some friends in Beijing, the emperor simply forgot to reply to Ma Tang's second memorial but remembered one day about the gifts to be presented by some foreigners. On expressing his desire to see the object described to him as a bell that "rang by itself," he was informed that the missionaries had not been granted permission to present themselves at court, whereupon he hastened to sign the authorization.

Faced with the imperial injunction, Ma Tang could only comply and gave orders that the missionaries were to be accompanied to Beijing at the expense of the state, in accordance with the law for visiting ambassadors. The Jesuits were hurriedly reunited with their baggage, and an imposing escort was assembled with over thirty bearers and eight horses led by an imperial official specially sent from Beijing. The former prisoners, now treated with the greatest respect, were ready to leave on January 20, 1601, eight months after their departure from Nanjing.

Ricci was already on his way when he noticed that the crate with his books of mathematics and astronomy was missing, and he immediately sent a servant back to Tianjin on the assumption that it had simply been forgotten in the haste of departure. He had no intention whatsoever of abandoning his scientific library, which he considered as essential to the success of the mission as the religious and moral works. His plan was in fact to go on teaching Western science in Beijing in order to acquire the authority needed to secure acceptance of the Christian religion by the Chinese elite. Ricci knew that the possession of mathematical and astronomical works without the emperor's permission was forbidden on pain of death by Chinese law, but also that this was seldom applied. He never imagined that Ma Tang had had the books placed in a special crate clearly labeled as containing prohibited material with the intention of using them as evidence against the Jesuits at the right moment.

By a stroke of luck, however, the servant sent to look for the books found the crate in the fortress and brought it straight back to the Jesuits because he was unable to read and therefore to understand the writing indicating its content. Ricci gave thanks to Divine Providence on receiving his books and reading the attached label. In any case, the work of spreading European knowledge that he was to perform in Beijing would have been impossible if that unwitting and illiterate servant had not restored Euclid's *Elements* and the other works of mathematics and astronomy by Clavius to the missionaries.

Notes

1. *Il Mappamondo cinese del Padre Matteo Ricci S.I.*, cit., pp. 77–80.
2. Cit. in J. Gernet, *Chine et christianisme*, p. 304.
3. FR, book IV, ch. VIII, p. 81.
4. The emperor alone was to be wished "ten thousand years of life."

5. For the relations between Wanli and Feng Bao, see R. Huang, op. cit.

6. FR, book I, ch. IV, p. 32.

7. OS II, p. 243.

8. Theodor N. Foss, "La cartografia di Matteo Ricci," in *Atti del convegno internazionale di Studi Ricciani, Macerata-Roma, 22–25 October 1982*, ed. Maria Cigliano (Macerata: Centro Studi Ricciani, 1984), p. 181.

9. No copy of this map has survived.

10. See also R. Smith, op. cit., p. 29.

11. FR, book IV, ch. IX, p. 94.

12. Letter dated August 14, 1599; OS II, pp. 246 ff.

~

CHAPTER TWELVE

In the Heart of the Empire

Beijing, 1601

My hope for those in high places.

> —Matteo Ricci, *Xiqin quyi bazhng* ("Eight Songs for
> the Western Harpsichord")

The Master said, "To quietly persevere in storing up what is learned, to
continue studying without respite, to instruct others without growing
weary—is this not me?"

> —Confucius, *Analects* (7, 2)

The Solemn Entrance into Beijing

The picturesque cavalcade of Western missionaries dressed as Confucian
literati traveling with gifts for the emperor made its solemn entrance into
Beijing on January 24, 1601. Li Madou was preceded not only by his reputation as a sage from a distant land and author of an extraordinary map of the
world, but also by rumors about the outlandish objects he was bringing, bells
that rang by themselves, stones that produced all the colors of the rainbow,
splendid paintings, and instruments for observation of the heavens. The
event was recorded by the historians of the Ming dynasty.[1]

Ricci was now forty-eight. Thirty-three years had gone by since his arrival
in Renaissance Rome, the capital of the Papal State. While it had never been
his intention to stay for long in the city that molded him in cultural and
religious terms, he was instead determined not to leave the Chinese capital

185

and was confident that he would be able to meet the emperor and ask his permission to preach the Christian religion freely.

Ricci entered with an escort of the Imperial Guard after traveling at the expense of the Chinese state like a foreign ambassador. After the brief and ill-fated experience of two years earlier, it was like seeing the city for the first time.

Beijing was the political center of the Ming, the last great Chinese dynasty, which had reigned for nearly three centuries over a country of glaring contrasts whose population of two hundred million had more than doubled over that time.

It was Yongle, the third Ming emperor, who decided to transfer the capital from Nanjing to Beijing after taking the throne in 1402. The new political hub of the empire was built not far from the site of Khanbalik, the capital of the Yuan dynasty, as a modernized version of the old Mongol city and its system of walls.

Considered the greatest Ming ruler after Hongwu, the founder of the dynasty, Yongle wanted a grand, orderly, and imposing capital to reflect the qualities he desired for his empire. The building work involved a quarter of a million craftsmen and a million peasants and took twenty years. The hundreds of thousands of bricks required were produced on the spot in ovens constructed in the northern part of the city, and the timber arrived in a constant flow from the southwest provinces by river. On completion of the work in 1421, the city was officially proclaimed the new capital with the name of Beijing and became the symbol of total power in terms of its structure as well. In order to increase its population, the emperor ordered the resettlement of ten thousand families from the Shaanxi province, whose capital Xi'an had also been one of the historical capitals of the Chinese empire.

The creation of the new capital in the north enabled the Son of Heaven to remain in the area where he had lived and built up his power before the civil war through which he usurped the throne. It also facilitated the defense of the northern frontiers against invasion by nomadic tribes, a historical threat to the Chinese empire. There were, however, considerable disadvantages too. On the one hand, the center of power was now detached from the economic and cultural heart of the country and from the major areas of agricultural and industrial production, situated mostly in the southeast. On the other, the transport of goods for the court along the Great Canal and the maintenance of that immense waterway entailed prohibitive costs for the state, which was now running a constant deficit.

When Ricci entered Beijing, the survival of the dynasty was threatened by power struggles between state officials and eunuchs, by the empire's dire financial straits, by pressure from the Manchurians on the frontiers, and by recurrent popular uprisings. Despite the crisis and decay of the Ming state, however, the country was prosperous and dynamic in other respects. Commerce and the crafts were thriving, and the cultural scene was characterized by development and revitalization. In point of fact, if the golden age was the Chinese Renaissance of the Song dynasty at the beginning of the first millennium, when China outstripped the rest of the world in the arts, sciences, and technology, then the last century of the Ming era can be regarded as a second renaissance by virtue of the powerful new ideas in circulation and the intensity and vivacity of its intellectual life.[2]

While the official interpretation of the Confucian classics in the imperial examination system was dogmatic and unchanged by any recent revision, culture and philosophy were exploring new avenues outside the corridors of power. Unorthodox thinkers and scholars sought fresh stimuli in the Buddhist and Taoist traditions with a view to moving beyond the established Confucian conceptions. Moral, cultural, and metaphysical questions were freely and eagerly discussed in the flourishing academies of all the major cities, as Ricci had seen for himself in Nanjing and Nanchang. If sciences such as mathematics and astronomy were neglected, there was renewed interest in other sectors of knowledge, above all in what the Chinese called "practical studies," as demonstrated by the immense production of books, manuals, and treatises about military, agricultural, and artisanal techniques, drugs and medicine, botany, geology, geography, and hydraulic engineering.

The same years saw unprecedented growth in the sector of popular literature in the vernacular. Reading had become a popular pastime with the spread of elementary schools and the ever-increasing literacy of the poorer classes and women. Manuals and popular encyclopedias provided useful information, and novels covered a broad range of genres from romance and eroticism to crime and satire. Printing works capable of producing books with illustrations in five colors sprouted everywhere to meet the demand. The entrepreneur Mao Jin[3] in Beijing employed twenty skilled craftsmen and used more than one hundred thousand wood blocks to print as many as six hundred different works a year. While manifesting disdain for mass literature in public, the *shidafu* read works of popular fiction and sometimes wrote them in secret to increase their incomes, like the anonymous author of *Jin Ping Mei*[4] ("The Golden Lotus," or "The Plum in the Golden Vase"), one of the most famous Chinese classics and considered the first ever novel of manners, which rumor attributed to the high-ranking official Wang Shizen. The book revealed the intrigues and debauchery of the ruling classes through the story of the rich, corrupt, and dissolute merchant Ximen and his six wives. Theater was also revitalized, and women, though traditionally marginalized in society, were given leading roles in two works of social satire, one of which tells how the young Mulan passes herself off as a man, takes her father's place in the war, and leads the army to victory.[5]

Beijing reflected the country as a whole to a greater extent than any other Chinese city. Matteo Ricci was soon to find responsive intellectuals eager to find out about "Western" knowledge in that environment with its wealth of new ideas and stimulating contradictions, where popular and official culture, and theoretical and practical knowledge, were apparently separate but actually influenced one another, and where the thirst for new forms of knowledge made itself strongly felt.

The missionaries were lodged in a palace owned by the *taijian* in the inner city, near the entrance to the Imperial City, and they immediately set about preparing the gifts for presentation to the emperor while Ricci drew up yet another list of the items accompanied by a new memorial. This document, which has survived,[6] is dated "the twenty-fourth day of the twelfth moon of the twenty-eighth year of the reign of Wanli," or January 27, 1601. In it, Li Madou presented himself to the Son of Heaven as a foreigner from far away attracted by the fame of China. After residing in various Chinese cities, trusting in the emperor's benevolence toward foreigners, he now came to offer the products of his country. Being a priest with no wife or children, he asked for no favors but would be delighted to place himself at his Majesty's service as an expert in astronomy, geography, calculation, and mathematics. This was followed by a detailed list of the gifts[7]: two paintings of the Virgin Mary, a small painting of Christ, a breviary with a gilded cover, a cross studded with precious stones, two mechanical clocks (one larger and made of iron with weights and the other of gilded metal with springs), a copy of the Ortelius atlas, two glass prisms, eight mirrors and bottles of various sizes, a rhinoceros horn, two hourglasses filled with sand, a New Testament, four European belts of different colors, five lengths of material, four European silver coins, and a portable table harpsichord decorated with two psalms in Latin in gilded letters. The musical instrument presented by the missionaries was a comparatively recent innovation in Europe consisting of a rectangular sound box horizontally strung with metal wires and played by means of a keyboard.[8]

Having delivered the gifts, the Jesuits were the guests of the eunuchs for three days while the request for an audience was processed through the requisite bureaucratic channels and the objects were transported into the Forbidden City. They then moved immediately into a rented house not far from the Imperial City to await a reply. Having arrived in Beijing and handed over the gifts, the missionaries hoped they had freed themselves of the unwelcome patronage of Ma Tang, but the eunuch was still determined to derive some benefit from their visit to the capital and kept them under the constant surveillance of a group of faithful servants. At the same time, in an effort to put an end to the stories of his avarice that had now reached the imperial court, he lavishly reimbursed the *taijian* who had provided the missionaries with accommodation.

The Golden Prison of the Emperor Wanli

The Forbidden City was surrounded by the Imperial City, a sort of shell separating it from the rest of the metropolis, which also produced everything necessary for the survival of the court. The square, walled citadel provided living quarters for twenty thousand eunuchs, divided into twenty-four departments, and the three thousand women employed in the palaces. Its inhabitants were all dressed in black, the color reserved for those connected with the life at court, apart from the bureaucrats closest to the emperor and the eunuchs of high rank, who were entitled to wear red.

The main entrance facing south, the *Tiananmen*, or Gate of Heavenly Peace,[9] was a great pavilion set on a platform of white marble with an imposing double-eaved roof that was covered, like every other roof in the imperial complex, with majolica tiles in the emperor's own bright yellow color. The eastern part of the city housed the factories that produced articles for the imperial palaces, the warehouses of provisions and every other kind of material required for the life of the court, and the office of entertainment, whose personnel were capable of organizing banquets for as many as fifteen thousand people even at short notice. The western part was occupied by a huge park with temples, multistory towers, and ponds inhabited by cranes and crossed by bridges of white marble.[10] The most luxurious villas were the homes of the most important *taijian*, surrounded by servants and personal secretaries and differing little from the eminent *guan* of the bureaucracy in terms of lifestyle. It was not unusual for them to live with women of the palace like married couples and to adopt children, having none of their own, or to act as guardians to young eunuchs.

At the heart of the Imperial City was the *Zi Jin Cheng*, or "Purple Forbidden City," a name derived from the color of the walls and buildings. Commonly known as the "Great Within," this was the home of Wanli, the fourteenth Ming emperor, now in power for twenty-eight years.[11] It was to him that the Jesuits presented their gifts and on him that they pinned their hopes of spreading Christianity on Chinese soil.

Ricci's studies on arriving in China told him that immense power was concentrated in the hands of the emperor, including the life and death of his subjects, which led him to conjure up the ideal image of a cultured and enlightened monarch, the personification of Confucian ethics, the supreme leader and source of inspiration for state officials and army officers. On closer acquaintance with the reality of Chinese life, however, he soon discovered that the Son of Heaven was the eunuchs' puppet and had no interest in handling the affairs of state, even though he still had no idea of the extent to which the monarch had relinquished authority and lived a segregated existence in the imperial palaces. Like other emperors before and after him, Wanli was very far from the ideal. Having withdrawn from public life long before, he lived in seclusion in his private apartments, where he met only the empress, the concubines, and the palace eunuchs, playing no part whatsoever in the government of the country. He had stopped attending the general audiences with members of the government at least ten years earlier, took no part in public ceremonies, no longer met the grand secretaries and ministers, glanced absentmindedly at the memorials brought to his attention, and seldom bothered to give an answer even when the documents contained requests for the authorization of new bureaucratic appointments. Years of neglect had brought the state machinery to the brink of paralysis.

Wanli has gone down in history as an idle, apathetic, irresolute emperor interested only in pleasure and collecting works of art. According to more recent historical studies,[12] however, he was an intelligent and able young man but too sensitive and submissive for such a dehumanizing role as that of emperor, which left no room for the expression of personality and feelings. The power of the Chinese emperor was in fact absolute only in principle. In reality, he performed above all a symbolic function and was strongly influenced and controlled by a bureaucracy in which honest, upright individuals still existed but alongside increasingly large numbers of corrupt figures, and where everyone was concerned above all to preserve their power and ensure survival against the ever-greater threat of the eunuchs' influence. Due to the organizational structure of the Chinese state, the Son of Heaven was in fact isolated, the prisoner of his role and of superfluous, energy-consuming rituals. When he was not endowed with a strong personality, he easily became the puppet of the dishonest bureaucrats and eunuchs in a court torn apart by internal power struggles.

Wanli lacked determination and had been exposed to the influence of court life since childhood. His youthful enthusiasms, desires, and manifestations of cultural interest, including a passion for calligraphy, had all been frustrated and repressed by the officials at his side ever since he came to the throne. Having become emperor when still a child, he was entrusted for nine years to the guardianship of his powerful tutor and grand secretary Zhang Juzheng, to whom he formed a strong attachment in the belief that he was an irreproachable servant of the state. When the mandarin was discredited after his death by a group of hostile bureaucrats, who accused him of having amassed an enormous fortune through corruption, and all his family fell into disgrace, Wanli was deeply disillusioned. Confused, upset, and wholly unable to establish who was telling the truth, the emperor began to feel increasing distrust for the *guan*, who were always ready for betrayal and intrigue and were far too busy writing memorials accusing one another to think about the good of the country. A weak emperor like him had few weapons against the bureaucracy, which could instead subject the decisions and conduct of the Son of Heaven to criticism, albeit indirectly, through memorials circulated among the most important mandarins or through calculated allusions during government meetings. The greater the emperor's fragility and passivity, the more ruthless the struggle for predominance between groups of officials. Added to this was the growing ambition of the eunuchs, a class even more corrupt than the bureaucrats, to which the monarch ended up delegating his power.

Wanli had never been free to decide if and when to leave the capital. His last journeys, which never lasted more than a week, had been allowed so that he might inspect the construction work on his mausoleum, situated a short distance from the capital and completed thirteen years before. Any ideas of further short trips had since been nipped in the bud on various pretexts, and the now resigned emperor no longer even moved outside the Forbidden City, where he was to live in segregation until his death. Wanli had eight wives, who gave him eight sons and ten daughters, and numerous concubines. In 1586, he made his favorite, the concubine Zheng, who enjoyed a reputation for intelligence, learning, and determination, the imperial consort, second in rank only to Empress Wang, and decided to designate his third son Zhu Changxun, Prince Fu, whose mother she was, as heir to the throne. This event, which was the talk of the whole country, gave rise to strenuous opposition on the part of the officials at the court. Wanli was finally forced to yield after a power struggle of fifteen years with the *guan*, but his already difficult relations with the bureaucracy had deteriorated still further. As a last, stubborn act of defiance against the mandarins, he waited for many years before deciding to exile his favorite son Prince Fu to the provinces in accordance with the dictates of dynastic law.

The Dialogue at a Distance with the Son of Heaven

The first indications of the emperor's reaction to the missionaries' gifts began to filter through from the Imperial City a few days after their delivery. According to rumor, the Son of Heaven had admired the religious images and said that the divinities looked like living beings. These words fired the popular imagination, and the Jesuits began to be pointed out as the people who had presented a "living god" at the court.[13] The overly intense expressions of the figures portrayed soon began to have a disquieting effect on Wanli, however, and he decided to get rid of them by presenting them in turn to the empress dowager on the assumption that being greatly devoted to the Buddhist and Taoist divinities, she would accept the presence of sacred images in her rooms more readily. Once the initial curiosity wore off, however, she also tired of those sternly staring faces, and the paintings were definitively consigned to the imperial treasury.

Wanli was instead captivated by the mechanical clocks. None of the ambassadors of the tributary countries had ever brought him anything that amazed him as much as those timepieces capable of making sounds like a musical instrument. To his great dismay, however, they ran down and stopped working. Not long after their last chime, a group of eunuchs arrived on horseback to take the missionaries back with them to the Imperial City immediately by order of the emperor. Ricci and Pantoja rode with them for the first time through the massive wall into a world forbidden to common mortals and found themselves in a huge courtyard. At the far end, by the second great gate of the Imperial City to the south of the Forbidden City, which Ricci describes as a "second wall," they saw the large clock on the ground surrounded by a group of eunuchs dressed in black.

Their leader, an authoritative member of the office of protocol, asked the reason for their presence in Beijing. Ricci put his mind at rest by answering that he was a priest who wished to live in peace in Beijing, honoring the Lord of Heaven, and that he had no intention of asking anything of Wanli in exchange for his gifts. The eunuch explained that it was his task to find out why the clock that so enchanted the Son of Heaven no longer chimed and asked for an explanation of the mechanisms that made the hands move and rang the hours. Ricci told him that they stopped working if the spring was not wound every two or three days. Summarily instructed on how to do this, the eunuchs disappeared into the Forbidden City to report. A *taijian* messenger called on the Jesuits a few days later with the news that the emperor had appointed four eunuch members of the court board of mathematicians to take charge of the clocks and wished the missionaries to teach them everything they needed to know in order to take care of the instruments and wind them whenever necessary.

Ricci and Pantoja were lodged in the Imperial City for three days to give the eunuch mathematicians a crash course on the working principles of mechanical clocks. Since there were no Chinese words for mechanisms and techniques devised in such a different culture, Ricci coined a specific vocabulary in Mandarin for the occasion. Terrified lest they might let some essential detail slip, the eunuchs paid the utmost attention and took meticulous notes on everything he said.

Once the lessons were over, the clocks were taken back to the imperial apartments. Wanli rewarded the eunuchs who had learned how to wind them with promotion to a higher rank and allowed them access to his private rooms every day to check on the smaller clock, from which he could never bear to be parted. The Jesuits' visit proved a godsend to these four *taijian*, who thus acquired greater influence at court and began to receive gifts and manifestations of deference from their colleagues. No object was as dear to Wanli as his clock, as demonstrated by an episode that someone related to the missionaries in violation of the rules of discretion. Intrigued by talk of the "bells that rang by themselves," the Empress Mother asked for the small clock to be brought to her rooms one day. Fearing that she might seek to appropriate it, the Emperor ordered the eunuchs to take it only after it had run down. Hearing no bells chime and being given no explanation as to how the device worked, the Empress found it most disappointing and sent it back to her son, as Wanli had hoped.

The large clock was instead placed in a garden close to the imperial apartments, as it was too cumbersome to be kept in the emperor's rooms. Before this, however, it was further embellished by the court craftsmen with a new and richly decorated wooden base and fitted with a new bell to ring the hours.

The positive response to the clocks enabled the Jesuits to establish a privileged channel of communication with the Son of Heaven, albeit with the *taijian* as intermediaries. The emperor was curious, and few days went by without a eunuch being sent from the court with some new question for the Jesuits. Wanli wanted to know how people lived, ate, dressed, and married in Europe, and what form a royal funeral took. The last question was probably motivated by a desire to compare his now completed mausoleum, to which he attached great importance, with similar edifices in the West. It was not difficult to satisfy his curiosity by describing the burial of Philip II of Spain, who had died just three years earlier. The Jesuits explained that the monarch's remains had been placed in a case of lead inside a wooden coffin in a stone sepulcher in a church.

It is probable that the eunuchs told the Jesuits in turn about the structure of Wanli's huge mausoleum, located about fifty kilometers outside the capital in the area accommodating the tombs of all the Ming emperors from Yongle on. The necropolis was surrounded by a red wall and was reached by means of a road called the Sacred Way lined with a series of imposing stone statues of real and mythological animals, including lions, elephants, unicorns, and camels, whose task it was to guard the burial places. Alongside these were statues of ministers and dignitaries of high rank who had acquired particular merit during their lives. Similar in structure to those of his predecessors, Wanli's tomb consisted of an edifice in which sacrifices were performed and the Soul or Stela Tower, beneath which were the chambers built to hold the remains of the emperor and empress, dressed in the costliest of garments and surrounded by votive objects and symbols of power.

This indirect dialogue with the Jesuits interested Wanli, who expressed a desire to know more about the two sages from the West. The reports of the *taijian* and their minute descriptions of the missionaries' physical appearance and habits were no longer enough. The emperor would have liked to see them for himself, but he was now so used to isolation that he preferred to order the eunuchs to paint life-size portraits and take them to his apartments.

Ricci and Pantoja were summoned to the court once more to pose for the painters. On the agreed day, they were admitted to an area deeper within the Imperial City and even through the second gate, but again without being allowed to meet the Son of Heaven, as they may have hoped. Wanli's curiosity was such that he had the portraits brought to him as soon as they were ready. On seeing the missionaries' long beards, he appears to have remarked that they looked like Muslims, which the *taijian* said was impossible as they had seen them eat pork. Still not satisfied with the information received on the world from which the Jesuits came, Wanli asked how the monarchs of the West dressed and how their palaces were constructed. Having nothing else at his disposal, Ricci sent him a small engraving of Christ surrounded by the kneeling figures of the angels from Heaven, the damned from Hell, and all men on earth, including the pope, the emperor, and the king and queen. Wanli appreciated the sacred image but was unable to distinguish the different figures, and he ordered his painters to produce a much larger copy. Once again, Ricci and Pantoja were summoned to the court to help the artists in their work.

In order to satisfy the emperor's curiosity about European palaces and houses, Ricci provided him with some reproductions of views of the Escorial, built by order of Philip II of Spain, and Saint Mark's Square in Venice. The eunuchs reported that Wanli was amused to see that the buildings in Europe developed vertically. Living like all the Chinese in a horizontal world of buildings and houses constructed at ground level, he saw those of the West as dangerous and inconvenient. Despite his misgivings, however, he appears to have remarked that this was obviously what the Europeans wanted. As

Ricci put it in his history of the mission, "We are all happy with what we have been brought up to."[14]

After an interval of a few days, the now customary scene was repeated, and four *taijian* of authoritative appearance turned up at the Jesuits' door. This time they were members of the imperial office of music with orders to learn how to play the harpsichord presented as a gift by the Jesuits, an instrument completely unknown to them. Ricci had been taught musical theory at the Roman College but appears to have been unable to play any instrument. The expert was Pantoja, who had been taught by Lazzaro Cattaneo when the missionaries were still in Nanjing.

When the missionaries went to the court for the first lesson, the four eunuch musicians bowed not only to them, addressing them solemnly as their masters, but also to the harpsichord as a propitiatory gesture, "as though it was alive." The lessons went on for a number of days, interrupted only by pauses for the abundant meals served in honor of the Western masters. Now well into the month of February, the Jesuits were beginning to feel at home in the Imperial City, where their visits never failed to attract inquisitive groups of high-ranking *taijian*.

Ricci soon left the lessons to Pantoja, who went on teaching the eunuchs with great commitment every day for a month. It was very difficult for his pupils, especially the two oldest ones, to master an instrument and musical technique based on criteria so very different from theirs, and progress was accordingly limited. It was decided that thirty days had to suffice. Before ending the course, they insisted on Pantoja teaching them some songs to perform to the accompaniment of Western music, feeling certain that the emperor would ask them to do so and not wishing to be caught unprepared. Ricci saw this as an excellent opportunity to convey a spiritual and religious message to the Son of Heaven and decided to write the words.

The Jesuit found some compositions on moral subjects in his books, transformed them into songs in Mandarin Chinese, and presented them in a slender volume entitled *Xiqin quyi bazhang* ("Eight Songs for the Western Harpsichord") dedicated to the Son of Heaven. The Jesuit also prepared a version with Chinese characters whose pronunciation reproduced the sounds of the Italian words so that the eunuchs could sing them in the original version.[15]

In line with Ricci's style as an expert in proffering ethical teachings with the light and graceful touch of a humanist, the verses of the songs were composed with the intention of "teaching the right way to live" and not just "delighting the ear."[16]

In the first composition, entitled "My Hopes for Those in High Places," Ricci urged the monarch to honor the Lord of Heaven, to do good, and to be impartial in judging his subjects. He then went on to give sage advice on how to cultivate the virtues and seek spiritual peace in the knowledge of being at the service of the Creator. The last song, "Death Makes Inroads Everywhere," addressed the subject of death, recalling that it strikes rich and poor, stupid and wise, all alike. While Wanli's reaction to this gift is not known, the songs enjoyed success also outside the imperial court. The literati were eager to read them and praised Li Madou for his highly Confucian intention "to teach their king to govern this reign well and to live virtuously in keeping with the demands of his position."[17]

Imprisonment in the "Foreigners' Castle"

While Pantoja went to the court for the daily lessons in Renaissance music, Ricci began the customary round of calls on mandarins whose names he had been given in Nanjing in the hope that they might help to establish his position in the city on a sound basis and thus free him from the tutelage of the eunuch Ma Tang. As these dignitaries were, however, all afraid of compromising themselves through dealings with a foreigner and refused to receive him, he was forced to admit that Ma Tang's intervention had proved useful in securing their arrival at the imperial court and even thanked the Lord for having brought them together.

The future looked very uncertain. Even though the missionaries had been well received at court, their position was precarious and ambiguous because their entry into the capital and presentation of gifts had not taken place under the supervision of the ministry of rites through the office of reception as required by protocol. The head of the office was offended because he had not met the Jesuits and inspected their gifts before their delivery to the Forbidden City, and he was particularly annoyed with Ma Tang for his interference. Being unable to take any action against the eunuch, the *guan* vented his anger on the missionaries by sending a group of guards and agents to order them to report to the ministry of rites and clarify their position.

The soldiers imprisoned the Jesuits in their house and tied them up for fear that they might escape. The agent of Ma Tang who kept constant watch over the missionaries came to their defense and offered them safer accommodation, but Ricci declined, thinking it preferable to give his own version of the facts to the officials at the ministry and show that he had acted in good faith.

The eunuch accompanied him to the ministry in order to intimidate the *guan* but was forced to stand aside. Ricci was taken before the head of the office of reception and kept kneeling for more than an hour before being questioned. Accused of failure to comply with the law, he explained that he had been unable to free himself of the tutelage of Ma Tang and added that he had been living in China for many years and therefore assumed that the protocol established for visiting foreign ambassadors did not apply in his case.

Even though the mandarin seemed to be convinced of the Westerners' good faith, he refused to free them and had them moved to what Ricci called the "foreigners' castle," where all foreign ambassadors were required to live until their audience with the Son of Heaven. This was a dilapidated building that provided accommodation for over a thousand people a year in small rooms with no doors or furnishings that seemed more appropriate for sheep than human beings, as Ricci observed on entering. Moreover, the "foreigners' castle" was a sort of prison. Those lodged there were allowed out only when summoned to the court or in order to return to their homeland. The only positive element in this very disagreeable situation was that Li Madou was granted preferential treatment because of his friends in high places. The director assigned the missionaries a small apartment with chairs, tables, mats, and silk blankets for the night, and invited them to dine with him more than once during their stay, displaying a keen interest in mathematics and astronomy. He was delighted to receive the gift of a celestial globe.

Ricci initially thought that the building accommodated only ambassadors from tributary countries, but he soon discovered that the guests were much more varied. Many were members of delegations sent from distant lands to pay homage to the Son of Heaven, the already high number of which had increased over the years during the Ming period, after Yongle, the third emperor, had initiated diplomatic relations with the countries of Central and Southeast Asia by sending out Chinese emissaries. Most of the countries in the neighboring regions were willing to accept the status of vassal states and adopt the Chinese calendar as a sign of submission to the emperor in exchange for access to the empire's products, most importantly silk, which was in great demand in every part of the world. The delegations of representatives of foreign governments had, however, been joined over the years by ever-increasing numbers of merchants passing themselves off as ambassadors, who arrived in China from more or less distant lands in search of business opportunities. The mechanism was very simple. All they had to do was turn up at the frontier, declare their desire to pay homage to the emperor, and display some gifts, not necessarily of any great value, whereupon permission would be granted for a certain number to continue their journey to the capital entirely at the expense of the Chinese government.

Once inside China, the merchants set about buying goods to sell in Beijing. After the presentation of their gifts at the court, they then bought Chinese goods for sale on return to their own countries. Even though the accommodation provided during their stay in the capital was the most unpleasant imaginable and their movements were kept under the strictest control, the bogus ambassadors obtained substantial financial benefits. Though well aware of the real purpose of these sham embassies, the Chinese government turned a blind eye and allowed the merchants to do good business, as they considered it an easy way to establish cordial relationships with foreign countries and discourage hostile actions. Ricci was astonished at this practice, which he describes as follows in his history of the mission: "They deceive the King of China into thinking that all the world is his and pays him tribute, to the great sorrow of those with a better understanding, who see that it is rather China that pays them tribute."[18]

Having clarified the identity of his fellow prisoners, Ricci took advantage of the opportunity to talk to merchants from Korea, Siam, Cochin China, Burma, Formosa, Tibet, and Mongolia, and he conversed at great length with a group of Muslims from Central Asia who were familiar with Europe. They had done very good business by purchasing crates of rhubarb at the border and selling it in the capital at a handsome profit, and now they planned to buy silk before leaving for their homeland to sell it. Their gifts for the emperor were jade, diamond tips used by the Chinese to work porcelain, and lapis lazuli, the only really precious objects that Ricci saw in the castle. Most of the other merchants brought worthless gifts like half-starved horses or swords and armor that were no more than rusty scrap iron. Ricci's long conversations with the "Saracen" merchants in the gloomy palace not only supplied precious information about their countries of origin and the regions of the empire they had traveled through, but also further evidence that China was Cathay and Beijing Khanbalik, as the Muslims again confirmed that the Middle Kingdom and its capital were still known in their lands by the names that Marco Polo used. The Jesuit wrote to his superiors in India and Europe immediately to reaffirm his discovery and assured them that they "could have all their maps of the world corrected." Once again, there was no reply.

Having adapted with some difficulty to the hardships of life in the castle, Ricci learned from his fellow prisoners that the arrival and departure of groups of ambassadors were marked by sumptuous banquets with musical entertainment and such an abundance of food that the leftovers were sufficient to feed the "guests" in the fortress for several days, as long as they managed to keep them safe from the avaricious guards. Ricci was astonished at this waste of public money, even though he did understand the reasons for such generosity. When those in charge let it be known that they would be willing to allow the missionaries to take part in these banquets in exchange for a small fee, Ricci answered that he had no interest in that kind of overindulgence and would, on the contrary, be willing to pay in order to be sure that nothing of the kind was organized in his honor.

Notes

1. FR, p. 123, no. 4.

2. Jacques Gernet, *Le Monde chinois* (Paris: A. Colin, 1972), [trad. it. Torino: Einaudi, 1978, p. 411].

3. See P. Buckley Ebrey, op. cit., p. 201.

4. Published in China in 1610 and translated into English by Clement Egerton as *The Golden Lotus*, 4 vols. (London: 1938). The translation by David Tod Roy (*The Plum in the Golden Vase, or Chin P'ing Mei*, Princeton University Press) is still incomplete at the time of this writing.

5. Mario Sabattini and Paolo Santangelo, *Storia della Cina* (Rome-Bari: Laterza, 1996).

6. FR, book IV, ch. XII, p. 124, no. 1.

7. FR, book IV, ch. XII, pp. 123–24, no. 5.

8. FR, book IV, ch. XII, pp. 123–24, no. 4.

9. Crowned by a gigantic portrait of Mao Zedong, this gate now provides access to the northern side of the huge square of the same name.

10. This area included the present-day Beihai Park and the Zhongnanhai district, where the most important offices of the People's Republic of China are now located, as well as the private homes of the highest officials.

11. Wanli reigned for forty-seven years, from 1573 to 1620, longer than any other Ming emperor. The second longest was the forty-four-year reign of Jiajing from 1522 to 1566.

12. The information in the following lines is drawn from the above-cited work by R. Huang.

13. FR, book IV, ch. XII, p. 125.

14. Ibid., p. 131.

15. See Pasquale D'Elia, "Sonate e canzoni italiane alla corte di Pechino in 1601," *Civiltà Cattolica* 96, no. 3 (1945): pp. 158–65; "Musica e canti italiani a Pechino (marzo–aprile 1601)," *Rivista degli studi orientali* 30 (1955): pp. 131–45.

16. FR, book IV, ch. XII, pp. 134–35, no. 6.

17. Ibid., p. 135.

18. Ibid., book V, ch. XIV, p. 433.

CHAPTER THIRTEEN

~

The Empty Throne

Beijing, 1601

I recently saw Ricci's map with his notes, the maps printed by Europeans, and the map of Nanjing printed on six sheets, and realized for the first time the immensity of the heavens and the earth.

—Liang Zhou[1]

The Master taught under four categories: culture, proper conduct, doing one's utmost, and making good on one's word.

—Confucius, *Analects* (7, 25)

The Audience in the Forbidden City

After the Jesuits had spent a few days in the "foreigners' castle" around the end of February and the beginning of March 1601, the director sent a messenger with the news that Ricci had been waiting for ever since he first set foot on Chinese soil. They had been granted an audience with the emperor.

The missionaries hoped for a meeting with Wanli that would constitute a turning point in their work, an opportunity to ask for permission to preach the Christian religion all through the empire, but this long-cherished dream was not so close to fulfillment. It was indeed clear that the Jesuits had only been admitted to a general audience and were very unlikely to be allowed to speak to Wanli, even though Ricci may have dreamed of thus initiating closer contact with the Son of Heaven.

In preparation for the ceremony, the two missionaries received instruction from officials responsible for protocol, who showed them how to kneel before the emperor and kowtow, bowing their foreheads to the ground three times. They also tried on the special robes of red damask silk and gold lacquered caps and were each given an ivory tablet called a *hu* to be held in front of the face as a sign of respect. Woken long before dawn on the great day, they were led through the dark and still deserted streets into the Imperial City all the way to a gate providing access to the Forbidden City, where they waited for hours in the bitter cold together with a group of foreign ambassadors and officials summoned to give thanks for favors, appointments, and awards.

The deep blue sky lightened and took on a rosy hue at sunrise as the golden beams spread over the Forbidden City and brought the colors to life. The dark red of the walls began to glow and the yellow of the roofs to shine. The gate finally opened, and the three thousand soldiers of the night guard emerged with five elephants. Ricci and Pantoja, the first Europeans to enter the heart of the Ming empire, passed through the massive wall and found themselves in a huge courtyard right in front of the arcade of the Palace of Supreme Harmony and the five doors to the chamber where the imperial throne of gilded rosewood normally stood, surrounded by dark red columns decorated with golden dragons. The throne had been moved outside for the audience and positioned to face the courtyard below.[2]

Ricci estimated that the enormous square could hold about thirty thousand people. The marble staircase rising to the imposing edifice was lined on either side by eunuchs holding colored imperial banners. Ambassadors, soldiers, and dignitaries were arranged in perfectly aligned rows and were positioned according to rank. Civilians occupied the eastern section, which was considered more prestigious, and military commanders the western. The courtyard was only one of the areas of the imperial complex made occasionally accessible to the public, while the rest of the citadel remained hidden and impenetrable.

The Forbidden City was a galaxy of palaces, gardens, streams, and pavilions,[3] each of which was endowed with an evocative poetic name exemplifying the sophisticated use of language in which the Chinese excelled. Rectangular in shape and covering an area of over seventy-two hectares, its typically Chinese structure still preserves its extraordinary charm intact today despite the passage of time. The layout of the buildings was designed to reproduce the celestial order and draw a parallel between the emperor and the pole star, the throne room and the pavilions for the imperial rites being located at the center of the great complex along the north-south axis, with the other buildings symmetrically arranged on either side to mirror the positions of the circumpolar stars. The similarity between the heavens and the earth was not perfect because the layout of the Forbidden City, unlike the nearby Temple of Heaven, was a triumph of straight lines and rectangular geometric shapes with no reference to the circularity of the celestial vault. The idea of cosmic space was suggested rather by the vastness of the courtyards and the succession of walls and gates, apparently all the same but actually differing in size and minute details, which spread out to give the idea of a closed but infinite universe.

The main gates were located at the four cardinal points of the compass, and the most important was the Meridian Gate or Wumen, a one-story construction with the customary double-eaved roof of yellow tiles and three arches. The central arch was for the exclusive use of the emperor, the only exceptions being the empress on her wedding day and the three candidates ranked highest in the third-level examinations held in the imperial palace. Running through the first large courtyard on the other side of the Meridian Gate was a small watercourse, known as the Golden Stream, crossed by five marble bridges. The Gate of Supreme Harmony to the north gave access to the true centers of power. Beyond it lay the huge courtyard into which Ricci had been admitted, where the three palaces of the imperial rites stood one after the other on an enormous marble platform. This was reached by three flights of steps, in the center of which a gigantic ramp of white marble carved with a pattern of intertwining lotus flowers looked like an unrolled carpet. In wet weather, the rainwater was channeled onto this surface from either side of the balustrade through the mouths of over a thousand stone dragons, thus transforming the structure into an unusual fountain. The first building was the Palace of Supreme Harmony, which housed the throne and provided the setting for the most important ceremonies, such as the coronation of the Son of Heaven. The smaller Palace of Perfect Harmony was where the emperor performed the preparatory rites before proceeding to the Temple of Heaven. Banquets in honor of the ambassadors of tributary countries and the third-level imperial examinations were held in the Palace of Protecting Harmony.

The way out of the elevated structure was by a staircase to the north adorned with the largest marble panel in the Forbidden City, a block of 250 metric tons decorated with clouds and dragons that had been hauled from the outskirts of Beijing one winter along a 50-kilometer road of ice created by pouring water onto the ground. Farther north, the Gate of Celestial Purity led to the imperial apartments, the most private part of the citadel and surrounded by yet another ring of walls. Located on a single-story marble platform were the Palace of Celestial Purity, where the emperor slept, the Pavilion of Union, containing the throne room, and the Palace of Earthly

Tranquility, where the empress lived. A garden to the north led to the Gate of Spiritual Value, the exit from the Forbidden City.

The buildings used for minor ceremonies and the quarters of the palace eunuchs and the emperor's other wives and concubines were located in the greenery on either side of the central axis where the six most important palaces stood. They too bore poetic names such as Benevolent Tranquility, Peaceful Longevity, Eternal Spring, Concentrated Beauty, and Admirable Benevolence.

Symbolism informed the choice of every color and decorative detail, a concentration of centuries of tradition that encompassed every element of the architecture and endowed it with ritual significance. The most recurrent image, painted on columns or carved in marble, was the emperor's dragon emblem, together with the phoenix of the empress. The four curved sides of every roof were crowned with a procession of small majolica sculptures of dragons, lions, and mythological beasts to provide protection against evil spirits, its length being proportional to the importance of the building. This was preceded in some cases by a guardian spirit on a winged horse, to which a small monkey, the symbol of dexterity, was added only above the throne room. In the gardens, enormous stone turtles symbolized longevity, strength, and endurance. The crane-shaped braziers of bronze on the terraces were emblems of good luck. The entrances of the most important buildings were flanked by the typical pairs of stone or bronze lions with curly manes and gaping jaws, symbols of power that served to intimidate visitors. The number nine, associated with the organization of the universe, was constantly recalled on the red gates providing access to the palaces and courtyards, each of which was adorned with eighty-one gilded studs laid out in nine rows of nine elements.

It was easy to lose track in observing the details of a world so rich in symbolic allusions, just as it was easy to lose your way on walking through the countless courtyards and the small side doors leading into long, narrow corridors like the passageways of a labyrinth. The Forbidden City has been described as a disorienting maze of straight lines, or a nightmare of déjà vu. The symbolic heart of the great and ancient Chinese empire unquestionably communicated the idea of power and strength but also a sense of peace and immensity. Matteo Ricci saw practically nothing outside the courtyard where the audiences were held and devoted only a few lines of his writings to a description of the Forbidden City, a place that was to remain as secret and distant for him as it was for all the emperor's subjects. Despite his subsequent visits to the Forbidden City, he was never able to explore it freely, and he never managed to form an overall impression, as his knowledge was limited to a few pavilions and corridors.

Ricci waited for the audience to begin, together with the others in that vast courtyard in front of the Palace of Supreme Harmony. The black-clad eunuchs in charge moved swiftly up and down the rows to make sure that everything was in order, and the censors kept watch for any suspicious movement. Finally, a precise order was echoed from line to line, and the ritual commenced.

The participants were taken onto the terrace in groups by officials who prompted them aloud in their performance of the ritual gestures and formulas so as to avoid any mistakes. On arrival before the imperial throne, they bowed and repeated the greeting "ten thousand years," a formula used exclusively to wish the Son of Heaven a long life, while keeping the *hu* in front of their faces. On looking at the throne, Ricci realized that there was no one seated there, but he knelt down just the same when his turn came and addressed the phrase to the empty seat like all of those before and after him. The audience, organized by palace officials in accordance with a set schedule out of respect for tradition, was a grotesque charade performed every time in the absence of the leading character, as Wanli had stopped taking part many years earlier. Even though Ricci had probably been warned that he was not going to meet the Son of Heaven, it is reasonable to assume that he felt some disappointment. There is, however, no mention of this in his surviving letters or his history of the mission, where the audience is described with no comment. Ricci did not see the emperor at the audience in February 1601 and was never to meet him. He simply had to resign himself to this.

Other Memorials on the Ricci Case

Having ascertained that direct contact with Wanli was impossible, the Jesuit was determined to obtain permission to live in Beijing and intended to do so in compliance with the set procedures. He thus lost no time in calling at the ministry of rites, where he was received by the vice minister. When he handed over his memorial and asked for it to be forwarded to the emperor, it was immediately clear that the mandarin was intent on handling the matter in his own way, raising the customary difficulties for the sole purpose of demonstrating his power. Ricci found himself in much the same situation every time he had any dealings with the bureaucracy, just as nerve-wracking in China as it probably was in pontifical Rome or the kingdom of Spain.

The vice minister explained that he could not deliver the missionary's memorial but would have to write a new one himself with his appraisal of the situation after a customary examination of the case. He thus ordered yet another inventory of the Jesuits' assets, which established that the *daoren* possessed no valuables but only books and holy relics, and then sent a memorial to the court with instructions that it was to be kept secret. Ricci ended up getting wind of its contents all the same. As was to be expected, it was by no means favorable. It can be summarized as follows: "Li Madou claims that he is from the Far West, but there is no mention of any such place in the Ming dynastic histories and it is therefore impossible to know whether he is telling the truth. Since he has come to offer tributes to the emperor after living on Chinese territory for twenty years, the law for the treatment of foreign ambassadors is not applicable in his case. The gifts he offered to the emperor are insignificant and of little value. Moreover, objects [the holy relics] have been found in his baggage that he claims to be the bones of spirits, but if spirits have no bodies, how can Li Madou have their bones?"[4]

The document went on to urge that no gifts should be accepted from the missionaries and accused Ricci of having presented objects through the intercession of the eunuch Ma Tang and therefore sharing his guilt in the violation of procedure. It ended with the suggestion that Li Madou should be given some lengths of silk, a hat, and a belt, and ordered to go back to his own country. He should not be allowed to reside in Beijing or Nanjing because of the risk that he might cultivate his good relations with the eunuchs and incite rebellion. Even though the suggested gift of a hat and belt, typical accessories of state officials, was a mark of consideration, the tone of the document left no room for doubt. The stance adopted by the vice minister was the result of a power struggle between the eunuchs and the ministry of rites over the case of Li Madou, and the Jesuits were to bear the brunt of it. Ricci felt sure, however, that the emperor and the palace eunuchs would be on his side, and events proved him right. The memorial received no reply, which was something quite extraordinary for a document sent by the ministry of rites. The emperor evidently did not agree.

Rumors filtered through from the court that Wanli had been furious to learn of Li Madou being locked up in the foreigners' castle. While it was of course impossible to establish whether the words attributed to the emperor—"Are these men perhaps robbers to have been treated in this way?"[5]—were actually spoken or instead simply circulated in order to favor the missionaries, the monarch clearly had no intention of expelling them and had decided to adopt the tried and tested tactic of passive resistance to the pressure of the bureaucracy. The eunuchs responsible for the clocks also clearly wanted Ricci to stay, as they were terrified at the idea of the precious devices breaking down with no possibility of asking the missionaries for advice about how to repair them.

A month after the delivery of the document to the court, the bureaucrats began to feel alarmed at the emperor's prolonged silence and the possibility of a vendetta on the part of the eunuchs in Li Madou's favor. For fear of repri-sals, the director of the foreigners' castle allowed Ricci to leave the building during the day for the customary courtesy visits but ordered four guards to keep constant watch over him and prevent any attempt to escape.

In the meantime, now realizing that he had made a mistake by asking for the missionaries to be expelled, the vice minister drew up a second and far more positive memorial and sent Ricci a copy to show his goodwill. Here too, however, there was no request for a residence permit for the Jesuits. The omission was intentional because the emperor was empowered by procedure to grant such authorization only in response to an explicit request on the part of the relevant authorities.

Time passed and it became known that the ministry of rites had sent another three memorials on the case of Li Madou to the court without once asking for the missionaries to be granted permission to reside in Beijing and without once receiving a reply from Wanli. Exasperated by the continuing deadlock and his restricted liberty, Ricci turned to Cao Yubian, an official of the ministry of personnel and the only bureaucrat to have displayed any friendliness toward him during the early days of his stay in Beijing, for help in obtaining permission to leave the foreigners' castle. The mandarin exerted pressure, and the director, who was of lower rank, was forced to come up with some expedient in order to free the Jesuits. It was decided that Ricci should write a letter indicating serious problems of health. For once in his life, the Jesuit agreed to resort to a stratagem for his own benefit. The falsehood was confirmed, and he was freed together with his companions in the month of May. The missionaries moved into rented accommodations but retained the right to be supplied with provisions and firewood free of charge by the state.

As Ricci wrote, "We were very glad and gave thanks to God at now being able to regain some of the good reputation lost during our semi-imprisonment in that castle."[6]

Ricci Settles in Beijing by Order of the Emperor

Now as free as a foreigner could be in imperial China, Ricci set about getting his own memorial delivered to the court while avoiding any involvement of officials of the ministry of rites, and he was astonished to succeed without encountering any obstacles at all. While his petition also remained unan-swered, the significance of the emperor's silence was very different in this case from his failure to reply to the ministry of rites, as those in the know were quick to explain. It was in fact now clearly established that Wanli wanted the missionaries to remain in Beijing, but also that he could not grant them residence permits without the ministry's prior approval. Wanli therefore preferred to make no specific pronouncement on the assumption that his prolonged silence already spoke volumes. So it was, without any official document having been drawn up or any order given, that Ricci learned from the palace eunuchs that his request had been granted. The missionaries would be allowed to reside in Beijing indefinitely and to receive a handsome stipend from the state with the emperor's consent and no possibility of any objection being raised. The ministry of rites was obliged to accept the situation, and the director of the foreigners' castle even summoned Ricci for the express purpose of congratulating him on his success, observing with uncommon deference that Beijing was big enough to accommodate one more foreigner.

When the news spread, all the missionaries' friends and acquaintances, starting with Cao Yubian, came to express their delight, and there was very soon a whole procession of dignitaries eager to meet Li Madou, Xitai, the scholar from the West who had obtained the emperor's protection. The influx was such that the street where the Jesuits lived was constantly blocked with litters and horses guarded by a host of servants.

A young literatus called one day with a gift and a request for lessons in Western mathematics. He declared himself a disciple of the illustrious scholar Feng Yingjing, a convinced anti-Buddhist and orthodox Confucianist who knew and admired the works of Li Madou. Feng Yingjing was one of the few mandarins who had had the courage to oppose a powerful eunuch, thus bringing about his own downfall. His story was well known in the city. Having become a *jinshi* in 1592, he was serving as provincial judge in Huguang (now divided between the provinces of Hunan and Hubei) and was greatly respected for his integrity. When the eunuch Chen Feng arrived in his district to organize the collection of taxes and began to employ the brutal methods for which the *taijian* were known, the *guan* took action by reporting his crimes in three memorials sent to the emperor. Wanli's only response was to have the mandarin recalled to Beijing, stripped of his position, and imprisoned.

On hearing this story, Ricci visited the *guan* in prison, and the two men soon came to know and respect one another. Having ascertained Feng Yingjing's readiness to learn about the Christian religion and feeling sure that he would be able to secure his conversion one day, Ricci asked him to read the manuscript of his catechism, which was still in progress. Feng Yingjing was so convinced of the value of Ricci's works and the importance of their circulation that he gave orders from prison that the treatises on friendship and the four elements and some of the maps were to be reprinted at his expense. He also penned an introduction for each work and referred to Ricci in all of his writings as a *jinshi*, the title used for scholars who successfully completed the third level of the imperial examinations. This decision influenced the other literati, and Ricci was customarily attributed this qualification henceforth. The Jesuit was flattered to have become an honorary metropolitan graduate and regarded this prestigious title as conferring added luster on the Society of Jesus, even though it had not been earned by sitting the examinations.

Ricci's friend, who did so much from prison to foster the circulation of the Jesuit's works, was never to convert. On being released three years later, when a general amnesty was granted for the appearance of a comet in the sky (October 10, 1604), he moved to Nanjing and died there without meeting the missionaries again. This provided further evidence that many Chinese intellectuals were as sincerely interested in Ricci's works on ethics and science as they were suspicious of his religious teachings, and that most of them preferred to take the prudent course of avoiding or delaying such a great commitment as the decision to convert to Catholicism.

The stream of visitors increased steadily, and not a day went by without a minister, vice minister, or military commander calling on the Jesuits. Ricci made them all gifts of globes, sundials, and small clocks, and engaged in lengthy discussions on philosophical and moral subjects with figures like the minister of personnel Li Dai and the scholar Feng Qi, who was soon to be appointed minister of rites.

The missionaries' social position was definitively established by a meeting with the grand secretary Shen Jiaomen, who called on Li Madou at home as a sign of respect and graciously accepted the gift of a precious ebony sundial. The *guan* then held a banquet in Ricci's honor and asked him a great many questions about the European way of life. According to the Jesuit's account, he was impressed above all by the fact that Westerners had only one wife. Being well aware that polygamy was one of the main obstacles to the conversion of mandarins, Ricci always laid great stress on this aspect of life in the West.

Many dignitaries followed the grand secretary's example and organized banquets in honor of Xitai, who seemed to have received more invitations during the first few months of his stay in Beijing than in all his previous years on Chinese soil, sometimes as many as two or three in the same day. The missionaries tired themselves out rushing from house to house in an effort to keep everyone happy and avoid giving offence, but they were obliged even so to decline some invitations due to the absolute lack of time. Now that they were treated as equals by the ruling class, Ricci was sorry to see that they received no visits from the poor in Beijing, who were unquestionably intimidated by their popularity with the rich and privileged.

One day they received a visit from the *taijian* responsible for the emperor's clocks, who had not called in a long time. Being very worried because the large clock had stopped working despite regular winding, they had brought it with them to make sure that Ricci would examine it immediately and left it with the Jesuits for repair.

The stream of visitors increased enormously as soon as it was known that an object belonging to the emperor was to be found in Li Madou's house. The opportunity to admire a unique work of art temporarily removed from the heart of the palace was something that happened only once in a lifetime.

Wanli was annoyed when he heard about this and ordered the eunuchs to take the clock back to the court immediately. It was never again to be taken out of the Forbidden City on pain of dire punishment. In the event of a breakdown, the Jesuits would be allowed to enter the imperial palace to repair it. Moreover, to ensure that these orders were always obeyed, Ricci decided to authorize the Jesuits in advance to enter the Forbidden City four times a year to service the clocks. Combined with the freedom already acquired to go in and out of the Imperial City at will, this right of access to areas kept strictly off limits to other subjects increased Ricci's prestige to the point that the wholly groundless rumor began to spread that the Jesuit had enjoyed the privilege of meeting the emperor.

Li Zhizao and Geography:
The Third Edition of the Map of the World

Friendship with the prisoner Feng Yingjing preceded a meeting that was to prove still more significant for the future of the mission. This came about in the customary way, when a young *guan* from Hangzhou in the southeastern province of Zhejiang called one day and asked to see Li Madou. Having worked in Nanjing as assistant to the minister of public works there, Li Zhizao had recently been called to Beijing to take up an analogous position.[7] Now aged thirty-six, thirteen years younger than Ricci, he had graduated as a *jinshi* three years before the Jesuits' arrival in Beijing, ranked eighth out of three hundred candidates. In the course of their long conversation, Li Zhizao examined the Jesuit's books and above all his map of the world. Geography was one of his own particular areas of interest, and he had in fact drawn a map of China with a description of the provinces of the empire some years earlier.

From geography, the two men went on to discuss other subjects in an exchange of ideas that continued over the next few days. Ricci realized that the *guan* was open to every new form of knowledge, and Li Zhizao that Li Madou was not only a sage who would tell him about faraway countries but also a man of great spiritual conviction willing to introduce him to an interwoven universe of mathematics, geometry, and moral values.

This new friend thus called assiduously at the missionaries' house in his free time to learn the secrets of Western knowledge. Ricci tells us that Li Zhizao studied with him for a year, making every effort to understand the Ptolemaic model of the universe and performing calculations for hours on end. On observing his determination to grasp the new concepts and verify the consistency of the geocentric system, Ricci realized that he had found an enthusiastic collaborator, and a fruitful intellectual relationship soon developed. It was now evident that many *shidafu* were aware of the importance of science and technology and were eager to explore new worldviews and philosophies other than the narrowly specialized and dogmatic knowledge required for success in the imperial examinations.

Li Zhizao was interested above all in geography and had little difficulty persuading Ricci to prepare a new edition of his map of the world. The Jesuit set to work at the beginning of the summer of 1601 and produced the *Kunyu wanguo quantu* ("Complete Map of the Countless Countries of the Earth") in the space of a year. It was printed between August and September 1602 on six panels of Chinese paper that could be mounted side by side on a screen measuring approximately four meters by two. As in the previous maps, the countries of the world were shown inside an oval to indicate the spherical nature of the earth, and China was placed in the middle, but there were also many new details. In addition to the equator, this new version showed the tropics of Cancer and Capricorn, which appeared here for the first time on a map in Chinese, and divided the globe into five climatic zones in relation to variations in latitude: the torrid zone cut by the equator, the two subtropical zones, and the two polar regions. Following the atlas of Ortelius, Ricci placed the zero meridian in the Fortunate Isles, the present-day Canaries, and drew the lines of latitude and longitude every ten degrees.

While employing the techniques introduced by European cartography, Ricci followed the Chinese tradition of combining the map with a large section of written text, as in the two previous editions. This version provided geographic, astronomical, naturalistic, and historical information in still greater detail, as well as descriptions of the ways of life and customs of the different peoples. The maps of Petrus Plancius, Mercator, and Ortelius were used as a basis for the characteristics of the Western countries, and the content of Chinese maps, probably with the help of Li Zhizao, were used for the description of China and other regions of Asia. Ricci is thought, for example, to have drawn on local cartography for the use of a series of dots to represent the desert, a convention unknown in the West at the time but commonly used in Chinese maps.[8]

Ricci, whose mastery of Chinese was now considerable, managed to include one thousand place names as against the thirty of the previous edition. He used the Chinese names found on the maps drawn during the voyages of discovery undertaken by the eunuch Zheng He at the beginning of the Ming era for some localities on the coast of Africa. As in the previous editions, Ricci used characters related to the meaning of the words or constituting phonetic transcriptions of the same in devising Chinese names for places unknown to the inhabitants of the Middle Kingdom. As Ricci's birthplace, the Marche was the first Italian region to have a Chinese version of its name. Ricci had the opportunity to create Mandarin names for the world, and many of his toponyms are still used in Chinese atlases today.

The text was closely written in small, neat characters on either side of the map, and in some panels text was inserted in the oceans or in the Antarctic region, where no names appeared. The descriptions of the countries are a curious mixture of objectivity and approximation. In presenting Italy, Ricci wrote that the pope, the head of the Catholic Church, lived in Rome, observed the vow of celibacy, and was revered by all of the other European nations. He noted that "there are no poisonous snakes and other types of insects" in England. He described China as "the land of the Great Ming Dynasty," "famous for its culture and its products," and gave details of its latitude.[9] All of the empire's tributary countries were included, and a great deal of space was devoted to Japan, emphasizing the warlike nature of its inhabitants. As usually happened when the imagination was still called upon to compensate for a lack of direct evidence, his description of the characteristics of various countries combined historical fact with fantastic details and bizarre legends of both Western and Chinese origin. He described people with bovine hooves or just one eye; races of dwarves preyed upon by cranes and obliged to take refuge in caverns, who gave birth at the age of five and reached old age at eight; and a land of spirits in northern Asia, whose inhabitants had mouths in their necks and fed on snakes and deer.

Ricci also endeavored to supply written lessons in astronomy and applied mathematics. Together with a representation of the Ptolemaic universe in the four corners of the panel, he included a drawing of an armillary sphere and added two small drawings of the southern and northern hemispheres as well as two diagrams to explain the mechanism of solar and lunar eclipses. He described the movement of planets, illustrated the method for measuring the size of the earth and the moon, provided a comparative table with the dimensions of the planets and their distance from the earth, and presented two methods for determining the altitude of a locality.

In the customary preface presenting the map to the Chinese public, Ricci paid tribute to his hosts by claiming that it was admiration for the greatness of China that had brought him from the West, but he did not forget to stress the magnificence of God, the Lord of Heaven and Earth. This was followed by presentations written by Li Zhizao and three other scholarly friends as well as the preface of Wu Zuohai for the Nanjing edition of the map of the world.

The new map was a great success, and Li Zhizao had countless copies printed for friends. The work proved so popular and the demand so great that the printers duplicated the wood blocks and ran off an unauthorized version that circulated at the same time as the official one. The map of 1602 was the most famous and had the greatest number of reproductions made, even outside of China. Five complete copies have survived, one of which is now in the Vatican Library.

Some of the printed copies were painted in different colors to differentiate the five continents. In addition to the printed copies, with or without coloring, hand-painted copies were also made, often by the eunuchs of the imperial palace. The Chinese continued to reproduce Ricci's map of the world over the years, and the copies painted by hand were embellished from the end of the seventeenth century on[10] with depictions of ships sailing across the oceans; denizens of the deep like whales, sharks, and walruses; and more or less fantastic land animals like ostriches, elephants, rhinoceroses, and dinosaurs. Of the six surviving copies of the complete map made by hand, one displays an extraordinarily good state of preservation. Of undetermined date, it is painted on paper with great delicacy in light colors and is decorated with sailing ships and animals. Found in the Liulichang district of Beijing in 1923 and held in the museum of the Forbidden City until 1936, it was then transferred to the archives of the Nanjing Museum, where it still remains. After passing through the hands of various collectors, the only part of a hand-painted copy surviving in the West, the third of the six panels containing a depiction of a whale, is now in a small museum of whale hunting at Sharon, Massachusetts, eighty kilometers south of Boston.[11]

Constellations, Arithmetic, and Christian Doctrine

Fully convinced of the importance of disseminating the knowledge he was acquiring in his studies among the other scholars and literati, Li Zhizao offered to help Li Madou translate some of the works in the Jesuit's possession, as Qu Taisu had done years earlier with the first book of Euclid's *Elements*.

Ricci accepted gladly, and together they translated the "Treatise on the Constellations"—a poem of 420 septenary verses that the missionary had found the time to write in the early months of his residence in Beijing—into Chinese as *Jingtian gai*. The work described the major Chinese constellations together with the names, relative positions, and brightness of the most important stars situated in the zodiac, the region of the sky around the pole star, and the intermediate area between the two. The use of the poetic form, something unusual for Ricci, may well have been a device to aid memorization.

The decision to devote the first book of astronomy in Chinese to the constellations was by no means fortuitous. Identifiable among the countless dots of light in the heavens by virtue of their characteristic conformations, these clusters of stars were in fact indispensable points of reference for any study of the celestial vault.

The Chinese astronomers of antiquity had already identified a larger number of constellations and stars than the Greeks. In the case of the Plow or Big Dipper, an asterism known to all the ancient peoples, the configuration was the same as described by the Greeks. Its name, *Bei Dou*, or "Northern Dipper," refers to a large wooden ladle that served as a unit of measurement for grain. In China as in the other countries of the world, peasants had learned to determine the period of the year by the angle of its handle to the horizon.

Having completed the translation of this small volume, Li Zhizao decided to continue with the study of Clavius's *Epitome arithmeticae praticae* (1583) under Ricci's guidance, and he began work on a translation of certain sections that was finished in 1608 and published in 1613 as the *Tongwen suanzhi* or "Treatise on Arithmetic." Aimed at all literati interested in learning the art of "calculation with the brush," it gave the rules for performing the operations of addition, subtraction, multiplication, and division as well as the extraction of roots in writing so as to dispense with the traditional Chinese abacus.

As Ricci wrote in his history of the mission, Li Zhizao "translated all of Father Clavius's *Practical Arithmetic* without omitting anything and indeed with the addition of the way to extract roots, square, cube and so on *usque to infinitum*, a source of great wonder in China. . . . And all this with pen and ink, something quite new in this land, where people can only count with a certain instrument [the abacus] made for that purpose."[12]

Even though Chinese mathematics was less backward in the Ming era than Ricci believed,[13] as we have seen, it is a fact that the Chinese had been outstripped by Westerners in the search for general theories for the solution of equations and had not yet begun to use symbols rather than words in writing mathematical expressions, as is commonly done today. Europe had already begun to introduce symbols into mathematics, and some recently adopted forms of modern notation were exported to China first by Ricci but above all by the Jesuits who were to come after him.

It was precisely during that period in Europe that rhetorical algebra, where a mathematical expression was described in words, gave way to syncopated algebra, where symbols and words were mixed as the first step toward the totally symbolic algebra that was to dispense entirely with words and use only letters of the alphabet. The process was gradual but unstoppable, as the adoption of symbols simplified calculations and made it possible to develop mathematical theories of an increasingly general character. While the Latin term *res* was still commonly used in the sixteenth century for the unknown in an equation (like *cosa* in Italy and *Coss* in Germany), Clavius had already adopted a sign analogous to the "x" generally employed today, together with other symbols that have since fallen into disuse, as outlined in his *Algebra*, published at the beginning of the seventeenth century, whose content may have been partially known to Ricci. The symbols + and − used today to indicate the operations of addition and subtraction were introduced in Germany halfway through the previous century, while the letters *p* (for *più*: plus) and *m* (for *meno*: minus) were used in Italy. The equals sign (=) appeared for the first time in the West in *The Whetstone of Witte*, written by the Welsh mathematician Robert Recorde (1510–1558) in 1557, but was not used in Clavius's work on algebra and was therefore probably unknown to Ricci, being introduced together with the other algebraic symbols by the Jesuits who arrived in China in later years. It is worth noting that Recorde also wrote a book on mathematics and astronomy entitled *The Castle of Knowledge* which he dedicated to English travelers intent on reaching the mythical land of Cathay.

Though delighted to have a collaborator as scientifically gifted as Li Zhizao, Ricci did not forget his religious mission and soon began to speak during the lessons of astronomy and mathematics about the Lord of Heaven, the creator of the heavens and the earth and supreme lawgiver of the universe, and to illustrate the principles of the Christian religion. The *shidafu* listened to the religious instruction with the same attention as he paid to the scientific teaching. As he was to write in the prefaces to some of Ricci's works, he was greatly impressed by the Jesuit's personality, strength of character, probity, and ability to address ethical and mathematical subjects with the same profundity. For him, Ricci was the "perfect" master and embodiment of the Confucian virtues, capable of improving himself through study and the practice of the virtues.[14] Li Zhizao was won over by the Jesuit's teaching and was willing to receive baptism but had to be dissuaded "due to the impediment of polygamy."[15] The scholar had a concubine that he had no intention of repudiating. Having secured Li Zhizao's promise that he would rectify his marital position sooner or later, Ricci resigned himself to waiting for the fruits ripened through the teaching of science.

Notes

1. Cit. in T. N. Foss, "La cartografia di Matteo Ricci," cit., p. 181.

2. This was the fourth courtyard encountered after entering by the southern gate of the Imperial City and passing through four gates one after the other. Those granted an audience were probably admitted through a side entrance to the Forbidden City and were taken to the courtyard by a shorter route.

3. Among the many descriptions available, readers are referred to May Holdsworth and Caroline Courtauld, *The Forbidden City* (Hong Kong: Odyssey Publications, 1995).

4. FR, book IV, ch. XIII, p. 147, no. 3.

5. Cited by Ricci: see FR, book IV, ch. XIII, p. 148.

6. FR, book IV, ch. XIII, p. 151.

7. For Li Zhizao and the other best-known Chinese converts, see Willard J. Peterson, "Why Did They Become Christians? Yang T'ing-yun, Li Chih-tsao, and Hsu Kuang-ch'i," in *East Meets West: The Jesuits in China, 1582–1773*, ed. Charles E. Ronan and Bonnie B. C. Oh (Chicago: Loyola University Press, 1988), pp. 129–52; Nicolas Standaert, ed., *The Handbook of Christianity in China* (Leiden: Brill, 2001), pp. 404 ff; Jacques Gernet, "Gli ambienti intellettuali cinesi all'epoca del Ricci," in *Atti del convegno internazionale di Studi Ricciani, Macerata-Roma, 22–25 ottobre 1982*, ed. Maria Cigliano (Macerata: Centro Studi Ricciani, 1984), p. 121.

8. T. N. Foss, "La cartografia di Matteo Ricci," cit., p. 183.

9. Ricci calculated from 15° to 42° of latitude north. It was impossible to calculate longitude precisely in his day. In the Ming era, China extended from 18° of the island of Mainan in the south to 42° north, from 70° to 125° east of Greenwich.

10. "I am inclined to believe that the maps of the world with wild animals, sea monsters, and caravels are all subsequent to 1672, the year in which they were first seen on the maps of Ferdinand Verbiest," (*Il Mappamondo cinese del Padre Matteo Ricci*, cit., p. 103, no. 2).

11. For Ricci's map of the world, see P. D'Elia, preface to *Il Mappamondo cinese del Padre Matteo Ricci*, cit.; Theodore N. Foss, "A Western Interpretation of China: Jesuit Cartography," in Charles E. Ronan and Bonnie B. C. Oh (eds.), op. cit., pp. 209, 251; T. N. Foss, "La cartografia di Matteo Ricci," cit., pp. 177–95; John D. Day, "The Search for the Origins of the Chinese Manuscript of Matteo Ricci's Maps," in *Imago Mundi* 47 (1995): pp. 94–117; Yu Dong and John D. Day, "The Mappamundi of Matteo Ricci," in *Miscellanea Bibliothecae Apostolicae Vaticanae, VI, Collectanea in honorem Rev.mi Patris Leonardi Boyle, O.P. septuagesimum quintum annum feliciter complentis* (*Studi e testi;* 385) (Vatican City: 1998); Isaia Iannaccone, "Matteo Ricci e l'introduzione delle scienze occidentali in Cina," in *Le Marche e l'Oriente, Atti del convegno internazionale di Studi Ricciani, Macerata, 23–26 ottobre 1996*, ed.

Francesco D'Arelli (Rome: Istituto Italiano per l'Africa e l'Oriente), 1998; Gaetano Ricciardolo, "Geografia e cartografia in Matteo Ricci S.J. La determinazione delle coordinate geografiche della Cina," in *Le Marche e l'Oriente*, cit.; R. Smith, op. cit.

12. FR, book IV, ch. XV, pp. 175–76.

13. See chapter 6 ("Doing Sums with Brush and Paper").

14. Li Zhizao's opinions of Ricci are taken from his prefaces to Ricci's "The Chapters of an extraordinary Man" and other works by the Jesuit. Cf. W.J. Peterson, "Why Did They Become Christians? . . . ," in Charles E. Ronan and Bonnie B.C. Oh (eds.), op. cit., pp. 138–42.

15. FR, book IV, ch. XV, p. 178.

CHAPTER FOURTEEN

~

The Lord of Heaven

Beijing, 1602–1603

There was something undefined and complete, coming into existence before Heaven and Earth. How still it was and formless, standing alone, and undergoing no change, reaching everywhere and in no danger (of being exhausted)! It may be regarded as the Mother of all things. I do not know its name, and I give it the designation of the Tao (the Way or Course).

—*Tao Te Ching* (25)[1]

Every state or country has [its own] lord. Is it possible that only the universe does not have a lord?

—Matteo Ricci, introduction to *The True Meaning of the Lord of Heaven*[2]

The Burning of "Idols" and Books, and the Fourth Edition of the Map of the World

Having finally settled in Beijing, the long-awaited goal of his wanderings on Chinese soil, Ricci resumed the work of evangelization, determined now to secure the results that he felt he deserved after so many years of effort, not least in the strength of the imperial protection he enjoyed. Diego de Pantoja had now mastered Mandarin Chinese and was able to talk to the literati on an equal footing, thus providing real assistance despite the somewhat strained relations between the two Jesuits due to their very different personalities.[3]

217

For all of Ricci's commitment, however, the mandarins who listened to his words and read his works with interest were seldom persuaded to adopt the Catholic faith. The obstacles were many. Christianity accepted no compromise and put forward absolute truths and dogmas, whereas the Chinese view—expressed by the monk Daguan, better known as "Complete Enlightenment"—was that "there are a thousand and ten thousand ways to reach the truth."[4] Accustomed to the coexistence of different religions as something completely natural and having little inclination toward exclusive choices, the Chinese intellectuals would have accepted the religion presented by Ricci more readily if they had been able to consider it on the same level as Buddhism and Taoism.

Another obstacle to spreading the Gospel among the *shidafu* was the well-known problem of polygamy, which Ricci called a "chain difficult to break," a way of life deeply rooted in society that still prevented the conversion of Qu Taisu and Li Zhizao. Neither was yet capable of making such a drastic choice entailing painful sacrifices and a break with the laws and customs of their land.

As the missionaries working primarily among the poorer and hence necessarily monogamous classes through the other Chinese residences founded by Ricci, Niccolò Longobardo in Shaozhou, João Soerio in Nanchang, and João da Rocha in Nanjing all realized through their everyday experience that the work of evangelization proved no simpler where the problem of polygamy did not arise.

For the Chinese peasants, the Christian religion was a form of devotion steeped in magic, as was the case also in Europe, where the Virgin Mary and the saints were worshiped as miracle-working dispensers of grace and favor. They converted only when convinced that the Western religion was more effective than the traditional cults or because the missionaries appeared more charitable than the Buddhist and Taoist monks. Christening did not prevent them, however, from remaining strongly attached to the forms of worship and the protecting spirits whose aid they had always called upon. The missionaries tried to put a stop to this by asking them to burn the effigies of the various local divinities they kept in their homes, but not always with success. During a period of drought in Shaozhou, as Longobardo informed Ricci in a report, the converted peasants joined all the others in turning to traditional gods like the Buddhist divinity Guanyin. Given the poor results, a fortune-teller proclaimed that the goddess was offended and was in pain from the wounds on her back inflicted by the Jesuits in burning her effigies. When the rain did finally fall, however, the three hundred converts of Shaozhou went back to destroying their pagan idols in order to keep the Western priests happy.

Ricci also went occasionally with Pantoja to preach among the poorer classes living on the outskirts of the city. When his work proved successful, the newly baptized converts handed over whole boxes full of idols for destruction, as he reported with some satisfaction in letters to Rome. It was, however, above all among the *shidafu* that Ricci and his brethren sought proselytes in Beijing. The first in the capital were the emperor's brother-in-law, two sons of the court physician, both of whom qualified as *xiucai* or "budding talents," a schoolmaster, a former governor, and a painter specializing in religious images of Buddha, who agreed to burn all his works after baptism. The conversion of the *shidafu* Li Yingshi was a very difficult process. Having fought in the war against Japan and been awarded a high rank in the Imperial Guard as a right to be handed down to his heirs in perpetuity, he lived on this pension in Beijing with his family and was a follower of the religion combining Confucianism, Taoism, and Buddhism. He was also a renowned astrologer and expert in *feng shui* (geomancy), called in for advice on choosing sites for houses and tombs and to tell the future. Li Yingshi had studied for a long time in order to attain his acknowledged degree of mastery and had a large library of specialized texts, mostly in manuscript form and including works on mathematics, another of his great interests.

This intellectual "of very lively intellect"[5] delighted in studying mathematics and geometry and persuaded Ricci to work with him on a new version of his map of the world, as the third edition proved so popular that the two series of wood blocks, both the originals and the ones produced by the printers, were not enough to meet the demand. This fourth edition, two copies of which have survived,[6] was entitled *Liangyi xuanlan tu*, or "mysterious visual map of the two forms," namely the earth and the heavens. Printed in January 1603 and divided into eight panels, it was larger but substantially identical to the previous one, the only change in content being the addition of two spheres to the diagram of the Ptolemaic universe: the tenth, or *primum mobile*, and the eleventh, the dwelling of the Lord of Heaven, with the saints and angels of paradise. Ricci wrote a new preface, as did five of his scholarly friends, including Feng Yingjing, who sent these words from prison: "Many are those who will see this Map in China. Some will get from it the pleasure of traveling while reclining at their ease [in their rooms]; others [seeing it] will enlarge their administrative plans; others [seeing the great size of other countries] will rid themselves of petty sentiments of excessive provincialism; still others will thrust away vain ideas of worthless gossip."[7]

After collaborating with Ricci fruitfully on the map of the world, Li Yingshi was subjected to the customary religious indoctrination and was won over by the Jesuit's scholarly arguments to the point of considering the possibility of conversion. When he realized that this would entail repudiating the knowledge that constituted the basis of his profession and his reputation, however, he was assailed by doubts. How could the beliefs that had enabled him to make correct predictions on so many occasions possibly be false? Ricci succeeded in convincing him, however, and the scholar was baptized with the name of Paul. As final proof of his devotion and as an example to the others, the new convert agreed to destroy his entire library in public on a bonfire that burned for three days.

"Paul Li" was followed in his conversion by all the members of his family and his household. One servant cut off a finger with an ax to show his determination not to become a Christian, but he was forced to yield to the master's orders. A total of seventy converts was reached in Beijing in just over two years.

Anti-Buddhist Persecution

As noted above, one of the greatest obstacles to the work of proselytism was the popularity of Buddhism, the religion with the most followers, which the missionaries loathed and branded as idolatry inspired by the devil. Buddhism had already been present in China for more than fourteen centuries when Ricci arrived there. Its period of greatest success was during the Tang dynasty at the end of the sixth century, when it nearly became the state religion due to the support of the empress Wu. The subsequent persecution of foreign cults in the eighth and ninth centuries reduced its influence and reasserted the supremacy of Confucianism. Buddhism had, however, evolved in typically Chinese forms and penetrated deeply into the culture. Some elements of its philosophy were even incorporated into Neo-Confucianism.

Even though the government exercised strict control over the construction of new temples and the recruitment of monks, Buddhism had a following in the population that could scarcely be challenged. There were about one thousand Buddhist temples in Beijing alone, and anyone entering was deeply impressed by the teeming crowds of devout believers and the imposing statues of the seated or reclining Buddha, his face illuminated by a faint smile of serene reflection. The believers burned bundles of incense in great bronze braziers emitting dense clouds of perfumed smoke and knelt down in prayer before the statues, bowing their forehead to the ground three times.

While most of the literati despised the monks, many of them knew and appreciated the Buddhist philosophy. Wanli was known to delight in reading Buddhist and Taoist writings and to have been generous in financing the construction of new temples in Beijing together with the empress mother.[8]

The empress consort Wang made no secret of her sympathies for the monk Daguan, treating a robe of his in her possession as a holy relic, and many concubines followed the teachings of the bonze Hanshan.

Even though the most authoritative monks thus enjoyed a certain degree of influence at the court, none of them had permission to enter the Imperial City freely, unlike the Jesuits, who were very glad of this privilege. The government's tolerance of religious practices and their underlying doctrines was in fact limited and circumspect, and the emperor was periodically forced to take a stand so as to forestall any attempt on the part of Buddhist sympathizers to challenge the supremacy of Confucianism and its political role in ensuring the stability of the empire. A decree issued by Wanli ten years earlier, in response to recommendations put forward by the minister of rites, prohibited the use of quotations from Buddhist and Taoist writings in all the imperial schools so as to reassert the superiority of Confucianism.[9]

As everyone was well aware, Ricci's attitude toward Buddhism was clear and uncompromising. The missionary regarded it simply as a form of idolatry and took every opportunity to manifest his contempt for the monks with no sign of the tolerance he could display in other circumstances. On realizing the hatred felt toward them by the foreign priests, the Buddhists repaid them in the same coin, not least because they feared that the Jesuits might succeed in converting the emperor and turning him against their religion. Given the circumstances, it was only a matter of time before the hostility of the Buddhists and of the *guan* opposed to the Jesuits' presence in Beijing began to manifest itself.

The mandarin Huang Hui—a member of the Hanlin Academy, expert calligrapher, renowned poet, and tutor of the emperor's firstborn son—secured an invitation to a banquet in order to meet Ricci and obtained a copy of the catechism, which was already circulating in manuscript form, in order to read it together with another Buddhist sympathizer. They noted their criticisms in the margins and sent it to the missionaries. The monk Daguan invited Ricci to his home shortly afterward, but the Jesuit declined, having no wish to be involved in another argument like the one at the banquet in Nanjing many years earlier.

The two episodes alarmed Ricci, not least because it was rumored among those in the know that a group of literati were about to send a memorial attacking the missionaries to the court and that Li Dai, regarded by the Jesuits as a friend, had adopted a hostile stance. Other and more serious events soon monopolized attention in the capital, however, completely overshadowing the problems caused by the presence of the Western missionaries.

The first episode, which was the talk of the town in 1602, was the condemnation and suicide of Li Zhi, the philosopher and Buddhist sympathizer whom

Ricci had met in Nanjing and in Jining and who had complimented the Jesuit on his treatise on friendship. Li Zhi's writings were discussed for their veiled criticisms of the state philosophy, but his latest work *Cangshu*, the "Book to Be Hidden," published a year before Ricci's arrival in Beijing, caused outcry by bringing to light the ideas of unorthodox intellectuals who had adopted an anti-Confucian stance. The arrival at the court of a memorial containing detailed charges against the troublesome intellectual obliged the emperor to recall him to Beijing and have him imprisoned. The 75-year-old philosopher cut his throat with a razor before the trial and died in his cell after two days of agony.

In the wake of this tragic event, the minister of rites Feng Qi, a good friend of the Jesuits, wrote a memorial attacking Buddhism and issued a decree prohibiting the citation of Buddhist works in the schools, a provision already taken in the past. Students disobeying this order would not be admitted to the imperial examinations, and officials manifesting Buddhist sympathies would lose their positions. The situation flared up again in December 1603, when an anonymous pamphlet was found on the doorsteps of the most important dignitaries in Beijing one morning at dawn. The "Discussion of the Danger of a Succession to the Throne" claimed that the emperor, having been forced to designate his firstborn son as heir against his wishes, intended to go back on this and alter the succession in favor of the third-born. As this was a very thorny subject that had already led to a clash between Wanli and the court mandarins, none of the *guan* wanted to see it raised again with the risking of disturbing the delicate balance of power established in the Forbidden City. The author of what immediately became known as the "pamphlet of bad luck" had to be found out and punished at all costs, and a witch-hunt was soon unleashed that many took advantage of to discredit their political rivals.

The hunt for the anonymous author did not spare the homes of the most influential monks, which were meticulously searched. A letter was found among Daguan's papers in which he criticized the emperor for lack of religious conviction and for showing insufficient respect for his mother. Wanli gave orders that the bonze was to be punished, and the officials complied with undue zeal by having him beaten to death with bamboo canes. The monk Hanshan also had compromising documents; his punishment was perpetual exile in the Guangdong province.

The first to be suspected of writing the pamphlet was a captain of the Imperial Guard and nephew of Li Dai, who was stripped of his rank and exiled to his hometown even though the accusations proved to be groundless. The search continued, and suspicion fell on a merchant who composed poems in a style considered similar to that of the illegal publication. The man refused to confess even under torture but was nevertheless sentenced to *lingchisi*, or death by a thousand cuts, the most terrible of Chinese tortures, which involved binding the victim to a wooden frame in a public place and then slowly removing 1,600 slices of flesh, the victim's head being left intact so as to witness his body's torture for as long as possible.

Though perhaps disturbed by the cruelty of the punishments, which were in any case not dissimilar from those meted out in the West, the missionaries were glad that the anti-Buddhist movement and the persecutions of the alleged authors of the pamphlet had temporarily neutralized their more direct adversaries. Ricci interpreted these events as "divine retribution" visited upon his rivals.[10]

Valignano's Help to Strengthen the Mission

On establishing that the missionaries had succeeded in settling in the capital, the superiors in Macao were very pleased with the results obtained. Replaced by Valentim Carvalho as rector of the Jesuit College in Macao, Manuel Dias visited Beijing during the summer of 1602, followed by Nanchang and Nanjing, and sent a glowing report to Valignano. News of the success of the Jesuits' endeavors also reached Rome. Superior General Acquaviva decided to send some more young missionaries to China, and the king of Spain pledged to provide the necessary funds. Meanwhile, in the wake of the achievements of the Society of Jesus, members of other religious orders, above all the Franciscans and Dominicans in the Philippines, made plans to found missions on Chinese soil.

Reassured by the encouraging news, the Visitor was intent on developing the China mission and reorganizing its hierarchical structure. He decided to make Ricci independent of Macao by allowing him to submit his decisions only to the Provincial and to dispense with the approval of the rector of the College in Macao. As Ricci commented in his history of the mission, "It was something very necessary and useful for the success of this work [because] the superiors of the College sometimes . . . have little experience in the matters of Christianity among unbelievers."[11]

In order to free Ricci from his other duties and enable him to concentrate exclusively on the mission in Beijing, Valignano placed Manuel Dias in charge of the three Jesuit residences in the south. More missionaries were assigned to China and began studying Mandarin in Macao, and three young Chinese men with Christian parents were admitted to the order. Valignano also obtained fresh funds and instructed the procurator of Japan and China to have the money delivered directly to China without obliging the missionaries to travel to Macao. His final act was to have various religious objects sent to the missions, including books and paintings to adorn the chapels and churches.

Ricci was reassured by this display of full support from his superior. As he wrote to Ludovico Maselli in February 1605,[12] "Valignano provides us with everything we need." He added that he intended to arrange for his superior to visit China the following year so that he could see the results achieved for himself.

The Portuguese Jesuit Gaspar Ferreira, one of those assigned to the China mission, began his journey to Beijing along the Grand Canal in the summer of 1604. The vessel following him with the gifts for the mission was lost on the way due to the torrential rains that had swollen the rivers and caused catastrophic flooding, and many objects were stolen. The altar wine disappeared into the waves as well as the precious *Biblia Regia* sent as a gift by Cardinal Giulio Antonio Santori of Santa Severina, a polyglot bible in eight volumes printed in Antwerp in 1569, which contained versions of the holy scriptures in Latin, Greek, Jewish, and Syro-Chaldean.

The crate containing the precious work floated along the river and was salvaged by some boatmen, who hoped to find rich pickings. On discovering only a few books inside, they returned it to the owners in exchange for a small sum of money. The event was celebrated in the Beijing mission on the Feast of the Assumption with a solemn ceremony. In an effort to recover some more of the religious articles, including a painting sent to adorn the altar, the Jesuits sought the aid of Feng Yingjing, who made arrangements from prison for some friends to find the guilty parties. The boatmen suspected of the theft were soon captured and imprisoned, but the missionaries secured their release, well aware that confessions were extracted by means of torture in China, as they were in Europe. Most of Valignano's gifts were thus lost forever.

The flood of July 1604 caused a great many deaths and was followed by a terrible famine. The emperor came to the people's aid by allocating funds equivalent to two hundred thousand *scudi*, ordering the free distribution of food, and selling rice from the imperial granaries at low prices. Ricci was so impressed by the generosity of the Chinese state that he commented on the episode in a letter to his father Giovanni Battista: "I was astonished at so much charity among unbelievers."[13]

Ricci's "Catechism," *The True Meaning of the Lord of Heaven*

At the end of 1603, after three years in the capital, Ricci was ready to publish the apologetic work to which he attached the most importance, namely what he called his "catechism," the fruit of at least ten years of study and reflection, and the spearhead of his method of evangelization based on cultural accommodation. In agreement with Valignano, he had decided to channel his greatest effort of persuasion into the medium of writing because he knew that the literati, being accustomed to study, would be more easily convinced of the validity of a doctrine by reading a text than by listening to a sermon. When he spoke about religion with scholars, they often asked him for a book on the subject so as to consider it with the necessary degree of concentration.

It was twenty years since the publication of the first catechism, drafted by Ruggieri and revised by Ricci in Zhaoqing. In that now distant period, the two Jesuits still dressed in Buddhist robes, had a limited grasp of the language, and knew nothing of the Confucian philosophy. While their first doctrinal work had nevertheless proved successful and been circulated also in Japan and Korea, Valignano found it unsatisfactory because terms of Buddhist origin were used to express religious concepts, and there was no reference to Confucianism. The Visitor therefore asked Ricci to write a new treatise more in line with the system of values espoused by the literati and ordered the destruction of the wood-block matrices of the Ruggieri catechism in 1596. Ricci set to work in Shaozhou between 1591 and 1594, in concomitance with his translation of the Confucian classics, and his superiors received the initial manuscript version in Latin in 1597.

The Visitor corrected the text with Duarte de Sande during the summer of 1598, but Ricci did not see the revised version until after his arrival in Beijing due to his unexpected departure from the south, the death of De Sande the following year, and various problems of transport. Ricci continued to improve the work in the meantime with the addition of new arguments against Buddhist doctrine drawn from discussions with the literati in Beijing. The Jesuits' friends arranged for numerous handwritten copies to be produced and circulated among the scholars, whose comments then enabled Ricci to make further improvements. The only thing now needed for publication was the indispensable imprimatur from the inquisitors in Goa. While Ricci was still awaiting this ecclesiastical authorization, his friend Feng Yingjing asked for permission to have the work printed at his own expense and wrote a preface. The Jesuit asked him to wait, but according to Ricci's account, the *shidafu* wrote back to say that China was "seriously ill" and the catechism was the only medicine that could cure it.

The Jesuit found this argument so cogent that he raised no further objections and allowed Feng Yingjing to have two hundred copies of the manuscript printed by his friends between October and December 1603 with the title *Tianzhu shiyi*, or *The True Meaning of the Lord of Heaven*.[14]

The substantial treatise was not at all a catechism in today's sense of the term but a work conceived and constructed specifically for the literati of imperial China, "the first attempt by a Catholic scholar to use a Chinese way of thinking to introduce Christianity to Chinese intellectuals."[15] The text is divided into eight chapters and is presented as a dialogue between two literati, one Western and the other Chinese. The former illustrates the Christian doctrine; the latter raises doubts, questions, and objections.

Since the boundary between religion and philosophy was very blurred in China, Ricci decided to present his arguments on the plane of speculation. In other words, he chose to illustrate only what could be demonstrated and understood through reasoning, not what was to be accepted as an act of faith. As he explained to Girolamo Costa, "It was a book about our religion, all according to natural reason."[16] In theological terms, he decided to speak only about what is called "natural revelation" and not about "positive revelation."

In short, his aim was to demonstrate to the literati that Buddhism and Taoism—based respectively on the "void" and "nothingness" according to his interpretation of part of their philosophical foundations—were to be irrevocably rejected. He chose, however, to refrain from making direct accusations against his adversaries: "It is better to refute [the teachings of Buddhists and Taoists] than to hate [the men who hold these opinions]."[17]

Ricci wanted to convince the Chinese that Christianity was not only compatible with the doctrine of Confucius but was also the only religion that fully reflected the teachings of ancient Confucianism before its contamination by Buddhist and Taoist ideas and Neo-Confucian interpretations. His was a bold undertaking, an ingenious effort to reconcile the irreconcilable, an attempt to bridge the abyss between Chinese and Western conceptions of the world, albeit so as to serve the ends of evangelization.

In order to achieve his goal, the Jesuit cited the classic texts of Confucianism and reinterpreted their numerous ambiguities to his own advantage. As he wrote in his history of the mission, "He endeavored to enlist Confucius, the leader of the sect of literati, on our side by interpreting in our favor some things left uncertain in his writings."[18] At the same time, he deliberately presented his precepts in the Confucian style, emphasizing the importance of self-improvement in the knowledge that this was one of the most important virtues taught by Confucius, and seeking to show that this could come about through learning to worship the Lord of Heaven.

The first subject of discussion is the existence of one god, the creator of all things. Ricci refutes the beliefs developed by Buddhists and Taoists and rejects the idea of *taiji*, or "Supreme Ultimate," the form of energy regarded by Neo-Confucianism as the origin of the universe, which is incompatible with the Christian idea of god. He then works back through the history of Chinese culture to rediscover the millennial roots of religious thought and claims that the idea of one personal god—called *Shangdi*, the Lord on High, or *Tian*, Heaven—is to be found in the Chinese classics of the third millennium BC. According to the missionary, both terms indicate the Eternal Father of Christianity—which he calls *Tianzhu*, the Lord of Heaven, in Chinese—and the recurrent expressions about respecting, fearing, and serving *Tian* are all references to God.

Ricci stresses the difference between human and divine nature and refutes the idea of mankind and the universe as forming a single organism, which is deeply rooted in Chinese culture. He then dedicates two chapters to the existence of the soul, which he describes as an entity of a spiritual nature separate from the body and the exclusive prerogative of humanity. The dualism of the spirit and the body was unknown to the Chinese, who believed that the various spirits attributed to people dissolved more or less quickly after death. They also believed that the human spirit was essentially the same as the animal, albeit of greater subtlety and agility. The catechism instead maintained that human beings and animals are different in nature because only the former have the ability to reason. One later chapter is entirely devoted to refuting the Buddhist doctrine of transmigration and another to presenting the Christian idea of heaven and hell, stress being laid on the capacity of human beings to choose between good and evil on the basis of reason.

The idea of otherworldly bliss juxtaposed with the possibility of being irrevocably condemned to eternal damnation was very difficult for the Chinese to accept. One of the recurrent criticisms made by the literati was that the catechism sought to attract the unwary by promising eternal happiness after death and terrifying them with tales of hellfire.

The last chapter speaks about the practice of celibacy and explains that Catholic priests are required to devote themselves entirely to their religious mission. Apart from a very brief mention of the Incarnation—"something is also said about the coming of Christ, our redeemer"—discussion of the mysteries of the faith was deliberately and prudently postponed to his subsequent work *Tianzhu jiaoyao* ("Christian Doctrine"), which was aimed at converts.

Ricci was satisfied with his work. As he wrote in a letter to the Alaleoni brothers, Jesuits from his hometown of Macerata, "It turned out very well."[19] He sent two copies to Superior General Acquaviva in the same year, asking him to show one to Pope Paul V and to anyone else interested in seeing it. While they would not be able to understand the Chinese, looking through the work would help to understand "how much effort these soldiers [of Christ] make to learn these characters [of the Chinese language] and how great their need of God's help is."[20]

The treatise enjoyed a large circulation, and the literati read it with interest as a moral and philosophical work. But there was of course no lack of criticism. As Ricci wrote to Ludovico Maselli in February 1605, reading the work "removed the suspicion of wicked ulterior motives from the minds of some but increased the hatred of others who cherished this suspicion."[21]

The Buddhist sympathizers kept to the plane of philosophical discussion in replying to Ricci's confutations. The possibility of sending the emperor a memorial against the Jesuits was considered by a small group but was soon abandoned due to awareness that the Westerners enjoyed Wanli's protection, and any challenge to this would be perilous.

Other editions followed. Valignano had a second one printed in Canton for Japan in 1605, and a third—a copy of which is to be found in the Jesuit Archives in Rome—was produced in Hangzhou in 1607. Numerous editions also appeared in the nineteenth and twentieth centuries, as well as translations in Manchurian, Korean, Vietnamese, French, Japanese, and English.

Notes

1. *Tao Te Ching*, 25, trans. James Legge, in The Sacred Books of the East, vol. 39 (Oxford: Oxford University Press, 1891).

2. Matteo Ricci S.J., *The True Meaning of the Lord of Heaven (T'ien-chu Shih-i)*, with an introduction by Douglas Lancashire and Peter Hu Kuo-chen S.J., Chinese-English edition, ed. Edward J. Malatesta S.J. (Taipei, Hong Kong, St. Louis: The Institute of Jesuit Sources, 1985), p. 57.

3. See chapter 17 ("The Paradoxes of an Extraordinary Man").

4. J. Gernet, *Chine et christianisme*, p. 110.

5. FR, book IV, ch. XX, p. 262.

6. One in Seoul, Korea, and the other in the museum of the Liaoning province, China. Cf. Y. Dong and J. D. Day, op. cit.

7. Pasquale D'Elia S.J., "Recent Discoveries and New Studies (1938–1960) on the World Map in Chinese of Father Matteo Ricci," in *Monumenta Serica* 20 (1961): pp. 129–30.

8. R. Huang, op. cit., p. 220.

9. R. Huang, op. cit.

10. FR, book IV, ch. XVI, p. 187.

11. FR, book V, ch. I, p. 274.

12. OS II, p. 260.

13. Letter dated May 10, 1605; OS II, p. 271.

14. Pasquale D'Elia refers to it as *Il solido trattato su Dio*.

15. M. Ricci S.J., *The True Meaning of the Lord of Heaven (T'ien-chu Shih-i)*, cit., introduction, p. 47.

16. Letter dated October 12, 1594; OS II, p. 122.

17. M. Ricci S.J., *The True Meaning of the Lord of Heaven* (*T'ien-chu Shih-i*), cit., p. 101.

18. FR, book V, ch. II, p. 296. Ricci speaks of himself in the third person in his history of the mission.

19. Letter to Giulio and Girolamo Alaleoni, July 26, 1605; OS II, p. 296.

20. Letter to Giulio and Girolamo Alaleoni, p. 294.

21. Letter to Giulio and Girolamo Alaleoni, p. 257.

CHAPTER FIFTEEN

~

Doctor Paul

Beijing, 1603–1605

Never in my life have I been so pressed for time, so much so that I sometimes hardly have enough to commend my soul to God when I need it most.

—Matteo Ricci, letter to Fabio de Fabii[1]

The Master said, "Learning without due reflection leads to perplexity; reflection without learning leads to perilous circumstances."

—Confucius, *Analects* (2, 15)

Paul Xu, the "Pillar" of the Mission

Life in the Nanjing mission proceeded smoothly, and Lazzaro Cattaneo and João da Rocha kept Ricci informed of any new developments. They often went to celebrate Mass in the home of the former soldier and extremely devout convert "Paul Chin," who had built a small chapel for religious functions where the family, all of whom were baptized, would gather for prayer in private. When the seventy-four-year-old patriarch died, his son Martin broke with tradition by obeying his wishes and refusing the Buddhist monks permission to attend his funeral. This was a small triumph for the Jesuits and a sign of the consolidation of their religious community, which had been joined by over a hundred new converts in the space of two years.

The most important event was, however, an unexpected visit in January 1603 from a scholar named Xu Guangqi, who asked for Li Madou, the author of the renowned map of the world, and explained that he had met him briefly three years earlier but had been unable to stop and talk for lack of time. According to Ricci's account in his history of the mission, on learning that Li Madou had moved to Beijing, the *shidafu* stayed and talked until late at night with João da Rocha, who showed him the manuscripts of the *Tianzhu shiyi* ("The True Meaning of the Lord of Heaven") and the *Tianzhu jiaoyao* ("Christian Doctrine").[2] He studied these works thoroughly over the next few days, he asked to be received into the Catholic Church soon afterward, and he was baptized with the name Paul. While the missionaries were glad to have a scholar of evident culture and the highest caliber like Xu Guangqi among their new converts, they would certainly never have imagined that he was to have such a brilliant career in the imperial bureaucracy, culminating with the positions of grand secretary, minister of rites, and tutor to the heir to the throne. Xu Guangqi was to be the most eminent Chinese Catholic and the most authoritative supporter of the Jesuits, fully deserving Ricci's description of him some years later as the "greatest pillar" of Christianity in China.[3]

Aged forty-one at the time, ten years younger than Ricci, Xu Guangqi was born in Shanghai, then a small town on the sea in the Jiangsu province. His father was a merchant of modest degree, but his mother was from a family of *shidafu*. Like all young people whose parents were able to afford the expense, he set off on the long path of study leading to a career in the imperial bureaucracy, albeit with some ups and downs, having now failed to pass the examination to qualify as a *jinshi* on two occasions.

There is no lack of allusions to prophetic dreams and omens in the account Ricci gives of the scholar's life and conversion in the history of the mission. His failure in the third-level examinations is in fact considered providential, as he would otherwise have been able to afford a concubine and would have found it much more difficult to embrace Christianity. Moreover, he would probably have been posted to a distant province and would thus have had no opportunity to visit Nanjing and be baptized.

Xu Guangqi's prefaces to Ricci's works provide some insight into the reasons why he decided to become a Catholic. Despite what he described as his natural inclination toward doubt and skepticism, on reading the works of Li Madou, it was as "a cloud lifting."[4] To quote one of his best-known remarks, the religion expounded by the missionaries was able to "supplement Confucianism and displace Buddhism."[5] Xu Guangqi also attached great importance to ascertaining that there was nothing in Ricci's writings incompatible with such Confucian principles as the fidelity of the subject to the monarch or the son to the father, and nothing that was not conducive to self-improvement or the common good.

While Xu Guangqi was becoming the Catholic Paul Xu in Nanjing, Li Zhizao returned to Beijing after serving as the head of a board of examiners in the Fujian province and resumed his visits to the Jesuits' house while awaiting another government assignment. He was pleased to be able to show Ricci the good use he had made of his teaching by telling him that he had included a mathematical question among those he was required to set for the examination. To the missionaries' regret, however, Li Zhizao had only been in the capital for a few months when he was appointed superintendent of the Imperial Canal in the Shandong province and set off without having decided to convert.

Examinations and Baptisms

In January 1604, a year after his baptism, Xu Guangqi went to sit the imperial examination for the third time in Beijing, where he and Ricci got to know each other and formed a strong attachment. Realizing the uncommon caliber of this scholar "of fine intellect and great natural virtue"[6] and the potential benefits of his collaboration with the missionaries, Ricci took a close interest in his preparation for the examination. Xu Guangqi was ranked 123rd out of the 310 successful candidates and finally obtained the longed-for title of *jinshi*, whereupon the missionaries began to refer to him simply as Dr. Paul. Martin Chin, the convert from Nanjing and son of Paul Chin, also graduated in the same session, passing the examinations of the highest level in the section reserved for army officers at his sixth attempt.

The Jesuits' delight at the success of their converts was tempered by regret that they would now have to leave the city, as only those topping the list of successful candidates could hope for a position in Beijing. Everyone else would have to obtain a post in a faraway province and then wait for promotion so as to move gradually toward the capital, or be recalled if lucky. As expected, Martin Chin was assigned to the Zhejiang province, where he remained for six years.

Xu Guangqi was also ready to accept a post on the outskirts of the empire, but Ricci was most reluctant to let him leave. He had no wish to lose the brilliant convert who resembled him so closely in terms of personality and might well prove an invaluable ally. In order to keep him in Beijing without harming his career prospects, Ricci advised him to take the examination for membership of the Hanlin Academy, which was based in the capital. The examination, which was extremely selective, was scheduled for the early summer. The *jinshi* accepted the challenge, took lodgings with the Jesuits to study, and succeeded in passing. Paul Xu would be able not only to stay in the capital but also to aspire to positions of great prestige and take Christianity into the upper echelons of the imperial bureaucracy. The academy was located in the vicinity of the southern gate of the Imperial City close to the ministries and the other government departments. In the space of a few months, Xu Guangqi found a house near the office in which he worked and was joined there by his family. His father was christened with the name Leo soon afterward, and his eldest son with James three years later.

Ricci was pleased with the results achieved and felt optimistic. Living with him in the mission were Pantoja, Ferreira, the two Chinese novices, and a small group of disciples. They were joined every day by numerous converts who attended the religious ceremonies regularly. One of the most fervent was the former geomancer Li Yingshi, or Paul Li, who helped the Jesuits "hunt for souls." Such was his zeal in following the doctrinal precepts to the letter, Ricci tells us, that the missionaries had to dissuade him from going all the way to Macao for confirmation, a long journey that would have cost him a fortune.

Now satisfied with the mission's progress, Ricci reported to his superiors on the results achieved, sometimes lingering over descriptions of the fervor shown by his converts and mentioning episodes considered miraculous. Together with the anecdotes and "prodigies" recounted in order to reassure the religious authorities as to the performance of the China mission, he endeavored to take stock of the situation objectively. There were about 150 conversions in the first three years of his stay in Beijing and about 1,000 in twenty-two years for China as a whole. While far higher figures were achieved in Japan and other countries where the Jesuits operated, Ricci pointed out that there were only fourteen priests and four lay brothers in "this never cultivated land,"[7] few indeed for a vast empire differing so radically in terms of language, culture, and mentality, especially as some of the brethren had still to acquire a mastery of Chinese. In agreement with his superior Valignano, Ricci stuck to the strategy of proceeding step by step and giving priority to conversion based on rational conviction—"few but good" rather than "many and imperfect," as he put it in a letter to Ludovico Maselli in February 1605.[8] This held above all for the Beijing residence, which baptized fewer converts than the others.[9] Ricci was unconcerned about this, however, as he was convinced that the converts in the capital, people in positions of authority who were assiduous in their observance of the sacraments, were "superior in quality."[10]

Confirmation of the validity of this approach came from the Nanjing mission with the good news that Qu Taisu, the "great old friend who helped us so much to earn the credit we have in China,"[11] had finally been baptized. The decision had not been easy. Qu Taisu had turned up at the missionaries' house and had asked them to take in his fourteen-year-old son and give him a Christian upbringing. After a short indoctrination, the missionaries baptized the youth with the name Mattew, after Ricci, and urged the father to receive the sacraments too. The scholar hesitated once again, having no wish either to leave his concubine or to be forced to relinquish the work he had recently been commissioned to undertake. By an ironic twist of fate, this was the publication of Buddhist works, which would have been a source of renown and guaranteed earnings.

It was the Chinese lay brother Francisco Martines, recently transferred to Nanjing, who came up with the right arguments to overcome his resistance and convince him after so much hesitation. Qu Taisu resolved the problem of his concubine by making her his lawful wedded wife in defiance of social conventions, and he abandoned the publication of the Buddhist works. He was immediately baptized with the name Ignatius on March 25, 1605.

Greatly pleased at this triumph, Ricci decided to publish his *Tianzhu jiaoyao*, or *Christian Doctrine*, a work long ready in manuscript form, in August of the same year. Designed specifically for converts and prepared "with great diligence," it contained Chinese translations of the Lord's Prayer, the Hail Mary, and the Creed, as well as the Ten Commandments and the seven sacraments. A further aim was to ensure the uniformity of the missionaries' teaching and to specify the terminology to be used in preaching by creating "many ecclesiastical words and new words in China."[12] Given the lack of any equivalent of a capital letter in Chinese, prominence being indicated by a higher position with respect to the other characters, Ricci adopted this practice for those designating God, Jesus, the Father, the Son, and the Holy Spirit, but not Mary.[13]

Commending Virtue: *The Twenty-five Discourses*

The increase in the number of converts encouraged Ricci in his attempt to reach as many Chinese intellectuals as possible with his teachings. It was now two years since the publication in 1603 of *The True Meaning of the Lord of Heaven*, in which the Jesuit had attempted to reconcile Christianity and Confucianism by taking a stance against Buddhism and Taoism. As he was well aware, the work had persuaded some people of the validity of the Christian doctrine but had also aroused great resentment against the Jesuits among sympathizers of the two Chinese religions. He therefore thought it better to avoid controversy and to resume the role of sage and moralist that he found so congenial.

The time had come to publish *Ershiwu yan*, or *Twenty-five Discourses*, an ethical work written at the end of 1599 in Nanjing addressing subjects of interest to Confucian literati regardless of their religious sympathies. The small volume published in August 1605 was a Chinese adaptation of the *Enchiridion* of the Greek Stoic philosopher Epictetus (AD 50–115),[14] who taught the renunciation of desire, passion, and worldly goods; the endurance of evil; and acceptance of one's fate. The subjects addressed were all part of the Jesuits' cultural baggage, as revised in the light of Christian morality, and were perfectly comprehensible to Chinese literati due to their similarities with Confucian ethics. While it is not known whether Ricci had a copy of the philosopher's work with him or he relied for the citations solely on his memory of his years of study at the Roman College, he adheres very closely indeed to the original text.

In offering this work to the Chinese, Ricci meant to present himself as a Christian philosopher who praised virtue without attacking the other religious doctrines. As he wrote to Ludovico Maselli shortly after its publication, "I do nothing but speak of virtue and living a good life in a very complete way as a natural philosopher but also as a Christian without refuting any sect."[15]

In much the same way that Jesuit thinkers reworked the subject matter of pagan morality in Christian terms, Ricci presented ancient Confucianism to the Chinese as though it were the Chinese version of Stoicism. The result was another small masterpiece of cultural accommodation, or indeed of twofold cultural accommodation, consisting as it did in the adaptation of Greek philosophy to Chinese philosophy and then both to Christianity. Ricci translated the aphorisms and the anecdotes of the *Enchiridion* with the modifications required to adapt them to Chinese culture, and he replaced the Greek word for the gods with the singular "God," the Lord of Heaven. He omitted references to typical aspects of the Greco-Roman world that would have proved incomprehensible or inappropriate to Chinese readers, including gladiatorial combat, sexual relations, and moments in the private life of Roman matrons, and he replaced them with Chinese equivalents. In place of Socrates, Zeno, Homer, and other figures of the Western classical world, he cited Confucius and the legendary founding fathers of ancient China, such as the first sovereigns of the Zhou dynasty. Where Epictetus complained of the abstruseness of an ancient philosophical work by Chrysippus, he referred instead to the *I Ching* or "Book of Changes," the best-known Chinese book of divination and one renowned for its cryptic utterances.

On completion of the work, Ricci decided to refrain from writing the expected preface, judging it inappropriate to praise a book that talked about disdain for worldly vanities. Introductions were instead written by Xu Guangqi and Feng Yingjing. The latter invited readers to compare the *Twenty-five Discourses* with the sutra of forty-two aphorisms, the first

Buddhist text translated into Chinese in the first century, and argued that Ricci's doctrine was to be preferred as more in keeping with the customs of the Chinese empire.

As with the earlier treatise on friendship, this moral essay enjoyed wide circulation and was greatly appreciated by a public of varied philosophical and religious inclinations: "It is read and very popular with everyone, regardless of their sect . . . and there are few of my visitors that do not urge me insistently to write more books, because we thus give credit to the things of our religion."[16] All of the Jesuits' friends wanted copies and could not believe that foreign culture could be capable of producing works of such value: "They were amazed to find something so accomplished from strange lands that they regarded as barbarian."[17]

The success of Ricci's works, the ever-greater number of visits from dignitaries, and the gradual increase in conversions made it a matter of some urgency to find a new residence capable of accommodating the three priests, the two lay brothers, the two new Chinese converts who lived with the missionaries, and the servants, not to mention the novices due to arrive from Macao. The Jesuits had already moved a number of times and would have preferred to buy a house, even though they knew their funds were insufficient. By a stroke of luck, a bargain turned up due to circumstances identical to those in Nanjing. A building of forty rooms located alongside the Xuanwumen gate—the westernmost of the three gates providing access to the inner city from the south—was put on the market at an exceptionally low price because it had been constructed some time earlier without respecting the geomantic criteria of *feng shui*, and was indeed said to be haunted by evil spirits. Caring little for superstition, the Jesuits asked their friends for a loan so as not to miss this excellent opportunity. With the aid of Xu Guangqi, they raised a sum equivalent to six hundred *scudi*, sufficient to cover the initial expenses; completed the transaction in three days; and were able to move in on August 27, 1605. Ricci considered the location so close to the main entrance of the Imperial City and all the major government offices "the most convenient to be found."

On being informed, Valignano sent money to pay the debts, buy furniture, dig a well, and add a new story. After registering the contract of purchase, the Jesuits should have begun to pay an annual tax on the property, but Ricci heard that some dignitaries were exempt and decided to consider himself so until someone turned up to demand payment. The situation came to the notice of the tax office some years later, and the Jesuits were asked to rectify matters. Fearing that they might be forced to pay a fine in addition to the arrears, Li Madou asked a mandarin friend to intercede on the grounds that he was entitled to exemption as a foreigner from far away. This move proved successful, and the Jesuits were freed of any such burden forever. As Ricci noted in his history of the mission, "This was how the Church came in some way to enjoy ecclesiastical immunity."[18]

The purchase of the house marked the beginning of stability, and Ricci now felt sure of Wanli's protection, even though he was well aware that he had many enemies. His privileged position was put to the test when the court officials responsible for sending the Jesuits the monthly stipend granted by the emperor were persuaded to stop the payments by mandarins hostile to the missionaries' presence. Ricci responded by sending a document to the court informing the emperor that the missionaries, having been deprived of their allowance from the state, were ready to return to their homeland and asked for an audience to take their final leave. Evidently viewing the Jesuits' presence in the city with favor, Wanli came to their aid once again and ordered the immediate resumption of payments. The incident was never to be repeated.

"Send Me an Astronomer"

On completion of the extensions, the building was big enough to accommodate sixteen people, including the novices from Macao and the servants, and to allow the faithful to attend the services held in the spacious chapel. Pleased to note that the house now functioned as a sort of Jesuit college,[19] Ricci was always the busiest of them all. In addition to religious activities such as prayer, the performance of spiritual exercises, and celebrating Mass, he taught Chinese by reading the Confucian classics with the novices, and he did not fail to devote part of the day and night to correspondence. As the superior, he kept in constant contact by letter with the missionaries in the other residences, he wrote the customary reports to Rome, he never forgot to write to his brethren in Europe, and he answered the letters of numerous mandarins in Chinese. As though this were not enough, he taught science to those willing to listen to him, he read books in Mandarin, and he devoted many hours to study.

The problem of the Chinese calendar was never far from his mind, and every year, after the presentation of the "Book of the Laws of Time" at court, he checked and saw that the imperial astronomers' predictions were inaccurate. As he told João Alvarez in a letter dated May 12, 1605, "Even though I have no book of astrology [astronomy] here, I sometimes predict eclipses more precisely than them with certain Portuguese ephemerides and tables."[20] Evidence of the imperial astronomers' ignorance was provided by the glaring error of three quarters of an hour in predicting the beginning of the solar eclipse two years earlier in May 1603.[21] Well aware of how important the accuracy of astronomical predictions was for the Chinese, Ricci repeated to Alvarez his customary request for brethren skilled in astronomy to be sent to China to help. He was convinced that the missionaries' reputation would benefit enormously if a Jesuit were to succeed in correcting the Chinese calendar:

> I want very much to make a request that I made many years ago but never received a reply, and it is one of the most useful things that could come from there for this court, namely for a father or brother who is a good astrologer [astronomer]. I say an astrologer because I know enough about other things like geometry, clocks, and astrolabes, and have enough books, but they do not say so much about this, about the movement and true place of the planets, the calculation of eclipses, and how to construct ephemerides. . . . If a mathematician came here, as I ask, we could turn our [astronomical] tables into Chinese characters, which I can do very easily, and undertake the task of amending the year [correcting the calendar], which would give us a great reputation, expand our foothold in China, and allow us greater stability and freedom.[22]

Ricci's activities while awaiting this long-desired scientific support included an increasingly busy social life. Deeply convinced that availability was an integral part of his missionary work, he never refused to receive anyone who wanted to see him, and he accepted every invitation. The influx of visitors was greater in the capital than at any other residence, not only because Beijing was so densely populated, but also because the city filled up every year with thousands of dignitaries and literati taking part in special events and celebrations. In addition to the arrivals and departures of *shidafu* and *guan*, there was an almost continuous stream of merchants arriving from other urban and rural areas to supply the Imperial City and the court. Many occasional visitors took advantage of their stay in Beijing to see Li Madou, and old friends gladly undertook the journey to the capital to visit him.

Ricci wanted the house to be always open: "Even though it is a lot of hard work, let everyone be warmly welcomed so as to gain the good wishes of all as well as the possibility of talking to them about the matters of our faith."[23] He knew that contacts with the most important mandarins were conducive to the progress of the mission and to the protection of the brethren in other cities, being sure that if officials passing through saw the respect that Li Madou enjoyed at court, they would have more consideration for the Jesuits resident in the provinces. He received up to twenty books of visits a day and as many as hundreds on festive occasions, and he went to return the invitations every two or three days, on foot or horseback, as required by etiquette.

Such zeal had its price, and the Jesuit felt his energy flagging. The post of superior of the China mission was now too much of a burden for him, and he wished with little real hope that Valignano would "lift it from his shoulders."[24] He confessed his weariness to Girolamo Costa on May 10, 1605: "The more the work proceeds, the more business they load upon me. . . . Responding to the visits of the important men that constantly come to see us and learn about our religion would be enough by itself for a man much abler than me."[25] He wrote to Fabio de Fabii in much the same vein: "Writing is all that is left to poor me, so close to the Tartars and very far away not only from Europeans and friends but also from the companions who are in China . . . but do not think that I am therefore idle, as never in my life have I found myself so pressed for time, so much so that I sometimes hardly have enough to commend my soul to God when I need it most."[26]

The Jew and the "Worshipers of the Cross"

The number of popular publications talking about the Jesuits resident in Beijing grew along with Ricci's renown. Some concentrated on the story of the priests' arrival and on vivid, admiring descriptions of the gifts brought for the emperor. Other more scholarly works examined the scientific, moral, and philosophical subjects addressed by Ricci in his writings, citing entire passages and reproducing parts of his maps of the world. The Jesuit often noted that the authors talked about him without even having read his works or met him. The Jesuits were described more or less as follows in a highly popular publication in vernacular Chinese entitled "Things I have heard":

They are two Westerners, one called Matteo Ricci and the other Cattaneo. Both have prominent foreheads, deep-set eyes, pink faces, and grey beards. They arrived in the Guangdong province after an eight-year voyage and stayed there for ten years. They built a house worth many thousands of *taels* and then abandoned it and traveled to Nanjing, each holding a bamboo umbrella. There an official of the water department possessed a house haunted by many evil demons, and anyone who entered it died immediately. These two men chased the demons out and lived there with no harm done to them. They say that in the West there is an extraordinary lord called the Lord of Heaven who loves good by nature, eats no meat, and has nothing to do with women. The entire country honors him as its sovereign. As regards customs, they esteem friendship and do not cultivate solitude. On arriving in the Middle Kingdom, they began studying the classics and histories day and night, and so have published many observations about friendship. It is impossible to count precisely all the precious objects they have with them. These are the strangest: a painting of the Lord of Heaven whose eyes follow you everywhere, a clock that rings the hours and is very precise for the minutes and quarters, a prism that makes even dead trees and broken down walls shine with the five colors as soon as it starts glowing before the eyes, a square harpsichord with strings of iron that makes sounds even when no one touches it and is played with a bamboo rod that moves over the strings.[27]

Even though Ricci made ironic fun of the "falsehoods," "bizarre lies," and "fantastic, unheard-of things" that he chanced to read, he was pleased to be mentioned together with his companions, as he believed that his reputation furthered the cause of Christianity: "They spread so many true and false reports that they will always be remembered for all the centuries in these lands, and mostly in a good way."[28]

The book with the description of the Jesuits had been read by a *shidafu* who visited the missionaries' home while he was in Beijing to sit the imperial examination. The man was not of the Chinese race but was a Jew named Ai Tian from the Henan province in central China. Being under the impression that the Jesuits shared his faith, he interpreted the images of Mary, Jesus, and John the Baptist in the chapel as depictions of Rebecca and her sons Jacob and Esau. Ai Tian called himself an Israelite and did not know the term "Jew." When Ricci showed him his copy of the *Biblia Regia*, he recognized the Hebrew writing even though he was unable to read it.

This unexpected visit was a precious source of information. Ai Tian told Ricci that there were many Jewish families in the city of Kaifeng, where he lived; that they were allowed to practice their religion in a great synagogue that had just been restored; and that there were also Jews at Hangzhou in the Zhejiang province and in other Chinese cities. He said that the Jews had arrived in the Middle Kingdom five centuries earlier and that the Chinese made no distinction between Muslims and Jews, even though the latter "loathed" the followers of Mohammed and hated being mixed up with them. He confessed that he was not a devout follower of his religion and that, having studied the Confucian philosophy in order to sit the imperial examinations, he would abandon his faith with no regret if he passed. He informed Ricci that the Chinese term *Huihui*, used by extension for the followers of all foreign religions, originally indicated an ethnic minority of the Muslim persuasion descended from Arabian and Persian immigrants,[29] reference being made to diet in order to differentiate the various religions. Saracens were thus *Huihui* that did not eat pork, Jews were *Huihui* that did not eat sinews (a reference to their particular way of butchering meat), and the descendants of Christians were *Huihui* that did not eat animals with hooves, because it was not their habit to use horses or mules for food. The latter were also known as *Huihui* of the number ten because of the similarity between the Chinese character for ten and a cross.

Ricci asked Ai Tian if he could confirm what he had heard from Muslim merchants about the existence on Chinese soil of Christian communities whose members were called "worshipers of the cross."[30] Ai Tian answered that there were some in Kaifeng and in other parts of China, characterized by their practice of making the sign of the cross over everything they ate or drank and marking their children's foreheads with a small black cross. His somewhat vague information was that they had been living in China for a long time and had distinguished themselves in the past as fearsome warriors. Fear of persecution had, however, caused most of them to abandon their ancient faith and to adopt Chinese religions or Islam.

Ricci was happy to learn that there were still communities of Christian origin in China, as he had always hoped, and he realized that Marco Polo had told the truth when he had claimed that there were Christians in Cathay, unquestionably in large numbers during the Yuan era. He hastened to inform Superior General Acquaviva in a letter dated July 26, 1605,[31] which also contained yet another exposition of his thesis that China and Cathay were certainly the same country, albeit with some confusion about the dates and names of the leaders of the Mongol invasions.

Three years after his meeting with the Jew, Ricci asked a Chinese Jesuit to trace these "worshipers of the cross" in the hope of being able to receive them into the Catholic Church. The mission proved a complete failure, however, as they had now forgotten their ancient religion, they wished to be considered Chinese in all respects, and they were afraid that contact with foreigners could prove harmful.

Equally disappointing was Ricci's contact with the rabbi. When the Jesuit wrote that he had the books both of the Old Testament and of the Gospel, which talked about the coming of Christ, the rabbi stated in his reply that the Messiah had yet to appear on earth and that the Jews would have many centuries to wait. He did, however, very obligingly offer the Jesuit the place of leader of the synagogue on condition that he altered his diet and moved to Kaifeng.

Notes

1. OS II, p. 262.
2. See the section "Examinations and Baptisms" in this chapter. FR, book V, ch. III, p. 308.

3. FR, book V, ch. III, p. 308. Ricci's remark led to the three most important Chinese converts, namely Li Zhizao, Xu Guangqi, and Yang Tingyun, being referred to as the "Three Pillars of Christianity in China."

4. W. J. Peterson, "Why Did They Become Christians?...," in Charles E. Ronan and Bonnie B. C. Oh (eds.), op. cit., p. 146. The translation of this passage is more emphatic in the Fonti Ricciane: "a veil had suddenly been torn apart and all indecision vanished." FR, book V, ch. II, p. 288, no. 3.

5. W. J. Peterson, "Why Did They Become Christians?...," in Charles E. Ronan and Bonnie B. C. Oh (eds.), op. cit., p. 147.

6. FR, book IV, ch. XIX, p. 252.

7. Letter to Girolamo Costa, May 10, 1605; OS II, p. 273.

8. Letter to Girolamo Costa, p. 253.

9. Letter to Fabio de Fabii, May 9, 1605; ibid., p. 263.

10. Letter to Fabio de Fabii.

11. Letter to Giulio and Girolamo Alaleoni, July 26, 1605; OS II, p. 295.

12. Letter to Fabio de Fabii, May 9, 1605; OS II, p. 266.

13. Letter to Fabio de Fabii.

14. Cf. Christofer Spalatin, "Matteo Ricci's Use of Epictetus' Enchiridion," in Gregorianum 56 (1975): pp. 551–57.

15. Letter to Ludovico Maselli, February 1605; OS II, p. 257.

16. Letter to Ludovico Maselli.

17. FR, book V, ch. II, pp. 286–87.

18. FR, book V, ch. VIII, p. 356.

19. Letter to Girolamo Costa, May 10, 1605; OS II, p. 274.

20. Letter to Girolamo Costa, p. 285.

21. Cf. H. Bernard, op. cit., ch. IV.

22. Letter to João Alvares, May 12, 1605; OS II, pp. 284–85.

23. FR, book V, ch. VIII, pp. 353–54.

24. Letter to Ludovico Maselli, February 1605; OS II, p. 258.

25. Letter to Ludovico Maselli, p. 273.

26. Letter to Fabio de Fabii, May 9, 1605; ibid., p. 262.

27. FR, book V, ch. IV, p. 316, no. 1.

28. FR, book V, ch. IV, p. 315.

29. Hui is the name still used for one of the Muslim ethnic minorities in China today.

30. This term was used officially for the first time during the Yuan era in an imperial decree of 1289 to designate the followers of various Christian churches in China. The earliest "worshipers of the cross" were the Nestorians, the first Christians to penetrate China from the Byzantine empire through Persia in the seventh century and settle there permanently until the fall of the Mongol dynasty.

31. OS II, pp. 291–92.

~

CHAPTER SIXTEEN

Euclid Becomes Chinese

Beijing, 1606–1607

The Master said, "Reviewing the old as a means of realizing the new—
such a person can be considered a teacher."

—Confucius, *Analects* (2, 11)

Nothing could be done without this book [Euclid's *Elements*], not least
because its proofs are so clear.[1]

—Matteo Ricci

The Death of Valignano

Alessandro Valignano, who had done more than anyone else to inspire and
encourage Ricci, decided to visit the China mission and see the results obtained for himself. Despite their constant contact by letter, Ricci had met
him only once since his arrival in the East and had long been awaiting this
moment. Now he would finally be able to take justified pride in showing his
superior and particular point of reference the progress that had been achieved
in the twenty-two years since the founding of the first residence in Zhaoqing.

Valignano's visit was to take in the three residences in Shaozhou, Nanchang, and Nanjing before culminating in the capital. He would be accompanied by Lazzaro Cattaneo, now resident in Macao since 1603 after moving
there from Shaozhou to recover after an illness, and Francisco Martines, the
eldest of the Chinese lay brothers. The missionaries prepared Valignano's
journey with the utmost care. Xu Guangqi used his influence to obtain the

indispensable permits to travel through the provinces and cities, and Minister Wang Zhongming secured authorization for the Visitor of Missions to travel at the state's expense, receiving horses and provisions at the posting stations and transport on vessels along the Imperial Canal free of charge.

The letters with the permits were entrusted to Martines, who set off from Nanjing for Macao, where Valignano was awaiting a ship from Japan carrying valuable objects and silver for the missions, which was expected to arrive in February or March.

When everything was ready, the kidney problems from which Valignano had been suffering for some years suddenly returned, and he died on January 20, 1606, at the age of sixty-six. The China mission was plunged into mourning. Like Frances Xavier forty-four years earlier, he had arrived on the threshold of China but had been unable to enter. As Ricci wrote with great sorrow in his history of the mission, "His death was felt and wept over by the fathers of the two Christian missions in Japan and China."[2]

Ricci knew that there would not be another Valignano, a superior with such a thorough understanding of the peculiarities and difficulties of missionary work in China and with such a capacity to inspire him "with great love and hard work." He felt like an orphan without this support, as he wrote to Superior General Acquaviva,[3] and he wondered how the gap could ever be filled.

While the Jesuits were still grief stricken at the death of their superior, some tragic events took place in Macao that endangered the continued existence of the missions in China. The peace of the city on the coast, where Portuguese merchants and priests of various congregations lived alongside the local population, had always been balanced on a knife edge. The Chinese fear of foreigners as potential invaders was held in check so as to allow trade, but it remained a latent source of friction.

The situation of comparative calm enjoyed by Macao for a few years began to deteriorate particularly when the Dutch arrived on the scene fired with determination to carve out a niche on the Asian markets. Having already attacked the Portuguese settlements in the Moluccas, Mozambique, and Malacca, they landed in the Chinese province of Fujian in the summer of 1604 in a bid to establish a trading outpost but were repulsed by the local population. Fearing a possible attack on Macao as well, the Portuguese built new fortifications, thus heightening tensions that led to manifestations of intolerance between the Chinese population and the missionaries. The most serious events, which also involved members of the Society of Jesus, were sparked off, however, by a dispute between Augustinians and Franciscans.

The Franciscan friars of the monastery of Our Lady of the Angels clashed with the vicar of the parish of Saint Lawrence and asked Valentim Carvalho, the rector of the Jesuit college, to arbitrate between the two sides. This choice angered the new bishop of Macao, the Augustinian Miguel Dos Santos, a former Jesuit expelled from the order, who felt that his authority had been slighted. After a reciprocal exchange of accusations, the bishop placed an interdiction on Macao and excommunicated a number of people, including Carvalho, and the city became the scene of a bitter struggle between the two rival factions. There was fighting in the streets, "not only with spiritual arms," Ricci wrote in dismay, "but also at times with swords and harquebuses, which caused a great shock and confusion and was a scandal for nonbelievers and new Christians alike."[4]

The clash between religious orders had serious consequences. A member of the faction hostile to the Jesuits took advantage of the turbulent situation to inform the Chinese authorities that members of the Society of Jesus led by Lazzaro Cattaneo were plotting to invade the Guangdong province and then penetrate the Chinese interior with a force of Portuguese and Dutch soldiers. News of these accusations reached Canton, and the provincial authorities took radical measures without bothering to ascertain the veracity of the accusations. The governor assembled the troops, and the *haidao*, the official in charge of the coastal areas, evacuated all the houses in Macao close to the Portuguese fortifications, thus causing panic among the population. All trade between Macao and Canton was forbidden, and the Chinese were ordered to receive no one with a tonsure into their homes. Rumors spread, and some even claimed that Cattaneo was really the famous Li Madou in disguise.

One innocent victim of this fraught situation was Francisco Martines, who arrived in Canton and was ready to continue to Macao with documents for Valignano when he was informed of the Visitor's death and stopped in the city despite the danger. Confined to bed by an attack of malaria, he had been in Canton for a month when he was captured, along with some servants and his host, and imprisoned as a spy working for enemies of China. The prisoners were all tortured, and the youngest sought to save his skin by claiming that the Jesuit had transported gunpowder from Nanjing for the rebels. When the Chinese discovered a tonsure hidden beneath the Jesuit's long hair and Western-style clothing in his baggage, his explanations were all rejected out of hand, and his permits were dismissed as forgeries. Subjected repeatedly to torture, he died in prison in March 1606 at the age of thirty-eight. The first Chinese to enter the order as a lay brother, Martines followed the Jesuit cause faithfully for fifteen years. Coming just two months after Valignano's, his death was another serious loss for the mission.

Hostility toward the Jesuits spread to the town of Shaozhou, where Niccolò Longobardo, who had tried in vain to help Martines through the local authorities, was falsely accused of adultery with a married woman. Even though the charge was dismissed, the continued presence of the mission there was in serious doubt.

Just when everything seemed to be on the verge of collapse, however, an investigation ordered by Zhang Deming, the provincial inspector of Guangdong, on his return from Beijing, where he had met Ricci, proved that the accusations against the Jesuits were wholly groundless. The governor and the *haidao*, who were behind the false accusations made against the Society of Jesus, were removed from office and from the Guangdong province, and peace finally returned to Macao as well. The Jesuits had their brother's body exhumed and transported first to Shaozhou for the funeral service and then to Macao for burial. Completely cleared of any wrongdoing, Lazzaro Cattaneo was able to enter China and proceed to the residence in Nanjing, to which he had been assigned. He traveled together with a thirty-one-year-old missionary from Lecce, Italy, named Sabatino de Ursis, who was to continue to Beijing, where he arrived in the first half of 1607.

The Search for Cathay: Confirmation of Ricci's Conjecture

Less than a month before the end of 1606, Ricci received a letter from Suzhou in the present-day Gansu province, bordering Mongolia in the northwest. It was signed by the Jesuit lay brother Bento de Góis, who said that he had been traveling for years in search of Cathay and had asked the missionaries to send money to help him continue his journey and escape from the Muslims who had robbed him. All trace had been lost of "Brother Benedict" since he set off from India five years earlier, and Ricci had been waiting for a long time for news. He realized immediately from the tone of the letter that the situation was desperate and hastened to send help. Even though Gansu was a three-month journey away and it was inadvisable to set off in the freezing cold of winter, he instructed Zhong Mingli (called João Fernandes in Portuguese and simply Giovanni in Italian[5]), a Chinese lay brother in his early twenties who was about to begin his novitiate, to leave for Suzhou with another convert to act as a guide and enough money to cope with any eventuality.

Despite his concern for the life of De Góis, Ricci was pleased because his arrival provided definite proof that China and Cathay were the same country, as he had suspected at least since his first journey to Nanjing twenty years earlier. Even though his superiors in Europe and India had been informed of this conjecture and of all the evidence gathered since, they were still not convinced. The belief in the existence of another country to the north of China that could be reached by following the silk roads, as the Polo family had in the thirteenth century, was so deeply rooted in European culture that Ricci's communications in sporadic letters that took years to reach their destination carried no conviction. Moreover, it was still commonly believed that Christian communities existed in Cathay, whereas Ricci claimed that there were only the "worshipers of the cross," who could no longer be called Christians, in China.

The strongest believers in the presence of fellow Christians lost in the immense Asian continent, cut off from the Western world and in need of the Church's support, were the Jesuit missionaries in India. The first to suggest that a mission should be sent beyond the Himalayas in search of Cathay was Rodolfo Acquaviva, one of Ricci's companions on the voyage from Portugal to India. Jerome Xavier, the nephew of Francis Xavier, then organized an expedition to ascertain the existence of the country described by Marco Polo and establish whether Ricci was right or wrong. His idea was to send a representative of the order with the caravans of merchants traveling the silk roads to Cathay. If the brother found Ricci at the end of his journey, it would prove beyond all doubt that China and Cathay were one and the same. The task fell on Bento de Góis, a Portuguese lay brother aged forty, who spoke excellent Persian and was familiar with Muslim customs.

The Jesuit set off on his mission to discover the *finis terrae orientalis*, the indefinite location of Cathay according to the ancient sources, from Agra in India on October 29, 1602, bound for Lahore, the capital of the Mughal empire. It was from there that a caravan of merchants left every year for Kabul, the present capital of Afghanistan, the first stage of a long journey to the easternmost parts.

Ricci was informed of this initiative and confidently expected to see "Brother Benedict" turn up one day safe and sound in Beijing. As the years went by with no news, he began to feel apprehensive and to ask all the merchants from Central Asia that he met in the capital whether they had come across a man called Bento de Góis in their travels. No information was forthcoming, however, until the arrival of the letter from Suzhou. Having sent out a rescue party, all he could do now was wait for them to return with De Góis.

João Fernandes returned to Beijing on October 29, 1607, with the news that Bento de Góis had passed away in Suzhou on April 10. Having buried him there, Fernandes had finally overcome a series of obstacles and had succeeded in leaving for the capital together with the Armenian servant Isaac, who had accompanied Bento all through his travels. He handed over to Ricci the gold cross that Bento had worn on his breast, the permits, and the letters from Jerome Xavier, jealously preserved to the very end. He then took from his bag a bundle of torn and crumpled sheets of paper that he had collected around the lay brother's deathbed, which proved to be fragments of his travel journal. Isaac explained through an interpreter that the journal in which De Góis kept a record of his long journey had been torn up by a group of Muslim merchants in order to eliminate all trace of the sums they owed the Jesuit. Ricci patiently reconstructed the writings and filled in the gaps with the help of Isaac, who stayed with the missionaries for a month to help them retrace the steps of the journey, of which he was the sole surviving witness.

The Armenian said that they had traveled four thousand kilometers in three years on foot and horseback, proceeding through the Mughal empire and the Taklamakan and Gobi deserts. He spoke of crossing some of the world's highest and least hospitable mountain ranges, frozen expanses of ice and snow, bleak, torrid steppes, and barren, burning deserts, and of scrambling across stony ground, up and down slopes of sheer rock, negotiating steep paths, and wading across raging torrents. He told of meeting peoples with bizarre customs that spoke incomprehensible languages, of fighting with bloodthirsty bandits, and of audiences with the sultans of kingdoms hidden in the innermost depths of Asia. During the journey they had encountered some Persian merchants returning from Cathay who had told them about a Christian missionary living in the capital and enjoying privileges unheard of for any foreigner, such as traveling in a litter and being admitted to private audiences with the Son of Heaven. Having recognized Ricci from the description, De Góis realized that China and Cathay were certainly the same country. He reached Suzhou on December 22, 1605, and tried to contact Ricci for the first time but with no success, not least because he did not know Ricci's Chinese name. After waiting three months for an answer in vain, De Góis sent a second letter, which is the one that Ricci finally received.

Having relived the events of the mission through Isaac's words and every surviving shred of writing from the journal, Ricci wrote a detailed report reconstructing his fellow Jesuit's travels from the beginning to the tragic end and sent it in two copies to Superior General Acquaviva. One was addressed to the superiors in India to be forwarded "by way of the West Indies" to Portugal and then Rome, and the other to the Jesuits in Japan for forwarding to Italy "by way of the East Indies," through the Philippines and Mexico. While the original document in Portuguese has been lost, a second version written in Italian has survived. The three chapters of the history of the mission that Ricci then devoted to his Portuguese brother's mission provide a unique account of a daring and dramatic endeavor. Despite its hagiographic overtones and some inevitable omissions and inaccuracies in the names of localities traveled through, the sequence of stages, the calculation of distances, and the documentation of dates, Ricci's painstaking account has prevented De Góis and his expedition from falling into oblivion.

Despite the definitive proof provided by this expedition, the myth of the existence of a country other than China called Cathay still lingered on. In 1624, less than twenty years after Brother Benedict's death, the Portuguese Jesuit Antonio de Andrade, superior of the mission in Agra, decided to set off again in search of the Christians of Cathay, crossing the Himalayas and entering Tibet from the south. The record of his journey was published in Rome in 1627 with a title that once again contradicted Ricci's thesis: "The Discovery of Great Cathay, the Kingdom of Tibet, by Father Andrade of Portugal."[6]

Mathematics at the Service of the Empire

Meanwhile, Paul Xu continued his assiduous collaboration with Ricci in Beijing. Like Li Zhizao and many other intellectuals of the day, he was dissatisfied with the state of scientific studies in China and realized that the almost exclusive focus of the imperial examinations on the mastery of literary style and the knowledge of history and Confucian philosophy was far too narrow.

Xu Guangqi understood that Li Madou's learning was the product of an ancient and developed culture that it would be useful to share. When Ricci illustrated his knowledge and displayed the European books he had brought with him, he never failed to refer appreciatively to the great thinkers of Western antiquity, whose works had been translated into Latin and the vernacular in the fifteenth and sixteenth centuries, after the oblivion of the Middle Ages, and were becoming the foundation and heritage of European culture. In China, the most ancient books of science and mathematics had instead been lost, and those still available proved almost incomprehensible because they were based on knowledge that was now all but forgotten. It was a fate similar to the one that had befallen the astronomical instruments constructed by Guo Shoujing in the thirteenth century, which Ricci had found lying abandoned on the terrace of the astronomical observatory in Nanjing, far too advanced for the imperial astronomers of the Ming era to use.

In the absence of continuity with the achievements of the past, it was difficult for Chinese intellectuals to link up constructively with the scientific tradition and take significant steps forward. Mathematics and its applications were, however, more necessary now than ever before. On the one hand, more advanced mathematics would make it possible to describe the movement of the celestial bodies with greater precision and create a more accurate calendar. On the other, progress in arithmetic and algebra was indispensable to meet the needs of commerce, cartography, engineering, and every other sector of human activity.

Xu Guangqi wanted to understand how Ricci's knowledge could help him revitalize Chinese mathematics and above all use it in the fields in which he had taken an interest for many years now, namely the technical and scientific disciplines that were referred to as "practical" or "concrete" studies in Chinese and would be called "applied" today. These included military sciences, agriculture, hydraulics, and geography, but also the techniques of surveying and calendrical calculation. A large number of intellectuals took an interest in these practical studies in the late Ming era and considered them important to the empire's development and prosperity.

Before his conversion and contact with Ricci, Paul Xu wrote a number of works identifying the problems to be addressed and solved by the imperial administration. The first was the inadequacy of the army, equipped with obsolete weapons and led by generals with no technical training. Even though the Chinese had invented gunpowder at least three hundred years before the Europeans and had developed rockets and grenades as well as land and underwater mines much earlier, they had never been interested in wars of conquest and had failed to develop either their military skills or the associated technologies. The defense of the empire was an absolute priority, however, and Xu Guangqi knew that it was essential to be ready to repel any possible new invasion from the north, like the Mongol conquest of China in the thirteenth century. The danger was real, and the Great Wall, a barrier of more symbolic than effective character, would not be enough to avert it.

The second unresolved problem was control over the always precarious waterways. The two greatest Chinese rivers, the Huang He and the Yangtze, and the system of smaller watercourses connected by the Imperial Canal were arteries connecting the remote provinces of the vast empire and served as precious reservoirs for irrigation, but they were also the cause of catastrophic floods. After studying the problem for a long time, Xu Guangqi submitted a plan for reorganization of the waterways to the authorities in Shanghai, and he wrote a treatise on the Great Canal suggesting possible improvements to China's main artery.[7] The ideas put forward were those of a truly innovative thinker. He urged government officials to put an end to the superstitious view of floods as the vengeance of Heaven on human or imperial wrongdoing and to take a pragmatic approach, explaining that floods could only be prevented by addressing the problem in methodical and global terms, which meant measuring the width, depth, and capacity of rivers and canals, studying the lay of the land, carrying out precise surveys, and drawing good maps.

Xu Guangqi took the same systematic approach to the study of agricultural technologies, using his in-depth knowledge to write an encyclopedia in which, among other things, he analyzed methods to improve the yield of land and ensure better harvests. His suggestions were invaluable in a vast country like China with a huge population that was constantly threatened by starvation through recurrent famines.

Contact with Li Madou was a unique and unrepeatable opportunity for an intellectual with an interest in technical matters like Paul Xu, not least because he was convinced that learning science and embracing the missionaries' moral doctrine were two complementary aspects of the self-improvement that it was the duty of every Confucian official to pursue.

Finding a convert of such intelligence and dynamism ready and willing to study with him was also an extraordinary opportunity for Ricci and one that he thought would prove very conducive to the progress of the mission. The Jesuit was right. Having formed an idea of the content of the scientific books shown to him, Xu Guangqi suggested with support from Li Zhizao that they should be translated into Chinese and published. He was well aware not only of the intrinsic value of the works presented to him by Ricci but also of the fact that their publication was the best way to enhance the Jesuits' prestige and facilitate the spread of the moral and religious doctrine they taught.

The Translation of Euclid's *Elements*

Ricci took up his friend's suggestion and set to work despite the immense labors with which he was burdened in the capital, being weighed down by visits in addition to his other tasks. He and his Chinese friends were to translate Clavius's works in order to explain the concepts and methods of European mathematics to the intellectuals of the Middle Kingdom. His only problem was the impossibility of obtaining the imprimatur from the inquisitors in Goa and his superiors in Rome for publications of a nonreligious character. With the exception of the *True Meaning of the Lord of Heaven* and *Christian Doctrine*, all of his books had so far been published by the Chinese on their own initiative with no authorization from the ecclesiastical authorities. This impediment did not, however, deter him from going ahead with his plans to spread the knowledge of Western science.

The Jesuit had no hesitation as regarded the choice of the first work to be presented to the Chinese public, namely the Clavius edition of Euclid's *Elements*. Unquestionably influenced by his former master, Ricci was convinced that arithmetic and geometry as addressed in accordance with the Euclidean hypothetical-deductive method constituted the ideal basis for studying every other sector of mathematics and science, as well as the problems of astronomy.

Preparing a Chinese version of the *Elements* promised to be a labor of herculean proportions. It would be necessary to translate concepts and methods of proof developed in the context of Greek culture—something quite alien to the Chinese—from Latin into Mandarin and to find the words most suitable for conveying their precise meaning. Ricci had already shown that this was possible some years earlier in Shaozhou by translating the first of the fifteen books together with his friend Qu Taisu. On that occasion, however, the results were not intended for publication. Now it was necessary to carry the project through to completion so as to reach a vast public with a work that would last through time.

As such a demanding task required a large number of hours during the day, Xu Guangqi advised Ricci to engage the services of a scholar he knew who was seeking employment. The man was engaged and was given accommodation in the Jesuits' house to work full time on the project, but he proved unsuitable after just a few days. Ricci then asked Xu Guangqi to take his place, being well aware that only an "intellect like his" would be able to complete the work.

Paul Xu set about the task with great commitment and devoted three or four hours a day to the translation for at least six months from the summer of 1606. The procedure was as follows. Using the Latin text, Ricci explained the concepts, clarified their meaning, translated orally, and discussed the possible alternatives in the choice of words with Xu, who advised him on the most appropriate expressions and wrote the results down in perfect literary Chinese with a "clear, sober, and elegant" style. The difficulties were obvious, as described by the Jesuit in the preface:

> The grammars of East and West vastly differ, and the meaning of words corresponds in a vague and incomplete manner. As long as one gives oral explanations, it is still possible to do one's best to find solutions, but when wielding the writing brush in order to produce a text, it becomes hard to realize. . . . We turned the meanings of the original upside down, and investigated them from all angles, in order to find the best equivalent in the Chinese language.[8]

Their efforts were rewarded, and many of the expressions coined by Ricci and Xu on that occasion have become an integral part of Chinese mathematical terminology and are still in use today. The first six books of Euclid's work, devoted to the geometry of plane figures and the theory of proportions between magnitudes, were translated entirely by the beginning of 1607. Every bit as determined and untiring as Ricci, Xu Paolo wanted to continue with the other nine.[9] The Jesuit decided to stop, however, partly in order not to divert too much time from the mission's other activities and partly to see how the Chinese public would respond to the first part of the work.

Described as a milestone in the history of translation,[10] the work was entitled *Jihe yuanben*, which literally means "the origin of quantity." Since then, however, the word *jihe*, meaning quantity, has been considered a synonym of geometry in China, and the text is commonly known as the "Elementary Treatise of Geometry."

Euclid's work was written in Greek in the third century BC, was translated into Arabic in the eighth century AD, and into Latin in the twelfth century. Published for the first time in the original Greek version in 1533, it appeared fifty years later, probably in May 1607, in Mandarin Chinese, with prefaces by Ricci and Xu Guangqi. The Jesuit sent copies to his superiors, including two for Clavius,[11] who must have been pleased to see the work that he himself had helped to make known now printed in Chinese characters.

The complete Chinese edition of the *Elements* did not appear until 1856, two and a half centuries later, after the translation of the other nine books by the English missionary Alexander Wylie and Li Shanlan. The part already translated by Ricci and Xu Guangqi was preserved unchanged, together with their Chinese title *Jihe yuanben*, a great tribute to the two pioneers who first introduced Euclid to the Chinese.

The Perfection of Geometry

"Li Madou from the Great West," the name Ricci used to sign the preface, was aware that the presentation of such an innovative work to the Chinese public would require a very convincing introduction constituting an authentic manifesto in defense of mathematics.[12] He decided to take Clavius's preface to the Latin edition as his model, adding Confucian concepts in keeping with the culture of his readers and adopting the richly metaphorical literary style typical of Chinese writings, things that he was now able to do very well indeed. He started by pointing out that the moral duty to extend one's knowledge and to study nature was felt by both Chinese and Christian scholars and that mathematics was the indispensable starting point of the path to knowledge: "For depth and solidity, nothing surpasses the knowledge that springs forth from the study of mathematics."

He continued as follows:

My country in the Far West, although small as far as its area is concerned, by far surpasses its neighbours by the strict analytical method by which the various schools study the phenomena of nature. . . . Savants only accept what has been proved by reason. . . . From the very first moment I set foot on Chinese soil, I noticed that those who study mathematics put all trust in their manuals, and that there is no discussion on fundamental issues. Without solid roots and firm fundaments it is difficult to build something up.

Ricci presented Euclid as the greatest mathematician of all time, the sage who had brought his discipline "to great perfection," and the author of a book that had become "the daily food for the mathematician." Nor did he fail to mention Clavius, the great commentator and translator of Euclid, referring to his former professor as Master Ding, the Chinese word for nail and hence equivalent in meaning to Clavius. Ricci asserted that the German Jesuit's version of Euclid's work was so soundly commented that it could be used as "a ford in the river . . . a bridge, a shelter in case of danger."

In the preface to his Latin version of the text, Clavius had sung the praises of mathematics with great emphasis in order to persuade the Jesuit authorities of the need to include the discipline in the syllabuses of their colleges. Ricci did the same, omitting the philosophical arguments that were unsuitable for the Chinese public and instead lingering over an impassioned presentation of the innumerable applications of arithmetic and geometry. Clavius compared mathematics to a fountain from which the other branches of science gush; Ricci compared it to a ladder leading up to the peaks of knowledge. Mathematics, he wrote, makes it possible to penetrate the mysteries of the cosmos, to measure the breadth of the celestial spheres, to draw maps, to predict the course of the seasons, and to create the calendar. It all should be used by all, including men of state. How indeed is it possible to implement an effective foreign policy if you cannot calculate the distances between countries and cities, if you cannot draw the frontiers? Physicians too, he continued, need mathematics if they are to understand the influence of the heavenly bodies on human life. It is hardly surprising that Ricci referred to astrology, since the belief in the influence of the stars on life and health was as widespread in China as in the West.

The Jesuit's stress on the importance of mathematics in improving military techniques may well have been suggested by his friend Xu Guangqi, who attached great importance to this aspect. Ricci wrote that courage alone was not enough to win a war. It was also essential to calculate precisely the amount of food needed for the soldiers, the distance of the armies from the enemy, the formation to be adopted in battle, and the strategy of attack. He continued in this vein, overlooking no field in which the use of mathematics was of assistance.

Ricci followed this exercise in propaganda by illustrating the hypothetical-deductive method of the *Elements* to his readers. He explained how the

Greek mathematician took definitions and axioms as his starting point to derive five hundred theorems and constructions, each of which consisted in a proposition followed by the proof: "The . . . propositions . . . unroll themselves in a straight line from beginning to end. Nowhere can the order be reversed; it is one unbroken chain."

Aware of the difficulty of the work, Ricci assured readers that the "undoubtable principles at the beginning are extremely simple and clear." When they encountered "hidden and subtle arguments," they should be patient because their meaning would become manifest step by step. With a very Chinese touch of poetry, he compared the unveiling of a solution to a mathematical problem to "tense eyebrows that relax into a smile." Immediately afterward, in more concrete terms, he stated that anyone ambitious and intelligent could understand the *Elements*.

On drawing close to the conclusion, Ricci dedicated the book to his Chinese friends out of gratitude for their confidence in him. Describing himself as a "humble traveler," he made no attempt to conceal the hard work involved and recalled being forced to pause repeatedly by the difficulties encountered along the way despite the aid of willing helpers: "All beginning is difficult."

The work of translation would have been impossible without the help of Xu Guangqi, just as the active support of this authoritative scholar was essential to its circulation among Chinese intellectuals. Paul Xu wrote a second preface in praise of Western geometry and published a short essay entitled *Reflections on Euclid*. In accordance with the Confucian approach of seeking confirmation for present-day knowledge in the past, he endeavored to draw arguments in support of the Greek work from the most ancient Chinese traditions, pointing out that mathematics was considered a crucial tool for the management of the state and social life in China during the reigns of the first dynasties in the first and second millennium BC, and that there was a rock-solid tradition of mathematical knowledge handed down from master to pupil. This transmission of knowledge was, however, interrupted in 213 BC, when Ying Zheng, the founder of the Qin dynasty and the first to unify the Chinese empire—known to history as Shi Huangdi, the First Emperor—ordered the burning of all ancient writings so that nobody might invoke tradition to challenge his authority.[13]

According to Xu Guangqi, that drastic act severed the continuity of knowledge. Since then, mathematicians had been left with no guidance, groping blindly like someone desperately trying to examine an elephant in the dark with just one candle and managing only a small piece at a time, seeing the head but losing sight of the tail. The remedy in order to salvage the lost tradition was precisely the study of mathematics, a form of "lucid," "solid," "well-grounded" knowledge that sharpened the intellect. Moreover, the great strength of Euclid's work lay in its exposition of the method used to arrive at the results presented. In order to convince his scholarly friends, the *guan* also used the ethical arguments cherished by Confucianism, asserting that the study of mathematics made self-improvement possible and that "hasty people, coarse people, those satisfied with themselves, jealous people, and the arrogant" would be unable to understand it. If the text seemed "obscure," it was necessary to have trust and persevere. Understanding would come:

> It is like when walking through thick mountains you look in all four directions and you don't see a passage; but then you reach a spot and suddenly the passage opens itself.

The prefaces of Li Madou and Xu Guangqi said everything there was to say in support of the work, and once the book came out in Beijing and was circulated among their friends and the friends of friends in the other provinces, they could only hope for a favorable response on the part of the public.

It was not easy, however, to judge the impact of such an innovative text in a short period. Full appraisal would entail waiting for the new ideas to take root in Chinese culture and to undergo gradual development at the hands of specialists. The honest judgment that Ricci gives in his history of the mission is that the work was "admired more than understood." In actual fact, far from being unnoticed, the book was discussed and commented on all through the seventeenth century and into the eighteenth and stimulated scholars to compare it with Chinese texts, thus fostering the progress of autochthonous mathematical research. The translation by Ricci and Xu Guangqi is still remembered today in Chinese history books, where it is referred to as a work translated by the latter with the help of Li Madou.

Prompted by a certain desire for revenge on the literati who were hostile to him, Ricci did detect one immediate effect of the book's circulation even before objective assessment of the publication was possible. In his view, the treatise on geometry was the first book written in Chinese that the *shidafu* found difficult to understand:

> [The publication of the *Elements*] served very well to humble Chinese pride, as it forced their greatest scholars to confess that they had seen a book in their writing and studied it with great attention but had failed to understand it, something that had never happened to them before.[14]

The Fruits of the School of Mathematics: Works of Trigonometry and Astronomy

Ricci maintained that Euclidean geometry was the foundation of every other sector of mathematics and science. Xu Guangqi was aware that it offered a method of analysis and investigation of nature that would serve in a variety of spheres. In developing the studies commenced with Ricci in greater depth, Paul Xu ascertained that the ideal geometric figures and theorems of Euclid's geometry, though abstract and apparently far removed from the real world, were extraordinarily effective tools serving to address and solve the practical problems that interested him so much. The first proof of this came when he studied and translated with Ricci part of Clavius's *Practical Geometry*, published in 1604, and saw how geometry could be applied to the study of the position of bodies in the sky and to the techniques of topographical surveying used to describe the configuration and dimensions of the earth's surface on paper. The result was *Celiang fayi* ("Explanations of the Methods of Measurement"), published in 1607, which explained how to construct a geometric quadrant and use it to measure heights and distances. In accordance with the typical approach of Chinese mathematical works, Xu Guangqi presented a list of fifteen concrete problems, such as calculating the depth of a well, the height of a hill, or the altitude of the sun over the horizon at a given hour of the day, and showed how they could be solved with the methods of Western geometry.

In contemporary terms, the calculations involved were above all a matter of trigonometry, the branch of mathematics that studies the relations between the sides and angles of a triangle. Derived from the Greek for measuring triangles, the term "trigonometry" was very recent in Ricci's day, having been introduced in a work published in Heidelberg at the end of the sixteenth century by the German mathematician Bartholomaeus Pitiscus. The origin of the discipline was, however, ancient. Hipparchus, the greatest astronomer of the Greek world, used rudimentary trigonometric techniques to measure the diameter of the earth and the distance of the moon and the sun from our planet as early as the second century BC. While the discipline had developed over the centuries and had experienced further growth in the sixteenth century in Europe, it remained at a somewhat primitive stage in China. According to the historian of Chinese science Joseph Needham, the work by Ricci and Xu Guangqi was the first modern work of trigonometry to appear in the Chinese language.[15] In presenting the book to readers with the customary preface, Xu Guangqi wrote that, even though the Western techniques were similar to the Chinese, they were to be preferred because they made it possible to solve more complex problems and also provided an explanation of how they worked.

While working with Paul Xu in Beijing, Ricci kept in contact by letter with Li Zhizao, who had not been back to the capital for nearly four years. In 1606, the year before, the Jesuits' friend unexpectedly lost his position as superintendent of the Imperial Canal and was demoted as a disciplinary measure, the reasons for which are not known. Deeply embittered, he chose to withdraw to the Zhejiang province, his homeland, rather than return to Beijing. He continued to study during this voluntary exile, however, and published a book about astronomy based on the works by Clavius that he had read with Ricci in Beijing. Entitled *Huangai tongxian tushuo* ("Diagrams and Explanations Regarding the Sphere and the Astrolabe"), it presented the Ptolemaic theory of the universe and described techniques for the construction of astrolabes and other equipment of astronomical observation, which Li Zhizao had himself learned to make.[16]

Ricci was very pleased with his friends' work and realized that his dream of teaching European science systematically to the Chinese was finally coming true with their aid. Unfortunately, however, the fruitful collaboration with Paul Xu was also interrupted by the unexpected death of his father at the end of 1607, which obliged him to leave the Hanlin Academy and return to Shanghai for the customary three-year period of mourning. Even though he could no longer work side by side with Ricci, Xu Guangqi continued his studies and kept in constant contact with the Jesuit by letter. He was determined to develop his grasp of Western knowledge, not in order to repudiate his own culture but to rediscover its peculiar characteristics and revitalize them with the aid of the new skills and the new method he had learned from Ricci.[17] To this end, he devoted himself to the study of ancient Chinese works of mathematics and in 1608 published *Celiang yitong* ("Similarities and Differences in Measurement"), in which he compared the Western and Chinese methods of surveying and planimetry with respect to six problems. Written together with his pupil Sun Yuanhua in 1609, *Gougu yi* ("Principles of the Right Triangle") applied the Pythagorean theorem to fifteen problems in accordance with the classical Chinese methods and then put forward a new solution based on the methods taught by Ricci.

Xu Guangqi and Li Zhizao also worked together in later years, and in 1613, after Ricci's death, they published *Tongwen suanzhi* ("Rules of Arithmetics Common to Cultures"), in which the Jesuit's methods of arithmetic and algebra were once again compared to those presented in the classical texts. Their work in rediscovering Chinese mathematics and comparing it with its Western counterpart in search of an original synthesis, which was continued by other Chinese scholars after their death, is regarded by historians as part of the essential heritage of Chinese science.

Notes

1. FR, book V, ch. VIII, p. 356.
2. FR, book V, ch. IX, p. 364.
3. Letter dated August 15, 1606; OS II, p. 299.
4. FR, book V, ch. X, p. 372.
5. Born into a Christian Chinese family in the Guangdong province in 1581 and the younger brother of Zhong Mingren, baptized Sebastião Fernandes.
6. FR, book V, ch. XIV, p. 444, no. 3.
7. Cf. P. M. Engelfriet, *Euclid in China*, cit., pp. 78 ff and 289 ff.
8. P. M. Engelfriet, appendix 1, pp. 459–60. An Italian translation of Ricci's preface can be found in Pasquale D'Elia, "Presentazione della prima traduzione cinese di Euclide," *Monumenta Serica* 15 (1956): pp. 161–202.
9. Devoted to number theory, incommensurables, and solid geometry.
10. P. M. Engelfriet, *Euclid in China*, cit.
11. Letter to Claudio Acquaviva, August 22, 1608; OS II, p. 359.
12. For an English translation of the prefaces by Ricci and Xu Guangqi, see P. M. Engelfriet, *Euclid in China*, cit., pp. 454 ff, pp. 291 ff. An Italian version can be found in P. D'Elia, "Presentazione della prima traduzione cinese di Euclide," cit.
13. Shi Huangdi is remembered for having commenced the building of the Great Wall and for the huge army of terracotta soldiers found in his tomb at Xi'an during the last century, one of the most important archeological discoveries of all time.
14. FR, book V, ch. VIII, p. 360.
15. J. Needham, op. cit., p. 138.
16. Letter to Claudio Acquaviva, August 22, 1608; OS II, p. 363.
17. See *Statecraft and Intellectual Renewal in Late Ming China: The Cross-cultural Synthesis of Xu Guangqi*, ed. Catherine Jami, Peter Engelfriet, and Gregory Blue (Leiden: Brill, 2001), esp. p. 279.

~

CHAPTER SEVENTEEN

The Open Door
Beijing, 1608–1611

The extraordinary man is extraordinary for other men but compatible with Heaven.

—Zhuangzi[1]

The Master said, "From fifteen, my heart-and-mind was set upon learning; from thirty, I took my stance; from forty, I was no longer doubtful; from fifty, I realized the propensities of *tian*; from sixty, my ear was attuned; from seventy, I could give my heart-and-mind free rein without overstepping the boundaries."

—Confucius, *Analects* (2, 4)

The Paradoxes of an Extraordinary Man

Sabatino de Ursis arrived in Beijing in the first half of 1607 and proved a great comfort to Ricci, who was able to start speaking to him in Italian, a language he now found "as strange to me as to anyone who has not spoken it for thirty years"[2] and spoke less fluently than Portuguese. Moreover, even though his new companion from Lecce was not the expert astronomer awaited by Li Madou for years now, he did have a good grasp of mathematics and was able to make a valid contribution to their scientific work. Ricci also had a good relationship with Gaspar Ferreira, who had made remarkable progress in the study of the Chinese language and philosophy in the space of just four years and was now master of the novices.

Relations were not so smooth with Pantoja, the Spaniard who had been at his side during the difficult early days in Beijing. Ricci referred explicitly to problems with this companion two years earlier in a letter to Superior General Acquaviva in connection with a difficulty regarding Ferreira. The latter had not had time to finish the course of theological studies before being sent to China and was therefore barred by the regulations from taking the special vow of obedience to the pope and holding positions of responsibility in the order. Ricci told Superior General that an exception should be made for Ferreira because moral qualities and virtues should count for more than years of study, especially in the case of missionaries working in such a difficult country as China. He went on to say that Ferreira had a far better knowledge of theology than other priests who had completed their studies and taken the four vows, like Diego de Pantoja, "who has given us little edification, is regarded by the brethren and other people in the house as lacking in virtue and prudence, and has created problems for everyone, and for me in particular, in the five or six years that he has been here."[3] Hardly a flattering portrait.

Apart from the problem of relations with Pantoja, the true extent of which is not known, the mission continued its normal life as a hive of activity. It was now three years since the publication of the *Twenty-five Discourses*, and the work's favorable reception prompted Ricci at the beginning of 1608 to bring out another short treatise, written over the previous two years, in which he addressed the moral questions cherished by Chinese literati from a new viewpoint.

Ricci called his new work the *Ten Paradoxes* to highlight the fact that while the moral truths asserted were considered self-evident by Christians, they would prove contrary to current opinion and hence paradoxical for most of the Chinese public. The purpose of this friendly challenge to the common sense of his host country was to persuade readers to free themselves from some beliefs deeply rooted in their culture and to accept his spiritual message. Drawing on his own exchanges of views with scholarly friends, he presented ten short conversations in accordance with a customary rhetorical device of the Western philosophical tradition. The participants included his faithful allies Xu Guangqi and Li Zhizao as well as some of the best-known bureaucrats in the capital, such as Li Dai, the minister of personnel, and Feng Qi, the minister of rites. As in his previous ethical works, Ricci reworked the writings of Greek philosophers and Christian thinkers in a Confucian style.

The subjects addressed by drawing upon the words of great figures from the past included death, which the Chinese feared to the point of avoiding all mention of it as something most inauspicious. Ricci knew that many mandarins spent huge sums on potions promising immortality. In contrast to the Chinese dread of the "nothingness" that awaited them at the end of life, according to their culture, Ricci put forward the paradoxical view that death was not to be feared and even urged his readers to keep it serenely and constantly in their thoughts, to await in hope the eternal life that all believers would receive when, according to Catholic doctrine, earthly sorrows came to an end and those who had suffered and acted correctly would be rewarded in paradise.

Recourse to fortune-tellers, the purveyors of vain prophecies offering their services on every street in the capital, was another Chinese custom connected with the fear of death that Ricci attacked as incompatible with Christian morality. By his calculations, there were at least five thousand fortune-tellers in Beijing, and he endeavored to warn the "poor" Chinese of every social class who paid them for the privilege of being hoodwinked. Proceeding from one paradox to another, the Jesuit invited the Chinese to meditate on the preciousness of time and to prefer correct actions to vain discourse, he explained the meaning of fasting and penance, he urged them to examine their consciences every day, he illustrated the harm done by avarice, and he criticized the accumulation of riches.

In actual fact, not all of the forms of austerity cherished by Christian morality and proposed in the treatise would have appeared unreasonable or outlandish to Chinese readers. Many literati practiced asceticism and delighted in meditation. Some remained immobile and controlled their breathing, a form of yoga of Buddhist origin known as "crouching in calm"; others carried out the equivalent of soul-searching every day in silent reflection on their bad actions called "solitary self-surveillance," motionless in front of a bowl of water and a stick of incense.[4] None of them, however, saw these practices as atonement for sins committed against God's laws. The Jesuit therefore endeavored to direct their actions toward deeper moral awareness with religious aims.

Before publication, Ricci circulated the manuscript among his friends in order to gauge their reactions, and many agreed to write laudatory prefaces in accordance with normal practice. The academician Wang Yazi prepared a version of the book in poetic form with an introduction referring to Ricci as "the long-bearded man of few words from the Great West" and acknowledging the good results of cultural accommodation in flattering terms:

Despite having the heavens and the earth [in common with us], the kingdoms of the West at a distance of ten thousand *li* [a Chinese unit of measurement corresponding to about three hundred meters] from China could not communicate with it. If they are in communication with China today, this began with the scholar Ricci. . . . Having entered China, he learned its language . . . the classics no longer hold any secrets for him. He has changed his ways and adopted the clothing of China. Knowing his plans in depth, I sigh deeply in saying that the scholar Ricci is an extraordinary man.[5]

In calling Ricci "an extraordinary man," Wang Yazi cited a celebrated work of the Taoist tradition known as the *Zhuangzi* after the name of its author, in which Confucius is attributed with these words: "The extraordinary man is extraordinary for other men but compatible with Heaven." It is from this aphorism that the work derived its definitive title *Jiren shipian*, "Ten Chapters of an Extraordinary Man."

The book proved as successful as Ricci's other moral works, and two more editions soon appeared in Nanjing and Nanchang. As Ricci wrote in the history of the mission with his customary emphasis and perhaps a little exaggeration, "They were all so pleased with this book that there was nobody who did not confess that it was something of great benefit to human life and that they learned more in ten chapters of this book than in many other books put together."[6]

Li Zhizao also wrote a preface, published in a later edition, in which he expressed his admiration for Li Madou, describing him as a free and independent spirit capable of bringing out the truth and combating false knowledge, a man of vast culture and an extraordinary memory devoted to study, and deeply versed in disciplines neglected by Confucian culture, such as astronomy, geography, geometry, and arithmetic. He ended by asserting that it was right to consider Li Madou an "extraordinary" man because he had no fear of death, he believed in the existence of Heaven, and he imparted teachings of sublime significance to the Chinese. Above all, he practiced what he preached.

The History of the Mission

Well aware that in China, the land of literati, the written word was much more effective than the spoken, Ricci emphasized its importance in the short introduction to some religious prints that he delivered to the ink merchant and publisher Cheng Dayue for publication in a collection of works of graphic art entitled *The Ink Garden of the Cheng Family*:

Those who will live one hundred generations after us are not yet born, and I cannot tell what sort of people they will be. Yet thanks to the existence of written culture even those living ten thousand generations hence will be able to enter into my mind as if we were contemporaries. As for those worthy figures who lived a hundred generations ago, although they too are gone, yet thanks to the books they left behind we who come after can hear their modes of discourse, observe their grand demeanor, and understand both the good order and the chaos of their times, exactly as if we were living among them.[7]

Prompted by the desire to leave some trace of his work for posterity and sensing that he did not have much time left, Ricci decided to make haste in writing another work to which he attached great importance, namely the history of the Jesuit mission in China aimed at European readers. He chose to write this in his now somewhat shaky Italian and began filling sheets of Chinese paper, each of which was stamped with the Jesuit symbol "IHS Maria," in his closely spaced handwriting during his free moments at the end of 1608. Now in the Jesuit archives in Rome, the manuscript of *Della entrata della Compagnia di Giesù e Christianità nella Cina* ("The Entrance of the Society of Jesus and Christianity into China") is a small volume of 131 pages with a soft cover of thick brown leather.

The first of the five parts provides a description of China and Chinese life, giving information about the country's geography and telling the European public for the first time how the system of imperial examinations worked, how the bureaucracy was organized, and how life was lived every day in the urban and rural areas. Widely circulated and drawn upon by scholars of the Eastern world, these precious and largely unprecedented observations make Ricci the first Western sinologist. The other four parts are a detailed account of the Jesuits' adventures in China told in the third person, where Ricci reconstructs the stages of his missionary work from the first foothold in Zhaoqing, through the move to Shaozhou and the creation of the other residences in Nanchang and Nanjing, up to the final arrival in Beijing and the founding of the mission there.

The missionary states in the introduction that his aim is to present the "simple truth" to readers as recorded in his memory so as to preserve the history of the Jesuits' work on Chinese soil from oblivion and hand the great efforts of the pioneers on to their successors. He stresses that it is important for posterity to know how much the Society of Jesus suffered in order to enter the "wild forest" of China and how much "sweat and diligence" accompanied the missionaries' efforts in the Middle Kingdom.

While Ricci was busy reconstructing the history of the mission from the very beginning, the brethren kept him constantly informed about the progress and difficulties of the other residences. Niccolò Longobardo wrote from Shaozhou to say that there was no increase in the number of conversions and that the hostility of the local population was palpable, which worried Ricci so much that he started planning to move the mission to a safer locality. João Soerio, the head of the Nanchang mission, had died of pulmonary tuberculosis two years earlier and had been replaced by new brothers. There were now two hundred converts, including some relatives of the emperor, but this comparative success did not prevent a group of mandarins from circulating a pamphlet accusing the missionaries of belonging to a heretical sect and of undermining the stability of the empire. This was a clear sign that the Chinese authorities were beginning to fear that the spread of Catholicism among the lower classes might endanger social peace. The Christians in Nanjing—where Xu Guangqi had been baptized by João da Rocha five years earlier and where he often returned on visits from Shanghai—had also been forced to defend themselves against accusations of plotting against China and had succeeded in proving their innocence.

In the meantime, Li Zhizao had been persuaded by Ricci and his *shidafu* friends to end his voluntary exile and return to Beijing. Now fully rehabilitated, he soon obtained a new appointment as district magistrate in the central province of Hubei. While awaiting the preparation of the documents required for his investiture, he persuaded the servants in his building to convert, but once again, to the missionaries' renewed regret, he refused to do so himself. The reluctance of Li Zhizao and other intellectuals to convert showed that it was by no means a foregone conclusion that Ricci's friends and admirers would allow themselves to be persuaded to make such a drastic choice as the one urged by the missionaries, even though many of them were genuinely interested in Western knowledge.

Li Zhizao strenuously resumed the translation of scientific works in the conviction that their circulation was indispensable in order to persuade the Chinese authorities to reform the calendar with the aid of the Jesuits, a project to which he attached as much importance as Ricci did. They worked together on *Yuanrong jiaoyi* ("The Meaning of [Compared] Figures Inscribed in a Circle"), a work illustrating the peculiar properties of the circle and the sphere, figures that the ancients regarded as perfect by virtue of their total symmetry and regularity. Published at the end of 1609, this short volume was based on Clavius's comment on the *De Sphaera mundi* of Johannes de Sacrobosco.[8] The purpose of these geometric dissertations was in reality astronomical, as the demonstration of the perfection of the sphere served to confirm the validity of the Aristotelian and Ptolemaic model of the universe, the elegant system of concentric spheres studded with the celestial bodies and with the earth in the geometric center. Following Clavius, Li Zhizao wrote as follows: "The Lord of Creation has wrapped the small earth and the countless forms living on it in the great round heavens. . . . On the large scale, we have the trajectories of the sun and the moon; on the small scale, raindrops."

Ricci send the work to Superior General Acquaviva, emphasizing that the mission's scientific work was essential to its success in preaching the Gospel and asking to be sent books so that he would no longer be forced to rely solely on memories of what he had learned at the Roman College. This subject had also been mentioned in a letter to Girolamo Costa the previous March: "My lack of books is such that most of the things I publish are what I can remember."[9] The letter to Acquaviva also reiterated his request for a Jesuit astronomer "capable of continuing what I have begun with my limited strength, few books, and little knowledge."[10] The indefatigable Jesuit was never to see this entreaty answered.

The Imperial Map of the World

In taking stock of the situation, as was inevitable after a quarter of a century in the Middle Kingdom, Ricci reflected on the validity of his method of spreading the Gospel. He was more strongly convinced than ever that in a country as peculiar as China—where the state administration was entrusted to a bureaucracy of literati, religion played a marginal role, and absolute, exclusive faith in one personal God was an alien concept—the decision to accord priority to the quality of conversions, even at the expense of quantity, was still the right one. As he wrote to Girolamo Costa, "We intend to be few but good rather than many but less deserving to be called Christians. As the fruit is now being planted rather than harvested, what we are doing at present cannot be judged on the number of Christians."[11]

There were now "more than two thousand" converts in China,[12] by his reckoning, as against a total of twenty-one missionaries—thirteen Jesuit fathers and eight lay brothers and young Chinese novices. Ricci regarded these figures as satisfactory and saw the great prestige enjoyed by the Society of Jesus among nonconverts—due above all to the circulation of his own religious, moral, and scientific writings—as proof of success as well.

If the publications helped to make the Society of Jesus known and esteemed, the stability of the China mission was ensured primarily by the special status the Jesuits enjoyed in Beijing, where they lived at the state's expense under the protection of the emperor, a privilege that shielded them from any hostile initiative. With the conversion of Xu Guangqi, an exemplary official who was to rise to the highest ranks of the imperial bureaucracy, the Christian religion reached the upper echelons of the Chinese state. Paul Xu was the prototype Confucian Christian, the finest example of how religious faith and fidelity to the state could coexist. If a larger number of important *guan* could be persuaded to convert, as Ricci hoped, it would be easier to spread the faith through the other layers of society.

Even though Ricci envisaged a bright future for the China mission and was optimistic about the results that his successors would obtain, the Jesuit authorities still considered the position of the missionaries in China precarious and insisted on the need to obtain imperial permission to reside indefinitely on Chinese soil and preach the Christian religion. This recognition alone, in Rome's view, would guarantee the continuity of the mission after the deaths of its founder and the emperor Wanli.

Ricci thought for a long time about how to comply with his superiors' instructions but could see no realistic way of doing so. Xu Guangqi suggested sending a memorial announcing his readiness to relinquish the imperial stipend, but Ricci decided against following this advice in the belief that the Jesuits' greatest form of protection was precisely the fact of living at the state's expense. Ricci knew that he still enjoyed Wanli's protection, as demonstrated by the fact that he could go in and out of the Imperial City without having to ask for permission and he visited the Forbidden City regularly with Pantoja to check on the clocks. One day they were even invited by a group of eunuchs to join some dignitaries on the wall surrounding the imperial palace and to enjoy the extraordinary privilege of gazing upon the world forbidden to common mortals from above.

The emperor, as the eunuchs reported, continued to live in the voluntary seclusion of his apartments, a condition of total isolation that not even the wedding of his fifteen-year-old daughter in 1608 induced him to alter. Wanli's silence was broken shortly afterward, however, just when the missionaries had given up any hope of further contact with him. One day Ricci and Pantoja were summoned to the offices of the mathematicians in the Imperial City and were told that Wanli wanted twelve copies on silk of the 1602 edition of the map of the world[13] as gifts for the princes of the court.

Though deeply flattered, Ricci was very surprised at the request because he had never made the emperor a gift of one of his famous maps for fear that the Son of Heaven might take offense on seeing China represented as a comparatively small part of the entire world. Someone had evidently had the courage to show the emperor one of the many copies of his work, possibly one of those painted in color by the eunuchs in the peace and quiet of the Forbidden City, and Wanli had evidently not been affronted by the size attributed to China. The emperor, in Ricci's view, thus demonstrated far better judgment than the many mandarins who criticized his representation of the world.

The Jesuit told the eunuchs that he would be honored to comply with Wanli's wishes but there was a serious obstacle. The wood blocks used for printing were no longer in Beijing. Li Zhizao had taken them to his home-town, and the unauthorized copies produced by the printers had been lost during the great flood that struck the capital in the previous year of 1607. The missionaries hastened to remedy the situation by gathering together the eight blocks commissioned by Li Yingshi for the edition of 1603 and sug-gested that the eunuchs use them instead. As the *taijian* had no intention of presenting to Wanli any edition of the map other than the one he had asked for, Ricci offered to have a new set of matrices produced that were identical to those of 1602, calculating that this could be done in a month. He promised to embellish them with some new details and also decided to take advantage of this opportunity to include some information about Catholicism reserved exclusively for the Son of Heaven. The eunuchs accepted this proposal and hastened to report it, but the emperor, who was evidently impatient to satisfy his desire, let it be known that there was no need for Li Madou to concern himself so much, and he ordered the *taijian* to produce new matrices on the basis of the existing drawings. This "imperial edition" of just twelve copies[14] was completed within the first few months of 1608, and Ricci confined him-self to creating two small maps for the emperor, to be hung on either side of the throne.[15] Thus it was that the Western representation of the world made its way into the most important chamber in the whole of China.

The End of the Journey: Ricci's Death

Even though he was always active in embarking on new projects, Ricci felt weaker all the time, and the obligation to receive and return visits, whose frequency showed no sign of slackening, was an "immense labor."[16] It was now 1609, and he was fifty-seven years old, twenty-seven of them spent in China. He often felt weary, the ankle injured years before was becoming increasingly painful, the headaches he had suffered for some time were more frequent, and he was more prone to moments of reflection tinged with bit-terness than in the past. As he wrote to Girolamo Costa just one year earlier, "When this [letter] reaches your hands I will have sixty years on my back and will thus be very close to the grave. May it be God's will that I can complete the last action still left for me to perform in His service and make amends for the past failings."[17]

Ricci was now sure that he would never see Europe again. Even if he wanted to do so, he knew that the Chinese would prevent him because the law forbade anyone who had lived in China for too long to return to their native land lest they might hatch some plot against the empire. One day he found himself reflecting on the fact that he was on his own, the sole survivor of the small group of missionaries who had first entered China. Michele Ruggieri had died in Salerno in 1607; Antonio de Almeida and Duarte de Sande, the superior of the mission, had been dead for many years;[18] and the irreplaceable Valignano, the man who had supported the China mission most of all, had also passed away, leaving a great void. The new Visitor was Francesco Pasio, the fellow student who had traveled with Ricci and Ruggieri on the carracks bound for the East. Having lived for years in Japan, he had only a superficial knowledge of China, and Ricci feared that he might not understand the principles that he shared with Valignano and that informed his work. Sensing that he had little time left, he thought it his duty to provide his superior with all the information required so that he could continue the work of supporting the mission begun by Valignano and guide the brethren who would be arriving in China in the same spirit after his death.

Wishing to state his position clearly once again, Ricci wrote Pasio a long letter on February 17, 1609, encapsulating the essence of his vision of the missionary work in China.[19] The concepts explained so many times to superiors were systematically arranged in consecutive points and were expounded with a certain degree of pedantry and repetition indicative of the importance he attached to defending his work and its underlying principle of cultural accommodation. Ricci sensed that his views were not shared by all the brethren and feared that the work to which he had devoted his entire life might be ruined after his death.

Since Pasio had also evidently been urging the missionaries to obtain authorization from the emperor to preach the Gospel in complete freedom for some time, Ricci explained that only people living in China could imagine the difficulties to be encountered in simply requesting such a concession, let alone being granted it. This was beyond the grasp even of the brethren living in the Chinese provinces far from Beijing, who had no idea of the complex unwritten rules that governed life at the court and the quicksand into which documents addressed to the emperor could sink. Ricci instead had firsthand experience of the complexity of the bureaucratic procedures regarding a memorial and knew that the Son of Heaven was not free to decide by himself even if he was favorably disposed toward the Jesuits. If the request was submitted to the palace eunuchs or officials, Ricci would never know which offices it would be sent to, who it would be read by, what the final decision would be, and what consequences it might give rise to.

Ricci was, however, sure that the missionaries would be able to go on living in peace in China after his death, especially if they demonstrated their independence from the Portuguese in Macao. He declared his optimism as regarded the future of the work of evangelization because the Jesuits enjoyed a good reputation—"Great is the hope of the great harvest to be reaped in this immense realm"—and he considered the results achieved as something of a miracle in view of the initial difficulties. He defended his decision to work with the literati as well as the apostolic strategy based on scientific teaching. After many years of contact with the *shidafu*, Ricci respected them greatly—"The natural intellect of the Chinese is fine and acute"—and was convinced that they could excel in the sciences. He explained to Pasio that the gratitude he had earned by teaching science was a legacy that should not be squandered. If the literati proved so receptive to mathematics, he asked, how would they respond if taught "more abstruse" sciences of a "physical, metaphysical, theological, and supernatural" nature?

Ricci regarded the literati not only as brilliant intellectuals but also—and contrary to the opinion of them current in the West—as inspired by moral principles akin to those of Christianity. He was indeed convinced that the Chinese had practiced a very similar form of religion in ancient times. He rejected the view put forward by some Buddhist sympathizers that the decision to forge an alliance with the literati instead of fighting them was not a form of "flattery," and he hoped that the new missionaries would take the same approach, as there was enormous potential in China for spreading the Gospel. Given the structure and stability of the Chinese state, if it ever proved possible to convert the emperor, as Ricci sometimes dreamed, the entire population would become Christian and remain so over the years. He earnestly recommended that the new missionaries not neglect the study of the Chinese language and philosophy, which were indispensable if they were to be accepted.

In another shorter letter written on February 17, 1609, to the Portuguese Jesuit João Alvarez,[20] his last known missive, Ricci described himself as "old and weary but healthy and strong," and he expressed the hope that good and numerous reinforcements would be sent to China: "We need a lot of people because the field is so great . . . good people and of good intellect, because our dealings are with shrewd and educated people." As though wishing to make sure for the last time that his discovery about the identity of the Middle Kingdom had been acknowledged, he then asked if there were still any doubts in Europe that China and Cathay were one and the same.

According to the subsequent reconstruction of events by his brethren, Ricci began to act as though he sensed the end drawing close the following year, in 1610. He commenced negotiations to purchase a site outside the city for use as a burial place for priests. When everything appeared to have been settled, the Chinese owner of the land changed his mind, but Ricci was not in the least put out and astonished his companions by saying that they would soon find an even better burial plot. Shortly after this, he decided to start building a church because the chapel was no longer big enough to hold the numerous believers. It was to be built in the European style so as to avoid its being mistaken for a Buddhist temple, and De Ursis was to supervise the work. After the various chapels used so far, this would be the first Catholic church ever constructed on Chinese soil.

Ricci was overjoyed at the return to Beijing of Li Zhizao, who fell seriously ill however soon after his arrival. The Jesuit rushed to his friend's bedside and watched over him day and night for two weeks until he was out of danger. This devotion was rewarded because Li Zhizao finally decided after so many years, as a token of gratitude, to make Li Madou happy and convert. He was baptized with the Christian name of Leo.

Ricci finished writing his history of the mission in the early months of 1610, put his study full of books in order, collected all his papers, and burned his letters. He then wrote two documents, one containing instructions for the brethren in Beijing and the other addressed to Niccolò Longobardo, who was to become the superior of the mission after his death. He wrote Lazzaro Cattaneo a letter to say farewell forever.[21]

The city began to fill up in March as thousands and thousands of candidates arrived for the imperial examinations in April, as well as countless *guan* for their customary three-year assessment in the capital. The influx of people also meant the customary increase in the number of visitors, some of whom had no qualms about turning up at the Jesuits' house even in the night and asking to meet the famous Li Madou. Ricci skipped his meals in order to receive them all, but the increased workload was now more than he could bear.

On May 3, after the end of the examinations, the Jesuit felt his strength fading fast and took to his bed in a room on the ground floor, where it was easier to receive visitors. When asked by the brethren how he felt, he answered serenely that the illness would lead to his death.

Li Zhizao, still convalescent, was informed immediately and sent his own physician to Ricci's bedside, but the remedies administered proved ineffective. The brethren then called in the six most famous doctors in the city, who disagreed on the diagnosis and prescribed different medicines. As the news of Li Madou's illness spread, the house filled up with neophytes praying for the missionary's life. Ricci confessed to De Ursis on the sixth day and managed on the seventh to get out of bed to kneel down and pray and take communion. He then fell into a state of delirium in which he talked about the mission and mentioned the conversion of the emperor. The last rites were administered during a spell of lucidity on the eighth day, May 10. He spoke to the brethren on the ninth and gave them his blessing. When one of them begged him not to abandon the missionaries in such need of his aid, he answered that he was leaving them in front of "a door open to great merits" but not devoid of "danger and suffering." He asked them to give a loving welcome to the new missionaries from Europe, who would have to face the difficulties of life in a distant country. Then, with the approach of evening, he slipped away almost imperceptibly from life into death.

Wanli's Tribute

The news of Li Madou's death spread, and the minister of rites informed the emperor. The missionaries' house was invaded by friends and converts wishing to present their condolences and see the remains. There was, however, also a constant stream of literati, academicians, ministers, and important government officials, demonstrating with their presence the respect felt for Li Madou, the sage from the West, the author of the map of the world, the book of geometry, the treaty on friendship, and the catechism.

Li Zhizao helped the priests to receive their guests in accordance with the ritual procedures laid down by Chinese tradition for such sad events. The brethren wore the typical white mourning robes of literati and adorned the room containing the remains with funeral vestments of the same color. The visitors announced at the entrance were ushered into a room where they could change into mourning dress and were then taken to see the body, before which they bowed four times. After the second or third bow, one of the missionaries would approach the visitor and say that there was no need to complete those acts of great courtesy, being well aware that the mandarin would continue. The visitor was then taken back to the room to change his dress and was escorted to the threshold of the house for leave-taking. In accordance with another Chinese tradition, the missionaries asked the lay brother You Wenhui, known as Manuel Pereira in Portuguese, to paint a portrait of the deceased. This was the only depiction of the Jesuit produced in China, as Ricci had always refused to pose for portraits except when requested to do so by Wanli. The painting is now in the Church of the Holy Name of Jesus in Rome.

The remains were placed in a wooden coffin obtained by Li Zhizao at his own expense and were taken into the newly built church. Deciding how the burial was to take place, however, presented a serious problem. While the remains of all the Jesuits deceased in China had hitherto been taken back to Macao, the priests were convinced in this case that the journey from Beijing would take too long and that it would be better to find a burial place in the city where the missionary had spent the last nine years of his life. By law, Chinese citizens could be buried only far away from inhabited areas, and it was customary for the deceased to be placed in a wooden casket sealed with a layer of varnish and kept in the family home for as long as two or three years until the burial plot was ready. For foreigners like Ricci, the possibility of burial in China was not even contemplated, even though exceptions were made for the ambassadors of tributary countries who passed away during official visits.

In order to resolve this delicate issue, a friend of the Jesuits advised Pantoja to submit a request asking the emperor to grant a burial plot even though there were no precedents for such an act in the whole of Chinese history. An imperial grant for a tomb was an exceptional privilege even for the Chinese, reserved exclusively for mandarins of great merit or for those whose families made very substantial donations to the state. At the same time, however, everyone knew that Ricci was a special case. Pantoja drafted the request for Wanli, Li Zhizao corrected its style, and other friends read it and promised to facilitate the bureaucratic procedures. The document was submitted to the court on May 18, 1610.

Now as expert as Ricci in dealing with the mandarins, Pantoja busied himself with paying his respects and making gifts to the *guan* capable of assisting the request through the intricate bureaucratic maze and securing its approval. As it was a memorial regarding Li Madou, all of the officials contacted were very willing to help. One of the grand secretaries promised his full support and observed that Xitai certainly deserved not only a burial plot but also the erection of a temple and a statue, as was customary for those performing services of great benefit to society.

Li Zhizao's contacts at the ministry of rites, Pantoja's visits of courtesy, and above all the great respect that Ricci had enjoyed at court all served to accelerate the procedures. Just three days after its presentation, the request was shown to Wanli, who gave his consent for it to be examined by the relevant officials and returned for definitive approval in the event of a favorable decision. The request was returned to the Son of Heaven with the blessing of the minister of rites after a month, an exceptionally short period by comparison with the time it normally took for any other memorial, and approval was granted on June 17, 1610. Ricci was to be buried in a plot of land assigned by order of the emperor. It was the greatest honor a foreigner could possibly receive in China.

The imperial officials selected four possible sites and asked the Jesuits to choose the one they thought most suitable for the tomb of the founder of the China mission. Their choice fell on a huge villa of brick and wood with thirty-eight rooms surrounded by a vast plot of land in the locality of Zhala just outside the Fuchengmen, the western gate of the inner city. Built thirty years earlier, it was the property of a *taijian* now in disgrace and imprisoned to await execution. As it had since been transformed into a Buddhist temple and was therefore under the jurisdiction of the ministry of rites, the machinations of the owner's eunuch friends could not prevent it from being handed over to the Jesuits. Two edicts signed by Huang Jishi, the governor of Beijing, and Wu Daonan, the minister of rites, attested its donation "by order of the emperor." The missionaries were granted permanent exemption from taxes on their new property, and a plaque was placed over the entrance with the inscription "By Imperial Largess." The governor then sent a solemn procession with a wooden panel bearing the words "To one who came attracted by justice, to the author of many books, to Li Madou from the Great West" for the tomb that was to be erected there.

Once the house had been cleared of all the Buddhist paintings and ornaments, which the missionaries burned in public in a great bonfire, Ricci's coffin was taken there on April 22, 1611, nearly a year after his death. Niccolò Longobardo arrived in Beijing on May 3 as the new superior of the mission to supervise the preparations for the burial. After the "cleansing" of the building, a hexagonal chapel was erected at one end of the garden with two semicircular walls stretching out to enclose the area reserved for the graves of missionaries. Ricci's tomb was placed in the center surrounded by four cypresses, which are considered emblems of mourning in China too. The funeral took place on November 1, All Saints Day, and was attended by the Jesuit brethren together with all of Li Madou's closest friends, including Xu Guangqi, who returned to Beijing from Shanghai six months after Ricci's death. As Nicolas Trigault wrote in his account of the ceremony, everyone manifested great sorrow when the coffin was buried, "but above all Doctor Paul, who had always loved the Father in particular, apart from his love for us and the Christian religion." Xu Guangqi held on to one of the ropes used to lower the coffin and wept, "finding no other way to show his love and grief."[22]

A fitting epitaph is provided by this moving description of the missionary's lot contained in a letter about Ricci's life in the Far East sent to his brother Orazio five years earlier:

> I remember writing in other [letters] to tell my brothers to think often of us priests living in these lands as in voluntary exile, far away not only from our loved ones, our parents, brothers and sisters and relatives, but also from Christian folk and our countrymen, sometimes in places where not one European is

to be seen for ten or twenty years. Some, like us in China, never eat bread or drink wine; some, like those in Malacca, live on flour made from trees and others on the roots of plants; some go barefoot with the fierce sun beating down on their heads and the ground scorching their feet, and all in outlandish dress.

Here we are with long beards and hair down to our shoulders in houses even poorer than those of our workers; and many times we have to flee from enemies come to do us harm, as once happened to me, when I jumped out of a window and twisted my ankle, which still causes me pain.

Some are shipwrecked in seas and rivers, and I have had my share of that. Some are crucified by the enemy, some pierced with arrows and others with darts. And those of us that live always have death before our eyes, being among millions of heathens, all of them our enemies; and all this for the love of God, and so that God may forgive us our sins and save us from hell: and with all that, we weep and shed many tears every day, not knowing what God's judgment will be.

What then must be done by those who are at home with their families and friends in the midst of comfort and pleasure? . . . I cannot in truth look forward to many years more and my hair is already all white. These Chinese wonder that I should be so old at no great age and do not know that they are the cause of my white hair.[23]

Notes

1. FR, book V, ch. II, p. 302. The work is attributed to Zhuang Zhou, a philosopher who lived in the fourth century BC, also known as Zhuangzi or "Master Zhuang."

2. Letter to Giulio and Girolamo Alaleoni, July 26, 1605; OS II, p. 295.

3. Letter to Claudio Acquaviva, August 15, 1606; OS II, pp. 303–4.

4. J. Gernet, *Chine et christianisme*, cit., p. 194.

5. Pasquale D'Elia, "Sunto Poetico-ritmico di I Dieci Paradossi di Matteo Ricci S.I.," in *Rivista degli studi orientali* 27 (1952): pp. 111–38.

6. FR, book V, ch. II, pp. 303–4.

7. Cit. in Antonella Cotta Ramusino, *Matteo Ricci Li Madou* (Rimini: Guaraldi, 1996), with an introduction by Paolo Aldo Rossi, p. 9; and in J. Spence, *The Memory Palace of Matteo Ricci*, cit., p. 22.

8. See chapter 6 ("Euclidean Geometry and the Achievements of Chinese Mathematics").

9. Letter dated March 6, 1608; OS II, p. 336.

10. Letter dated March 8, 1608; OS II, p. 343.

11. Letter dated March 6, 1608; OS II, p. 338.

12. Letter dated March 6, 1608; OS II, p. 331.

13. This was the third edition, produced with the aid of Li Zhizao. See chapter 13 ("Li Zhizao and Geography: The Third Edition of the Map of the World").

14. J. D. Day, "The Search for the Origins of the Chinese Manuscript of Matteo Ricci's Maps," cit., p. 96.

15. FR, book V, ch. XVII, p. 474, no. 2.
16. Letter to Claudio Acquaviva, August 22, 1608; OS II, p. 367.
17. Letter dated March 6, 1608; OS II, p. 338
18. Almeida died in 1591 and Duarte de Sande in 1599.
19. OS II, pp. 377–87.
20. OS II, p. 388.
21. FR, book V, ch. XXI, p. 546, no. 1.
22. FR, book V, ch. XXII, pp. 627–28.
23. Letter to Ricci's brother Orazio, May 12, 1605; OS II, p. 279.

~

CHAPTER EIGHTEEN

After Matteo Ricci

The Scientific Legacy, Triumph, and Persecution

All in all, the contribution of the Jesuits, chequered though it was, has characteristics of noble adventure. If the bringing of the science and the mathematics of Europe was for them a means to an end, it stands for all time nevertheless as an example of cultural relations at the highest level between two civilisations theretofore sundered.

—Joseph Needham[1]

Those who believe that the religion they profess is true must desire tolerance: in the first place, in order to be themselves tolerated in the countries in which their religion is not dominant; and then, so that their religion can conquer all minds.

—Voltaire, *Treatise on Tolerance*

The Jesuit Mathematicians and the Scandal of the Eclipse

A few days after Ricci's funeral, a eunuch asked the grand secretary Ye Xiangao why Li Madou had been accorded such an extraordinary mark of imperial favor as the granting of a burial plot. The mandarin answered that the translation into Chinese of Euclid's work would have sufficed by itself to merit such an honor.[2]

The remaining brethren and the new arrivals intended to continue the dissemination of Western scientific knowledge begun by the founder of the mission with the crucial aid of their faithful allies Xu Guangqi and Li Zhizao.

Just as Ricci had done so many times before, Sabatino de Ursis asked his superiors to send scientific books from Europe along with missionaries skilled in astronomy. As he wrote in a letter dated September 2, 1610, if the mission was to function, it was indispensable to work with both hands, the right for "the things of God" and the left for the spreading of science.[3] The new superior of the mission, Niccolò Longobardo, echoed these sentiments two months later in urging the Jesuit authorities to send "good mathematicians" to China.[4] All this insistence was prompted by the conviction that the time was now ripe to suggest to the Chinese authorities that the task of reforming the calendar might be assigned to the Jesuits.

This belief proved quite correct, and the long-awaited opportunity to demonstrate the validity of their methods soon presented itself. On December 15, 1610, the imperial astronomers calculated the beginning of the solar eclipse with an error of half an hour and supplied incorrect data also as regarded its duration.[5] This blunder, the latest in a long series, caused great outcry. While the minister of rites consulted experts in search of a solution to a problem that now threatened the stability of imperial power, Paul Xu came forward and submitted a memorial suggesting that the correction of the calendar should be entrusted to the Jesuits. While the emperor raised no objection, the proposal aroused the utmost hostility among the court mandarins who were opposed to the involvement of foreigners in matters of state, and the memorial remained unanswered.

Meanwhile, De Ursis set about studying the characteristics of the Chinese calendar with a view to pinpointing possible modifications, and he drew up a report for his superior Pasio in 1612.[6] Given the fundamental differences in approach between Chinese and Western astronomy and the fact that the Chinese divisions of time were unlike the European units, the Jesuit was convinced that radical alteration of the calendar used in the Middle Kingdom was impossible, and it would be better to introduce the adjustments needed to improve the accuracy of astronomical predictions and the calculation of eclipses while maintaining the basic structure. Though limited, the project was still very demanding and necessitated, as Ricci had always maintained, the assistance of numerous specialists.

Longobardo took it upon himself to ask Superior General Acquaviva for reinforcements once again on the same grounds as his predecessor. As he wrote on October 15, 1612, "It is an established fact for us that mathematics will open the way to what we are seeking. . . . We should be able to offer the king philosophy and theology in the shadow of mathematics."[7] A few months later, fearing that his pleas would be ignored, he dispatched the young French Jesuit Nicolas Trigault, newly assigned to the China mission, to Rome with instructions to illustrate the missionaries' needs to the Superior General and the pontiff.

Trigault left on February 9, 1613, with Ricci's portrait[8] and the completed manuscript of his history of the mission. During the journey and his stay in Rome, where he arrived at the end of 1614, the Belgian prepared a Latin version of the original with the addition of seven chapters of his own,[9] two of which were devoted to Ricci's death and the events connected with his burial and the others to the activities of the residences outside Beijing. This was published under his name in 1615.[10] While Ricci's original manuscript was left in the archives and forgotten after being handed over to the Jesuit authorities, Trigault's Latin version enjoyed considerable circulation and was not only translated into French, German, and Spanish but was also retranslated into Italian in 1622.[11]

After meeting with the Jesuit authorities in Rome, Trigault traveled through Europe for two years in search of funds as well as scientific books and instruments. He was accompanied on part of his travels by Johann Schreck (1576–1630), known as Terrenz, or Terrentius in Latin, a German Jesuit and eclectic scientist highly esteemed as a physician, botanist, mathematician, and astronomer. Schreck was also the seventh member of the Accademia dei Lincei, which he joined in 1611, just eight days after his friend Galileo and a few months before deciding to enter the Society of Jesus. He met Trigault in 1614 and agreed to follow him to China. Being aware that one of the tasks awaiting him was the reform of the Chinese calendar, he wrote to Galileo from Milan asking for the most recent astronomical tables and some advice on the correct calculation of eclipses. Unquestionably embittered at having been warned not to hold, teach, or defend the Copernican theory by the Jesuit cardinal Roberto Bellarmino on February 26, 1616, the scientist did not reply.

On April 15, 1618, after three years of preparations, Trigault left for China from Lisbon, together with another twenty-two Jesuits assigned to the missions in the East. The five merchant ships were loaded with scientific and astronomical instruments of every type and hundreds of books encompassing the latest developments in Western science.[12] While the astronomical books did not include the work by Copernicus presenting the heliocentric system, which the Church considered heretical, Galileo's observations of the heavens were discussed in others. Schreck did not forget to take a copy of Galileo's most recent telescope, a gift from Cardinal Federico Borromeo in Milan that he intended to present to the emperor.

Some of the missionaries died during the voyage or soon after their arrival in Goa, and only eight of the survivors entered China. In addition to Schreck, two of them were the skilled mathematicians that Ricci had requested so many times, namely Giacomo Rho from Milan and the German Johann Adam Schall von Bell. It would be their task to continue at a more highly specialized level the dissemination of Western knowledge begun by the founder of the mission thirty years before.

Scientific Work

While Trigault was in Europe enlisting Jesuit scientists, an edict issued in 1615 by Valentim Carvalho, the Provincial of Japan and China, called the work of the missionaries in China into question once again. Having been forced to move to Macao the previous year as a result of anti-Christian persecution in the Land of the Rising Sun, the Provincial forbade the Jesuits resident in China to teach mathematics and philosophy or to undertake the correction of the calendar. While this decree fortunately had no real effect, as Carvalho left his post soon afterward, the episode showed that not everyone in the order agreed with the approach of the founder of the China mission.

This unpleasant incident was the least of the problems that beset the mission in the years immediately after Ricci's death, when the Jesuits were faced with the first manifestation of an anti-Christian attitude on the part of the Chinese government in the thirty-plus years of their stay in the Middle Kingdom.

It all began in Nanjing with a series of memorials sent to the court by the vice minister of rites Shen Que in 1616 accusing the Jesuits of being a dangerous influence, turning the people against the government, and leading the literati astray from the Confucian tradition. Xu Guangqi tried to defend his friends with the support of another eminent scholar, namely Yang Tingyun,[13] who had been baptized after Ricci's death with the name of Michele. The situation grew worse, however, and culminated on February 14, 1617, with the issuing of an imperial edict ordering the Jesuits' arrest and expulsion from China.

When the anti-Christian persecution finally came to an end in 1623,[14] many things had changed in the China mission. Pantoja died in 1618 and De Ursis two years later without either having been able to return to Beijing. Wanli, the invisible monarch who had helped and protected Ricci, also died in 1620 after forty-seven years on the throne. The new emperor Taichang died of a mysterious illness within a few months—many suspected poisoning—and was followed by Tianqi, who ruled until 1627. His successor, Chongzhen, was to be the last emperor of the Ming dynasty.

With the end of anti-Christian hostilities, the life of the missions slowly returned to normal, and it was possible to resume the work of spreading the

Gospel. It was, however, now evident that the Chinese state could react violently if it thought Catholicism was a threat to its stability. The existence of a religion not subordinated to imperial authority was in fact inconceivable.

Johann Adam Schall von Bell and Giacomo Rho were held up in Macao and were involved there in the defense of the city against attack by the Dutch in 1622. Schall moved to Beijing the following year and joined Schreck, who was already there devoting his energies to work in science and astronomy. The German Jesuit immediately demonstrated his skill as an astronomer by accurately predicting the duration of the solar eclipse of September 1624,[15] and Xu Guangqi had his calculations printed in a small volume that he presented to the minister of rites as proof that the new arrivals were ready and able to make a contribution to Chinese astronomy. Published by Schall in 1626, "The Lens That Sees Faraway" was the first book in Chinese about the telescope, described as an "instrument that sharpens the sight and delights the scientist," and it also presented the astronomical discoveries of Galileo, albeit without mentioning him explicitly by name.[16] After four years of work in the capital, Schall left for Xi'an to join the mission established in the Shaanxi province.

Schreck also devoted himself to scientific work.[17] In addition to writing a medical treatise in 1626 entitled "Western Theories about the Human Body," which was not published until after his death, he embarked on a meticulous collection and classification of herbs and plants unknown in Europe in order to study their curative properties. He worked with some Chinese collaborators on a mathematical work entitled "Great Measurement," which presented the most recent developments in trigonometry,[18] and he wrote the treatise "The Explanation and Illustration of Wonderful Instruments" together with Wang Zheng. Published in 1628, this work described machines used to lift and transport heavy objects with an explanation of how they worked based on the principles of geometry. The third Jesuit scientist, Giacomo Rho, who was based in the Shaanxi province, devoted his energies above all to mathematics and writing a book on anatomy and medicine.

The works of the new arrivals joined those that the other missionaries had continued to write after Ricci's death, combining scientific work with evangelization.[19] Chinese converts were also involved in the production of these volumes by helping the missionaries with their translations, writing prefaces to their works, or providing funds for wood-block printing.

The intense and fruitful period that crowned Ricci's pioneering efforts culminated in 1628 with the publication of the Jesuits' twenty most significant works in the *First Collection on the Learning from Heaven*, compiled by Li Zhizao. The term "Learning from Heaven," considered equivalent to "Western studies," was used by Chinese intellectuals for the whole of what the missionaries had to impart, placing ethics, religion, science, and engineering all together at the same level. The works in the collection were in fact divided into the two categories of "general principles," encompassing the ethical and philosophical works, and "concrete phenomena," regarding the technical and scientific disciplines.[20] The missionaries allowed such different subjects to be presented together under the name of "learning from heaven" because this reflected the combination of science and religion that had always characterized their work of evangelization. For the Jesuits, the heavens were an object of study but also the dwelling place of God, the supreme lawgiver of nature.[21]

Li Zhizao explained in his preface to the collection that the writings provided true insight into various sectors of human knowledge, a doctrine that Confucius "would not change if he came [back to life]."[22] The works on "general principles" included Ricci's *Ten Chapters of an Extraordinary Man, Twenty-five Discourses,* and *The True Meaning of the Lord of Heaven.* The collection also included a work on the Nestorian Stele, a renowned monument dating from AD 781 and bearing inscriptions in ancient Chinese and Syriac about the Nestorian religion and the history of the Christian mission in China during the Tang period. On its discovery in Xi'an in 1623, large numbers of Chinese scholars attempted to decipher the Syriac inscriptions with no success until a converted literatus sent Li Zhizao a copy to show to the missionaries. It was Schreck, an expert on Semitic languages, who completed the translation.[23]

A pall was cast over the pride the missionaries had in the published collection of their works by Trigault's suicide in November the same year.

The Reform of the Calendar

The Jesuits did not abandon their hopes of being asked to assist in the reform of the calendar, which they felt sure would come about sooner or later. Having received no reply from Galileo, Schreck addressed his astronomical queries to the German astronomer Johannes Kepler, who sent answers as well as the highly up-to-date Rudolphine Tables in 1627.[24]

An opportunity to try out Kepler's suggestions and make use of the new astronomical tables presented itself in 1629, when Chongzhen had been on the throne for a year. A solar eclipse was predicted for June 21, and the Son of Heaven, deeply concerned about the consequences that another mistake on the part of the imperial astronomers might have, asked Schreck and Longobardo to perform the necessary calculations so as to check their results against those of the Chinese and Muslim astronomers. The Jesuits' data proved more accurate, and Xu Guangqi felt justified by this further demonstration of the effectiveness of Western methods in submitting a proposal once again to undertake reform of the calendar with their aid.

An imperial edict[25] issued on September 1, 1629, ordered the creation of a new calendrical office, with Xu Guangqi as its director, to undertake the reform of the Chinese calendar "in accordance with the Western methods." It was thirty-five years since Minister Wang of Nanjing had first spoken to Matteo Ricci of the possibility of assigning the Jesuits the task of carrying out the astronomical calculations. Li Madou's dream was becoming reality.

Xu Guangqi asked Schreck to prepare a plan of work together with the now elderly Longobardo, Li Zhizao, and a group of Chinese experts. He drew up a large-scale project for translating the European works brought back by Trigault into Chinese; for writing new treatises on a whole range of subjects including arithmetic, geometry, hydraulics, optics, mechanics, and music; and for the construction of the indispensable scientific equipment for observation and measurement. The plans were solemnly presented to Chongzhen by Xu Guangqi on September 13, 1629.

The work had just begun when Schreck died in 1630, followed shortly afterward by the seventy-five-year-old Li Zhizao, the Jesuits' precious ally for so long. Rho and Schall were recalled to Beijing to take the missionary's place. The first translations were presented at court one year later by Xu Guangqi, who had meanwhile been appointed minister of rites and then grand secretary and tutor to the heir to the throne. The Jesuits' satisfaction at the presence of such an authoritative and illustrious convert at the very top of the government ladder was short-lived, however, as Xu Guangqi fell ill and died on November 8, 1633, at the age of seventy-one. Paul Xu had always done his utmost for the Jesuit cause with devotion and friendship and without ever deviating from fidelity to the Confucian system of values. The cycle begun by Matteo Ricci came to a close with his death.

The Western astronomical office continued to operate under the guidance of Li Tianjing, a scholar designated by Xu Guangqi before his death. Even though the new director was not a convert and lacked the authority of his predecessor in coping with the inevitable disputes aroused by the Jesuits' work,[26] the studies, research, and translation continued, and the new works were presented to the court at regular intervals. The Son of Heaven received a telescope as a gift in 1634 and was so impressed that he asked for more of those instruments immediately.

The huge project was completed by the end of 1636: an encyclopedia of Western knowledge in 137 volumes entitled *Chongzhen lishu* ("Writings on the Calendar from the Chongzhen Reign") and containing Chinese translations of European works, new works in Mandarin written by the Jesuits and

Xu Guangqi together with a group of Chinese assistants, and two celestial atlases. In addition to Schreck's book on trigonometry, the mathematics section included a dozen works by Rho, one of which, entitled "Calculus," presented logarithms—a major innovation of sixteenth-century European mathematics and an indispensable tool for the simplification of astronomical calculations—for the first time in China.

The cosmological works in the astronomy section offered the Chinese a description of the universe differing from the geocentric Ptolemaic system that Ricci had presented to them. In European science, despite the Church's opposition to the heliocentric system and Galileo's forced recantation in 1633, the Copernican revolution was sweeping the Ptolemaic vision of the world away forever. Being well aware of the most recent developments in astronomy but unable to embrace the Copernican system, the missionaries of the new generation presented to the Chinese the model of the universe devised in the second half of the sixteenth century by the Danish astronomer Tycho Brahe, an elegant compromise between the heliocentric and geocentric systems accepted temporarily in the West because of its compatibility with the dictates of religious authorities. According to Brahe, the earth remained at the center of the universe with the sun rotating around it and the planets rotating in turn around the sun. The Jesuits continued to put this system forward even after it had been discarded in Europe in favor of the Copernican system, which was not presented in China until 1760, a century later, by the French Jesuit Michel Benoist.

The adoption of an incorrect cosmological system such as Brahe's model had no effect on the validity of the calculations performed for the calendar, as demonstrated by the fact that the Chinese had produced excellent calendars in the past without employing any geometric model of the solar system.[27] The superiority of the Jesuits' predictions was due to the use of more advanced astronomical tables, methods of calculation, and instruments of observation. And the effectiveness of the "Western methods" was confirmed every time they were challenged by the Jesuits' adversaries.

At the same time, the authority that was gained through the formidable feat of cultural transmission facilitated the work of evangelization, and the missions flourished. Even though the converts numbered no more than a few thousand, there were now sixteen Jesuit residences scattered throughout Chinese territory, including one in Xu Guangqi's hometown Shanghai. Christianity also obtained a foothold inside the Forbidden City thanks to Schall, who succeeded in converting dozens of eunuchs and ladies of the court. Now enjoying a position at court that was at least equal to Ricci's, the German Jesuit even succeeded in repairing the harpsichord given by his predecessor to Wanli, which had been rediscovered in the imperial apartments after so many years. Chongzhen was so pleased with the success of the Western methods in reforming the calendar that he bestowed the inscription "Imperial Praise on the Learning from Heaven" on Rho and Schall. Rho died in 1638 at the age of just forty-five, and it was Schall, the most long-lived of the three Jesuit mathematicians that had arrived from Europe twenty years earlier with Trigault, who continued the work of the astronomical office and the dissemination of scientific knowledge pioneered by Ricci.

The End of the Ming Dynasty

While Ricci's heirs were altering the physiognomy of the China mission, the Ming empire, already worn out by economic and political problems, was on the verge of collapse. The most serious threat was from the northeast, where the Manchu tribes, unified by Nurhaci in the early years of the seventeenth century, had become stronger and battle hardened.

The danger from outside was combined with the internal threat of peasant revolts unleashed from the 1620s in the northern region of the empire, especially in the Shaanxi province. A rebel leader named Li Zicheng conquered Xi'an in 1643 and marched on Beijing. Incapable of organizing any resistance, Chongzhen hanged himself from a tree on the Jingshan Hill behind the imperial palace, thus bringing the Ming dynasty to an end after 276 years of power.

The rebellious peasants were unable to consolidate their gains, however, because the Chinese general Wu Sangui, in charge of the Ming imperial troops in the northeast, formed an alliance with the Manchu and succeeded in defeating Li Zicheng. Having established themselves in Beijing, the Manchu invaders proclaimed the new Qing, or "Pure," dynasty in 1644 and succeeded in regaining control of the entire territory within a few years.[28] The child emperor Shunzhi took the throne, and the regent Dorgon implemented a policy of stabilization so as to facilitate transition to the new dynastic order. Even though the Manchu were foreigners, the Qing dynasty was not totally barbarian because Chinese influence in Manchuria had partly sinicized the tribes, and the conquest of China itself had taken place with the assent of many of the Chinese military leaders involved in the wars against the rebels. The majority of the Ming bureaucrats therefore sided with the victors.

The advent of the new dynasty was relatively painless for the Jesuits, even though Schall had enabled the Ming troops to obtain Portuguese cannons from Macao to fight the Manchu invaders during the conflict and had himself helped the Chinese to construct a foundry in 1642 and to cast and test about twenty cannons, whose functioning he described in a treatise on military techniques.

Needing to consolidate their power and therefore wishing to introduce an accurate calendar as an unmistakable sign of their harmony with Heaven, the new rulers realized that the Jesuits' astronomical skills constituted a precious asset that it would be foolish to relinquish. The regent Dorgon offered to appoint Schall director of the astronomical office, one of the most important posts in the imperial bureaucracy. The Jesuit hesitated for a long time over this extraordinary proposal, which would place him in a wholly unprecedented position for a missionary, but he was finally persuaded to accept by the insistent recommendations of Francisco Furtado,[29] the superior in charge of the Jesuit residences in northern China. His appointment was the highest mark of recognition ever obtained by the Jesuits in China and crowned the pioneering efforts of Matteo Ricci thirty-four years after his death.

Schall reorganized the office and closed down the Muslim observatory. Predictions were henceforth to be made solely in accordance with the "new rules," as the Chinese called the Western methods. Unlike Ricci, who had never been able to meet Wanli, Schall succeeded in establishing a very close and personal relationship with the young Son of Heaven.

The emperor was very grateful to the Jesuit for his work at the astronomical office and bestowed many honors upon him, including the title of "master who understands the mysteries" and the honorary qualification of bureaucrat of the first rank in 1658. With his approval, Schall built a new residence for the missionaries in Beijing and a new church, later known as the "southern church." The work of evangelization continued in the meantime, and the number of converts rose to some tens of thousands, still a very modest figure in view of the fact that the empire had a population of about 250 million. Zhang Weixin,[30] the first Chinese Jesuit, was ordained in Rome a few years later in 1664.

As historians have established, progress in evangelization was achieved above all among the lower classes, with no more conversions of illustrious literati and leading bureaucrats being obtained after the first two decades of the seventeenth century. Moreover, the widespread sympathy and curiosity shown by unconverted intellectuals for the "learning from heaven" until the collapse of the Ming dynasty gave way in the Manchu era to a sharper awareness of the radical difference between the Jesuit and Chinese visions of the world. Partly for his own ends but also out of sincere conviction, Ricci had endeavored to identify similarities between Confucian and Christian conceptions, interpreting the former in relation to the spreading of the Gospel and using the dissemination of science to pave the way for religious instruction. With the passing of time, however, Chinese intellectuals realized that the superficial parallels between Chinese and Catholic ethics concealed fundamental differences.

At the same time, the members of the bureaucracy began to fear that Catholicism might undermine the foundations of the Chinese state, where no form of power not subordinate to imperial authority was permissible, not even one of a religious character. The acknowledged value of the teaching of Western science was also kept within precise limits. As Jacques Gernet writes, it became normal in the Manchu era to divide the missionaries' teaching into two parts, namely the scientific and technical, which was to be preserved, and everything connected with religion, which was to be banned. This concept was expressed early in the eighteenth century by one of the compilers of a remarkable Chinese bibliography. Citing the collection of missionaries' works published by Li Zhizao in 1628 in a note, he comments as follows: "The superiority of Western teachings lies in calculations, their inferiority in the worship of a Lord of Heaven, which tends to disturb people."[31]

The loss of sympathy on the part of Chinese intellectuals seems to be demonstrated by the sharp decline as from 1616 in the number of laudatory introductions written for works published by Jesuit missionaries.[32] The attitude of the literati had no influence, however, on the esteem the Jesuits enjoyed at court, where they were held in great consideration above all as foreign experts.

Despite the increase in the number of converts and the important position established in the imperial court, Schall was as significant as he was controversial and found bitter opponents within the Jesuit order.[33] One of the charges laid against him regarded his acceptance of the post of director of the calendrical office. Since the astronomical calendar was published together with the almanac of auspicious and inauspicious days, his critics accused him of endorsing Chinese superstitions instead of combating them, which was inadmissible for a Jesuit. The heated disputes on this subject, which continued until the death of the German missionary, were also addressed by several boards of theologians, and the religious authorities decided in 1664 that Schall would be permitted to retain his position on condition that he worked exclusively on the astronomical part of the calendar.

Schall's influence at the imperial court and with the emperor declined over the years, and Shunzhi turned to Buddhism toward the end of a reign that lasted just under twenty years. This decision gave new strength to the Jesuits' opponents, who sought revenge for being ousted from the astronomical office. The Muslim astronomer Wu Mingxuan accused the missionaries of making false predictions, and the literatus Yang Guangxian wrote a defamatory pamphlet against them. These charges would have had no serious consequences if Shunzhi had not died in 1661 and been succeeded by Kangxi, a child of just seven, under the tutelage of four regents, one of whom, Oboi, turned against the Jesuits. It was 1664, and the seventy-three-year-old Schall had just been struck by partial paralysis when formal charges were submitted to the minister of rites accusing the Jesuits of professing subversive doctrines and being involved in suspicious relations with the merchants of Macao. Schall in particular was accused of the serious crime of indicating an inauspicious day for the burial of Shunzhi's third son, who died in 1658 when still a child. The old missionary was imprisoned together with Ludovico Buglio, Gabriel de Magalhães, the young Flemish Jesuit Ferdinand Verbiest (1623–1688) who had assisted him for four years in his astronomical work, and some Chinese assistants. The ensuing trial lasted six months.

Charged with treason, spreading a false religion, and teaching a false astronomy, Schall was sentenced to death. While the Jesuits were released after the empress mother made a plea for clemency, their Chinese collaborators were executed. The wave of persecution had extended in the meantime to the other missionaries on Chinese soil, many of whom were held in prison in Canton until 1671. Severely weakened by his long imprisonment, Schall died on August 15, 1666, a year after his release. Ferdinand Verbiest, an engineer, mathematician, and man of eclectic culture, was ready to continue his work together with the other brethren.[34]

The Jesuit Verbiest, Emperor Kangxi, and Ricci's Geometry

The situation returned to normality for the Jesuits in 1667, when Kangxi decided, on turning thirteen, to get rid of the regent Oboi and take control of the empire. Unlike his father, the new emperor was endowed with capacity, energy, an open mind, and an interest in culture, science, and mathematics. His relations with the Jesuits were to be close and fruitful for a long period.

One of Kangxi's first decisions regarded the calendrical office, where Schall's main adversary, Yang Guangxian, had been appointed director after his removal from office. The new Chinese calendar brought out at the end of 1688 contained errors in calculation, however, which Ferdinand Verbiest brought to the emperor's attention and offered to correct. On proving his skill, the missionary became the second Jesuit to direct the calendrical office. He also secured the rehabilitation of Schall von Bell, whose remains were finally laid to rest on Ricci's right in the Jesuit cemetery in Zhala.

A relationship of mutual esteem and consideration was soon established between Verbiest and the sovereign, thirty-one years his junior. Considered one of the great Chinese emperors, Kangxi was to reign for sixty years as an authoritative and enlightened monarch. One of the things the missionary and the emperor shared was an interest in science. Starting in 1670, Verbiest went to the court every day for four years to give the Son of Heaven lessons in mathematics. The first book that Kangxi asked to study was the translation of Euclid's *Elements* by Li Madou and Xu Guangqi, a work still renowned sixty years later.

With the emperor's support and encouragement, Verbiest continued the dissemination of European culture in which his predecessors had so distinguished themselves. He drew maps of the world that continued the tradition inaugurated by Ricci, he translated Western works into Manchu, and he wrote about forty books on scientific, moral, and religious subjects.

The Jesuit left his most significant imprint on the study of the heavens. He produced a calendar containing predictions for the next twenty years, published "The Astronomical Laws of the Reign of Kangxi," and constructed at the emperor's request six great pieces of astronomical equipment in bronze that can still be seen today on the terrace of the ancient observatory in Beijing. Combining Chinese aesthetics and the sophisticated art of metallurgy with Western astronomical conceptions,[35] these instruments took the place of the ancient ones produced four centuries earlier by Guo Shoujing for the Great Khan, which were very similar to the ones seen by Ricci on the terrace of the observatory in Nanjing.[36]

Verbiest's work also became invaluable in the military field when Kangxi had to deal with revolts that broke out in some parts of the empire and he asked the missionary to organize a foundry, as Schall had done many years earlier, capable of producing hundreds of light cannons. The Son of Heaven was so pleased with the help received that the Jesuit was made honorary vice minister of public works. When the Flemish missionary died in 1688 at the age of sixty-five, he was given a solemn state funeral with the participation of the most important government officials.

Collaboration between Kangxi and the Jesuits continued after the death of Verbiest, who had sent Philippe Couplet and Shen Fuzong to Paris in 1680 with a request to Louis XIV to send missionaries skilled in astronomy to China. This aroused the interest of the astronomer Giovanni Domenico Cassini, then director of the Paris observatory, and of the members of the French Academy, who assigned the five Jesuits selected—Joachim Bouvet, Jean-François Gerbillon, Jean de Fontaney, Louis Le Comte, and Claude de Visdelou—the task of carrying out studies in the fields of geography, astronomy, surveys, and natural history. On reaching Beijing after Verbiest's death, the French Jesuits resumed Kangxi's lessons in mathematics, and it was by his request that they organized a team of cartographers that traveled all over the territory of the empire in the decade from 1708 to 1718 and produced the "Complete Map of the Kingdom of Kangxi."

Kangxi was so delighted with the missionaries' assistance that he issued what has been described as the "edict of tolerance"[37] for the Christian religion in 1692. While Catholicism was not accorded a privileged status with respect to the other religions, the document recognized it as coexisting peacefully with the state and completely extraneous to any of the sects regarded as endangering the balance of civil life. The doctrine professed by the missionaries was acknowledged to foster a climate of social harmony and to cultivate the best virtues of citizens, and Catholicism was therefore permitted as a private religion subordinate to the orthodoxy of the Confucian state, like Buddhism. Despite the limitations, the document marked the moment of greatest harmony in relations between the Chinese state and the Jesuits, confirming the success of the policy of cultural accommodation eighty years after Ricci's death. As a further gesture, Kangxi granted them a plot of land inside the walls of the Imperial City, where they built the Bei Tang, or "northern church," in 1693. The same year, the Jesuits used quinine for the first time in China to treat the emperor for malaria, and he appointed one of them court physician. In the meantime, the number of converts in the country as a whole rose to two hundred thousand.

In the second half of the seventeenth century, the abundant literature on China produced by the missionaries and the correspondence between many of them and men of culture stimulated growing European interest in that remote empire—totally cut off just a century before—governed by literati. Works like the *Novus Atlas Sinensis* (1653) of Martino Martini and the *China Illustrata* (1667) of the German Jesuit Athanasius Kircher, a richly illustrated book based exclusively on the reports of missionaries, made China known again nearly four centuries after the publication and popularity of Marco Polo's *Travels*. Produced by a team of about thirty missionaries under the supervision of Philippe Couplet and published in Paris by order of Louis XIV in 1687, the *Confucius Sinarum Philosophus* presented the Chinese philosophy of state to Western scholars nearly a century after Ricci's first translation of Confucius into Latin.[38] China fascinated Europe, and one of the most enchanted was Leibniz, who was in close correspondence with the Jesuits Joachim Bouvet and Filippo Grimaldi, Verbiest's successor as director of the calendrical office.

The Chinese Rites Controversy and
the Suppression of the Society of Jesus

The period of intense cultural exchange between China and the West at the court of Kangxi was to prove short-lived due to disputes that had already been undermining the stability of the Jesuit order and the Church for decades.

It became clear immediately after Ricci's death that not all of the missionaries agreed with his choices. Niccolò Longobardo, the new superior of the mission, did not approve of the terms *Tian* (Heaven), *Shangdi* (Lord on High), and *Tianzhu* (Lord of Heaven) introduced by its founder to indicate God, and he raised the question with the ecclesiastical authorities. The choice of religious terminology was, however, only one of the problems opened up by missionary work in China. Far more serious disputes arising outside the Society of Jesus and prompted by competition between religious orders were to follow.

Following Matteo Ricci's approach, the Jesuits always allowed Chinese converts to observe the traditional rites in honor of the deceased and the ancestors, and to participate in the celebrations of Confucius. It had never seemed inappropriate for baptized literati to go to the temple of Confucius for the customary ceremonies of thanksgiving after passing the imperial examinations because the missionaries saw this as an exclusively secular practice. The Jesuit missionaries' tolerance of Chinese rites was, however, considered an unacceptably permissive attitude to idolatry by the members of some orders, especially the Franciscans and Dominicans who had begun to gain a foothold in China after 1632. The "question of rites" dragged on for over a century in an interminable dispute accompanied by countless in-depth studies.[39]

It all started in 1643, when the missionary Juan Bautista de Morales, who entered China with the first Dominicans in 1633, accused the Jesuits of the Beijing mission of permitting idolatrous practices. Having obtained no satisfaction from the Visitor, he appealed to the Holy See and submitted his accusations in seventeen specific articles. Pope Innocent X decided in his favor in 1645, decreed the practice of Chinese rites incompatible with the Catholic faith, and thus condemned the interpretation of the same put forward by Matteo Ricci and his brethren.

The Jesuits did not submit to this decree, however, and sent Martino Martini to Rome in 1651 to defend their views. Alexander VII reversed his predecessor's decision in favor of the Jesuits in 1656, and Martini returned to China in 1658 with papal backing and thirty-five new missionaries, including Ferdinand Verbiest.

In 1669, after further discussions on the subject, Clement IX ruled that the decisions of both his predecessors were to be considered valid and that choices were to be made "on the basis of particular circumstances, cases, and questions."

This compromise rested on weak foundations, and the problem resurfaced just one year after Kangxi's edict of tolerance toward Christianity. Charles Maigrot, the apostolic vicar of the Fujian province, issued a decree in 1693 forbidding converts within his jurisdiction to practice the Chinese rites and asked the pope to reconsider the issue. Soon afterward, five French bishops asked the faculty of theology at the Sorbonne to pronounce on works written by the Jesuits Le Comte and Le Gobien in defense of the practices of their order. The verdict delivered by the French theologians in 1700 was that the Jesuits' theses were to be considered "reckless, scandalous, erroneous, and injurious to the holy Christian religion."

The Jesuits then asked Kangxi to clarify the Chinese standpoint, and the emperor confirmed that Confucius was considered a sage rather than a god and that the ceremonies in honor of the dead were not religious in character. Offended by what he considered the interference of a secular authority in the religious domain, Clement XI responded in 1704 with the approval of a decree drawn up by a committee of cardinals that forbade Chinese Christians to take part in rites in honor of Confucius and the ancestors or to designate God with the names *Tian* or *Shangdi* adopted in the classical texts. *Tianzhu* was the only term to be used. The papal legate Charles-Thomas Maillard de Tournon was dispatched to China immediately to carry out an investigation into the conduct of the Jesuits.

In his second audience with Kangxi in the summer of 1706, the legate made the inappropriate choice of the apostolic vicar Maigrot, one of the Jesuits' fiercest opponents, to act as his interpreter. Even though he had lived in China for twenty years, Maigrot had a poor grasp of the language and failed to recognize some characters that Kangxi gave him to read during the audience. He was also unable to identify the Chinese name "Li Madou" and admitted that he had not read Ricci's *Christian Doctrine*. Irritated by this unjustifiable demonstration of ignorance, the emperor took offense at Maigrot's presumptuous arrogation of the right to teach the Chinese how to judge practices that formed an integral part of their millennial culture and dismissed him from his presence. He then issued a decree in December requiring every missionary to carry a document promising to remain in China for the whole of his life and to accept Li Madou's interpretation of the Chinese rites. The period of tolerance toward the Christian religion was over forever.

Tournon reacted in February 1707 by drawing up a list of instructions for missionaries on how to respond to the emperor's demands. Kangxi had him arrested and handed over to the Portuguese in Macao, who imprisoned him for violating their right of *padroado*, or jurisdiction, over missions in the East.

The Chinese rites were definitively condemned eight years later in the papal bull *Ex Illa Die* of 1715, and the patriarch of Alexandria, Ambrogio Mezzabarba, was sent as a new legate to ask the emperor to allow his subjects to practice Christianity in the form approved by Rome and to recognize the pope's jurisdiction over Chinese Christians in matters of religion.

Indignant that a "barbarian" should presume to teach the Chinese how to interpret the "Great Doctrine" of Confucianism, Kangxi threatened to prohibit the Christian religion. The papal legate made some concessions to moderate the condemnation of the rites, but these were annulled by the new pope, Innocent XIII.

China continued to fascinate European intellectuals in that period, not least because of the *Lettres édifiantes et curieuses*, a collection of letters sent by missionaries from China and published on a regular basis as from 1702 by the French procurator of the missions in China and Japan, Charles Le Gobien. Leading figures in the French Enlightenment admired the ethical and political wisdom of Confucian philosophy, grounded on reason and natural morality, and saw the third Qing emperor as an enlightened sovereign.

Kangxi died in 1722, and two years later the ministry of rites endorsed accusations put forward by the general governor of the Fujian province and declared the Catholic Church the most pernicious of all the false sects. The new emperor, Yongzheng, banned Catholicism and ordered the confiscation of the churches. With the sole exception of those serving as court astronomers in Beijing, all the missionaries were originally to be expelled to Macao but then were confined to Canton. Any priests attempting to continue their activities clandestinely were henceforth to be expelled or arrested. The religious authorities gave orders in 1742 that missionaries leaving for China were to swear they would treat those practicing the Chinese rites as idolaters.[40] In 1736, only a few years earlier during the reign of Qianlong, various works by Ricci, including his treatise on friendship and his translation of Euclid's *Elements*, had been included in the "Complete Collection of the Four Treasuries," the official edition of the most important books published in China.

As regards developments in Europe, the *Description géographique, historique, chronologique, politique, et physique de l'empire de la Chine et de la Tartarie chinoise* by the French Jesuit Jean-Baptiste Du Halde—one of the most celebrated eighteenth-century works on the Middle Kingdom and based entirely, like Kircher's, on the reports of missionaries—was published in 1735, and the Sinophily of the French Enlightenment reached its peak in 1740 with Voltaire, who judged the Chinese empire the best organized in the world and appreciated Confucianism. The Middle Kingdom was also the subject of his *Orphelin de la Chine*, based on a Chinese theatrical work of the thirteenth century and performed in Paris on August 20, 1755.

The main source of information on the empire so idealized by the Enlightenment dried up, however, when Jesuit missionaries stopped sending reports back from China. In 1773, after nearly two centuries during which some five hundred Jesuits had worked in China along the path indicated by Matteo Ricci, the Society of Jesus was suppressed by Clement XIV, and the missions in the Middle Kingdom were handed over to the Lazarists. The members of the abolished order occupied important positions in the calendrical office until the death in 1774 of the last director, Augustin de Hallerstein, who had held the position since 1746.[41]

Even after the suppression of the Society of Jesus,[42] missionaries formerly belonging to it remained at the imperial court as astronomers or experts in other disciplines and continued the work of cultural dissemination in which they so excelled. During the reign of Qianlong, a group of Jesuits designed the "Complete Map of the Empire," and the Milanese lay brother Giuseppe Castiglione,[43] known in Chinese as Lang Shining, the court painter since the reign of Kangxi, designed the Yuan Ming Yuan, the imperial summer residence just outside Beijing, together with other former Jesuits as a fusion of Chinese and European architectural styles.

Remembrance of Matteo Ricci: Writings and Monuments

After three centuries of total oblivion, Ricci's manuscript was rediscovered in 1909 by the Jesuit historian of religion Pietro Tacchi Venturi, who brought out the first edition in 1911 under the title *I Commentarj della Cina* as well as part of Ricci's correspondence. After Tacchi Venturi, the Jesuit sinologist Pasquale D'Elia brought out the three-volume edition *Fonti Ricciane, Storia dell'Introduzione del Cristianesimo in Cina* between 1941 and 1949. This was to have been followed by an edition of the letters, which D'Elia was unable to complete before his death.

Ricci's tomb in Beijing continued to attract visitors during the seventeenth century. Around 1650, when Johann Adam Schall von Bell was still alive, it was embellished with a large stone adorned with the symbols of the dragon and the cross as well as eight Chinese characters meaning "Tomb of Mr. Ricci of the Society of Jesus" and two inscriptions in Latin and Chinese recalling the most significant events in the missionary's life.[44] Under the Jesuits until the suppression of the order, and then the Lazarists, the cemetery became part of a great complex of Catholic buildings. In 1900, during the Boxer Rebellion, the burial ground was destroyed, and the bones of the missionaries were scattered.[45] Ricci's tombstone was later salvaged and set in a new structure on a new base between the graves of Schall von Bell, on the right, and Verbiest, on the left.

In 1954, when plans were made for the construction of a Chinese Communist Party training school on the property at Zhala, Zhou Enlai decided that the graves of Ricci, Schall, and Verbiest were to be left in their place and the remains of the other missionaries moved to another cemetery. The Red Guards destroyed the cemetery in 1966 during the Cultural Revolution, damaging all the gravestones and defacing the inscriptions. These were successfully restored in the early 1980s, and the graves of Ricci, Schall, Verbiest, and sixty other missionaries were returned to their original location in the grounds of the former school, now an administrative college.

Surrounded by cypresses and a stone wall with a gate, the cemetery is today a small, timeless oasis of peace, totally isolated from the frenetic life of the Chinese capital encircling it with its fifteen million inhabitants. This secluded spot evocative of a past of heroism and hardship is still visited by many figures passing through Beijing and wishing to pay homage to the memory of Matteo Ricci, the pioneer of dialogue between China and the West. It is also possible to visit the church of the Immaculate Conception south of Tiananmen Square, built on the place where Li Madou once lived.[46]

Notes

1. J. Needham, op. cit., p. 556.

2. As recalled by the Jesuit Giulio Aleni in *Daxi Xitai Li xiansheng xingji* ("The Life of Matteo Ricci from the Great West"), a biography of Ricci published in Chinese in 1630 and now in the Vatican Library.

3. P. D'Elia, "Echi delle scoperte galileiane in Cina," cit., pp. 154–55.

4. Letter dated November 23; P. D'Elia, "Echi delle scoperte galileiane in Cina," p. 155.

5. See H. Bernard, op. cit., p. 69.

6. See H. Bernard, op. cit.

7. P. D'Elia, "Echi delle scoperte galileiane in Cina," cit., pp. 155–56.

8. The painting was hung in the Jesuit headquarters in Rome together with the portraits of Ignatius Loyola Francis Xavier in 1617.

9. Book IV, chapters XVII and XVIII in Portuguese; book V, chapters XVIII, XIX, and XX in Portuguese and XXI and XXII in Latin.

10. The Latin title is De Christiana Expeditione apud Sinas suscepta ab Societate Iesu. Ex P. Matthaei Ricij eiusdem Societatis Comentarijs Libri V.

11. Matteo Ricci and Nicolas Trigault, *Entrata nella Cina de' Padri della Compagnia del Gesù (1582–1610)* (Naples: printed by Lazzaro Scoriggio, 1622).

12. There is no agreement as to the number of volumes. Some scholars say six hundred, others seven hundred, and the seventeenth-century Chinese sources say seven thousand.

13. Considered one of the "three pillars of Christianity in China" together with Li Zhizao and Xu Guangqi.

14. The vice minister Shen Que was appointed grand secretary in Beijing in 1621. The rebellion of the White Lotus sect unleashed further persecution of foreigners, and hence Christians, in 1622. The situation began to return to normal in 1622, when Shen Que left his post.

15. P. M. Engelfriet, *Euclid in China*, cit., pp. 335 ff.

16. Schall mentioned the moons of Jupiter and the phases of Venus, a phenomenon first predicted by Copernicus and observed by Galileo. He also described two stars apparently flanking Saturn, which were actually effects of optical distortion caused by the planet's rings, and spoke about sunspots, observed by Galileo thirteen years earlier and described by the same in his *Istoria e dimostrazioni intorno alle macchie solari*.

17. Cf. Isaia Iannaccone, "Scienziati gesuiti nella Cina del XVII secolo," in *Scienze tradizionali in Asia. Principi ed applicazioni, Atti del convegno, Perugia 26–28 ottobre 1995* (Perugia: Fornari Editore, 1996).

18. The work illustrated the trigonometric functions of sine, cosine, and tangent.

19. Cf. Isaia Iannaccone, "Le fasi della divulgazione della scienza europea nella Cina del XVII secolo," in *La missione cattolica in Cina tra i secoli XVII–XVIII, Emiliano Palladini . . . , Atti del convegno, Lauria 8–9 ottobre 1993*, ed. Francesco D'Arelli and Adolfo Tamburello (Naples: Istituto Universitario Orientale, 1995).

20. Dennis Twitchett and Frederich W. Mote, eds., *The Cambridge History of China*, vol. 8, part 2: The Ming Dynasty 1368–1644 (New York: Cambridge University Press, 1998), p. 833.

21. D. Twitchett and F. W. Mote, op. cit., p. 789.

22. D. Twitchett and F. W. Mote, op. cit., p. 833.

23. The Jesuit Manuel Dias the Younger published a commentary on the discovery a few years later in 1644.

24. Named in honor of the Holy Roman Emperor Rudolph II, the Rudolphine Tables were published by Kepler in 1622 on the basis of data drawn from Tycho Brahe's observations.

25. D. Twitchett and F. W. Mote, op. cit., p. 834.

26. D. Twitchett and F. W. Mote, op. cit., p. 836.

27. J. Needham, op. cit., pp. 542–43.

28. Some imperial princes fled to the south and sought to maintain their power but were defeated. Zhou Yulang, who adopted the era name of Yonglu, held out

the longest, and some Jesuit missionaries moved with his court to Guilin and then into the Yunan province. One of these was the German Andreas Wolfgang (later Xavier) Koffler, who was able to convert a number of women including the empress mother. Baptized with the name of Helena, she sent a letter to Pope Innocent X, now in the Vatican archives, seeking aid and support for the Ming dynasty.

29. George H. Dunne, *Generation of Giants* (London: Burns & Oates, 1962), p. 325.

30. George H. Dunne, *Generation of Giants*, p. 174.

31. J. Gernet, *Chine et christianisme*, cit., p. 84.

32. Adrian Dudink, "Sympathising Literati and Officials," in *The Handbook of Christianity in China*, ed., N. Standaert, cit., pp. 479–80.

33. For information about Schall, see G. H. Dunne, op. cit., or Roman Malek, ed., *Western Learning and Christianity in China: The Contribution and Impact of Johann Adam Schall von Bell, 1592–1666*, 2 vols. (Sankt Augustin, China-Zentrum, Monumenta Serica Institute, 1998).

34. See *Ferdinand Verbiest, Jesuit, Missionary Scientist, Engineer and Diplomat 1623–1688*, ed. John Witek (Steyler Verlag, Nettatal, 1994). See also N. Cameron, op. cit., ch. XI.

35. Verbiest used the system of coordinates based on the ecliptic whereas the Chinese used the equatorial coordinates.

36. Guo Shoujing's instruments reflected the Chinese conception of the universe better than the Jesuit's and used the system of equatorial coordinates, which was soon to be adopted also in the West. See chapter 10 ("The Forgotten Astronomical Observatory").

37. N. Standaert, ed., *The Handbook of Christianity*, cit., p. 516.

38. See chapter 7 ("Confucius, 'Another Seneca': The Translation of the Confucian Classics"). See also L. M. Jensen, op. cit., pp. 122, 325.

39. The literature of the "Chinese rites controversy" or the "Chinese rites question" is endless, and the dispute is also discussed in nonspecialized works such as P. Rule, op. cit.; Giorgio Borsa, *La nascita del moderno in Asia Orientale* (Milan: Rizzoli, 1977); G. H. Dunne, op. cit.; Davide Mungello, *Curious Land* (Honolulu: University of Haway Press, 1985); J. Waley-Cohen, op. cit.

40. The ban on Chinese rites was lifted by Pope Pius XII in 1939.

41. G. H. Dunne, op. cit., p. 211.

42. The reconstitution of the Society of Jesus was officially sanctioned by Pius VII in 1814 with the bull *Sollicitudo omnium Ecclesiarum*. The order, which had about twenty-three thousand members in 1773, was reborn as a group of six hundred brethren.

43. Having arrived in China in 1715, he remained at the court for fifty-one years.

44. FR, book V, ch. XXII, p. 626, no. 2.

45. Some bones found near Ricci's grave are kept in an urn at the Jesuit archives in Rome, but their authenticity has yet to be established. See Angelo Lazzarotto,

"Le onoranze cinesi a Matteo Ricci," in *Atti del convegno internazionale di Studi Ricciani, Macerata-Roma, 22–25 ottobre 1982* (Macerata: Centro Studi Ricciani, 1984), p. 123. For the history of the Jesuit cemetery, see also Edward J. Malatesta, *Departed, Yet Present: Zhalan, the Oldest Christian Cemetery in Beijing* (San Francisco: The Ricci Institute, University of San Francisco, 1995).

46. This was the "southern church" built in 1650, during Schall's lifetime, reconstructed in the twentieth century.

Chronology

1552   October 6. Birth of Matteo Ricci in Macerata, Italy.

1571   August 15. Begins novitiate to enter the Society of Jesus in Rome.

1572   September 17. Start of attendance at the Roman College.

1578   March 24. Departure from Lisbon for India.

        September 13. Arrival in Goa.

1582   April 26. Leaves Goa for Macao.

        August 7. Arrival in Macao.

        September 10. Arrival in Zhaoqing.

1583–1588   Compilation of a Portuguese-Chinese dictionary together with Ruggieri.

1584   Translation of the Ten Commandments, Hail Mary, and Credo, Zhaoqing.

        First edition of the Ricci map of the world, Zhaoqing.

1589   Translation of the Gregorian calendar.

        August 15. Expulsion from Zhaoqing.

        August 26. Arrival in Shaozhou.

1591–1594   Translates the Four Books of Confucianism into Latin.

1595   May 18. Departure from Shaozhou for Beijing with the vice minister of war.

        May 31. Stop in Nanjing.

        June 28. Arrival in Nanchang.

        Writes the *Treatise on Friendship*.

1596   Writes the *Treatise on Mnemonic Arts*.

1597   August. Appointed superior of the China mission and instructed to move to Beijing.

1598   June 25. Departure from Nanchang with minister Wang.

      July. Stop in Nanjing.

      September 7. Arrival in Beijing.

      November. Leaves Beijing for Nanjing.

      December. Stop in Linqing.

1599   January. Arrival in Danyang.

      February 6. Arrival in Nanjing and decision to move there.

      Writes the *Twenty-five Discourses*, published in Beijing in 1605.

1599–1600   Writes the *Treatise on the Four Elements*.

1600   Second edition of the Ricci map of the world.

      May 19. Departure for Beijing on a eunuch's junk.

      July. Arrives in Linqing and is taken prisoner by Ma Tang.

      August. Transferred to Tianjin.

1601   January. The emperor gives orders for Ricci to be brought to Beijing.

      24 January. Entry into Beijing.

      27 January. Presentation of gifts and a memorial to Emperor Wanli.

      Writes *Eight Songs for the Western Harpsichord*.

      Writes the *Treatise on the Constellations* and translates it with Li Zhizao.

1602   Third edition of the map of the world.

1603   Fourth edition of the map of the world.

      Publication of the *True Meaning of the Lord of Heaven* (Ricci's "Catechism").

1605   Publication of the *Christian Doctrine*.

1607   Writes the *Elementary Treatise on Geometry* with Xu Guangqi.

      Writes *Diagrams and Explanations regarding the Sphere and the Astrolabe* with Li Zhizao.

      Writes *Explanations of the Methods of Measurement* with Xu Guangqi.

1608   Writes the *Ten Chapters of an Extraordinary Man*.

      Writes the *Treatise on Arithmetic*, published in 1613, together with Li Zhizao.

      Starts work on his history of the mission (*Della entrata della Compagnia di Giesù e Christianità nella Cina*).

      Printing of the "imperial edition" of the Ricci map of the world.

1609   Writes *Principles of the Differences between Figures Inscribed in Round* together with Li Zhizao.

1610   May 11. Dies after nine days of illness.

          June 19. Wanli grants the Jesuits a burial plot for Ricci.

1611   22 April. Ricci's remains are transported to Zhala.

          November 1. Ricci's burial.

1613   February 9. Nicolas Trigault leaves for Rome with Ricci's manuscript.

1615   September–October. First edition of Ricci's manuscript expanded and translated into Latin by Nicolas Trigault.

1622   Publication of the Ricci-Trigault history in Italian as *Entrata nella China de' Padri della Compagnia del Gesù*.

1629   September 1. Emperor Chongzhen gives orders for the calendar to be reformed with the Jesuits' help.

1644   The Jesuit Adam Schall von Bell is appointed director of the office of astronomical observations.

1692   Kangxi issues an edict of tolerance toward the Christian religion.

1724   Catholicism is banned in China.

1773   Pope Clement XIV orders the suppression of the Jesuit order.

1774   Death of the last director of the astronomical office, a member of the suppressed Jesuit order.

~

Chinese Dynasties[1]

XIA
3rd millennium–18th century BC
SHANG
18th–16th century BC
ZHOU
11th century–256 BC
Western Zhou (11th century–771 BC)
Eastern Zhou (770–256 BC)
Spring and Autumn (722–481 BC)
Warring States (403–256 BC)
QIN (first emperor)
221–207 BC
HAN
206 BC– AD 220
Western Han (206 BC– AD 9)
Xin (reign of Wang Mang) (9–23)
Eastern Han (25–220)
WEI (Three Kingdoms)
220–265
WESTERN JIN
265–316

---

1. Based on Anne Cheng, *Histoire de la pensée chinoise* (Éditions du Seuil, 1997).

NORTHERN AND SOUTHERN DYNASTIES
317–589
North
Tuoba Wei
Eastern and Western Wei
Northern Qi
Northern Zhou
South
Eastern Jin
Liu Song
Qi
Liang
Chen
SUI
581–618
TANG
618–907
FIVE DYNASTIES (period of division)
907–960
SONG
960–1279
Northern Song (960–1127)
Liao (Khitan in Mongolia) (916–1125)
Southern Song (1127–1279)
Jin (Jürchen in Manciuria) (1115–1234)
YUAN (Mongols)
1264–1368
MING
1368–1644
QING (Manchu)
1644–1912
CHINESE REPUBLIC
1912 (on Taiwan since 1949)
PEOPLE'S REPUBLIC OF CHINA
1949–present

~

Glossary

Bei Tang—Northern church.

Beijing—Northern capital, formerly known as Peking.

Cha—Tea.

Chan—School of meditation, Chinese variant of Buddhism. Zen in Japanese.

Da Ming—"Great Ming," China.

Dadu—"Great Capital," Beijing.

Daoren—Master of the Way.

Datong—Calendar introduced during the Yuan era and used in the Ming dynasty.

Ding—Chinese name used by Ricci for Christopher Clavius.

Feng shui—Geomancy, literally "wind-water."

Fuchengmen—Western gate of the Inner City.

Fuchu—"Restorer," Chinese honorific adopted by Michele Ruggieri.

Guan (or **Guanyuan**)—Official of the imperial bureaucracy.

Guanxi—personal network of social relations.

Haidao—Superintendent of the coastal areas.

Hao—Honorific.

Hu—Ivory tablet to be held in front of the face during imperial audiences.

Huangdi—Emperor.

Huihui—Term originally indicating a Muslim ethnic minority and used by extension for all those practicing foreign religions.

Hutong—Narrow lanes.

Jinshi—"Literatus presented [to the court]," or metropolitan graduate, a graduate of the third level of the imperial examinations.

Juren—"Literatus recommended [to the court]," or provincial graduate, a graduate of the second level of the imperial examinations.

Kang—Sleeping platform of brick heated with hot air from the cooking area.

Kowtow—Act of kneeling and bowing the head to the ground.

Ling—dew drop, term used for zero.

Lingchisi—Slow slicing or death by a thousand cuts.

Nanjing—Southern capital, formerly known as Nanking.

Qi—Flow, vital energy.

Qing qing—Polite expression of invitation, encouragement, or the like.

Ren—Benevolence, humanity.

Shangdi—Lord on High, Lord Above.

Shenfu—Spiritual fathers.

Shi Huangdi—First emperor of a unified China.

Shidafu (or **Wenren**)—Scholar or literatus.

Shuyuan—Academy.

Taiji—Cosmological term translated as "Supreme Ultimate" or "Supreme Pole."

Taijian—Eunuch.

Tian—Sky or heaven.

Tao—Way.

Tao Te Ching—*The Classic of the Way and Virtue*, the basic text of Taoism.

Tianzhu—Lord of Heaven, God.

Wumen—Meridian Gate, southern entrance to the Forbidden City.

Wuqi—game of war.

Xie zhai—Mythological animal embroidered on the mandarin square of a censor.

Xitai—"From the Farthest West," honorific adopted by Ricci.

Xiucai—"Budding talent," a graduate of the first level of the imperial examinations.

Xuanwumen—Westernmost of the three southern gates of the Inner City.

Yin and **Yang**—Male and female principles in Chinese philosophy.

Yuan Ming Yuan—"Gardens of Perfect Brightness," the Old Summer Palace.

Zhong Guo—Middle Kingdom, China.

Zi Jin Cheng—Purple Forbidden City.

Bibliographic Sources

The primary sources of this biography are the history written by Ricci himself and the letters from China to his superiors, family, and friends. The edition of the *Fonti Ricciane, Storia dell'Introduzione del Cristianesimo in Cina*, 3 vols., ed. Pasquale D'Elia S.J. (Rome: La Libreria dello Stato, 1942–1949) is the essential text of reference together with the edition of the correspondence in *Opere storiche del P. Matteo Ricci S.I.*, 2 vols., Comitato per le onoranze nazionali, with introductions, notes, and tables by Fr. Pietro Tacchi Ventura S.J. (Macerata: Stab. Tipografico Giorgetti 13, 1911–1913), *I Commentarj della Cina, Le lettere dalla Cina*.

Attention is also drawn to the previous edition of the history: Matteo Ricci and Nicolas Trigault, *Entrata nella China de' Padri della Compagnia del Gesù (1582–1610)* (Naples: printed by Lazzaro Scoriggio, 1622); new edition with an introduction by Joseph Shih and Carlo Laurenti: *Entrata nella China de' Padri della Compagnia del Gesù (1582–1610)* (Rome: Edizioni Paoline, 1983).

The most recent editions of the history and correspondence are *Della entrata della Compagnia di Giesù e Christianità nella Cina*, ed. Maddalena del Gatto (Macerata: Quodlibet, 2000) and *Matteo Ricci, Lettere*, ed. Francesco D'Arelli (Macerata: Quodlibet, 2001).

~

Acknowledgments

Every book has its own history. Given my scientific background and my experience in scientific journalism, why did I decide to write a biography of Matteo Ricci? I owe the idea of a book on the dissemination of European science in China by a Jesuit from the Italian town of Macerata to someone I met at the beginning of my stay in China, namely Umberto Colombo (former Italian Minister of University and Research). Even though the initial project changed in shape over time, this book would never have come into being without his vigorous encouragement. I must, however, also thank Gian Arturo Ferrari for his suggestion to broaden the original concept and embark on the more demanding but also more engrossing task of writing a biography.

While Ricci used science as a means to the end of conversion, his commitment to the translation of scientific works into Chinese was of crucial importance and left an imprint on the history of the Jesuit mission in China. Biographers have not always given this aspect of his activity the attention it deserves. The aim here is not only to present an overall description of Ricci's life and work but also to highlight the constant attention that he and the most authoritative Chinese converts focused on science. The switch from outlining the new developments in contemporary science to reconstructing the life of a missionary who lived in China in the late sixteenth and early seventeenth century was a challenge that I endeavored to address in the same spirit as my work of popularization, seeking to understand the meaning of the events and ideas in order to convey it to my readers.

Taking Ricci's writings as my essential starting point, I present the events in accordance with his own reconstruction of them, and the China that emerges is seen through his eyes. His Western views and prejudices often seem to be of extraordinary present-day relevance. I therefore hope that the specialists will forgive me for according priority to the narrative and not always bothering to keep up with the latest historiographic interpretations. Though rigorously documented, this is a work aimed at the general public.

My warmest thanks to all the experts who lent me a hand along the way, in particular Eugenio Menegon of the History Department of Boston University for his advice, explanations, and bibliographical recommendations as well as for agreeing to read through the text and providing invaluable suggestions. I am also most grateful to Isaia Iannaccone, professor at the European School in Brussels and researcher at the astronomical observatory in Paris, for useful suggestions. His works on the dissemination of Western science in China by the Jesuits were an important point of reference for my book.

Vital help and support were provided both during and after my stay in Beijing by Mario Sabattini, professor in the Department of East Asian Studies at the Ca' Foscari University of Venice, then director of the Italian Cultural Institute in Beijing. The personnel of the Institute, and in particular Patrizia Liberati, were most helpful in the search for material in Chinese libraries. Precious assistance was also received from Hengda Yang and Ron Anton, then respectively director and international director of the Beijing Center for Language and Culture, and in particular from Thierry Meynard, now in the Philosophy Department at Sun Yat-Sen University, Guangzhou, who allowed me to make full use of their library's resources.

I am indebted to Ren Yanli, director of the Christianity Department at the Institute of Research on World Religions of the Chinese Academy of Social Sciences in Beijing, not least for allowing me unlimited access to the *Fonti Ricciane*; to the director Liu Dun and Han Qi of the History of Natural Sciences Institute of the Chinese Academy of Sciences in Beijing for useful indications and help with bibliographical research; to Gu Wei Min of the History Department at Shanghai University for taking me on a guided tour of the places where Xu Guangqi lived; to Xu Huping, the director of the Nanjing Museum, for granting me a private viewing of the Ricci map held there and for agreeing to show it to a broader public at the Italian Cultural Institute in Beijing; to Xiaoxin Wu, director of the Ricci Institute for Chinese-Western Cultural History, San Francisco, for the support and helpfulness shown in particular during the convention "Encounters and Dialogues," held in Beijing in October 2001. The many specialists who were so kind as to make fruitful suggestions during this convention include Father Gianni Criveller, researcher at the Holy Spirit Study Centre in Hong Kong. Particular thanks to Catherine Jami of the Centre National de la Recherche Scientifique and Paris University for useful clarification on the introduction of Western mathematics into China, and to Roger Hart of the University of Texas at Austin.

Among my friends in Beijing, I thank Davide Cucino, now director of the Italian Chamber of Commerce in China, for bibliographical suggestions and Franco Amadei, Fiat representative in China, for help in organizing my visit to Nanjing. I am very grateful to Anna Jaguaribe Bruni, who provided support and encouragement during the gestation of this project, and to the Beijing International Society for giving me the opportunity to ascertain how much interest still attaches to Ricci for an international public.

For help with my research in Italian libraries, I thank Father Giuseppe de Cock, then director of the Archivium Romanum Societatis Iesu, who showed me the manuscript of Ricci's *Della entrata della Compagnia di Giesù e Christianità nella Cina*; Monsignor Pier Francisco Fumagalli, cultural director at the Ambrosian Library in Milan, and Giliola Barbero; Father Lorenzo Chiesa, the director of the Papal Institute of Foreign Missions in Milan, and all the staff there; Ambrogio Piazzoni, vice prefect of the Vatican Library, and Clara Yu Dong; and Anna Pieroni of the Mozzi-Borgetti Library of Macerata.

Thanks also to Umberto Bottazzini (Department of Mathematics), Claudia di Filippo and Letizia Arcangeli (Department of History of Science and Historical Documentation), and Pasquale Tucci (Institute of Applied General Physics) of Milan University; Fabrizio Bònoli of Bologna University (Department of Astronomy); Flavio Rurale of Udine University (faculty of humanities and philosophy); Silvia Toniato of the University of Savoie; and Donatella Guida of Naples University (Department of Asian Studies).

Needless to say, I bear sole responsibility for the end result.

I am particularly indebted to Nicoletta Lazzari for her constant dedication and invaluable aid in the pursuit of quality, and to Roberto Armani for his acute and meticulous checking of the text.

I am deeply indebted to Paul Metcalfe, the excellent translator of the English edition, who succeeded in bringing the best out of the text with skill, dedication, care, and all the precision I could have wished for. A special thank-you to Barbara Venturi and Mario Curti at Scriptum in Rome for their fundamental contribution to the English version of this work.

I would also like to express my gratitude to all the friends who offered encouragement and support, especially Gisèle Geymonat. Thanks to Diego, who kept me company while doing his homework during the afternoons of work in Beijing.

I am most grateful to my father Angioletto, who read through the first draft of the book together with my mother and displayed such enthusiasm that I had yet another reason for continuing with the work. He would have been so happy to see it finally published. Special thanks to my husband for his unfailing concrete help and indispensable support during the four years it took me to complete the demanding work of writing this biography.

Index of Names

~

About the Author

Michela Fontana, holding a degree in mathematics, is a science journalist and writer. She has won the Glaxo Prize for science journalism and the Pirelli International Award for popularization of science for her book *Percorsi calcolati* (A Calculated Journey), and she received the 2010 Grand Prix de la Biographie Politique in Touquet, France, for the French edition of *Matteo Ricci*. She is the author of the theater play *Matteo Ricci, a Jesuit Scientist at the Ming Court*. She lived for four years in China.

CPSIA information can be obtained at www.ICGtesting.com
Printed in the USA
BVOW01*1559050614

355475BV00001B/1/P